A Survey of Classical Roman Literature

Volume I

A Survey of
CLASSICAL
ROMAN
LITERATURE

D.P. Lockwood

Volume I

THE UNIVERSITY OF CHICAGO PRESS

The University of Chicago Press, Chicago & London.
The University of Toronto Press, Toronto 5, Canada.
Copyright 1934 by
Prentice-Hall, Inc.
First University of Chicago Press Edition 1962.
Printed in the U.S.A.

Matris
Patris
arte docendi
peritissimorum
memoriae
sacrum

Preface

THE pedagogical principles upon which this book is based have been amply set forth in two articles by the author.[1] The book comprises a complete *fifth-year* Latin course, designed to crown the intensive work of the first four years with a rapid comprehensive survey of national or classical Roman literature— tracing the evolution of that literature from its beginnings to its dissolution, and presenting as complete as possible a picture of Roman civilization, through the medium of selections from literary masterpieces. For comparison and discussion, of course, supplementary reading may be assigned in standard histories of Roman literature (if there is sufficient time), but the present book is in itself a history of Roman literature, emphasizing tendencies and movements, and containing, I believe, enough facts to serve as a basis for true literary appreciation.

Is a bird's-eye view of classical Roman literature, based on reading of the original Latin, possible for American fifth-year students? In spite of the fact that the first four years of Latin study have been cut to the bone, I believe that it is possible, and I have tried in this book to demonstrate that possibility.

Frankly, the present *Survey* is designed to be at once a finishing course for those—and they are the great majority—who will take no more Latin, and an orientation course for those who will continue their study of the subject and will either delve deeper in the classical field or extend their range of work into the patristic or medieval or modern domains of Latin literature.

The Latin selections have been chosen to meet needs which, though sometimes conflicting, were nevertheless deemed essential:

(1) Ease of comprehension, both in style and in content. Especially suited to this purpose are the comedies of Plautus and Terence; the extracts from the *Rhetorica ad Herennium;* the letters

---

[1] "The Haverford Plan," *Journal of Higher Education,* June, 1930; and "Latin in the College," *Education,* June, 1934.

vii

of Caesar and Cicero; many of the poems of Catullus; the extract
from Sallust; the selections from Tibullus, Propertius, and Ovid;
Seneca's *Apocolocyntosis;* the poems of Phaedrus and of Martial;
many of the letters of Pliny; and the selection from Suetonius.
Teachers who wish to follow the line of least resistance may con-
centrate on this material. In no case, however, should these
authors be omitted from any program, for they offer a welcome
opportunity for *rapid reading*, as an antidote to the snail's pace
of the earlier preparatory years.

(2) Grasp of Roman literature as a whole. To accomplish
this, an acquaintance with even the more difficult authors is
necessary. No general survey can omit Cicero's essays, Lucretius,
Livy, Vergil, Horace, Seneca's philosophical works, Petronius,
Tacitus, and Juvenal. In style or in content, or in both, these
authors generally prove more difficult for the student, and on the
whole they are more academic and more "classic," lacking the
humor or the vivid human appeal of Plautus, Terence, Catullus,
the Elegists, Martial, and Pliny. But the great immortals
(Cicero, Vergil, Horace, and others) have been the torchbearers
of classic influence through the ages, and to offset the difficulties
entailed in studying their writings, emphasis may be laid on their
place in world literature.

The general view also calls for brief extracts from certain minor
authors, some of whom are (or were) milestones in the evolution.
of Roman literature, others, representatives of an era or a phase
of Roman achievement. As a matter of principle, I have included as few minor authors as possible: only Andronicus, Naevius, Ennius, Cato, Vitruvius, Statius, and Gaius have been
admitted.

Above all I wish to emphasize that, although there is room for
difference of opinion as to choice, the selection of both major and
minor authors in this book is based on a definite design of relative
values for the purpose in hand; namely, a comprehensive but
rapid survey of classical Roman literature. Furthest from my
desire is a collection of samples—a few paragraphs or pages from
every known classical author, with Catullus and Ovid faring
no better than Phaedrus and Statius; and Cicero and Pliny, no

better than Velleius Paterculus and Mela. Such an anthology
of samples, philological rather than literary, may possibly meet
the needs of graduate students, but not of high-school seniors or
college freshmen.

So important is the matter of relative values that I must re-
capitulate author by author—and here I must confess that I find
myself expressing disapproval of the traditional intensive Latin
course for college freshmen, as well as justifying my selection of
authors and works for this *Survey*.

Plautus. It is a godsend that the initiation of the college
freshman into a more mature and primarily *literary* study of
Latin can begin with Plautus. There are few students who are
not delighted and astounded when they discover that the Latin
language can be the vehicle of Plautine wit and humor. To
restrict the beginner's knowledge of Plautus to a scene or two
is a pedagogical crime and a tactical blunder (and blunders, for
the hard-pressed classical teacher, are worse than crimes). But
at once we are faced with the chief practical problem of the whole
Survey—the need for economy of time and space. Frankly, I
advocate abridging (not simplifying) comedies. A comedy remains a comedy, though "cut." (If that be a crime, it is one
of which every modern producer of Shakespeare is guilty.)
Those, however, who feel that sacrilege has been committed in
abridging the *Miles Gloriosus*, may read the *Epidicus*, shortest
and easiest of the plays of Plautus (save in the complexity of its
plot—which, however, is easily elucidated in plain English).

Terence. Plautus always takes the edge off Terence. The
Adelphoe, however, with its ever-fresh psychological problem, is
one of the truest representatives of the urbane comedy of manners
and the best foil for Plautus' farces. On the other hand, if ever
a playwright's essence may be got from a *scene*, it is from the
vivid exposition dramas (stories or plays within a play) which
open the *Heautontimorumenos* and the *Andria*.

Auctor ad Herennium. The vivid scenes from the comedy and
tragedy of life, which illustrate the unknown author's simple and
lucid theory of style, are unique masterpieces.

Caesar. It is the obvious duty of the teacher (whether or not he succeed in his effort) to reintroduce what he can of an author, utterly ruined for the student by youthful struggles with grammar and syntax.[2]

Cicero. A few letters can be read with pleasure, but the essays —one of my own greatest enthusiasms—soon pall. For the most part they require too much literary and philosophical background, and their stylistic glory is lost on the beginner. I have chosen a few extracts requiring the minimum of erudition.

Lucretius. A glimpse through the open portal is all that can be attained, but it is worth while.

Catullus. To include every suitable short poem of Catullus is one of the aims of this book, and I make no apology for regrouping the poems and supplying them with titles, the former process being a great improvement over the method of arrangement adopted by the unknown ancient editors of Catullus' *Carmina*, and the latter, a universal modern improvement over ancient custom.

Sallust. His philosophy is more important than his actual historical canvases. A brief selection therefore suffices.

Livy. If Livy's rhetoric does not leave the modern student cold, I know nothing of the undergraduate mind. Only a few historical episodes or "short stories" can be included. His grand effects can be appreciated only by those who read him *in extenso* (a truth that applies to *all* historians), and this appreciation is practically impossible for the undergraduate.

Vitruvius. Brief selections reveal an interesting facet of Roman character.

Vergil. A bit of the *Eclogues* and *Georgics* will suffice to indicate their literary importance, but of course they do not stir the blood.

Horace. In spite of difficult reading, as much of Horace must be covered as possible—both satires and odes. Horace is the keystone of the classic arch. As a gradatim approach to the odes,

---

[2] The same might be said of Cicero's orations, but they—as well as Vergil's *Aeneid* and Ovid's *Metamorphoses*—do not suffer quite so badly, and they are fresh enough in the student's memory to take their place in the comprehensive survey without further reading.

I have grouped together some of the easiest and briefest *carmina* along with easy extracts from *carmina* of lesser importance.

Tibullus, Propertius, and *Ovid.* Though not profound, the Elegists offer some of the simplest and most human material for rapid reading.

Phaedrus. The fable is a genre that deserves at least brief mention.

Seneca. Too often neglected by classicists, Seneca the philosopher affords an insight into the coming Christian and medieval ages—but only a glimpse is possible for beginners. As a masterpiece of humor, on the other hand, the *Apocolocyntosis* cannot be passed over.

Petronius. A brief selection is, unfortunately, all that beginners can master.

Statius. A sample of his writings suffices.

Martial. His work is perennially enjoyable—provided it is not reduced to a text for the study of *minutiae* of Roman private life.

Tacitus. The *Dialogus* and the *Agricola* have no appeal for the young; the *Annals* and *Histories,* difficult for freshmen, must be read *in extenso* to be appreciated; but the *Germania* is uniquely interesting to all—and valuable in the modern college curriculum as a link with medieval history.

Pliny. The letters offer a fascinating and indispensable pageant of human life.

Juvenal. A sample of the vitriolic satirist and arch-rhetorician will suffice.

Suetonius. The brief life of Titus is a welcome picture of the Empire and a revelation of the coming intellectual decline.

Gaius. Roman Law, honored by classicists more in the breach than in the observance, deserves at least a modest place in a survey.

As a practical demonstration, the following schedule illustrates what can be done to cover the maximum number of authors at maximum speed: [3]

---

[3] I assume the usual three-hour course in a college year of thirty-four weeks; that is, fifteen weeks or forty-five recitation periods in each semester, less one hour for a mid-semester test.

VOLUME I—FIRST SEMESTER

Number of recitations:

- (2) Introduction, Andronicus, Naevius
- (8) Plautus
- (1) Ennius and Cato
- (6) Terence
- (3) Auctor ad Herennium
- (3) Caesar
- (6) Cicero
- (2) Lucretius
- (13) Catullus

Total (44)

VOLUME II—SECOND SEMESTER

- (1) Sallust
- (3) Livy
- (1) Vitruvius
- (2) Vergil
- (10) Horace
- (6) Elegists (and Phaedrus)
- (3) Seneca
- (1) Petronius
- (1) Statius and Martial
- (3) Tacitus
- (6) Pliny
- (3) Juvenal
- (3) Suetonius
- (1) Gaius

Total (44)

I do not mean to imply that in following this schedule one can read all the selections of each author. The amount of material covered will depend upon the ability of the class and the degree of preparation. I have purposely included enough material for a wide latitude of choice and to vary the content of the course in successive years. In the second semester, particularly, minor writers may be omitted and more time devoted to major authors, if the teacher so prefers.

Much care has been expended on the notes, to make them concise and helpful, and to avoid learned technicalities, superfluous erudition, and pedantic mystification. The pedants—as that wise old Auctor ad Herennium says—*ne parum multa scisse viderentur, ea conquisiverunt quae nihil attinebant, ut ars difficilior cognitu putaretur.*

To help the student with the problem of vocabulary, I have included in the notes the meaning of practically every word not appearing in the *Latin Word List* of the College Entrance Examination Board, except those words which are obvious as compounds or have English derivatives. A complete vocabulary, after the fashion of those usually appended to elementary readers, would be entirely out of place in a fifth-year Latin book of this sort. Convenient though such a vocabulary may be, as a short cut for the indifferent student, it is pedagogically unsound and much of it is superfluous. Of course, students should, to a certain degree, be frankly and definitely helped with new and unusual words—as I have done in the notes—but the *basic* vocabulary must be acquired by rapid reading, supplemented by consultation of a good unabridged lexicon, in which more information is contained than meets the need of the moment. Above all a correct approach to problems of vocabulary must be inculcated in class, and the student must be rescued from the slough of incessant lexicon-thumbing—one of the worst pitfalls in language study.

The numbering of lines has been made complete. I know from experience that this slight departure from tradition will be found helpful. Marks of quantity and other visual helps have been freely used wherever they facilitate rapid reading. Standardized forms and spelling have been adopted throughout (period spelling, like period furniture, is generally more artistic than comfortable).

I wish to express my appreciation to successive colleagues in the Latin department of Haverford College, who have patiently endured years of experimentation with mimeographed texts: to Dr. Raymond T. Ohl, Dr. Frederic M. Wheelock, Dr. John L. Heller, and Dr. Howard Comfort. I am especially indebted to Professor Casper J. Kraemer, Jr., of New York University, for his invaluable help and encouragement.

D. P. L.

Contents

Introduction

Introduction

I

FOREWORD ON LATIN LITERATURE AS A WHOLE

IN WESTERN civilization no language has played so important a rôle nor endured so long as Latin, which for over two thousand years has been—and still is—a living literary language.

The literature composed in the Latin tongue during the past twenty-two centuries falls into the following general divisions or periods:

[1] **Native Latin Literature** (from prehistoric times to about the middle of the third century B.C.). Native Latin literature was pre-Roman in its origin, but endured as the sole medium of expression of all Latin tribes, Romans included, until Rome had begun her march to world empire by winning the First Punic War and had been subjected to the full tide of Greek cultural influence. During this entire time native Latin literature remained crude, provincial, and meager—inadequate to mirror completely the life and thought of the Latin peoples.

[2] **Classical, or National, Roman Literature** (240 B.C.–*125* [1] A.D.). Classical, or national, Roman literature comprises the complete record of the Romans during their rise to world power and during their period of dominance in international affairs. It is a rich and vital literature, closely modeled on that even greater Greek literature which had already passed through its national or classical period in the preceding five hundred years.

[3] **International Roman Literature** (*125–500* A.D.). International Roman literature is the record of occidental civilization, denationalized and gradually christianized, under the later Roman Empire.

[4] **European Latin Literature** (500 A.D.–the present). Until the twelfth century, European Latin literature was practically

---

[1] Dates in italics are approximate.

3

the sole record of the life and thought of the various nations of Western Europe. Thereafter, during the late Middle Ages and Renaissance, Latin retained its preëminence as the international language of diplomacy, science, and the arts. Not until the seventeenth century did it begin to lose ground. Today Latin has its strongest hold in Italy and in the Church.

European Latin literature may be subdivided into the following distinct, though overlapping, epochs:

> Medieval......................... *500–1500.*
> Renaissance..................... *1400–1700.*
> Modern......................... *1600*–the present.

Our purpose in this book is to study the second general literary period, that of national or classical Roman literature. This literature was the resultant of two forces: Roman character and Greek culture; or, more specifically, it was a fusion of two literary traditions: primitive Latin and mature Greek. An understanding and appreciation of national Roman literature therefore calls for some knowledge of both native Latin literature—which gave genuine, although much restricted, expression to the heritage of the race—and Greek literature—which had already embodied the supreme artistic and intellectual standards of the western world long before the Romans emerged from barbarism.

It was in 240 B.C., at the close of the First Punic War, that the Romans definitely yielded to the pressure of Greek intellectual influence and—like the Japanese after 1853—publicly adopted certain ideals and standards of an alien civilization. No great literature has ever been so dependent on foreign influence as has the Roman. But we must know something of the native forms of composition (which the Romans abandoned but never wholly forgot) in order to comprehend the evolution of national Roman literature.

II

NATIVE LATIN LITERATURE

Little is known and still less has been preserved of native Roman literature before the triumph of Greek influence. Inasmuch as the Romans were a branch of the Latin race, it is safe to assume that the crude and meager literature which they seem to have possessed was the common heritage of primitive Latin peoples. We may therefore speak of the literature of Rome before the middle of the third century B.C. as native Latin literature.

The primitive Romans were a people of marked national traits. Practical, hard-headed, and conservative, they were ruthless in maintaining law and order; they were a puritanical folk, hostile to art and the artistic temperament. They compensated for their lack of creative imagination by moral stability and devotion to civic duty.

Artistic expression among them was extraordinarily backward, and their language, rough-hewn, inelastic, and matter-of-fact. It is true that for centuries they had preserved laws and rituals, as well as meager or even childish annals, but none of these compositions—or compilations—had any genuine literary merit. The Romans possessed only the most primitive type of verse, of which the commonest form was subsequently styled the *Saturnian* (i.e., primeval, or belonging to the mythical golden age of Saturn)— a crude accentual rhythm, fundamentally different from the polished quantitative meters of Greek origin used by a Vergil or a Horace. Apparently this native verse form was not used for poetical compositions of any length or elaborate design; only charms, wise saws, religious chants, and epitaphs for the dead are known. Rude extemporaneous satire is also believed to have existed.

Such were the limited forms of self-expression with which the Romans were still content at a time when they had subjugated the entire Italian peninsula! Had these native and spontaneous modes of expression been further developed without foreign influence, the history of Latin literature—and of western civilization —would have been very different.

Let us now turn to a few brief and fragmentary examples of native Latin literature.

Primitive Latin Verse

There has been much speculation regarding the principles of Saturnian versification, for most of the later Roman and Greek grammarians who treated of metrics knew little and cared less about such relics of a benighted past. It is now generally agreed, however, that Saturnian verse, like English, is accentual. Saturnians consist of a half line (normally of seven syllables) with three stress accents, followed by a half line (normally of six syllables) with two stress accents. Alliteration is frequent, and the kinship with primitive Teutonic verse (e.g., Beowulf) obvious.

Stray verses, quoted and garbled by later writers, are all that we possess today of primitive Latin poetry. Every scholar has his pet theory of how to "restore" such verses to their original form—much as an architect, giving free rein to his judgment, might restore a ruined temple. The following may be taken as conjectural specimens:

[1]

A line from the very ancient hymn of the *salii*, or leaping priests of Mars, god of the farm lands:

> Quóme tónas Leucésie   praé tet tremónti
>
> > i.e., Cum tonas, Leucesie, prae te tremunt.
> > *When you thunder, o Light God, they tremble before you.*

[2]

A primitive charm to cure the gout—sing it twenty-seven times, touch the ground, and spit:

> Térra péstem tenéto,   sálus hic manéto.

[3]

A wise saw, ascribed to Marcus the Seer:

> Póstrémus dícas,   prímus táceas.

[4]

Maxims of Appius Claudius the Blind. Living at the end of the fourth and beginning of the third centuries B.C., Appius seems to have been the first native Roman with a sense of authorship; his parliamentary speeches were read by Cicero:

> [a] Amícum cúm vídes,   oblíscere misérias
>
> > i.e., obliviscere miseriae, *you forget your misery.*

[b] Éscit súas quísque   fáber fortúnas

> i.e., *Everyman is master of his fate.* **Escit,** *est;* **suas fortunas,** genitive singular.

[5]

Perhaps another simple type of primitive accentual verse, different from the Saturnian, is found in the ancient weather proverb:

Hibérno púlvere,   vérno lúto
grándia fárra,   camílle, métes

> lit., *From winter dust, from spring mud, much grain, my lad, shalt thou harvest* (i.e., *A dry winter and a wet spring make a big harvest*).

[6]

The famous pasquinades in Saturnian verse exchanged between the poet Naevius (see p. 24) and the consul Metellus, although coming a little later than the period under consideration, are probably characteristic of primitive Latin satire:

NAEVIUS: Fáto Metélli Rómae   cónsules fíunt.
METELLUS: Dábunt málum Metélli   Naévio poétae.

> In Naevius' attack **fato** is sarcastic: *None but the Metelli have a chance to become consuls!* Metellus' retort was no empty threat, however—Naevius was imprisoned for free speech.

[7]

More reliable is the evidence produced by archaeology—e.g., the epitaph of L. Cornelius Scipio (consul in 259 B.C.), which was found among others in the Tomb of the Scipios. Although carved on stone, it is not necessarily a contemporary document, as it was probably copied from the original painted epitaph after the lapse of a century or so. The right-hand end of the stone has been broken off, but very little is missing. Unfortunately the literary value of the epitaph is not high—then, as now, actual epitaphs were rarely inspired:

```
HONC.OINO.PLOIRVME.COSENTIONT.R[
DVONORO.OPTVMO.FVISE.VIRO.
LVCIOM.SCIPIONE.FILIOS.BARBATI
CONSOL.CENSOR.AIDILIS.HIC.FVET.A[
HEC.CEPIT.CORSICA.ALERIAQUE.VRBE
DEDET.TEMPESTATEBVS.AIDE.MERETO
```

i.e., Hónc oíno ploírume   coséntiont R[ómai]
duónóro óptumo   fuíse víro
Lúciom Scípióne.   Fílios Barbáti,
cónsol cénsor aidílis   híc fuet a[púd vos].
Héc cépit Córsica   Alériaque úrbe.
Dédet Témpestátebus   aíde méreto.

i.e., Hunc unum plurimi consentiunt Romae
bonorum optimum fuisse virum,
Lucium Scipionem.   Filius Barbati,
consul censor aedilis hic fuit apud vos.
Hic cepit Corsicam Aleriamque urbem.
Dedit Tempestatibus aedem merito.

> **1. Romae,** locative; missing words have been supplied from comparison with the epitaphs of other Scipios.
> **2. virum,** genitive plural.
> **6.** *He dedicated a temple to the Storm Gods as a thank offering.*

Primitive Latin Prose
[1]

The earliest piece of intelligible Latin that has been preserved to us is a prose epigram—i.e., an inscription placed upon an object in order to give the object utterance, to enable it to tell its own story. In this instance the object is a piece of jewelry (found at Praeneste near Rome)—a bronze *fibula* or brooch, which bears after a lapse of 2500 years the message its maker intended: *Manius made me for Numerius*—or, in its own quaint phrase (written from right to left):

IOISAMUN DEKAHFEHF DEM SOINAM

[2]

THE SO-CALLED "LEGES REGIAE"

Although ascribed by Roman antiquarians to the regal period (*753–509* B.C.), these fragments of laws are surely not so old—at least not in the form in which they have been preserved to us. These too have been much "restored":

[a] A concubine must not touch the altar of Juno, goddess of wedlock:

Pellex aram Iunonis ne tangito.   Si tagit, Iunoni, crinibus demissis, agnum feminam caedito.

> **Pellex,** *concubine;* **tagit,** *tangat;* **agnum feminam,** *agnam.*

[b] The corpse of a man struck by lightning must be left lying, or lifted as little as possible from the ground, and must be buried without ceremony:

> Si hominem fulmen Iovis occisit, ne supra genua tollito.
> Homo si fulmine occisus est, ei iusta nulla fieri oportet.

occīsit, *occīderit;* **iusta,** *funera.*

[c] Definition of murder:

> Si quis hominem liberum dolo sciens morti duit, paricidas esto.

dolo sciens, *with malice aforethought;* **duit,** *det;* **paricidas,** *murderer.*

[3]

THE LAWS OF THE TWELVE TABLES

These laws were originally codified in 451–450 B.C., but the few extracts quoted by later Roman authors and thus preserved to posterity probably belong to a revised version. At any rate, schoolboys in Cicero's time were still obliged to memorize these laws in full:

[a] Laws of inheritance and guardianship:

> Uti legassit super pecuniā tutelāve suae rei, ita ius esto.

As one shall have willed concerning his fortune or the guardianship of his estate, so be it valid. **legassit,** *legaverit.*

> Si intestato moritur cui suus heres nec escit, adgnatus proximus familiam habeto.

If one who has no natural heir dies intestate, the nearest agnate (or next of kin in the male line) shall take his estate. **nec escit** *non est.*

> Si adgnatus nec escit, gentiles familiam habento.

If there be no agnate, the clansmen shall have the estate.

[b] An eye for an eye and a tooth for a tooth:

> Si membrum rupsit, ni cum eo pacit, talio esto.

Note the extreme brevity: *If he shall have maimed a member, if he come not to terms with him, let there be retaliation* (i.e., *If A harm B, and A does not pay damages to B, B shall have the right to retaliate*).

[c] Breaking and entering:

> Si nox furtim faxsit, si im occisit, iure caesus esto.

>> Brevity is carried to the point of ignoring necessary change of subject: *If one commit theft by night, if he kill him, he shall be justifiably killed* (i.e., *If A commit theft from B, and B kill A in the act, A shall be justifiably killed*).   **nox,** adverb, *by night;* **faxsit,** *fecerit;* **im,** *eum.*

[d] A public thoroughfare must be kept in repair by the property owner over whose land it lies:

> Vias muniunto.   Ni sam delapidassint, qua volet iumenta agito.

>> *They shall construct roads.   If they have not paved it, let one drive his cattle where he will* (i.e., *one need not stick to the road, if it is not clearly defined*).

[e] Fragment of a sumptuary regulation which states that gold is not to be buried or burned with the dead—except gold teeth:

> (The beginning is lost) . . . neve aurum addito; at cui auro dentes iuncti escunt, ast im cum illo sepeliet uretve, se fraude esto.

>> . . . *nor add gold; but he whose teeth are joined with gold, if one shall bury or burn him with it, one shall be without guilt.*   **ast,** *si;* **se,** *sine.*

III

GREEK LITERATURE

The second of the two cultural forces that molded classical Roman literature was the Greek.

Early in the third century B.C. the Romans came into direct contact with the Greeks of Southern Italy, or *Magna Graecia.* This is not the place to discuss all the channels of Greek influence, direct and indirect, which had tended toward Rome from early times.   Suffice it to say that the Romans "officially" adopted Greek literary standards in the year 240 B.C., after a generation of political ascendancy over the cultured Greeks of Southern Italy.

Let us now turn far back in time and consider the civilization of the Greeks.   Artistically and intellectually the Greeks, or

Hellenes, were the most gifted race the world has ever seen. They were the pioneers of occidental civilization; the greater part of our intellectual heritage, theoretical knowledge, and artistic standards is derived from them. Even at present our ideas and capacities—except in the field of natural science—have not gone beyond those of the Greeks.

It is scarcely fair, however, to compare the Greeks with the Romans. The Romans were a *single tribe*, which gradually conquered and organized an ever-widening circle of neighbors, until its sway extended over and beyond the entire Mediterranean world. On the other hand, the Greeks were (and are) a *race* with many subdivisions and ramifications—a race which had occupied a large part of the Near East for many centuries, and which, through first one and then another of its groups or political units, had made far-reaching advances in human thought and civilization. Ultimately, when the Romans began conquering their oversea empire, they had already fused the entire Italic race into a single unit under Roman leadership; so that a comparison of Greeks and Romans at the time of Cicero is really one between two races: the Greek and the Italic, or Latin. Even as races, however, the two were not on a par, for the Greeks far outnumbered and outshone the Latins.

The Greek race had always been extraordinarily diversified, mobile, and plastic—its language had scores of dialects; no two of its states had the same institutions; its colonies of adventurous emigrants settled the coasts of every known sea; and its inventive and creative genius gave rise to infinite local variations. Thus the Greeks were the torchbearers of culture and civilization, but lacked that uniformity of organization which enabled the Romans to conquer Italy and, later, the Romanized Latins to conquer and rule the world.

The Greeks were as precocious in artistic expression as the Romans were backward. No race has ever produced such great literature at so early a stage in its evolution from primitive barbarism.

To our knowledge, Greek literary achievement dates from Homer's *Iliad* and *Odyssey*, greatest of the world's epics. These poems were probably composed about 1000 B.C., or at any rate so long before the dawn of western history that we are dependent solely on legend and conjectures for our knowledge of their origin and authorship. Although prehistoric, these epics are far from being crude; they were the first and are still the greatest poetic achievement of the occidental world.

The products of Greek genius were cumulative. In successive epochs first one branch, then another, of the Greek race created new channels of human thought or expression, every one of which became a permanent tradition. The old was not discarded when the new came in. Thus, by stages, a vast and enduring structure was built up—Greek literature, Greek art, Greek civilization in its entirety.

But to return to the steps or stages of development: in the eighth century B.C. the Ionian Greeks were the first to produce subjective or reflective poetry (elegiac and iambic); in the seventh century "personal" lyric was developed by the Aeolic Greeks and choral lyric by the Dorians; in the sixth century the Ionians added scientific and philosophic speculation; and in the fifth and fourth centuries the Athenians led the way in artistic creation by perfecting drama (both tragedy and comedy), oratory, history, political and ethical speculation, and a combination of the fine arts—architecture, sculpture, and painting—such as the world has never seen.

These achievements—given only in hasty and inadequate summary—were all the product of the hundreds of local units that made up the Greek, or Hellenic, race, each stimulated by local rivalry and even by warfare, but all conscious of the larger racial unity that differentiated them from "barbarians." The "classic" period of Greek literature, which extended from about 1000 to about 350 B.C., had as its keynote freedom of the mind.

External forces brought this period of Greek civilization to an end about a century before the Romans began to be directly influenced by contact with the Greek race. By the latter half of the fourth century internecine wars and rivalries had more or less exhausted the Greeks, with the result that Alexander the Great—who belonged to one of the outlying and less civilized

Greek tribes (the Macedonian)—conquered the Near East and established a vast empire. This empire endured, with varying fortunes and under various leaderships (first Greek, then Roman, then Byzantine), until its conquest in the eighth century of our era by the Mohammedans. Thus, in the fourth century B.C., a new phase of Greek civilization was inaugurated. The old spirit of freedom and of intense expression of provincial community life was superseded by a cosmopolitan world that spoke and wrote a "common" Greek dialect (the language of the New Testament); by an age of scholarship, of great libraries, of science and ethics, of polished and pedantic poetry—an age which found escape for itself and from itself in religion and in realms of fancy, such as historical fiction, the romantic novel, the pastoral idyl, the short story, and the moralizing fable. There arose with the growth of metropolitan life (in the old cities, like Athens, as well as in the new, like Alexandria) new problems of ethics, a new consciousness of individual sin and responsibility, and a craving for salvation. This produced the great world religions and philosophies (such as the cult of Isis, and later, that of Mithras), the schools of Stoicism and Epicureanism; and finally Christianity.

Such was the Greek "empire" with which the Romans came in contact. The influence upon the Romans of both phases of Greek thought was immediate; the first of these phases being the classic or Hellenic, which was enshrined in the literature of that earlier period of Greek independence; and the second, the Alexandrian or Hellenistic, which, having arisen less than a century before, continued its course, contemporary with, and parallel to—in the end even outliving—Roman thought.

The Chief Greek Authors

[1]

Classical, or Hellenic, Period (National Greek Literature)

(?) X Century B.C.

Homer: Epic (hexameter)—influenced Vergil and all Roman epic poets.

VIII Century

HÉSIOD: Didactic poetry (hexameter)—influenced Vergil in the *Georgics*.

VII–VI Centuries

ARCHÍLOCHUS, SOLON, ETC.: Reflective poetry (iambic and elegíac) —influenced Horace.

VI Century

ALCAÉUS, SAPPHO, ANÁCREON: Melic poetry, or "personal" lyrics —influenced Catullus, Horace, and all Roman lyric poets.

VI–V Centuries

PYTHÁGORAS, HERACLÍTUS, EMPÉDOCLES, HIPPÓCRATES, ETC.: Didactic poems and prose treatises on philosophy and science—influenced Lucretius; supplied material for Cicero's philosophical essays.

SIMÓNIDES, PINDAR, ETC.: Choral lyrics—influenced Horace.

V Century (in Athens)

HERÓDOTUS, THUCÝDIDES: History—influenced Sallust, Livy, and all Roman historians.

AÉSCHYLUS, SÓPHOCLES, EURÍPIDES: Tragedy—influenced all Roman tragedians, of whom only Seneca survives.

V–IV Centuries (in Athens)

ARISTÓPHANES: Political comedy (none in Roman literature).

IV Century (in Athens)

XÉNOPHON: Historical romance, biography, essays—influenced Cicero and all Roman historians.

DEMÓSTHENES, ISÓCRATES, etc.: Oratory—influenced all Roman orators.

SÓCRATES,[1] PLATO, ÁRISTOTLE, ETC.: Philosophical and ethical dialogues and treatises—influenced Cicero and all Roman speculative thinkers.

MENÁNDER, ETC.: Comedy of manners—influenced all Roman comedians, of whom only Plautus and Terence survive.

[1] Socrates inspired, rather than wrote, literature.

[2]

Post-Classical or Hellenistic Period (International Greek Literature)

[a] Alexandrian Era (contemporaneous with the early stages of national Roman literature):

III Century B.C.

Theócritus: Pastoral poetry—influenced Vergil in the *Eclogues*.
Callímachus, etc.: Lyrics, elegies, epigrams—influenced Catúllus, Tibúllus, Propértius, Ovid.
Apollónius of Rhodes: Epic—influenced Vergil.
Zeno, Epicúrus: Stoic and Epicurean philosophy—influenced Lucrétius, Cicero, and Seneca, and profoundly affected all Roman life and thought.

II Century B.C.

Polýbius: History—influenced Livy and other Roman historians.
The Epigrammatists (belonging chiefly to the post-classical period)—influenced Catúllus, Martial, and all Roman epigrammatists.

[b] Roman Era (the Greek world or Eastern Empire under the dominion of Rome):

I Century B.C.

Dionýsius of Halicarnassus: History.

I–II Centuries A.D.

Epictétus, Marcus Aurelius:[1] Moral philosophy.
Dio Chrýsostom: Lectures and essays.
Plutarch: Biography and essays.
Árrian, Áppian: History.
Lúcian: Satiric essays and romances.

Note that in a broad, general way every type of Greek literature *except* the political comedy of Aristóphanes—a fruit of radical democracy which could never be tolerated in Rome—was transplanted and reproduced on Roman soil. Conversely, Greek

[1] Roman emperor from 161–180.

models were closely and exactly followed in every field of
Roman authorship save satire—i.e., the type of satire exemplified
in Horace and Juvenal.[1]   The lack of precise models for other
types of satire is insignificant; Horace, however, believed, and
not without reason, that his satires were *inspired* by Aristophanic
comedy.   In accepting his point of view, we bridge all gaps in
the formative influence of Greek literature on Latin.   On the
other hand, the famous Roman critic Quintilian stressed Roman
independence and sounded the patriotic note when he declared:
Satira tota nostra est.   By his use of *satira* in its narrower and
purely Roman sense, however, Quintillian really begged the
question.

National Roman literature came to an end early in the second
century of the Christian era.   Hence we see how brief its course
was, compared with that of Greek literature.   The later phases
of Greek literature (of the Roman and Byzantine periods) continued to the fall of Constantinople (Byzantium), in 1453 A.D.;
thereafter the Romáic, or modern Greek, *language* and literature
prevailed, and the Mohammedan Turks severed the chain of continuity between ancient and modern Greek.   The later phases
of the Latin language, on the other hand, sloughed off the spontaneous or spoken element—gradually becoming purely literary
and cultural—and have continued in unbroken continuity down
to our own times.

IV

NATIONAL ROMAN LITERATURE

A new national literature, modeled on the Greek, came into
being at Rome about the middle of the third century B.C.   Not
all Romans felt the lure of Greek civilization and culture, but
enough influential nobles were attracted by Greek thought and
Greek art to turn the tide in favor of adopting Greek forms of
literary expression.   The decisive step occurred in 240 B.C., and
it is remarkable that we can date the beginnings of a great literature with such precision.   In this year (immediately after the
close of the First Punic War) the aediles decided to add to the

---

[1] See Vol. II.

horse racing and other entertainments of the fall carnival (or *ludi Romani*) the production, in the Latin language, of two Greek plays—a tragedy and a comedy. The innovation was a great success. It was the entering wedge. Steadily the range of interest in Greek modes of expression widened, and the process of assimilation became effective. Henceforth the growth of national Roman literature from meager and unpromising beginnings to splendid achievement was rapid.

National Roman literature falls into the following six periods, of which the first two constitute the era of growth, and the last four that of maturity:[1]

[1] 240–*150* B.C.: Period of the hasty adaptation of Greek materials to Roman use.

[2] *175–85* B.C.: Period of apprenticeship to classical Greek models of style.

[3] *85*–43 B.C.: Ciceronian Era—first of the mature periods.

[4] 43 B.C.–14 A.D.: Augustan, or Golden, Age.

[5] 14–96 A.D.: Period of the growth of internationalism and the decline of classicism.

[6] 96–*125* A.D.: Silver Age, or the revival of Augustan ideals.

---

[1] Bear in mind that chronological periods are bound to overlap—i.e., the last conservatives of one period and the advance guard of the next are often contemporaries.

National or Classical Roman Literature

FIRST PERIOD

(240–*150* B.C.)

THE PERIOD OF THE HASTY ADAPTATION
OF GREEK MATERIALS TO ROMAN USE

The First Period

FIVE authors may be grouped together and regarded as the pioneers of national Roman literature, and the years over which their activity extends may consequently be called the first period. It must be remembered however that, by this method of grouping, the second period will begin before the first has ended. The years thus comprising the first period amount to nearly a century—namely, 240–*150* B.C.; and the authors are Andronícus, Naevius, Plautus, Ennius, and Cato. It is significant that Cato was the first genuine Roman author. Andronícus was actually Greek; Ennius, probably Oscan—perhaps even Greek; Plautus, who was born in Umbria, was probably of Umbrian blood.[1] Of those who preceded Cato, Naevius alone was a pure Latin, but a Latin of Campania—i.e., that portion of the Latin domain nearest to *Magna Graecia*.

This first period of national Roman literature was a transitional one. Old and new standards existed side by side or were imperfectly blended. The content of Greek literature—mythology, history, and philosophy—had to be assimilated, as well as the major literary forms—drama, elegy, epic, and lyric. The new literature was almost wholly in verse. In their epic or narrative compositions, poets clung for a generation or more to the native accentual meter, the Saturnian; then Ennius, "the father of Latin literature," began adapting the quantitative Greek hexameter to the Latin tongue—a considerable feat of scholarship and literary technique. In their dramatic compositions, however, these same poets made use from the very first of various Greek quantitative meters, ranging all the way from the iambics and trochaics of dramatic dialogue—which were rather free and easy and not so foreign to the genius of the Latin language—to

---

[1] The Oscans and Umbrians were non-Latin peoples of Italic stock; their languages were no more closely related to Latin than Italian is to Spanish.

21

the more elaborate choral rhythms—which were sustained by musical accompaniment. The Latin language remained stiff and inflexible; it could be set to rhythm arbitrarily, but it could not be endowed with melodious cadences. Poets simply used it as they found it, for better or for worse. In comedy they had the advantage of a more colloquial and lively variety of the same rude tongue.

Prose literature made less of an advance during this period. There were no epoch-making innovations comparable to the introduction of epic, dramatic, and lyric poetry and the adoption of quantitative, in place of accentual, rhythms. Prose writing continued in the old channels, with little, if any, improvement in style. Greek influence in the field of prose hardly accomplished more than fire men's ambition to extend the range and increase the dignity of their native oratory and history. Pride in the effectiveness of simple Roman eloquence is manifested as early as 280 B.C. (over a generation before the official "birth" of national Roman literature), when the speech of Appius Claudius the Blind, advising the senate to reject Pyrrhus' terms of peace, was copied and preserved in written form. A century or so later, Cato laid the foundations of Roman prose literature by publishing all of his speeches, and by producing a history of Rome and a collection of treatises on practical subjects (medicine, agriculture, military science, and so forth). Little is known of these works, but to judge by the only one that has been preserved—the treatise on agriculture—Cato's ability as a prose writer had progressed but little beyond that of the jurists and annalists of primitive Rome.

L. LIVIUS ANDRONICUS

(BORN IN ?; ACTIVE FROM 260–204 B.C.)

Andronícus, the earliest "Roman" author, was a native Greek who came to Rome as a youthful prisoner of war after the capture of Tarentum, in 272 B.C. The date of his birth is unknown. He became the slave of M. Livius Salinator and ultimately the tutor of Salinator's children. He was manumitted, took the name of L. Livius Andronicus, and settled permanently in Rome.

The first Latin work by Andronicus was merely a forerunner of the new Roman literature; for as early as 260 B.C. (or thereabouts) Andronicus, who wished to teach "grammar" and could find no Latin literature on which to base his teaching, translated the *Odyssey* into Saturnian verse—probably the first occasion on which that meter was used for a long poem. This bald and crude translation did not have the effect of Andronicus' later work, that of starting a new movement or cultural epoch. Nor, on the other hand, does it belong in spirit and content to the old native Latin literature. It was solely a textbook for the *grammaticus*, or teacher of poetry. We must remember, however, that it was still used as a textbook in the grammar schools when Horace was a boy. Only a few fragments of this crude translation have been preserved:

[1]

Nausicaä tells Odysseus to wait until she has reached home in the mule cart before he starts to follow her (*Odyssey* VI, 295–6):

íbi mánens sedéto   dónicum vidébis
mé, carpénto vehéntem,   dómum venísse.

donicum, *donec;* **vehentem,** *riding.*

[2]

" . . . for I know of naught
That more severely tries the strongest man,
And breaks him down, than perils of the sea."
(*Odyssey* VIII, 138–9; Bryant's Translation 172–4)

námque núllum péius   mácerat humánum
quámde máre saévom.   Víres cui sunt mágnae,
tópper cónfríngent   ímportunae úndae.

i.e., namque nihil peius macerat hominem quam mare saevum. Cui vires sunt magnae, [eum] protinus confringent importunae undae.

The fact that this translation and the even more venerable *Laws of the XII Tables* were still a part of the pabulum of the schools in the Ciceronian era, indicates the tenacity of the older traditions and proves that the native Latin genius was still a force to be reckoned with in classical Roman literature.

In 240 B.C. Andronicus was commissioned to make versions of a Greek tragedy and a Greek comedy for the Roman carnival. He thus took what proved to be the first step in the creation of the new national Roman literature. After this memorable year Andronicus continued to exercise his function of "playwright," and the Greek drama grew steadily in popularity.

Upon occasion Andronicus also composed original Latin hymns for religious festivals. Before his death, in 204 B.C., literature was established at Rome and (with characteristic Roman philistinism) poets were recognized as legitimate artisans, with the right to form a guild like other workmen!

CN. NAEVIUS

(Born in ?; active from *240*–199 B.C.)

The second "Roman" author, a contemporary of Andronicus, was a native free-born Latin of Southern Italy. Since the Latins of Southern Italy were in closer contact with the Greeks, they were more fully cultured and Hellenized than the Romans. Naevius, the date of whose birth is unknown, came to Rome about 240 and lived there till 199 B.C. His chief literary works were: (a) dramas, which included not only paraphrases from the Greek but also two original tragedies (closely modeled on Greek style, of course)—one dealing with the pseudo-Roman legend of Romulus and Remus; the other, with contemporary history, after the analogy of the *Persians* of Aeschylus and other famous Greek "chronicle plays"; and (b) an original epic in Saturnian meter, entitled *de Bello Punico*, from which even Vergil borrowed—for it dealt with Roman legend and history from Aeneas to the First Punic War.

The satiric epigrams exchanged between Naevius and the Metelli have already been mentioned (p. 7). They seem to have

arisen from an enthusiastic, but misguided, attempt on the part
of Naevius to introduce into Rome the freedom of speech for
which the great Athenian literature of the fifth and fourth centuries B.C. was famous.

A few of the extant fragments of his works are worth glancing
at:

[1]

A witty description of a coquette has been preserved from his
comedy *Tarentilla*.   The meter is trochaic, in the free and easy
style of comedy:

> Quási in choró ludéns, datátim dát se et cómmuném facít;
> álii adnútat; álii adníctat; álium amát; aliúm tenét;
> álibi mánus est óccupáta; álii pércellít pedém;
> ánulúm dat álii spéctandum; á labrís alium ínvocát;
> cum álio cántat; át tamen álii suó dat dígito lítterás.

> Quasi . . . dat se, *as if playing* [*ball*] *in a group* [*of maidens*],
> *she gives herself to and fro;* the subject throughout is *she*—i.e.,
> the coquette.

[2]

Fragments of his *Bellum Punicum* in Saturnian meter were preserved by scholars who wrote commentaries on the *Aeneid* in the
late Roman Empire.

[a] Servius on *Aeneid* III, 10 says: Naevius enim inducit uxores
Aeneae et Anchisae cum lacrimis Ilium relinquentes his verbis:

> . . . ambórum uxóres
> nóctu Tróiad exíbant   capítibus opértis,
> fléntes ámbae, abeúntes   lácrimis cum múltis.

> **Troiad,** *Troiā* (i.e., *from Troy*).

[b] Servius on *Aeneid* II, 297 says: Naevius, Bello Punico primo
(i.e., in Book I), de Anchisa et Aenea fugientibus haec ait:

> Eórum séctam sequóntur   múlti mortáles;
> múlti álii e Tróia   strénui víri
> úrbi fóras cum aúro   íllic exíbant.

> **sectam,** *band;* **urbi,** ablative.

At the death of Naevius, Saturnian meter disappears from
formal literature.

T. MACCIUS PLAUTUS

(BORN IN ?; ACTIVE FROM *220*-184 B.C.)

His Life and Works

Of the real life of Plautus nothing is known, but tradition records that, like Shakespeare, he was of humble origin and trained in practical stagecraft. Plautus wrote only comedies. A collection of twenty-one of his plays has survived in fairly good condition; these were selected in the time of Cicero as the best and most authentic of the many ascribed to his name.

Of all the forms of Greek literature that the Romans tried to master, none was so quickly and successfully assimilated as the comedy of manners. The Romans had a natural .bent for the satiric rather than for the sublime; and they found the comedy of manners, which belonged to the Greek world of their own day, easier to comprehend than the classic Greek literature of an earlier and remoter age. In fact, the comedy of manners—dealing, as it does, with familiar and traditional types of humanity—is always universal in its appeal and always entertaining. Moreover, fate has been kind to the Romans; for the Greek originals, which were undoubtedly superior to the Roman adaptations, have almost entirely perished. Thus the excellence of the Greek comedy of manners is today reflected almost exclusively in the existing Latin versions—i.e., the plays of Plautus (which were produced from about 220 to 184 B.C.) and the six plays of Terence (which belong to the next period of Roman literature and were produced from 166 to 160 B.C.). As regards the relative merits of Greek and Roman comedy, it is probably safe to say that the baser elements of farce and caricature appeared more often in the latter. Moreover, modern imitators like Ben Jonson, Molière, and (in a few plays) Shakespeare have improved the characterization considerably.

The "comedy of manners" (called variously the "comedy of character," the "comedy of humors," and so forth), as presented by the Greeks and Romans, was highly conventional. No matter what the play, the setting was always the same: the long narrow

stage was a street, and the background was formed by the fronts
of three buildings facing the street. All action, therefore, had to
take place outdoors; there were no interior scenes. These limitations become more plausible, however, when one reflects that
in southern cities of today (such as Naples) there is hardly any
happening, domestic or otherwise, which cannot and does not
take place on the street! The Greek and Roman comedies were
also conventional in that all plays drew their characters from
the same set of stock figures: the irate father, the prodigal son,
the fawning parasite, the cunning servant, the bragging soldier,
the cook, the courtesan, the indulgent mother, and so forth.

Such Latin adaptations were presented to the Romans as pictures of *Greek* life. Names of the characters remained Greek;
and actors wore the Greek national costume, the *pallium* (so
different from the toga)—whence the plays were called *fabulae
palliatae*. Not for a minute would the Romans—those of this
period, at least—have allowed such a gay and dissolute life as
these comedies generally portrayed to be presented as Roman.
The plays appealed to a Roman audience just as risqué Parisian
farces now appeal to a puritanical Anglo-Saxon audience—i.e.,
they were entertaining and, provided they did not reflect on
Roman morals, could be safely, if not too frequently, enjoyed.
(It was almost 200 years after the introduction of Greek drama
into Rome before the conservative prejudices against the stage
could be sufficiently overcome to allow the building of a permanent theater.)

Plautus handles his Greek originals with great freedom—either
paraphrasing and reshaping single plays, or inserting and adapting scenes from other plays (the latter process being known as
contaminatio, a practice as common in modern as in ancient
times). His plot structure is somewhat slipshod, but his humor
rough and ready. At his hand, Greek subtlety of delineation is
changed into vigor of action. Although still essentially primitive
Latin, the language of Plautus is used with colloquial rapidity
and exuberance. Thus, despite the fact that they are borrowed
from the Greek, his plays are among the most racy of European
dramatic productions; their spirit is genuinely Italic.

Of the twenty-one plays of Plautus, nineteen are complete or almost complete. The best of these are: *Aulularia*, or *The Pot of Gold* (the original of Molière's *l'Avare*); *Menaechmi* (Shakespeare's *Comedy of Errors*); *Miles Gloriosus*, or *The Swashbuckler; Mostellaria*, or *The Haunted House; Rudens*, or *The Shipwreck; Amphitruo*, or *The Birth of Hercules* (a parody of mythology, or "tragi-comedy"); *Captivi*, or *The Captives; Trinummus*, or *Thrippence* (the latter two are "moral" plays, without female characters); and four comedies of intrigue, named in each instance for the chief character or characters: *Pseudolus, Curculio, Bacchides*, and *Epidicus*.

The Meters of Plautus' Plays

The greatest handicap to our appreciation of all ancient drama, both comedy and tragedy, is the loss of the music that was an integral part of a performance. With the music was associated the dance—all definite knowledge of that has likewise perished. In Roman comedy certain scenes, particularly those having greater emotional intensity, were sung and danced to the accompaniment of the flute. These scenes, called *cantica*, were composed sometimes in familiar meters, sometimes in more unusual ones, which are too difficult for the beginner. Without their musical accompaniment, the more elaborate meters cannot be satisfactorily interpreted even by the greatest scholars. No attempt has been made in this book, therefore, to indicate the scansion of the more difficult *cantica*.

The spoken passages in Roman comedy (*diverbia*) were always in either iambic or trochaic rhythms. These two rhythms are essentially one, the only difference being that in the trochaic the accent begins on the first syllable of a line, in the iambic on the second. For instance, a fifteen-syllable line, consisting of alternate short and long syllables ($\smile - \smile - \smile - \smile - \smile - \smile - \smile - \smile$) might be scanned theoretically either as a seven-and-a-half foot iambic ($\smile \acute- \; \smile \acute- \; \smile \acute- \; \smile \acute- \; \smile \acute- \; \smile \acute- \; \smile \acute- \; \smile$) or as a seven-and-a-half foot trochaic ($\smile \; \acute- \smile \; \acute- \smile \; \acute- \smile \; \acute- \smile \; \acute- \smile \; \acute- \smile \; \acute- \smile$). Following the traditional nomenclature, however—i.e., "trochaic," when the accent begins on the first syllable of a line; "iambic," when it begins on the second—we find that the *diverbia*, or spoken passages of Roman comedy, consist of six-, seven-, and eight-foot iambics and of seven- and eight-foot trochaics.

The next point to note is that usage allowed the trochaics and iambics of comedy to become practically loose rhythms instead of exact meters. To illustrate—"pure" iambics may be seen in an epigram of Catullus, composed with almost mathematical precision:

$$\smallsmile \acute{\,}\; \smallsmile \acute{\,}\; \smallsmile \quad \acute{\,} \quad \smallsmile \acute{\,} \smallsmile \quad \acute{\,} \quad \smallsmile \acute{\,}$$

Phasellus ille quem videtis hospites.

But it is obvious that such a rigid meter as this would be too monotonous for comic dialogue, which must be informal and naturalistic, approximating everyday conversation. Consequently it had become the tradition of comedy (long before the Romans borrowed their drama from the Greeks) to allow the substitution of almost any other foot for the iamb or the trochee—provided it contained the same number of musical units, or not more than one additional unit. *Only the accent* had to remain iambic or trochaic, as the case might be. Since every long syllable is regarded as the equivalent of two shorts, it is evident that the iamb (˘ ´), like the trochee (´ ˘), contains three musical units. We may therefore substitute for the *iamb* (a) the tribrach (˘ ˘́ ˘), which contains the same number of units, and (b) any of the following four-unit feet: spondee (– ´), dactyl (– ˘́ ˘), ánapaest (˘ ˘ ´), and proceleusmáticus (˘ ˘ ˘́ ˘). These same substitutions may be made for the *trochee*, but with trochaic accent: tribrach (˘́ ˘ ˘), spondee (´ –), dactyl (´ ˘ ˘), ánapaest (˘́ ˘ –), and—very rarely—proceleusmáticus (˘́ ˘ ˘ ˘). Occasionally even five-unit feet are substituted.

Let us now look at some examples of the loose rhythms of comedy. The numerous substitutions and elisions render these verses comparatively easy to compose, but difficult to scan:

SIX-FOOT IAMBIC

Communicabo semper te mensā meā (*Miles*, l. 31)

–	´	˘	´	–	´	˘	´	–	´	˘́
Commun		ica		bosemp		erte		mensa		mea

Nimia est miseria nimis pulchrum esse hominem. Immo ita est (l. 44)

˘	˘́	˘	˘ ˘́	˘ ˘́ ˘	–	´	˘ ˘ ´	˘́
Nimia'st		miseri	animi'	pulchr'ess'	homin'Imm'		ita'st	

"Seven-Foot" [1] Iambic

Cum me in locis Neptuniis templisque turbulentis (*Miles*, l. 187)

Cumm'in locis Neptun i i s templis queturb ulent is

Non edepol tu illum magis amas quam ego, mea, si per te liceat (l. 503)

Nonede polt'ill ummagis amas qu'egomea siper telice at [2]

Eight-Foot Iambic

Id modo videndum est, ut materies suppetat scutariis (*Epidicus*, l. 37)

Idmodo viden dum'stut materi essup petat scuta r i i s

"Seven-Foot" [1] Trochaic

Mussitabis: plus oportet scire servum quam loqui (*Miles*, l. 232)

Mussi tabis plusop ortet scire servum quamlo qui

Consilium est ita facere. Pede ego iam illam huc tibi sistam in viam
(l. 161)

Consili um'stita facere Ped'ego j'ill'huc tibisist' invi am

Eight-Foot Trochaic

Quia perire solus nolo, te cupio perire mecum (*Epidicus*, l. 77)

Quiaper ire solus nolo tecupi oper ire mecum

Anapaestic

For the pure anapæst (˘ ˘ ´) may be substituted: the spondee (- ´), the dactyl (- ´ ˘), or the proceleusmáticus (˘ ˘ ´ ˘).

"Seven-Foot" [1] Anapaestic

Quia tis egeat, quia te careat. Ob eam rem huc ad te missa est
(*Miles*, l. 389)

Quiatis e g e a t quiate careat Obeam r'hucad temiss a'st

Ab illa quae digitos despoliat suos et tuos digitos decorat (l. 401)

Abil'a quaedigi tosde spoliat suoset tuosdigi tosdecor at.

---

[1] There are really seven and a half feet to a line.

[2] Note that the last syllable of a line may be either long or short, regardless of the requirements of the meter—a universal rule of Latin verse.

Spelling

The standardized spelling, familiar to students, has been used for all Latin authors in this book from Plautus on. To help a student over the difficulty of homonyms, the circumflex accent has been introduced as an arbitrary sign to distinguish relative and demonstrative adverbs (in so far as they are ambiguous) from their corresponding adjectives and pronouns: hîc, *here;* istîc, istî, illîc, illî, *there;* quô, *whither;* quoquô, *whithersoever;* eô, istô, istôc, istûc, illô, illôc, illûc,[1] *thither;* eôdem, *to the same place;* aliquô, *to some place;* quôlibet, quôvis, *to any place;* quâ, *where;* quaquâ, *wherever:* eâ, istâ, istâc, illâ, illâc, *that way;* eâdem, *the same way, at the same time;* aliquâ, *some way;* quâlibet, quâvis, *any way;* quî, *how;* aliquî, *somehow;* and so forth. A few nondemonstrative adverbs have been similarly treated to differentiate them from adjectives, nouns, or verbs: rectâ, *directly;* unâ, *together;* modô, *only, just, now;* citô, *quickly;* intrô, *into the house;* and so forth.

I

Miles Gloriosus, or The Swashbuckler

(A SIMPLE FARCE, ABRIDGED FOR EASY READING.)

DRAMATIS PERSONAE

(All names are Greek.)

(1) PYRGOPOLINÍCES (or *Citadel-Stormer*): the *miles gloriosus*, a braggart and lady-killer, now resident commander of a mercenary force in Éphesus.

(2) ARTOTRÓGUS (or *Trencherman*, lit. *Bread-Devourer*): parasite or hanger-on of Pyrgopolinices.

(3) PALAÉSTRIO (or *Nimble*, from *palaestra* or *wrestling ground*): a clever and cunning servant of Pyrgopolinices, still faithful to his former master Pleusicles (see below).

(4) SCÉLEDRUS (or *Rapscallion*, lit. *dirt* in the Greek, but also suggesting *scelus* and *sceleratus* to a Latin audience): a blundering servant of Pyrgopolinices.

(5) PLEÚSICLES (or *Rover*, from the Greek root *to sail*): a young gallant of Athens; lover of Philocomasium.

(6) PHILOCOMÁSIUM (or *Mardigras*, suggesting that she is fond of

---

[1] *Huc* needs no special accent, for it has no homonym.

revels): former sweetheart of Pleusicles in Athens; abducted by
Pyrgopolinices and brought to Ephesus.

(7) PERIPLECTÓMENUS (or *Twining*, alluding to his accomplishments
in the dance): a wealthy and gay old bachelor of Ephesus; old family
friend of Pleusicles.

(8) ACROTELEÚTIUM (or *Perfection*): a young woman of Ephesus;
client of Periplectomenus.

(9) MILPHIDÍPPA (or *Bat-Eye*, suggesting that she stays out late
nights): maidservant of Acroteleutium.

SCENE

The scene is laid in a street in Éphesus, a gay Greek city of Asia
Minor.   On the right the street is supposed to lead to the market
place (*forum*) and center of the town; on the left, to the harbor and
foreign parts.   Two adjoining dwellings face the street and the spectators.   The house on the right belongs to PYRGOPOLINICES; that on
the left, to PERIPLECTOMENUS.

INDUCTION

Meter: six-foot iambic.

[*Enter* PYRGOPOLINICES *from his house, in full regalia, accompanied by his bodyguard and his fawning, black-robed parasite.
The soldiers halt.*   PYRGOPOLINICES *struts across the stage, followed
deferentially by* ARTOTROGUS.]

[1] **Py.** [*with haughty condescension*] Ubi Ártotrógus núnc est?
    Ar. [*at his elbow*] Stát proptér virúm

2   fortem átque fórtunátum et fórma régiá,

3   tum béllatórem . . . [*at a loss for words*] . . . Márs haud
    aúsit díceré

4   neque aéquiperáre suás virtútes ád tuás.

5   **Py.** [*just to make conversation*] Quemne égo servávi in cámpis
    Cúrculióniís,

6   ubi Búmbomáchides Clýtomestóridysárchidés

7   erat ímperátor súmmus, Néptuní nepós?

8   **Ar.** Meminí: nempe íllum dícis cum ármis aúreís,

9   cuius tú legiónes dífflavísti spíritú,

[10] quasi véntus fólia. [*He pauses expectantly, but gets no re-
     ply.*]   Vél elephánto in Índiá . . . [*he stops to think what
     to say*]

11   quo pácto ei púgno praéfregísti brácchiúm.

12   **Py.** Quid "brácchium"?   **Ar.** Íllud díceré voluí "femúr."

13   **Py.** At indíligénter ícerám.   **Ar.** Pol sí quidém

14   conníxus ésses, pér coriúm, per víscerá,

15   perque ós elephánti tránsminéret brácchiúm.

[16]   **Py.** [*waving him aside*] Nolo ístaec núnc.   **Ar.** [*to the audience, confidentially*] Hasce áerumnás ventér creát,

17   et ádsentándum 'st quídquid híc mentíbitúr.

18   **Py.** [*beckoning to* Artotrogus] Habés . . . ?   **Ar.** [*interrupting him*] Tabéllas vís rogáre: habeo—ét stilúm.

19   **Py.** Facéte advértis túum animum ád animúm meúm.

20   **Ar.** Novísse móres tuós me méditaté decét

21   curámque adhibére ut praéolat míhi quod tú velís.

22   **Py.** [*laughingly testing him*] Ecquíd meminísti?   **Ar.** [*resuming his flattery with gusto*] Mémini céntum in Cíliciá

23   et quínquagínta; céntum in Scýtholatróniá;

24   trigínta Sárdos; séxagínta Mácedonés . . . [*stopping for breath*] . . .

25   sunt hómines quós tu . . . [*pausing to think what to say next*] . . . óccidísti unó dié.

26   **Py.** Quanta ístaec hóminum súmma 'st?   **Ar.** [*with noble disregard for arithmetic*] Séptem míliá.

27   **Py.** Tantum ésse opórtet: récte rátioném tenés.

28   **Ar.** At núllos hábeo scríptos: síc meminí tamén.

29   **Py.** Edepól memória 's óptimá.   **Ar.** [*frankly*] Offaé monént.

30   **Py.** Dum tále fácies quále adhúc, adsíduo edés:

31   [*with mock solemnity*] commúnicábo sémper té mensá meá.

32   **Ar.** [*in a burst of gratitude*] Quid tíbi ego dícam quod ómnes mórtalés sciúnt:

33   Pyrgópoliním te únum in térra víveré

34   virtúte et fórma et fáctis ínvictíssimís?

35   Amánt ted ómnes múlierés—neque íniuriá,

36   qui sís tam púlcher; vél illae quaé here pálló

37   me réprehendérunt.   **Py.** [*interested*] Quíd eae díxerúnt tibí?

38   **Ar.** Rogitábant: "hícine Achílles ést?" inquít mihí.

39   "Immo éius fráter" ínquam " 'st."   Ibi íllarum álterá

40 "ergó mecástor púlcher ést" inquít mihí
41 "et líberális; víde, caesáries quám decét."
42 **Py.** [*eagerly*] Itane áibant tándem? **Ar.** Quaén me ambae
    óbsecráverínt,
43 ut te hódie, quási pompam, íllâ praéterdúcerém?
44 **Py.** [*sighing*] Nimiá 'st miséria nímis pulchrum ésse homi-
    nem. **Ar.** Ímmo itá 'st.
[45] Molestaé sunt múlierés: oránt, exóbsecránt,
[46] ut té videánt; ad sése te árcessí iubént . . . [*pausing*] . . .
[47] ut tuó non póssim dáre operám negótió.
48 **Py.** [*brusquely*] Vidétur témpus ésse ut eámus ád forúm,
49 nam réx Seleúcus me ópere orávit máximó,
50 ut síbi latrónes cógerem ét conscríberém.
51 **Ar.** Age, eámus érgo. **Py.** [*to his men-at-arms*] Séquiminí,
    satéllités. [*Exeunt right.*]

PROLOGUE
Meter: six-foot iambic.

[*As the soldiers march off, enter* PALAESTRIO *from the house of*
PYRGOPOLINICES. *He makes a grimace at the departing swash-*
buckler and then addresses the audience.]

[52] **Pa.** Erús meus ílle 'st, glóriósus, ímpudéns.
53 Ait sése ultro ómnis múlierés sectáriér:
54 is déridículo 'st, quáquâ incédit, ómnibús.
[55] Ego haú diu apúd hunc sérvitútem sérvió.
56 Id vólo vos scíre, quómodo ad húnc devénerím
57 in sérvitútem ab eó cui sérviví priús.
58 Erat érus Athénis míhi aduléscens óptimús,
[59] qui amábat múlierem Átticam, et ílla illúm simúl.
60 Is públicé legátus Naúpactúm fuít.
61 Intéribi hic míles fórte Athénas ádvenít,
62 eamque húc invítam múlierem ín Ephesum ádvehít.
63 Ubi amícam erílem Athénis ávectám sció,
64 ego, quántum vívus póssum, míhi navém paró;
65 inscéndo, ut eám rem Naúpactum ád erum núntiém.
66 Ubi súmus provécti in áltum, fít quod dí volúnt:
67 capiúnt praedónes návem illam úbi vectús fuí.

68 Ille quí me cépit dát me huic dóno mílití.

69 Hic póstquam in aédis me ád se déduxít domúm,

70 video íllam amícam erílem, Athénis quaé fuít.

71 Ubi cóntra aspéxit me, óculis míhi signúm dedít

72 ne se áppellárem; deínde póstquam occásió 'st,

73 conquéritur mécum múlier fórtunás suás:

74 ait sése Athénas fúgere cúpere ex hác domú;

75 sese íllum amáre, méum erum, Athénis quí fuít,

76 neque péius quémquam odísse quam ístum mílitém.

77 Ego quóniam inspéxi múlierís senténtiám,

78 cepí tabéllas, cónsignávi, clánculúm

79 dedi mércatóri cuídam, qui ád illum déferát

80 (meum erúm qui Athénis fúerat, qui hánc amáverát),

81 ut is húc veníret. Ís non sprévit núntiúm;

82 nam et vénit et ís in próximo híc [*pointing to the house of* Periplectomenus] devértitúr

83 apúd patérnum suum hóspitém, lepidúm seném,

[84] qui operá nos cónsilióque adhórtatúr, iuvát.

85 Ítaque égo parávi híc [*pointing to the house of* Pyrgopoli- nices] íntus mágnas máchinás,

86 quí amántis únâ intér se fácerem cónvenás.

[87] Nam unúm concláve, múlieri ílli quód dedít

88 milés, quô némo nísi eapse ínferrét pedém,

89 in eó conclávi egó perfódi párietém,

90 quâ cómmeátus clam ésset hínc huc múlierí;

91 et séne sciénte hoc féci; is cónsiliúm dedít.

92 Sed fóris concrépuit hínc a vícinó sené;

93 ipse éxit. Hic ílle 'st lépidus, quém dixí, senéx.

ACT I: THE HOODWINKING OF SCELEDRUS
Scene 1

Meter: seven-foot trochaic.

[*Enter* Periplectomenus *from his own house, in great agitation.*]

[94] **Pa.** [*calling*] Quíd agis, Périplectómene? **Pe.** [*looking up*] Estne híc Palaéstrio? [*Impressively*] Óccisí sumús.

95 **Pa.** Quíd negóti 'st? **Pe.** Rés palám 'st. **Pa.** Quae rés palám 'st? **Pe.** De tégulís

96 módô nescióquis ínspectávit véstrum fámiliáriúm
97 pér nostrum ímpluvium íntus apúd nos Phílocomásium
   atque hóspitém
98 ósculántis. **Pa.** Quís homo id vídit? **Pe.** Túus consérvus.
   Pa. Quís is homó 'st?
99 **Pe.** Néscio, ita ábripuít repénte sése súbito. **Pa.** Súspicór
100 mé periísse. **Pe.** Ubi abít, conclámo: "heus, quíd agis tu"
   ínquam "in tégulís?"
101 Ílle mihi ábiens íta respóndit, sé sectári símiám.
102 **Pa.** Séd Philocómasium hícine étiam núnc est? **Pe.** Cum
   éxibam híc erát.
103 **Pa.** Í si's, iúbe transíre huc [*pointing to* Pyrgopolinices'
   house] quántum póssit, se út videánt domí
104 fámiliáres, nísi quidem ílla nós vult súpplició darí.
105 **Pe.** Díxi ego ístuc; nísi quid áliud vís? **Pa.** Volo; hóc ei
   dícitó:
106 út eum, quí se hîc vídit, vérbis víncat né is se víderít;
107 sí quidém centiéns hîc vísa sít, tamen ínfitiás eát.
108 Núnc sic rátionem íncipísso. [*He ponders for a moment.*]
   Hánc instítuam astútiám,
109 út Philocómasio hánc sorórem géminam gérmanam álterám
110 dícam Athénis ádvenísse cúm amatóre aliquó suó,
111 tám similém quam lácte lácti 'st.   Apúd te eos hîc devér-
   tiér
112 dícam hospítio. . . . **Pe.** [*interrupting him*] Euge eúge, lépide! Laúdo cómmentúm tuúm.
113 **Pa.** . . . út, si illíc concrímmátus sít advérsum mílitém
[114] hánc sesé vidísse cum álieno ósculári, ego árguám
[115] álterám vidísse apúd te cúm suo amátore. **Pe.** Óptimé:
116 ídem ego dícam, si éx me exquíret míles. **Pa.** Séd simílli-
   más
117 dícito ésse.   Et Phílocomásio id praécipiéndum 'st út sciát,
118 né titubét, si exquíret éx ea míles. **Pe.** Nímis doctúm do-
   lúm!
119 Séd si ambás vidére in úno míles cóncilió volét,
120 quíd agimús? **Pa.** Facilé 'st: trecéntae póssunt caúsae
   cólligí:

121 "nón domi 'st, ábiit ámbulátum, dórmit, órnatúr, lavát,
122 prándet, pótat, óccupáta 'st, óperae nón est, nón potést."
123 **Pe.** Plácet ut dícis. **Pa.** Íntrô abi érgo, et, si ístî 'st múlier,
    eám iubé
124 cítô domúm transíre; atque haéc ei díce, mónstra, praécipé
125 dé geminá soróre. **Pe.** Dócte tíbi illam pérdoctám dabó.
[126] Númquid áliud? **Pa.** Ábeas íntrô. [*Exit* PERIPLECTOME-
    NUS.] Ego ínvestígabó quidém,
127 quí fuerít consérvus qui hódie sít sectátus símiám.
128 Séd forés crepuérunt nóstrae; ego vóci móderabór meaé,
129 nam íllic est Phílocomásio cústos, méus consérvus qui ít
    forás.

SCENE 2

Meter: seven-foot trochaic.

[*Enter* SCELEDRUS, *sorely puzzled, from the house of* PYRGOPOLI-
NICES.]

130 **Sc.** [*to himself*] Nísi quidem égo hodie ámbulávi dórmiéns
    in tégulís,
131 cérte edepól scio mé vidísse hîc próximaé vicíniaé
132 Phílocomásium erílem amícam síbi malám rem quaéreré.
133 **Pa.** [*pricking up his ears*] Híc illam vídit ósculántem, quán-
    tum hunc aúdiví loquí.
134 **Sc.** [*overhearing him*] Quís hic est? **Pa.** Túus consérvus.
    Quíd agis, Scéledre? **Sc.** [*eagerly*] Té, Palaéstrió,
135 vólup est cónvenísse. **Pa.** [*pretending ignorance*] Quíd iam?
    Aut quíd negóti 'st? Fác sciám.
136 **Sc.** Símiam hódie súm sectátus nóstram in hórum tégulís:
137 fórte fórtuná per implúvium húc despéxi in próximúm,
138 átque ego illî áspicio ósculántem Phílocomásium cum álteró
139 néscioquo ádulescénte. **Pa.** Quód ego, Scéledre, scélus ex
    te aúdió?
140 **Sc.** Prófecto vídi. **Pa.** Tútin? **Sc.** Égomet—duóbus hís
    oculís meís.
[141] **Pa.** Ábi, nón verisímile dícis. **Sc.** Haéc vidísse egomét
    sció.

142 **Pa.** [*feigning wrath*] Pérgi'n, ínfelíx?   **Sc.** Quid tíbi vis dícam, nísi quod víderím?

143 Quín etiám nunc íntus hĩc in próximó 'st.   **Pa.** [*innocently*]
Eho an nón domí 'st?

144 **Sc.** Víse, abi íntrô túte, nam égo mi iám nil crédi póstuló.

[145] **Pa.** Cértum 'st fácere.   [*Exit, dashing into* Pyrgopolinices'
house.]   **Sc.** Hĩc te oppériar [*planting himself before the
door of* Periplectomenus' *house*]: múlieri ínsidiás dabó.

[*Enter* Palaestrio, *running out of* Pyrgopolinices' *house.*]

[146] **Pa.** Scéledre, Scéledre, quís homo in térra té 'st audációr?
Sc. Quid ést?

147 **Pa.** Iúbe'n tibi óculos écfodíri, quíbus id quód nusquám
'st vidés?

148 **Sc.** Quam ób rem iúbeam?   **Pa.** Phílocomásium eccám
domí, quam in próximó

149 vídisse áibas te ósculántem atque ámplexántem cum álteró.

[Philocomasium *looks out of* Pyrgopolinices' *house.*]

150 Séd fores cóncrepuérunt nóstrae.   **Sc.** [*like a cat watching a
mousehole*] At ego ílico óbservó forés:

151 nám nihil ést quâ hinc húc transíre ea póssit nísi recto
óstió.

152 **Pa.** [*exasperated*] Quín domi éccam!   Néscioquaé te, Scéledre, scélera súscitánt.

153 **Sc.** [*refusing to look*] Míhi ego vídeo, míhi ego sápio, míhi
ego crédo plúrimúm:

154 mé homo némo déterrébit quín ea sít in his aédibús.

155 **Pa.** Ví'n iam fáciam utí stultívidúm te fáteare, . . . **Sc.**
[*interrupting him defiantly*] Áge facé.

156 **Pa.** . . . néque te quícquam sápere córde néque oculís utí?
Sc. Voló.

157 **Pa.** Scí'n tu núllum cómmeátum hínc esse á nobís?   **Sc.**
Sció.

158 **Pa.** Quíd nunc?   Si éa domí 'st—si fácio ut eam éxire hínc
videás domó—

159 dígnu'n és verbéribus múltis?   **Sc.** Dígnus.   **Pa.** Sérva istás
forés,

160 né tibi clám se súbterdúcat ístinc átque huc tránseát.

161 **Sc.** [*calmly*] Cónsiliúm 'st ita fácere. **Pa.** Péde ego iam íllam huc tíbi sistam ín viám. [*Exit into* Pyrgopolinices' *house.*]

162 **Sc.** [*keeping his vigil*] Séd ego hoc quód ago, id me ágere opórtet: hóc obsérvare óstiúm.

Scene 3

Meter: seven-foot iambic.

[*Enter* Palaestrio *and* Philocomasium *from* Pyrgopolinices' *house.*]

163 **Pa.** [*triumphantly*] Quid aís tu, Scéledre? **Sc.** [*not budging an inch*] Hanc rém geró. Habeo aúris: lóquere quídvis.

164 **Pa.** Respícedum ad laévam. [Sceledrus *looks.*] Quis íllaec ést muliér? **Sc.** Pro di ímmortáles!

165 **Ph.** [*stepping forward*] Ubi isté 'st bonus sérvus quí probrí me máximi ínnocéntem

166 falso ínsimulávit? **Pa.** [*pointing to* Sceledrus] Ém tibi! Híc mihi díxit, tíbi quae díxi.

167 **Ph.** [*to* Sceledrus] Tun mé vidísse in próximo híc, sceléste, ais ósculántem?

168 **Pa.** [*egging her on*] Ac "cum álieno ádulescéntuló" dixít. **Sc.** [*defiantly*] Dixi hércle véro.

169 **Ph.** Tun mé vidísti? **Sc.** Atque hís quidem hércle oculís . . . **Ph.** [*interrupting him angrily*] Carébis, crédo,

170 qui plús vidént quam quód vidént. **Sc.** Numquam hércle déterrébor,

171 quin víderim íd quod víderím. **Ph.** [*haughtily*] Ego stúlta et móra múltum,

172 quae cum hóc insáno fábulér: quem pól ego cápitis pérdam!

[173] **Sc.** [*shouting after* Philocomasium *as she goes into* Pyrgopolinices' *house*] Nolí malúm minitári mí: certe égo te híc íntus vídi.

174 Sed [*with less confidence*] paúcis vérbis té voló, Palaéstrio: óbsecro, únde

[175] exít haec húc? **Pa.** Unde nísi domó? **Sc.** Domó? **Pa.** Quid ní? **Sc.** [*wavering*] Sed támen

176 nimis mírum 'st fácinus, quómodo haéc hinc húc transíre
pótuit.

177 **Pa.** [*jeering*] Sci'n té periísse?   **Sc.** [*deep in thought*] Núnc
quidém domi cérto 'st.   [*Rousing himself*] Cérta rés est,

[178] nunc nóstrum obsérvari óstiúm, ubiubí 'st amíca erílis.
[*Still puzzled, he stands guard at the door of his own house,
and continues to mumble to himself.*]

179 Nesció quid crédam egomét mihí iam: ita quód vidísse
crédo,

180 me id iám non vídisse árbitrór.   **Pa.** Ne tu hércle sérô,
opínor,

181 resipísces: si ád erum haec rés prius praévenít, períbis púlchre.

182 **Sc.** [*paying no attention to him*] Nunc démum expérior mi
ób oculós calíginem óbstitísse.

183 Nihil hábeo cérti, quíd loquár: non vídi eam, étsi vídi.

184 **Pa.** Ne tu édepol stúltitiá tuá nos paéne pérdidísti!

185 Sed forés vicíni próximí crepuérunt: cónticíscam.

Scene 4

Meter: ll. 186–198, seven-foot iambic; ll. 199–235, seven-foot
trochaic.

[*Having used the secret passage,* Philocomasium *enters uncon-
cernedly from* Periplectomenus' *house and pretends to be her own
twin sister, recently arrived from Athens.* Sceledrus *is watching
at the wrong door, but upon hearing her voice, turns and recognizes
her.*]

186 **Ph.** [*to a servant within*] Inde ígnem in áram, ut agám gratís
laeta Éphesiaé Diánae,

187 cum me ín locís Neptúniís templísque túrbuléntis

188 servávit, saévis flúctibús ubi sum ádflictáta múltum.

189 **Sc.** [*excitedly*] Palaéstrio, ó Palaéstrió.   **Pa.** [*mocking him*]
O Scéledre, Scéledre, quíd vis?

[190] **Sc.** Estne haéc Philocómasium án non ést ea?   **Pa.** [*judi-
cially*] Opínor, éa vidétur,

191 sed [*quoting* SCELEDRUS' *own words*] "fácinus mírum 'st quómodo haéc hinc húc transíre pótuit"—

192 si quídem ea 'st.   **Sc.** Án dubiúm tibí 'st, eam ésse hanc?
Pa. Éa vidétur.

193 **Sc.** Adeámus, áppellémus.   [*To* PHILOCOMASIUM, *who of
course pays no attention to him*] Heús, quid istúc est,
Phílocomásium?

194 Quid tibi ístîc in ístisce aédibús debétur?   Quíd negóti
'st?

195 [*Growing more exasperated*] Quid núnc tacés?   Tecúm loquór.   **Pa.** [*laughing at him*] Immo édepol túte técum,

196 nam haec níhil respóndet.   **Sc.** [*trying again, with more ve-
hemence*] Te ádloquór, vití probríque pléna,

197 quae círcum vícinós vagás.   **Ph.** [*coolly*] Quicúm tu fábuláre?

198 **Sc.** Quicúm nisi técum?   **Ph.** Quís tu homó 's, aut mécum
quid ést negóti?

199 **Sc.** Mé rogás, hem, quí sim?   **Ph.** Quín ego hóc rogém,
quod nésciám?

200 **Pa.** [*to* PHILOCOMASIUM] Quís ego sum ígitur, si húnc ignóras?   **Ph.** Míhi odiósu's, quísquis és—

201 ét tu et híc.   **Sc.** Non nós novísti?   **Ph.** Neútrum.   **Sc.**
[*aside, to* PALAESTRIO] Métuo máximé . . .

202 **Pa.** [*interrupting him*] Quíd metuís?   **Sc.** . . . enim né nos
nósmet pérdidérimus úspiám.

203 **Pa.** [*resuming the attack*] Tíbi ego díco, heus Phílocomásium!
Ph. [*angrily*] Quaé te intémperiaé tenént,

204 quí me pérperám perpléxo nómine áppellés?   **Pa.** Ehó!

[205] Quís igitúr vocáre?   **Ph.** Dícea.   **Sc.** Fálsum nómen quáre
habés?

206 **Ph.** Égone?   **Sc.** Túne.   **Ph.** Quaé heri Athénis Éphesum
advéni vésperí?

207 **Pa.** Quíd hîc tibi ín Ephesó 'st negóti?   **Ph.** Géminam
gérmanám meám

208 hîc sorórem esse índaudívi: eam véni quaésitúm.   **Sc.**
[*rudely*] Malá 's!

209 **Ph.** Ímmo ecástor stúlta múltum, quaé vobíscum fábulér.

210 [*Turning her back*] Ábeo. **Sc.** [*seizing her roughly by the arm*]
Abíre nón sinám te. **Ph.** [*struggling*] Mítte. **Sc.** Mánifestáriá 's:

[211] nón omítto. [*To* PALAESTRIO, *who holds aloof*] Quíd stas
ístîc? Rétine hanc, sí's, altrínsecús.

[212] **Pa.** [*shrugging his shoulders*] Níl morór negótiósum esse.
Ého tu, Scéledre, quí sció,

213 án ista nón sit Phílocomásium, atque ália eiús similís siét?

[214] **Sc.** [*dragging her*] Té rapiám domum. **Ph.** [*indignantly*]
Ímmo Athénis mí domus ést. Istám domúm

[215] níl morór. **Sc.** Te núsquam míttam, nísi das fírmatám
fidém,

216 te húc [*pointing to* PYRGOPOLINICES' *house*], si omísero, íntrô
itúram. **Ph.** Ví me cógis, quísquis és:

217 dó fidém, si omíttis, ístô me íntrô itúram quô iubés.

218 **Sc.** Écce omítto! **Ph.** [*as she runs into the house of* PERI-
PLECTOMENUS] At ego ábeo omíssa. **Sc.** [*chagrined*] Mú-
liebrí fecít fidé.

[219] **Pa.** [*pretending to be aroused*] Mánibus ámisísti praédam.
Ví'n tu fácere hoc strénué?

220 **Sc.** Quíd faciam? **Pa.** Écfer míhi machaéram huc íntus.
Sc. Quíd faciés eá?

221 **Pa.** Íntrô rúmpam réctâ in aédis: quémque hîc íntus víderó

222 cúm Philocómasio ósculántem, eum ego óbtruncábo extém-
puló.

223 **Sc.** Vísané 'st ea ésse? **Pa.** Immo édepol pláne eá 'st.
Sc. Sed quómodó

224 díssimulábat! **Pa.** Ábi, machaéram huc écfer. **Sc.** Íam
faxo hîc erít. [*He dashes into the house and out again, but
does not find* PHILOCOMASIUM, *for she has slipped into her
own room via the secret passage.*]

[225] **Sc.** [*completely baffled*] Níhil opú'st machaéra. **Pa.** Quíd
iam? **Sc.** Eccám domi; ín lectó cubát.

226 **Pa.** [*impressively*] Édepol né tu tíbi malám rem répperísti,
ut praédicás.

227 **Sc.** Quíd iam? **Pa.** Quia hánc attíngere aúsu's múlierem
hínc ex próximó.

228 **Sc.** Mágis herclé metuó. **Pa.** Sed númquam quísquam fáciet quín sorór

229 ístaec sít gemina húius: eám pol tu ósculántem hîc víderás.

230 **Sc.** Íd quidém palám 'st: eam ésse, ut dícis. Quíd propiús fuít

231 quam út perírem, si élocútus éssem ero? **Pa.** Érgo, sí sapís,

232 mússitábis: plús opórtet scíre sérvum quám loquí.

233 Égo abeo á te, néquid técum cónsilí commísceám,

234 átque apud húnc eró vicínum; tuaé mihi túrbae nón placént.

235 Érus si véniet, sí me quaéret, hîc ero: hínc me arcéssitó.

[*Exit into the house of* Periplectomenus.]

Scene 5

Meter: six-foot iambic.

[*Enter* Periplectomenus *from his house; he pretends to be in high dudgeon and rushes at* Sceledrus.]

[236] **Sc.** [*aside*] Perii! Ád me accédit. **Pe.** Tún, Sceledre, hîc, scelerúm capút,

237 meam lúdificávisti hóspitam ánte aedís modó?

238 **Sc.** Vicíne, auscúlta, quaéso. **Pe.** Ego aúscultém tibí?

239 **Sc.** Purgáre vólo me. **Pe.** Tún ted éxpurgés mihí,

240 qui fácinus tántum támque indígnum fécerís?

241 **Sc.** Licétne? **Pe.** At íta me dí deaéque omnés amént:

242 nisi míhi supplícium vírgarúm de té datúr,

243 dedécoris pléniórem erúm faciám tuúm

244 quam mágno vénto plénum 'st úndarúm maré.

[245] **Sc.** [*abjectly*] Vicíne, etiám nunc nésció quid víderím:

246 itá 'st ista húius símilis nósträi tuá,

247 siquídem non éadem 'st. **Pe.** [*relenting*] Víse ad me íntrô, iám sciés.

248 **Sc.** Licétne? **Pe.** Quín te iúbeo; et plácide nóscitá.

249 **Sc.** Ita fácere cértum 'st. [*He starts for the door; at the same time* Periplectomenus *runs to* Pyrgopolinices' *door and calls in.*] **Pe.** Heús, Philocómasiúm citó

250 transcúrre cúrriculo ád nos: íta negótiúm 'st.
251 Post, quándo exíerit Scéledrus á nobís, citó
252 transcúrrito ád vos rúrsum cúrriculó domúm.
[253] [*Returning to his own house*] Nunc métuo, haec né titubét.
Sed áperitúr forís.
[*Enter* SCELEDRUS *from the house, crestfallen.*]
[254] **Sc.** Pol múlierem hércle símiliórem nón reór
255 deos fácere pósse.   **Pe.** Quíd nunc?   **Sc.** Cómmeruí malúm.
256 **Pe.** Vidístin ístam?   **Sc.** Vídi et íllam et hóspitém
257 compléxam atque ósculántem.   **Pe.** Éane 'st?   **Sc.** Néscio.
258 **Pe.** Vi'n scíre pláne?   **Sc.** Cúpio.   **Pe.** Abi íntrô ad vós
domúm:
[259] sitne ístaec, víse.   **Sc.** Iám ego ad te éxibó forás.   [*He
again dashes in and out.*]
260 **Pe.** [*to the audience, gleefully*] Numquam édepol hóminem
quémquam lúdificáriér
261 magís facéte vídi et mágis mirís modís.
262 Sed éccum, egréditur!   **Sc.** [*humbly*] Périplectómene, te óbsecró
263 per deós atque hómines pérque stúltitiám meám [*clasping
his knees*]
264 perqué tua génua. . . **Pe.** [*laughing*] Quíd obsecrás me?
Sc. . . . inscítiaé
265 meae ét stultítiae ignóscas.   Núnc demúm sció
266 me fuísse excórdem, caécum, incógitábilém:
267 nam Phílocomásium eccam íntus!   **Pe.** Quíd nunc, fúrcifér?
268 **Sc.** Nunc hóc mi ignósce, quaéso.   **Pe.** Víncam animúm
meúm,
269 ne málitióse fáctum id ésse abs te árbitrér.
270 Ignóscam tibi ístuc.   **Sc.** Át tibi dí faciánt bené!
271 **Pe.** Ne tu hércle, sí te dí ament, línguam cómprimés
272 posthác: etiam íllud quód sciés nescíverís,
273 nec víderís quod víderís.   **Sc.** Bene mé monés:
[274] ita fácere cértum 'st.   Númquid áliud vís?   **Pe.** Abí.
[*Exit* SCELEDRUS.]
[275] Palaéstrió nunc ést apúd me: ibó domúm.   [*Exit.*]

ACT II: THE RESCUE OF PHILOCOMASIUM AND THE DOWNFALL OF PYRGOPOLINICES

Scene 1

Meter: seven-foot trochaic.

[Palaestrio *pokes his head out at the door of* Periplectome-nus' *house, peering cautiously to left and right; he then speaks to his fellow conspirators within.*]

276 **Pa.** Cóhibéte intra límen étiam vós parúmper, Pleúsiclés.

277 Sínite mé prius pérspectáre, ne úspiam ínsidiaé siént.

278 [*Reconnoitering again*] Stérilis hínc prospéctus úsque ad últimám 'st plateám probé.

279 Évocábo. Heus, Périplectómene et Pleúsiclés, progrédiminí.

[*Enter the conspirators from the house; they line up like soldiers.*]

280 **Pe.** Écce nos tíbi oboédiéntes. **Pa.** [*assuming the air of a generalissimo*] Fácile 'st ímperium ín bonís.

281 Núnc hoc ánimadvértite ámbo. [*To* Periplectomenus] Míhi opus ést operá tuá,

282 Périplectómene; nám ego invéni lépidam sýcophántiám,

[283] quî ádmutilétur míles íllic, ét Philocómasiúm sibí

[284] híc amans [*pointing to* Pleusicles] ábducát habeátque. **Pe.** Dári istanc rátioném voló.

285 **Pa.** Át ego mi ánulúm dari ístunc tuúm voló. **Pe.** Quam ad rem úsuí 'st?

286 **Pa.** Quándo habébo, igitúr rationém meárum fábricarúm dabó.

287 **Pe.** [*giving up his ring*] Útere, áccipe. **Pa.** Áccipe á me rúrsum rátioném dolí:

[288] érus meús ita amátor mágnus múlierúm 'st, ut néminém

289 fúisse aéque néque futúrum crédo. **Pe.** Crédo ego istúc idém.

290 **Pa.** Ísque Aléxandrí praestáre praédicát formám suám,

291 ítaque omnís se ultró sectári in Épheso mémorat múlierés.

292 Écquam tú potís reperíre fórmā lépidā múlierém,

293 cuí facétiárum cór pectúsque sít plenum ét dolí?

294 **Pe.** Íngenuámne an líbertínam? **Pa.** Aequi ístuc fácio, dúmmodó

[295] eám mihi dés, quae sít lepidíssima ádulescénsque máximé.

[296] **Pe.** Hábeo eccíllam [*pointing toward her house*] meám clién-
tam, féminam ádulescéntulám.

297 Séd quid ea úsus ést? **Pa.** Ut ád te eám iam déducás domúm,

[298] ét ita ornés ut crínis cómptos hábeat ádsimulétque sé

299 túam esse uxórem: ita praécipiéndum 'st. **Pl.** Érro quam
ínsistás viám.

300 **Pa.** [*to* Pleusicles] Át sciés. [*To* Periplectomenus] Sed
écqua ancílla 'st ílli? **Pe.** Ést primé catá.

301 **Pa.** Eá quoque ópus est. Íta praecípito múlieri átque an-
cíllulaé:

302 út simulét se túam esse uxórem et déperíre hunc mílitém;

303 quásique hunc ánulúm faveaé suae déderit; éa porró mihí,

304 míliti út darém; quasíque ego reí sim intérpres. **Pe.** Aúdió.

305 Nón potuít reperíre, si ípsi Sóli quaérendás darés,

306 lépidióres duás ad hánc rem quám ego. Hábe animúm
bonúm.

307 **Pa.** Érgo adcúra, séd propere ópu'st. [*Exit* Periplectomenus *hurriedly, to fetch the two women.*] Núnc tu auscúlta mi, Pleúsiclés.

308 **Pl.** Tíbi sum oboédiéns. **Pa.** Hoc fácito: míles dómum ubi
advénerít,

309 méminerís ne Phílocomásium nóminés. **Pl.** Quem nómi-
ném?

[310] **Pa.** Díceam. **Pl.** Mémineró. **Pa.** Sed íntereá tace, átque
núnc abí.

311 **Pl.** Éo ego intrô ígitur. **Pa.** Ét praecépta sóbrie út curés,
facé. [*Exit* Pleusicles.]

Scene 2

Meter: seven-foot iambic.

[*Enter* Periplectomenus, *escorting* Acroteleutium *and her
maid* Milphidippa.]

[312] **Pe.** [*with a gesture toward his house*] Hâc íntrô séquimini,
Ácroteleútium átque Mílphidíppa.

313 **Pa.** [*to* Periplectomenus, *pompously*] Veníre sálvum gaúdeó; lepide hércle ornátus cédis.

314 **Pe.** Bene ópportúneque óbviam és, Palaéstrio. Ém tibi
ádsunt,

315 quas mé iussísti addúcere ét quo ornátu. **Pa.** Eu! Nóster
ésto.

316 [*To* Acroteleutium] Palaéstrio Ácroteleútiúm salútat. **Ac.**
[*to* Periplectomenus] Quís hic, amábo, 'st,

317 qui tám pro nótā nóminát me? **Pe.** Hic nóster árchitéc-
tu'st.

318 **Ac.** Salve, árchitécte. **Pa.** Sálva sís. Sed díc mihi, écquid
híc [*pointing to* Periplectomenus] te

319 onerávit praéceptís? **Pe.** [*answering for her*] Probé medi-
tátam utrámque dúco.

320 **Pa.** [*to* Acroteleutium] Nempe tú novísti mílitém, meum
erúm? **Ac.** Rogáre mírum 'st.

321 Populi ódium quídni nóverím, magnídicum, cíncinnátum,

[322] pulchrum, únguentátum? **Pa.** Num ílle té nam nóvit?
Ac. Númquam vídit.

323 **Pa.** Age, Périplectómene, has núnciám duc íntrô; ego ád
forum íllum

324 convéniam atque ílli hunc ánulúm dabo, átque praédicábo

325 a túa uxóre mihí datum ésse, eamque íllum déperíre.

326 Hanc [*pointing to* Milphidippa] ád nos, cum éxtemplo á
foró veniémus, míttitóte,

327 quasi clánculum ád eum míssa sít. **Pe.** Faciémus: ália cúra.

328 **Pa.** Vos módô curáte; ego illúm probé iam onerátum huc
ácciébo. [*Exit to the forum.*]

329 **Pe.** Abeámus érgo intrô, haéc utí meditémur cógitáte,

330 ut áccuráte et cómmode hóc quod agéndum 'st éxsequámur,

331 ne quíd, ubi míles vénerít, titubétur. **Ac.** Tú moráre.
[*Exeunt.*]

Scene 3

Meter: seven-foot trochaic.

[*Enter* Palaestrio *with* Pyrgopolinices *from the forum.*]

332 **Py.** Vólup est, quód agas, si íd procédit lépide atque éx
senténtiá.

333 Nam égo hodie ád Seleúcum régem mísi párasitúm meúm,
334 út latrónes, quós condúxi, hinc ád Seleúcum dúcerét,
335 qui éius régnum tútaréntur, míhi dum fíeret ótiúm.
[336] Pa. Quín tu tuám rem cúra pótius quám Seleúci, nám tibí
337 cóndició nova et lúculénta fértur pér me intérpretém.
338 Py. Ímmo omnís res pósterióres póno atque óperam dó tibí.
339 Pa. Círcumspícedum né quis nóstro hîc aúceps sérmoní siét,
340 nam hóc negóti clándestíno ut ágerem mándatúm 'st mihí.
341 Py. Némo adést.   Pa. Hunc árrabónem amóris prímum a
    me áccipé.
342 Py. Quíd hic?   Únde 'st?   Pa. [speaking slowly and im-
    pressively] Á luculénta ác festíva féminá,
343 quaé te amát tuamque éxpetéssit púlchram púlchritúdiném.
344 Éius nunc mi ánulum ád te ancílla pórro ut déferrém dedít.
345 Py. Núptane 'st án viduá?   Pa. Et núpta et vídua.   Py.
    Quó pactó potís
346 núpta et vídua esse éadem?   Pa. Quía aduléscens núpta 'st
    cúm sené.
347 Py. Eúge!   Pa. Lépidā et líberáli fórmā 'st.   Py. Cáve
    mendáciúm.
348 Pa. Ád tuam fórmam illa úna dígna 'st.   Py. Hércle púl-
    chram praédicás.
349 Séd quis eá 'st?   Pa. Senis húius úxor Périplectómeni e
    próximó.
350 Éa demóritur te átque ab íllo cúpit abíre: odít sením.
[351] Py. Séd volo scíre, quíd faciémus múliere íllā quaé domí 'st?
352 Pa. Quín tu illám iube ábs te abíre quó libét, sicút sorór
353 éius huc gémina vénit Éphesum et máter, árcessúntque eám.
354 Py. Ého tu, advénit Éphesum máter éius?   Pa. Áiunt quí
    sciúnt.
355 Py. Hércle occásiónem lépidam, ut múlierem éxcludám
    forás!
356 Pa. Ímmo ví'n tu lépide fácere?   Py. Lóquere, et cón-
    siliúm cedó.
357 Pa. Ví'n tu illam áctutum ámovére, a te út abeát per grá-
    tiám?

358 **Py.** Cúpio. **Pa.** Túm te hoc fácere opórtet: tíbi divítiarum ádfatím 'st.

359 Iúbe sibi aúrum atque órnaménta, quae ílli instrúxti múlierí,
360 dóno habére, abíre, auférre ábs te quô libeát sibí.

361 **Py.** Plácet ut dícis; séd ne istánc amíttam et haéc mutét fidém,

362 víde modô. **Pa.** Vah! Délicátu's: quaé te támquam oculós amét.

[363] Séd forés crepuérunt. Écce ancíllula égreditúr forás,

[*Enter* MILPHIDIPPA *from the house; she peers about cautiously.*]

364 quae ánulum ístunc áttulít quem tíbi dedi. **Py.** [*always susceptible*] Édepol haéc quidém

365 béllulá 'st. **Pa.** Pithécium haéc est praé illā et spínturníciúm.

SCENE 4

Meter: ll. 366–374, seven-foot trochaic; ll. 375–414, seven-foot anapaestic.

366 **Mi.** [*aside*] Díssimulábo, hos quási non vídeam néque esse hîc étiamdúm sciám.

367 **Py.** [*to* PALAESTRIO] Táce, subaúscultémus écquid dé me fíat méntió.

[368] **Mi.** [*aside*] Quaéro hunc hóminem nímium lépidum et nímia púlchritúdiné,

369 mílitém Pyrgopólinícem. **Py.** [*excitedly, to* PALAESTRIO] Sáti'n haec quóque me déperít?

[370] Meám laudát speciem. Haéc ancíllula súbigit me út amem. **Pa.** [*hastily*] Hercle hánc quidém

371 níhil tu amássis: mihi haéc despónsa 'st. Tíbi si illa hódie núpserít,

372 égo hanc contínuo uxórem dúcam. **Py.** [*peevishly*] Quíd ergo hanc dúbitas cónloquí?

373 **Pa.** Séquere hâc me érgo. **Py.** [*following*] Pédisequús tibi sum. **Mi.** [*to herself*] Útinam, cúius causā forás

374 sum égressa, éius cónveniéndi míhi potéstas évenát!

375 **Pa.** [*raising his voice so that she can hear*] Homo quídam 'st, quí scit, quód quaerís ubi sít. **Mi.** [*feigning alarm*] Quem ego hîc audívi?

376 **Pa.** Sociúm tuorúm concíliorum ét partícipem cónsiliórum.

[377] **Mi.** [*cautiously*] Cedo sígnum, si hórunc sóciorum és. **Pa.**
[*mysteriously*] Amat múlier quaédam quéndam.

378 **Mi.** Pol istúc quidem múltae. **Pa.** At nón multaé de dígito
dónum míttunt.

379 **Mi.** Sed hîc númquis adést? **Pa.** [*cautiously*] Vel adést vel
nón. **Mi.** Cedo té mihi sólae sólum.

380 **Pa.** Brevine án longínquo sérmoní? **Mi.** Tribus vérbis.
Pa. [*to* PYRGOPOLINICES] Iam ád te rédeo. [*He starts
toward* MILPHIDIPPA.]

381 **Py.** [*protesting*] Quid ego? Hîc astábo tántispér cum hac
fórma et fáctis frústra?

382 **Pa.** [*turning back*] Patere átque astá; tibi ego hánc operám
do. **Py.** [*correcting him testily*] Próperandó: excrúcior.

383 **Pa.** [*appealing to reason*] Pedetémptim—tu haéc scis—trác-
taré soles hásce huiúsmodi mércis.

384 **Py.** [*yielding, but still irritated*] Age age—út tibi máxime
cóncinnúm 'st! **Pa.** [*aside*] Nullúm 'st hoc stólidius
sáxum.

[385] [*To* MILPHIDIPPA] Redeo ád te. Quíd me vóluistí? **Mi.**
[*whispering*] Quid agam? **Pa.** Ádsimulés. . . . **Mi.** [*interrupting him*] Teneo ístuc.

[386] **Pa.** Conlaúdató formam ét faciem ét virtútis. **Mi.** Né for-
mída.

387 **Pa.** [*briskly, as he returns to* PYRGOPOLINICES] Adsum: ím-
pera, sí quid vís. **Py.** Quid illaéc narrát tibi? **Pa.** Lámentári

388 ait íllam, míseram crúciari ét lacrimántem se ádflictáre,

389 quia tís egeát, quia té careát. Ob eám rem huc ád te
míssa 'st.

390 **Py.** Iube adíre. **Pa.** [*whispering to* PYRGOPOLINICES] At
scí'n quid tú faciás? Face té fastídi plénum,

391 quasi nón libeát; me inclámató, quia síc te vúlgo vúlgem.

392 **Py.** [*to* PALAESTRIO] Memini ét praecéptis párebó. **Pa.** [*in
a loud voice and official manner*] Vocone érgo hanc quaé
te quaérit?

393 **Py.** [*in the same manner*] Adeát, si quíd vult. **Pa.** Sí quid vís, adi, múlier. **Mi.** [*salaaming to* PYRGOPOLINICES] Púlcher, sálve.

394 **Py.** [*flattered; to* PALAESTRIO] Meum cógnoméntum cómmemorávit. [*To* MILPHIDIPPA] Di tíbi dent quaécumque óptes.

395 **Mi.** Tecum áetatem éxigere út liceát. . . . **Py.** [*haughtily, thinking she has finished*] Nimium óptas. **Mi.** [*hastily*] Nón me díco,

396 sed erám meam quaé te démoritúr. **Py.** Aliaé multae idem ístuc cúpiunt,

397 quibus cópia nón est. **Mi.** Écastór hau mírum, sí te habes cárum,

398 hominém tam púlchrum et praéclarúm virtúte et fórma et fáctis!

399 **Pa.** [*aside, to* PYRGOPOLINICES] Quin tu huíc respónde. [*Assuming the grand manner and in a loud voice*] Haec íllaec ést ab illá quam dúdum díxi.

400 **Py.** [*to* PALAESTRIO, *haughtily*] Qua ab íllarúm? Nam ita mi óccursánt multaé: meminísse hau póssum.

401 **Mi.** Ab illá quae dígitos déspoliát suos ét tuos dígitos décorat.

402 [*Pointing to the ring on his finger*] Nam hunc ánulum áb tui cúpientí huic [*pointing to* PALAESTRIO] détuli, híc porro ád te.

403 **Py.** Quid núnc tibi vís, muliér? Memora. **Mi.** Út, quae té cupit, eám ne spérnas,

404 nam nísi tu illí fers súppetiás, iam illa ánimum déspondébit.

405 [*Falling on her knees*] Mi Achílles, fíat quód te oró: serva íllam púlchram púlchre.

406 Expróme benígnum ex te íngeniúm—urbícape, occísor régum.

407 **Py.** [*thundering at* PALAESTRIO] Eu hercle ódiosás res! Quótiens hóc tibi, vérbero, ego ínterdíxi,

[408] ne cóndiciónem témere póllicitére! **Pa.** [*to* MILPHIDIPPA] Audí'n tu, múlier?

[409] [*Aside, to* PYRGOPOLINICES] Quin tu huíc respóndes áliquid

núnc? **Py.** [*to* MILPHIDIPPA, *curtly*] Iube eámpse exíre huc ád nos.

410 Dic me ómnia quaé vult fácturúm.   **Mi.** Facis núnc ut té facere aéquum 'st.

411 **Pa.** [*to* MILPHIDIPPA] Quin érgo abis, quándo résponsúm 'st?   **Mi.** [*to* PALAESTRIO] Ibo átque illam húc addúcam,

412 proptér quam operá 'st mihi.   [*To* PYRGOPOLINICES] Númquid vís?   **Py.** [*with a blasé air*] Ne mágis sim púlcher quám sum:

413 ita mé mea fórma habet sóllicitúm.   **Pa.** [*to* MILPHIDIPPA] Quid híc núnc stas?   Quín abis?   **Mi.** Ábeo.

414 **Pa.** [*aside to* MILPHIDIPPA, *as she leaves*] Philocómasió dic, sí 'st istíc, domum ut tránseat: húnc [*pointing to* PYRGOPOLINICES] híc ésse.

SCENE 5

Meter: six-foot iambic.

[415] **Py.** [*to* PALAESTRIO, *impatiently*] Quid **vís** nunc fáciam? Nám nulló pactó potést

[416] prius haéc recipí quam Phílocomásium amíserím.

417 **Pa.** [*shrugging his shoulders*] Quid mé consúltas, quíd agas? Díxi equidém tibí,

418 quo id pácto fíeri póssit clémentíssimé:

419 aurum átque véstem múliebrem ómnem habeát sibí;

420 dicásque témpus máxime ésse, ut eát domúm;

421 sorórem géminam adésse et mátrem dícitó,

422 quibus cóncomitáta récte déveniát domúm.

423 **Py.** Quî tú scis eás adésse?   **Pa.** Quía oculís meís

[424] vidi híc sorórem.   **Py.** [*eagerly, as usual*] Ecquíd bellá 'st? **Pa.** [*disgusted*] Nempe ómniá

425 vis óbtinére.   **Py.** Ubi mátrem esse áiebát sorór?

426 **Pa.** Cubáre in návi líppam atque óculis túrgidís

427 nauclérus díxit, qui íllas ádvexít, mihí.

428 Is ad hós [*pointing to* PERPLECTOMENUS' *house*] nauclérus hóspitió devértitúr.

[429] **Py.** [*fearing to face* PHILOCOMASIUM] Te vérba fácere cúm Philocómasió voló.

430 **Pa.** [*resolutely*] Quî pótius quám tute ádeas, tuám rem túte agás?

431 Dicás uxórem tíbi necéssum dúceré;

432 cognátos pérsuadére, amícos cógeré.

433 **Py.** Itán tu cénses? **Pa.** Quíd ego ní ita cénseám?

434 **Py.** [*screwing up his courage*] Ibo ígitur íntrô. Tu hîc ante aédis ínterím

435 speculáre, ut, ubi íllaec pródeát, me próvocés.

[436] [*Swaggering toward his own door*] Si nólet, ví Philocómasium éxtrudám forás.

437 **Pa.** [*calling after him and bringing him to a halt*] Istúc cave fáxis; quín potiús per grátiám

438 bonam ábeat ábs te. Atque íllaec quaé dixí dató.

439 Sed abi íntrô. Nóli stáre. **Py.** Tibí sum oboédiéns. [*Exit.*]

440 **Pa.** [*alone*] Nunc ád me ut véniat úsu'st Ácroteleútium aút

441 ancíllula éius aut Pleúsiclés. [*The door of* PERIPLECTOME- NUS' *house is slowly and cautiously opened.*] Pro Íuppi- tér,

[442] omnís video éxeúntis hínc e próximó.

SCENE 6

Meter: seven-foot trochaic.

[*Enter the conspirators from the house of* PERIPLECTOMENUS.]

443 **Ac.** [*to* MILPHIDIPPA *and* PLEUSICLES] Séquiminí. Simul círcumspícite né quis ádsit árbitér.

444 **Mi.** Néminém pol vídeo, nísi hunc quem vólumus cónven- tum. **Pa.** Ét ego vós.

445 Dáte modô óperam. **Ac.** Íd nos ád te, sí quid vélles, véni- mús.

[446] **Pa.** Mílitém lepide ét facéte lúdificáriér voló.

447 **Ac.** Némpe ut ádsimulém me amóre istíus dífferrí. . . . **Pa.** [*interrupting her*] Tenés.

448 **Ac.** . . . quásique, istíus caúsā amóris, éx hoc mátrimónió

449 ábierím, cupiéns istíus núptiárum. **Pa.** Omne órdiné—

450 nísi modô únum hoc: hásce esse aédis dícas dótalís tuás;

451 hínc senem ábs te abiísse, póstquam fécerís divórtiúm:

452   ne flle móx vereátur íntroíre in álienám domúm.

[453]   **Ac.** Béne monés.   **Pa.** [*to* Pleusicles] Nunc tíbi vicíssim
quae ímperábo, ea díscitó:

[454]   cum éxtemplo íntro haec [*pointing to* Acroteleutium]
ábierít, tu quási gubérnatór siés,

455   húc veníto et mátris vérbis Phílocomásium arcéssitó,

456   út, si itúra siét Athénas, eát tecum ád portúm citố,

457   átque ut iúbeat férri in návim síquid ímponí velít:

458   nísi eat, té solúturum ésse návim; véntum operám daré.

459   **Pl.** Sátis placét pictúra: pérge.   **Pa.** Ille éxtemplo íllam
hortábitúr

460   út eat própere, né sit mátri mórae.   **Pl.** Múltimodís sapís.

461   **Pa.** Égo illi dícam ut me ádiutórem, qui ónus feram ád
portúm, rogét.

462   Ílle iubébit me íre cum flla ad pórtum.   Ego ádeo (ut tú
sciás)

463   prórsum Athénas prótinam adíbo técum.   **Pl.** Atque úbi
illố vénerís,

464   tríduúm servíre númquam té, quin líber sís, sinám.

465   **Pa.** Ábi citố átque orná te.   **Pl.** Númquid áliud?   **Pa.**
Haéc ut méminerís.

466   **Pl.** Ábeo.   [*Exit to the harbor.*]   **Pa.** [*to* Acroteleutium *and*
Milphidippa] Et vós abíte hinc íntrô actútum; nam íllum
huc sát sció

[467]   iam éxitúrum esse íntus.   [*Exeunt* Acroteleutium *and*
Milphidippa.]   Écce cómmodum áperitúr forís.
[Pyrgopolinices' *door opens.*]

Scene 7

Meter: seven-foot trochaic.

[*Enter* Pyrgopolinices, *looking pleased with himself.*]

[468]   **Py.** [*to* Palaestrio] Quód volui, út volui, ímpetrávi, nám
Philocómasió dedí

469   quaé voluít, quae póstulávit: té quoque eí donó dedí.

470   **Pa.** [*concealing his delight*] Étiam mé?   Quomódo ego vívam
síne te?   **Py.** [*condescendingly*] Áge, animó bonó 's.

471 **Pa.** Étsi istúc mi acérbum 'st, quía ero té caréndum 'st óptimó,

[472] sáltem id vólup est, cum égo vicínam hanc cóncilió tibi núnciám.

[473] **Py.** Si ímpetrás eam, tíbi ego actútum mágnas dívitiás dabó:

[474] [*sentimentally*] géstio. **Pa.** Át modicé decét. [ACROTELEU-TIUM *opens the door and looks out.*] Eccíllam ipsam: égre-ditúr forás.

SCENE 8

Meter: seven-foot iambic.

[*Enter* ACROTELEUTIUM *and* MILPHIDIPPA *from* PERIPLECTO-MENUS' *house; they stand by the door and pretend not to know that anyone is present.*]

[475] **Ac.** [*in an awestruck voice*] Tute ípsum cónvenísti? **Mi.** Etiám cum ipsó pol súm locúta.

476 **Ac.** O fórtunáta múlier és. **Py.** [*aside to* PALAESTRIO] Ut amári vídeor! **Pa.** [*to* PYRGOPOLINICES] Dígnu's.

477 **Ac.** [*to* MILPHIDIPPA] Permírum ecástor praédicás: te adiísse atque éxorásse.

478 Per epístolam aút per núntiúm, quasi régem, adíri eum áiunt.

479 **Mi.** Namque édepol víx fuít copia ádeúndi atque ímpe-trándi.

480 **Pa.** [*to* PYRGOPOLINICES] Ut tu ínclitú's apud múlierés! **Py.** Patiár, quando íta Venús vult.

481 **Ac.** Venerí pol hábeo grátiám, eandémque et óro et quaéso,

[482] benígnus érga me út siét; quod cúpiam né gravétur.

483 **Mi.** Spero íta futúrum, quámquam múltae illúm sibi éxpe-téssunt.

484 Ille íllas spérnit; ségregát hasce ómnis, éxtra te únam.

485 **Ac.** Ergo íste metús me mácerát, quod ílle fastídiósu'st.

486 ne óculi eiús senténtiám mutént, ubi víderít me.

487 **Mi.** Non fáciet; módó bonum ánimum habé. **Py.** [*aside*] Ut ípsa sé contémnit!

488 **Ac.** [*to* MILPHIDIPPA] Metuó ne praédicátió tua núnc meam fórmam exsúperet.

489 **Mi.** Istúc curávi, ut opínióne illíus púlchriór sis.

490 **Ac.** Si pól me nólet dúceré uxórem, génua ampléctar

[491] atque óbsecrábo; pól moriár, si nón quibo ímpetráre.

492 **Py.** [*to* PALAESTRIO, *impatiently*] Prohibéndam mórtem múlierí videó. [*He pauses for an answer.*] Adíbon? **Pa.**
Mínime:

493 nam tú te vílem fécerís, si te últro lárgiére.

[494] Sine últro véniat ípsa: pérdere ístam glóriám vis?

495 Nam núlli mórtalí scio óbtigísse hoc nísi duóbus,

496 tibi ét Phaóni Lésbió, tam múlier sé ut amáret!

497 **Ac.** [*to* MILPHIDIPPA, *still pretending ignorance of* PYRGOPO-
LINICES' *presence*] Eo íntrô, an tu íllunc évocás forás, mea
Mílphidíppa?

498 **Mi.** Immo ópperiámur dum éxeát aliquís. **Ac.** Duráre néqueo,

499 quin eam íntrô. **Mi.** Occlúsae súnt forés. **Ac.** Ecfríngam.
Mi. Sána nón es.

500 **Ac.** [*suddenly falling into* MILPHIDIPPA'S *arms*] Tene me,
óbsecró. **Mi.** Cur? **Ac.** Né cadám. **Mi.** Quid itá?
Ac. Quia stáre néqueo:

501 ita ánimus pér oculós meós meus défit. **Mi.** Mílitém pol

502 tu aspéxisti. **Ac.** Íta. **Mi.** Non vídeo. Ubí 'st? **Ac.**
Vidéres pól, si amáres.

503 **Mi.** Non édepol tu íllum mágis amás quam ego, méa—si
pér te líceat.

504 **Pa.** [*to* PYRGOPOLINICES] Omnés profécto múlierés te amánt,
ut quaéque aspéxit.

505 **Py.** [*loftily, to* PALAESTRIO] Nesció tu ex me hóc audíverís an
nón: nepós sum Véneris.

506 **Ac.** [*in pseudo-desperation*] Mea Mílphidíppa, adi, óbsecro,
ét congrédere. **Py.** Ut mé verétur!

507 **Pa.** [*to* PYRGOPOLINICES] Illa ád nos pérgit. **Mi.** [*advancing*]
Vós voló. **Py.** Et nós te. **Mi.** Út iussísti,

508 erám meam éduxí forás. **Py.** Videó. **Mi.** Iube érgo adíre:

[509] verbum édepol fácere nón potést. Iam, quaéso, víde, ut
extímuit,

510 postquám ted áspexít. **Py.** Virí quoque armáti idem ístuc
   fáciunt:
511 ne tú mirére, múlierém.   Sed quid ést quod vúlt me fácere?
512 **Mi.** Ad se út eas: técum víveré vult átque aetátem exígere.
513 **Py.** Egon ád illam eám quae núpta sít?   Vir éius me dé-
   prehéndat.
514 **Mi.** Quin tuá causā éxegít virúm ab sé.   **Py.** [*eagerly*]
   Quî id fácere pótuit?
515 **Mi.** Aedés dotáles húius súnt.   **Py.** Itan?   **Mi.** Íta pol.
   Py. Iúbe domum íre:
516 iam ego íllî eró.   **Mi.** Vide né siés in éxspectátióne,
517 ne illam ánimi excrúcies.   **Py.** Nón eró profécto.   Abíte.
   Mi. Abímus.   [*Exeunt* Acroteleutium *and* Milphidippa *into the house.*]
[*From a distance* Pleusicles *is seen approaching; he is got up
as a sea captain and disguised by a patch over one eye.*]
518 **Py.** Sed quíd ego vídeo?   **Pa.** Quíd vidés?   **Py.** Nescióquis
   éccum incédit
519 ornátu quidém thalássico.   **Pa.** Ít ad nós: vult té profécto.
520 Nauclérus híc quidem 'st.   **Py.** Vídelicét arcéssit hánc iam.
   Pa. Crédo.

Scene 9

Meter: six-foot iambic.

[*Enter* Pleusicles.   *He stops at* Pyrgopolinices' *door.*]
521 **Pl.** Pultábo.   Heus, écquis híc est?   **Pa.** Ádulescéns, quid
   ést?
522 Quid vís?   Quid púltas?   **Pl.** Phílocomásium quaéritó.
523 A mátre illíus vénio.   Sí iturá 'st, eát.
524 Omnís morátur: návim cúpimus sólveré.
[525] **Py.** Iam dúdum rés paráta 'st.   [*To* Palaestrio] Évoca eam
   húc forás.
526 Duc ádiutóres técum ad návim, quí feránt
527 aurum, órnaménta, véstem, prétiosa ómniá.
528 **Pa.** Eó.   **Pl.** [*calling after him*] Quaeso hércle, própera.
   [*Exit* Palaestrio.]   **Py.** [*to* Pleusicles] Nón morábitúr.

SCENE 10

Meter: seven-foot trochaic.

[*Enter* PALAESTRIO *from the house; he is leading* PHILOCOMASIUM, *who is shedding crocodile tears.*]

529   **Pa.** Quíd modí flendó, quaeso, hódie fácies? **Ph.** Quíd ego
      ní fleám?

530   Úbi pulchérrime égi aetátem, inde ábeo. **Pa.** [*pointing to*
      PLEUSICLES] Ém hominém tibí,

531   qui á matre ét soróre vénit. **Ph.** Vídeo. **Py.** Audí'n,
      Palaéstrió?

532   **Pa.** Quíd vis? **Py.** Quín tu iúbes écferri ómniá quae istí
      dedí. [PALAESTRIO *gives the order and hurries back again.*]

533   **Pl.** Phílocomásium, sálve. **Ph.** Ét tu sálve. **Pl.** Máterque
      ét sorór

534   tíbi salútem mé iussérunt díceré. **Ph.** Salvaé siént.

535   **Pl.** Órant te út eas, véntus óperam dúm dat, út velum éx-
      plicént;

536   nám matri óculi sí valérent, mécum vénissént simúl.

537   **Ph.** [*turning toward* PYRGOPOLINICES *and weeping again*]
      Ístuc crúcior, á viró me táli abálienáriér.

538   **Pa.** Nám nil míror, sí libénter, Phílocomásium, híc erás,

539   sí forma húius, móres, vírtus áttinére animum híc tuúm;

540   cúm ego sérvus, quándo aspício hunc, lácrimo, quía difungi-
      múr.

541   **Ph.** [*to* PYRGOPOLINICES] Óbsecró, licét complécti, príus-
      quam próficiscó? **Py.** Licét.

542   **Ph.** [*darting toward* PYRGOPOLINICES] Ó mi ócule, ó mi
      ánime! [*As she passes* PLEUSICLES, *she pretends to faint.*]
      Pa. Óbsecró, tene múlierém,

543   ne ádfligátur. **Py.** [*seeing her in* PLEUSICLES' *arms*] Quíd
      istuc, quaéso, 'st? **Pa.** [*to* PYRGOPOLINICES] Quia ábs te
      abít, animó malé

544   fáctum 'st huíc repénte míserae. **Py.** [*to* PALAESTRIO] Cúrre
      intrô átque ecférto aquám.

545   **Pa.** [*apprehensive of trouble*] Níl aquám morór; quiéscat
      málo. [*Restraining* PYRGOPOLINICES] Ne íntervénerís,

546 quaéso, dúm resipíscit. **Py.** [*angrily*] Cápita intér se nímis
nexa hísce habént:

547 nón placét. [*To* Pleusicles, *who is kissing* Philocomasium]
Labra á labéllis aúfer, naúta; cáve malúm.

548 **Pl.** [*to* Pyrgopolinices] Témptabám spirárent án non. **Py.**
Aúrem admótam opórtuít.

549 **Pl.** Sí magis vís, eam omíttam. **Py.** [*afraid that he will be
unable to get rid of her*] Nólo: rétineás. **Pa.** [*on pins and
needles*] Fió misér.

[550] **Ph.** [*pretending to wake from her swoon*] Quíd videó? Quid
hóc? **Pl.** [*in a loud voice*] Resipísti? **Ph.** [*feigning astonishment*] Óbsecró, quem ampléxa súm

551 hóminem? Périi. Súmne ego apúd me? **Pl.** [*whispering*]
Né timé, voluptás meá.

[*Enter servants with* Philocomasium's *luggage.*]

[552] **Py.** [*to the whole party*] Íte cúm dis bénevoléntibus. **Pa.**
[*to* Pyrgopolinices] Iám vale. **Py.** Ét tu béne valé.

553 **Pa.** [*aside to* Pleusicles *and* Philocomasium] Íte citô; iam
ego ádsequár vos; cúm ero paúca vólo loquí. [*Exeunt*
Pleusicles *and* Philocomasium *to the ship.*]

554 [*To* Pyrgopolinices] Quámquam aliós fidélióres sémper há-
buistí tibí

555 quám me, támen tibi hábeo mágnam grátiám rerum ómniúm.

[556] **Py.** Hábe animúm bonúm. **Pa.** Non póssum; amísi omném
libídiném.

557 **Py.** I, sequere íllos, né morére. **Pa.** Béne vale. **Py.** Ét
tu béne valé.

558 **Pa.** [*delaying longer, to give* Pleusicles *and* Philocomasium
a good start] Cógitáto idéntidém, tibi quám fidélis fúerím.

559 [*Slyly*] Si íd faciés, tum démum scíbis, tíbi qui bónus sit, quí
malús.

560 **Py.** Víx reprimór quin té manére iúbeam. **Pa.** [*hastily*]
Cáve istuc fécerís:

561 dícant té mendácem néc verum ésse, fidé nullā ésse té.

562 Nám si honéste cénseám te fácere pósse, suádeám:

563 vérum nón potést; cave fáxis. **Py.** [*impatiently*] Ábi iam.
Pa. [*with feigned reluctance*] Pátiar quídquid ést.

564 **Py.** Béne vale ígitur. **Pa.** [*to himself*] Íre méliu'st strénue.
[*Exit.*] **Py.** [*absent-mindedly*] Étiam núnc valé.

565 [*To himself*] Ante hoc fáctum, hunc sum árbitrátus sémper
sérvum péssimúm:

566 eúm fidélem míhi esse invénio. [*Thinking*] Cum égomet
mécum cógitó,

567 stúlte féci qui húnc amísi. [*Rousing himself from his
thoughts*] Íbo hinc íntrô núnciám

568 ád amóres meós. [*Pausing*] Sed sénsi, hinc sónitum féce-
rúnt forés.

Scene 11

Meter: six-foot iambic.

[*Enter* Milphidippa *from* Periplectomenus' *house.*]

569 **Mi.** [*speaking to those within*] Ne mé moneátis; mémini ego
ófficiúm meúm. [*She turns and sees* Pyrgopolinices.]

570 Ehém, te quaéro. Sálve, vír lepidíssimé,

571 duo dí quem cúrant. **Py.** Quí duó? **Mi.** Mars ét Venús.

[572] **Py.** Facéte dícis. **Mi.** Íntrô te út eas, óbsecrát;

573 te vúlt; te quaérit; téque expéctans éxpetít.

574 Amánti fér opem. Quíd stas? Quín intrô ís? **Py.** Eó.
[*Exit into the house; immediately a sound of howling and
fighting is heard.*]

575 **Mi.** Nunc ín tumúltum ibo: íntus clámorem aúdió. [*Exit.*]

Scene 12

Meter: seven-foot trochaic.

[*Enter* Perplectomenus *from his house; he holds the door open.*]

576 **Pe.** [*to the servants within*] Dúcite ístum; sí non séquitur,
rápite súblimém forás.
[*Enter the servants carrying* Pyrgopolinices.]

[577] Fácite intér terram átque caélum út sit; né moréminí.

578 **Py.** [*abjectly*] Óbsecro hércle, Périplectómene, té. **Pe.**
[*sternly*] Nequíquam hercle óbsecrás.

[579] **Py.** Périi.   **Pe.** Haud étiam: númerô hoc dícis.   [*To the servants*] Vérberétur fústibús.

580 [*To* PYRGOPOLINICES] Cúr es aúsus súbigitáre álienam úxorem, ímpudéns?

581 **Py.** Íta me dí ament, últro véntum 'st ád me.   **Pe.** [*to one of his servants*] Méntitúr: ferí.

582 **Py.** [*to* PERIPLECTOMENUS] Máne dum nárro.   **Pe.** [*to the servants*] Quíd cessátis?   **Py.** Nón licét me díceré?

583 **Pe.** Díce.   **Py.** Orátus sum ád eam ut írem.   **Pe.** [*seizing a club and beating him*] Cúr ire aúsu's?   Ém tibí!

[584] **Py.** [*howling*] Oíei!   Sátis est.   Óbsecro hércle té, mea vérba ut aúdiás.

585 **Pe.** Lóquere.   **Py.** Nón de nihílo fáctum 'st: víduam hercle ésse cénsuí;

586 ítaque ancílla, cónciliátrix quaé erat, dícebát mihí.

587 **Pe.** [*solemnly*] Iúra té nocitúrum nón esse hómini de hác re néminí,

588 quód tu hódie hîc vérberátu's aút quod vérberáberé,

589 sí te sálvum hinc ámittémus, Véneriúm nepótulúm.

590 **Py.** [*humbly*] Iúro pér Iovem ét Mavórtem mé nocitúrum néminí,

591 quód ego hîc hódie vápulárim, iúreque íd factum árbitrór.

[592] **Pe.** [*to the servants*] Sólvite ístunc.   **Py.** Hábeo grátiam.   **Pe.** Eámus núnc.   [*Exeunt into the house, leaving* PYRGO-POLINICES *alone.*]   **Py.** [*seeing his servants returning from the harbor*] Servós meós

593 éccos vídeo.   [*To* SCELEDRUS, *who is in the lead*] Phílocomásium iám profécta 'st?   Díc mihí.

594 **Sc.** Iám dudum.   **Py.** Heí mihi!   **Sc.** Mágis dícas, sí sciás quod égo sció.

595 Nam íllic quí ob óculum habébat lánam naúta nón erát.

596 **Py.** Quís erat ígitur?   **Sc.** Phílocomásio amátor.   **Py.** Quî tu scís?   **Sc.** Sció.

597 Nám postquám portā éxiérunt, níhil cessárunt ílicó

598 ósculári atque ámplexári intér se.   **Py.** Vaé miseró mihí!

599 Vérba mihí data ésse vídeo.   Scélus virí Palaéstrió!

[600] Ís me in hánc illéxit fraúdem.   Eámus ád me.   Plaúdité.

II

The Recognition Scene From Act V of The Poenulus

HANNO, an elderly Carthaginian, traveling the world over in search of his long-lost daughters, comes to the Greek city of Cálydon. Here he discovers that one AGORÁSTOCLES, adopted son of his former friend ANTÍDAMAS, is not only a Carthaginian by birth but also his long-lost nephew, kidnapped from Carthage in childhood. In the course of his travels Hanno has become a great linguist (perhaps Carthaginian traders were always good at that sort of thing); but in order to carry on his detective work, it is his policy, on meeting people, cunningly to conceal this linguistic ability. As the prologue says:

> . . . ómnis línguas scít sed díssimulát sciéns
> se scíre: Poénus pláne 'st.

In the present scene Agorastocles and his rather impudent servant, MILPHIO, see Hanno coming along the street, attired in a flowing "gabardine"; they recognize him as a Carthaginian. A natural bluffer, Milphio pretends to understand the Punic language. The humor of the scene lies in Milphio's rough and ready interpretation of foreign words; he is like the Irishman who told of meeting the French sentry:

> "Qui va là?" sez he.
> "Je," sez I, for I shpake the language.
> "Comment?" sez he.
> "Come on yerself," sez I—and so on.

Such bilingual puns may not be a very high form of wit, but they have been a favorite theme of humor in all ages.

The actual Punic words and phrases in this play have, for the most part, been corrupted by scribes who naturally had no understanding of what they were writing. Even had the text been correctly transmitted, the use of the Punic language in a Latin (or Greek) play—especially in Hanno's long prayer at the beginning of Act V—would still have remained something of a mystery. Did Plautus (or Menander) know Punic? Did the Latin and Greek audiences understand it well enough to enjoy and appreciate Milphio's mistranslations? Or was Punic entirely over the heads of the audience and used merely for effect? If so, is it genuine or just imitation Punic? At any rate, even from these garbled remains one can gather something of the Semitic dignity of the widely traveled Hanno.

Meter: six-foot iambic.

1 **Mi.** [*seeing* Hanno *approach*] Sed quaé illaec ávis est quae
 húc cum túnicis ádvenít?

2 Numnam ín balíneis círcumdúctu'st pállió?

3 **Ag.** Faciés quidem édepol Púnicá 'st. Guggá 'st homó.

4 **Mi.** Servós quidem édepol véteres ántiquósque habét.

5 **Ag.** Quî scís? **Mi.** Vide'n ómnis sárcinátos cónsequí?

6 Atque út opinór digitós in mánibus nón habént.

7 **Ag.** Quid iám? **Mi.** Quia incédunt cum ánulátis aúribús.

8 **Ha.** [*to himself*] Adíbo hósce atque áppellábo púnicé.

9 Si réspondébunt, púnicé pergám loquí;

10 si nón, tum ad hórum móres línguam vérteró.

11 **Mi.** [*to* Agorastocles] Quid aís tu?   Écquid cómmeminísti
 púnicé?

12 **Ag.** Nihil édepol.   Nám quî scíre pótui, díc mihí,

13 qui illím sexénnis périerím Cartháginé?

14 **Ha.** [*aside, having overheard* Agorastocles] Pro di ímmortáles! Plúrimi ád illúnc modúm

15 periére púeri líberí Cartháginé.

16 **Mi.** [*to* Agorastocles] Quid aís tu? **Ag.** Quíd vis? **Mi.**
 Ví'n appéllem hunc púnicé?

17 **Ag.** An scís? **Mi.** Nullús me 'st hódie Poénus Póeniór.

18 **Ag.** Adi átque appélla, quíd velít, quid vénerít,

19 qui sít, cuiátis, únde sít. Ne párserís.

20 **Mi.** *Avó.*   Cuiátes éstis aút quo ex óppidó?

21 **Ha.** *Hannó byn Mýtthymbálle Béchaedréanéch.*

22 **Ag.** Quid aít? **Mi.** Hannónem se ésse aít Cartháginé,

23 Cartháginiénsis Mýtthymbállis fíliúm.

24 **Ha.** *Avó.* **Mi.** [*to* Agorastocles] Salútat. **Ha.** *Dónni.*
 Mi. [*to* Agorastocles] Dóni vúlt tibí

25 dare híc nescióquid.   Aúdi'n póllicitáriér?

26 **Ag.** [*to* Milphio] Salúta hunc rúrsus púnicé verbís meís.

27 **Mi.** [*to* Hanno] *Avó donnim,* ínquit híc tibí verbís suís.

28 **Ha.** *Mehár bocca.* **Mi.** [*aside, referring to* Hanno] Ístuc
 tíbi sit pótius quám mihí.

29 **Ag.** [*to* Milphio] Quid aít? **Mi.** Miseram ésse praédicát
 buccám sibí.

30 Fortásse médicos nós esse árbitráriér.
31 **Ag.** Si itá 'st, nega ésse.   Nólo ego érrare hóspitém.
32 **Mi.** [*to* HANNO, *but forgetting to talk Punic*] Audí'n tu?   **Ha.**
       [*disregarding* MILPHIO'S *question*] Rúfeénnycchoíssam.
       Ag. [*continuing his instructions to* MILPHIO] Síc voló
33 profécto: véra cúncta huic éxpedíriér.
34 Roga númquid opús sit.   **Mi.** [*to* HANNO, *again omitting the
       Punic*] Tú qui zónam nón habés,
35 quid in hánc venístis úrbem aút quid quaéritís?
36 **Ha.** *Murphúrsa.*   **Ag.** Quíd ait?   **Ha.** *Mívlechiánna.*   **Ag.**
       Quíd venít?
37 **Mi.** Non aúdis?   Múres Áfricános praédicát
38 in pómpam lúdis dáre se vélle aedílibús.
39 **Ha.** *Lechláchanánilímniichót.*   **Ag.** Quid núnc aít?
40 **Mi.** Ligulás, canális aít se advéxisse ét nucés:
41 nunc órat óperam ut dés sibi, út ea véneánt.
42 **Ag.** Mercátor, crédo, 'st.   **Ha.** *Ássam.*   **Mi.** [*aside*] Árvi-
       nám quidém.
43 **Ha.** *Palumérgadétha.*   **Ag.** Mílphió, quid núnc aít?
44 **Mi.** Palás vendéndas síbi ait ét mergás datás—
45 [*drawing on his imagination*] ad méssim, crédo, nísi quid tú
       aliúd sapís,
46 ut hórtum fódiat átque ut frúmentúm metát.
47 **Ag.** Quid ístuc ád me?   **Mi.** Cértiórem te ésse vúlt,
48 ne quíd clam fúrtim se áccepísse cénseás.
49 **Ha.** *Suphónnimsýcoráthim.*   **Mi.** [*to* AGORASTOCLES] Hem!
       cáve si's fécerís,
50 quod hic te órat.   **Ag.** Quíd ait aút quid órat?   Éxpedí.
51 **Mi.** Sub crátim ut iúbeas sé suppóni átque eó
52 lapidés impóni múltos, út sesé necés.
53 **Ha.** *Gunébelbálsaményrasá.*   **Ag.** Narrá.   Quid ést?
54 Quid aít?   **Mi.** Non hércle núnc quidém quicquám sció.
55 **Ha.** At út sciás, nunc dehínc latíne iám loquár.
56 Servum hércle te ésse opórtet ét nequam ét malúm,
57 hominém peregrínum atque ádvenám qui inrídeás.
58 **Mi.** [*angrily*] At hércle te hóminem et sýcophántam et súb-
       dolúm,

59 qui huc ádvenísti nós captátum, mígdilíx,
60 bisúlci línguā, quási prosérpens béstiá.
61 **Ag.** [*to* MILPHIO] Maledícta hinc aúfer. Línguam cóm-
pescás facé.
62 Maledícere húïc témperábis, sí sapís.
63 Meis cónsanguíneis nólo te íniusté loquí.
64 [*To* HANNO] Carthágini égo sum gnátus, út tu sís sciéns.
65 **Ha.** O mí populáris, sálve. **Ag.** Et tu édepol, quísquis és.
66 Et sí quid ópus, quaéso, díc atque ímperá
67 populáritátis caúsā. **Ha.** Hábeo grátiám.
68 Sed ecquem ádulescéntem tu hĩc novísti Agorástoclém?
69 **Ag.** Siquidem Ántidamãï quaéris adóptatíciúm,
70 ego sum ípsus quém tu quaéris. **Ha.** Hém! quid ego aúdió?
71 **Ag.** Antídamae gnátum me ésse. **Ha.** Sí ita 'st, tésserám
72 conférre sí vis hóspitálem, eccam áttulí.
73 **Ag.** Agedum húc osténde. [*He looks at it.*] Est pár probé.
Nam habeó domí.
74 **Ha.** O mi hóspes, sálve múltum. Nám mi tuús patér
75 . . . . hóspes Antidamás fuít.
76 Haec mi hóspitális tésserá cum illó fuít.
77 **Ag.** Ergo hĩc apúd med hóspitiúm praebébitúr.
78 Nam haú repúdio hospítium néque Cartháginém.
79 Inde súm oriúndus. **Ha.** Dí dent tibi ómnes quaé velís.
80 Quid aís? Quî pótuit fíeri utí Cartháginí
81 gnatús sis? Hĩc autem hábuisti Aétolúm patrém.
82 **Ag.** Surrúptus sum íllim. Hĩc me Ántidamás hospés tuús
83 emit, ét is mé sibi ádoptávit fíliúm.
84 **Ha.** Ecquíd meminísti tuúm paréntum nóminá,
85 patris átque mátris? **Ag.** Mémini. **Ha.** Mémoradúm mihí,
86 si nóvi fórte aut sí sunt cógnatí mihí.
87 **Ag.** Ampsígura máter mihí fuít, Iahón patér.
88 **Ha.** [*sadly*] Patrem átque mátrem—víverént vellém tibí.
89 **Ag.** An mórtuí sunt? **Ha.** Fáctum—quód ego aegré tulí.
90 Nam míhi sobrína Ampsígura túa matér fuít.
91 Patér tuus—ís erat fráter patruelís meús.
92 Et ís me herédem fécit, cum súum obiít diém,
93 quo prívatúm med aégre pátior mórtuó.

94 Sed sí ita 'st, út tu sís Iahónis fíliús,
95 signum ésse opórtet ín manú laevá tibí,
96 ludénti púero quód momórdit símiá.
97 Osténde: inspíciam. . . .
98 **Ag.** Mi pátrue sálve. **Ha.** Ét tu sálve, Agorástoclés.
99 **Ag.** Iterúm mihi gnátus vídeor, cúm te répperí.

III

Epidicus, or Too Many Sweethearts

(A COMEDY OF INTRIGUE.)

Plautus himself pays a unique tribute to this play, for in one of his other comedies (*Bacchides*, l. 214) he makes a character say:

. . . Epídicum, quám ego fábulam aéque ac me ípsum amó.

DRAMATIS PERSONAE
(All proper names are Greek.)

STRATÍPPOCLES (or *Warrior-Bold*): a handsome young guardsman; he is more often involved in affairs of the heart than in engagements with the enemy.

CHAERIBÚLUS (or *Free-Advice*): his friend, who is long on words but short on cash.

THÉSPRIO (i.e., *the Thesprotian*): military servant of Stratippocles.

PERÍPHANES (or *Prominent*): wealthy father of Stratippocles, ex-soldier and pillar of the state.

APOÉCIDES: a man of affairs and friend of Periphanes.

PHILÍPPA: a woman with whom Periphanes had been infatuated in his youth in Epidaurus, but whom he deserted to marry another.

EPÍDICUS (or *Persistent;* lit. *one who claims his rights*): hero of the play, lifelong servant of Periphanes, master hand at intrigue, and staunch ally of young Stratippocles.

ACROPOLÍSTIS (or *Toast-Of-The-Town*): a pretty music girl; she is the sweetheart of Stratippocles and has been palmed off on Periphanes as his natural daughter.

TELÉSTIS (or *Perfection*): natural daughter of Periphanes by Philippa, and half sister of Stratippocles.

FIDICÍNA (Lat. for *music girl*): an unnamed hireling of Epidicus who is palmed off on Periphanes as Stratippocles' sweetheart, Acropolistis.

MILES (Lat. for *soldier*): an unnamed Rhodian soldier and ardent admirer of Acropolistis.

DANISTA (Lat. for *money lender*): an unnamed Theban usurer.

SERVUS (Lat. for *servant*): an unnamed slave of Periphanes.

The scene is laid in a street in Athens, which leads, on the right, to
the center of town; on the left, to the harbor and foreign parts. Two
adjacent dwellings face the street and the spectators. PERIPHANES
and his family inhabit the house on the right; CHAERIBULUS, friend
of STRATIPPOCLES, inhabits that on the left.

PLOT

[A full account of the plot was probably contained in the prologue,
which is now lost.]

Aided and abetted by his clever servant EPIDICUS, PERIPHANES had
had an affair in his youth with a young woman of Epidaurus, PHILIPPA
by name, but had deserted her to marry an Athenian heiress. The
latter had led him a dog's life until her death. After her desertion,
Philippa had moved to Thebes and there borne Periphanes a daughter,
TELESTIS.

Now, after twenty years, the widower Periphanes would like to
marry his old flame—especially since, as he fondly believes, he has
just found his daughter Telestis and taken her into his home to live.
Though Periphanes had not seen his former mistress for twenty years
and had not laid eyes on his daughter since she was an infant, he had
kept in touch with them off and on through Epidicus, who therefore knew them well. Only the fear that his grown son, STRATIP-
POCLES, will not approve restrains Periphanes from going immediately
to Philippa and marrying her.

The experienced Epidicus is at present guiding the amours of the
son Stratippocles, just as he had formerly guided those of Periphanes
—even though this brings him into conflict with his elderly master.
As the play opens, Stratippocles is serving in the campaign of the
Athenian army against Thebes—a very brief affair of course, as most
local Greek campaigns were. Just before leaving Athens for the front,
he had fallen violently in love with ACROPOLISTIS, a music girl. He
had commanded Epidicus to secure her for him; and had constantly
sent letters to Epidicus during the campaign reminding him of his
orders and avowing undying affection for the alluring Acropolistis.

In the absence of Stratippocles, Epidicus had therefore tricked
Periphanes into believing that Acropolistis was his natural daughter,
Telestis. Under this misconception Periphanes has just bought, freed,
and established her in his household—she being not at all loath to
connive with Epidicus, who triumphantly awaits the return of Stratippocles. Epidicus fully expects that his young master will be overjoyed to find the way so conveniently paved for a secret love affair
under the very nose of his father!

Meanwhile the Athenian army has won a great victory and many

Theban captives, male and female, are offered for sale. Among these is the virtuous and beautiful Telestis, with whom the mercurial young Stratippocles falls in love at first sight, unaware of the fact that she is his half sister. Having borrowed the necessary funds from a Theban usurer, he buys Telestis and orders that she be brought to Athens.

The play opens with the expected return of the victorious Athenian army.

ACT I

Scene 1

This scene is a *canticum*.[1] Its meters, however, are not difficult: seven-foot trochaics, ll. 1–2, 9–17, 23, 29–36, 44–45, 50–51, 53–57, 66, 68, 71–72, 79–84, 86, 88, 90–91, 93, 95, 97, 99–103; eight-foot trochaics, ll. 67, 69–70, 77–78; "four-foot"[2] trochaics, ll. 3–6, 52a, 73–76, 90a; six-foot iambics, ll. 24, 46–47, 65; eight-foot iambics, ll. 7–8, 18–22, 25–28, 37–43, 48–49, 58–59, 61–64; four-foot iambic, l. 60; two-foot cretics ($\angle \smile \angle$ $\angle \smile \angle$, with variations), ll. 52, 85, 87, 89, 92, 94, 96, 98.

[*Enter* Thesprio, *military servant of* Stratippocles, *from the left; he is carrying a knapsack and other impedimenta. Like master, like servant—he strides along with soldierly ferocity. Puffing and panting,* Epidicus *comes hastening after him; he had gone to the harbor to meet the returning troops, and spied* Thesprio *from a distance heading for home—but without* Stratippocles!]

1   **Ep.** [*pursuing* Thesprio] Heús, aduléscens. **Th.** [*stopping, but not looking around*] Quís properántem mé reprehéndit pállió?

2   **Ep.** Fámiliáris. **Th.** Fáteor. Nam ódio 's nímium fámiliáritér.

3   **Ep.** Réspice véro, Thésprio. **Th.** Óh!

4   Épidicúmne ego cónspicór?

5   **Ep.** Sátis recte óculis úterís.

6   **Th.** Sálve. **Ep.** Dí dent quaé velís.

7   Veníre sálvum gaúdeó. **Th.** Quid céterúm quod eô ádsolét?

8   **Ep.** Cená tibi dábitur. **Th.** Spóndeó. **Ep.** Quid? **Th.** Me ácceptúrum, sí dabís.

---

[1] See p. 28 for explanation.

[2] There are really three and a half feet to a line.

9 **Ep.** Quíd tu agis? Út valés? **Th.** [*swelling out his chest*] Exémplum adésse intéllego. **Ep.** Eúgepaé!

10 Córpuléntiór vidére atque hábitiór. **Th.** [*displaying his left hand—symbolical of thievery*] Huic grátiá.

11 **Ep.** [*laughing*] . . . quám quidém te iámdiu édepol pérdidísse opórtuít.

12 **Th.** [*shrugging his shoulders*] Mínus iam fúrtificús sum quam ántehac. **Ep.** Quíd ita? **Th.** [*grinning*] Rápio própalám.

13 **Ep.** Di ímmortáles te ínfelícent! Út tu 's grádibus grándibús!

14 Nam út apud pórtum té conspéxi, cúrriculo óccepí sequí.

15 Víx adipíscendí potéstas módô fuít. **Th.** Scurrá 's. **Ep.** Sció

16 te ésse equidem hóminem mílitárem. **Th.** [*condescendingly*] Audácter quámvis dícitó.

17 **Ep.** Quíd ais? Pérpetuén valuísti? **Th.** Várie. **Ep.** Quí varié valént,

18 capréaginum hóminum nón placét mihí neque pántherinúm genús.

19 **Th.** Quid tíbi vis dícam nísi quod ést? **Ep.** Ut íllae rés? **Th.** Satís probé.

20 **Ep.** Quid erílis nóster fílius? **Th.** Válet púgilice átque athléticé.

21 **Ep.** Voluptábilém mihi núntiúm tuo advéntu adpórtas, Thésprió.

22 Sed ubí 'st is? **Th.** Ádvenít simul. **Ep.** Úbi is érgo 'st? —nísi si in víduló

23 aút si in mélina áttulísti. **Th.** Dí te pérdant! **Ep.** Té voló . . . [*pausing for effect*]

24 percóntari. Óperam da: ópera réddetúr tibí.

25 **Th.** Ius dícis. **Ep.** [*pompously*] Mé decét. **Th.** [*dampening his spirits*] Iam tu aútem nóbis praéturám gerís?

26 **Ep.** Quem díces dígniórem esse hóminem hoc [*slapping himself on the chest*] hódie Athénis álterúm?

27 **Th.** At únum a praéturá tua, Epídice, abést. **Ep.** Quidnám? **Th.** Sciés:

28 lictóres duó, duo úlmeí fascés virgárum. **Ep.** Vaé tibí!
29 Séd quid aís tu? **Th.** Quíd rogás? **Ep.** Ubi árma súnt
   Stratíppoclí?
30 **Th.** Pól illa ad hóstes tránsfugérunt. **Ep.** Ármane? **Th.**
   Átque quidém citó.
31 **Ep.** Múlcibér, credo, árma fécit, quaé habuít Stratíppoclés:
32 trávoláverúnt ad hóstis. **Th.** [*sarcastically*] Túm ille pró-
   gnatú'st Thetí.
33 Síne perdát: alia ádportábunt Nérëí ei fíliaé.
34 **Ep.** Sérióne dícis ístuc? **Th.** Sério, ínquam, hostés habént.
35 **Ep.** Édepol fácinus ímprobum! **Th.** Át iam ante álii féce-
   rúnt idém.
36 Érit illi ílla rés honóri. **Ep.** Quí? **Th.** Quia ánte aliís fuít.
37 **Ep.** Id módô vidéndum 'st, út matéries súppetát scutáriís,
38 si in síngulís stipéndiís ad hóstis éxuviás dabít.
39 **Th.** Supérsede ístis rébus iám. **Ep.** Tu ipse, úbi libét,
   finém facé.
40 **Th.** Desíste pércontáriér. **Ep.** Loquere ípse: ubí 'st Stratíppoclés?
41 **Th.** Est caúsa, quá causá simúl mecum íre véritu'st. **Ep.**
   Quídnam id ést?
42 **Th.** Patrém vidére sé nevólt etiám nunc. **Ep.** Quáproptér?
   Th. Sciés:
43 quia fórmā lépidā et líberáli cáptivam ádulescéntulám
44 dé praedá mercátu'st. **Ep.** [*dumbfounded*] Quíd ego ex te
   aúdio? **Th.** Hóc quod fábulór.
45 **Ep.** Cúr eam émit? **Th.** Ánimi caúsā. **Ep.** [*desperately*]
   Quót illic hómo animós habét?
46 Nam cérto priúsquam hinc ád legiónem abiít domó,
47 ipse mándavít mihi, áb lenóne ut fídiciná,
48 quam amábat, émeretúr sibi. Íd [*with a touch of pride*] ei
   ímpetrátum réddidí.
49 **Th.** [*consolingly*] Utcúmque in álto véntu'st, Épidice, éxim
   vélum vértitúr.
50 **Ep.** [*overcome by disappointment*] Vaé miseró mihí! Male
   pérdidít me. Quíd ais tú? **Th.** Quid ést?

51 **Ep.** Quíd istanc quam émit? Quánti eam émit? **Th.** Víli.
Ep. Haud ístuc té rogó.

52 **Th.** Quíd igitúr? **Ep.** Quót minís?

52a **Th.** Tót [*counting on his fingers*]: quadrágintá minís.

53 Íd adeo árgentum áb danísta apud Thébas súmpsit fénoré,

54 ín diés minásque argénti síngulás nummís. **Ep.** Papaé!

55 **Th.** Ét is danísta advénit únâ cúm eo, qui árgentúm petít.

56 **Ep.** [*laughing in spite of his troubles*] Di ímmortáles! Út
ego intérii básilicé! **Th.** Quid iam, aút quid ést,

57 Épidice? **Ep.** Heí, me pérdidít. **Th.** Quis? **Ep.** Ílle qui
árma pérdidít.

58 **Th.** Nam quíd ita? **Ep.** Quía cottídie ípse ad me áb legióne
epístulás

59 mittébat—séd taceam óptimúm 'st. Plus scíre sátiu'st
quám loquí

60 servum hóminem: eá sapiéntiá 'st.

61 **Th.** [*twitting him*] Nescíó edepól quid tímidu's. Trépidas,
Épidice. Út vultúm tuúm

62 videó, vidére cómmeruísse hîc me ábsente ín te aliquíd
malí.

63 **Ep.** [*flaring up*] Poti'n út moléstus né siés? **Th.** Abeo.
Ep. [*regretting his hasty words*] Ásta. Abíre hinc nón
sinám.

64 **Th.** Quíd nunc mé retinés? **Ep.** Amatne ístam quam émit
dé praedá? **Th.** Rogás?

65 Deperít. **Ep.** Deagétur córium dé tergó meó.

66 **Th.** [*laughing*] Plúsque amát quam te úmquam amávit.
Ep. Íuppitér te pérduít!

67 **Th.** Mítte núnciám me. Nam ílle mé vetuít domúm veníre.

68 Ád sodálem Chaéribúlum iússit húc in próximúm.

69 Íbi manére iússit. Eó ventúru'st ípsus. **Ep.** Quíd ita?
Th. Dícam:

70 quía patrém prius cónveníre sé non vúlt neque cónspicári,

71 quám id argéntum quód debétur pró illa dínumeráverít.

72 **Ep.** Eú edepól res túrbuléntas! **Th.** Mítte me út eam
núnciám.

73 **Ep.** [*shrugging his shoulders*] Haécine úbi scibít senéx,

74   púppis péreundá 'st probé.
75   **Th.** Quíd istúc ad me áttinét,
76   quó tu íntereás modó?
77   **Ep.** [*sarcastically*] Quía períre sólus nólo: té cupió períre mécum,
78   bénevoléns cum bénevolénte.   **Th.** Abi ín malám rem máximam á me
79   cúm istac cóndicióne.   **Ep.** I sáne, síquidém festinás magís.
80   **Th.** Númquam hominém quemquám convéni, unde ábierím libéntiús.   [*Exit into the house of* CHAERIBULUS.]
81   **Ep.** [*soliloquizing*] Íllic hinc ábiit.   Sólus núnc es.   Quo ín loco haéc res sít vidés,
82   Épidicé.   Nisi quíd tibi ín tete aúxilí 'st, absúmptus és:
83   tántae in te ímpendént ruínae.   Nísi suffúlcis fírmitér,
84   nón potés subsístere: ítaque in te ínruúnt montés malí.
85   Néque, ego núnc quómodó
86   me éxpedítum ex ímpedíto fáciam, cónsiliúm placét.
87   Égo misér pérpulí
88   meís dolís senem, út censéret suám sese émere fíliám.
89   Ís suó fílió
90   fídicinam émit quam ílle amábat, quam ábiens mándavít mihí.
90a Sí sibí nunc álterám
91   áb legióne abdúxit ánimi caúsā córium pérdidí.
92   Nam úbi senéx sénserít
93   síbi data ésse vérba, vírgis dórsum díspoliét meúm.
94   [*With sudden resolution*] Át enim tú praécavé!
95   [*Giving up in despair*] Át enim—bát enim: níhil est ístuc. Pláne hoc córruptúm 'st capút.
96   Néquam homó 's, Épidicé.
97   [*Bracing up again*] Quí libído 'st mále loquí?   Quia túte téte déserís.
98   [*He reasons with himself.*]   Quíd faciám?   Mén rogás?
99   [*He scolds himself.*]   Tú quidem antehác aliís solébas dáre consília mútuá.
100 Áliquid áliquâ réperiéndum 'st.   [*He sighs and gives up the struggle.*]   Séd ego césso ire óbviám

101 ádulescénti, ut quíd negóti sít sciam. [*He sees* STRATIPPO-
CLES *approaching.*] Átque ipse íllîc ést.

102 Trístis ést. Cum Chaéribúlo incédit aéqualí suó. [*He hides
in the doorway of his own house.*]

103 Húc concédam, orátiónem unde hórum plácide pérsequár.

SCENE 2

Meters: ll. 104–163, seven-foot trochaic; ll. 164–165, eight-foot
iambic.

[*Enter* STRATIPPOCLES *from the left, walking slowly and in ear-
nest conversation with his friend* CHAERIBULUS, *who had evidently
met him at the harbor upon his arrival from Thebes.*]

104 **St.** [*finishing the tale of his doubts and fears*] Rém tibi sum
élocútus ómnem, Chaéribúle, atque ádmodúm

105 meórum maérorum átque amórum súmmam edíctaví tibí.

106 **Ch.** [*stopping in front of his house*] Praéter aétatem ét vir-
tútem stúltus és, Stratíppoclés.

107 Ídne pudét te, quía captívam génere prógnatám bonó

108 ín praedá 's mercátus? Quís erit vítio qui íd vertát tibí?

109 **St.** Qui ínvidént, omnés inimícos míhi illoc fácto répperí.

110 Át pudícitiae éius númquam néc vim néc vitium áttulí.

111 **Ch.** Iam ístoc próbior és meo quídem animó, cum in amóre
témperés.

112 **St.** [*impatiently*] Níhil agít qui díffidéntem vérbis sólatúr
suís.

113 Ís est amícus quí in re dúbia ré iuvát, ubi ré 'st opús.

114 **Ch.** Quíd tibi mé vis fácere? **St.** Argénti dáre quadrágintá
minás,

115 quód danístae détur, únde ego íllud súmpsi fénoré.

116 **Ch.** Si hércle habérem, póllicérer. **St.** [*sarcastically*] Nám
quid te ígitur rétulít

117 béneficum ésse orátióne, si ád rem auxílium emórtuúm 'st?

118 **Ch.** Quín edepól egomét clamóre dífferór, difflágitór.

119 **St.** [*turning away in disgust*] Málim istíusmodí mihi amícos
fúrno mérsos quám foró.

120 Séd operam Épidicí nunc me émere prétio prétiosó velím.

121 Quém quidem égo hominem írrigátum plágis pístorí dabó,
122 nísi hodié prius cómparássit míhi quadrágintá minás,
123 quam "árgentí" fuero élocútus éi postrémam sýllabám.
124 **Ep.** [*concealed; aside, sarcastically*] Sálva rés est: béne pro-
        míttit.   Spéro, sérvabít fidém.
125 Síne meó sumptú parátae iám sunt scápulis sýmbolaé.
126 Ádgrediár hominem.   [*He emerges from concealment and
        approaches* STRATIPPOCLES *from behind, with lordly dig-
        nity.*]   Ádveniéntem péregre erúm Stratíppoclém
127 ímpertít salúte sérvus Épidicús.   **St.** [*startled*] Ubi is ést?
        Ep. Adést.
128 Sálvum te ádvenísse huc. . . . **St.** [*interrupting him*] Tám
        tibi ístuc crédo quám mihí.
129 **Ep.** [*ignoring the last remark*] Bénene usqué valuísti?   **St.**
        A mórbo válui, ab ánimo aegér fuí.
130 **Ep.** [*ingratiatingly*] Quód ad me attínuit, égo curávi.   [*He
        waits in vain for* STRATIPPOCLES *to answer.*]   Quód tu
        mándastí mihí,
131 ímpetrátum 'st.   [*Another pause ensues.*]   Émpta ancílla
        'st, quód tute ád me lítterás
132 míssiculábas.   **St.** [*gruffly*] Pérdidísti omnem óperam.   **Ep.**
        Nám quî pérdidí?
133 **St.** Quía meó neque cára 'st córdi néque placét.   **Ep.** Quid
        rétulít
134 té tantópere míhi mandáre et míttere ád me epístulás?
135 **St.** [*calmly*] Íllam amábam olim: núnciam ália cúra impén-
        det péctorí.
136 **Ep.** [*aside*] Hércle quî miserúm 'st ingrátum esse hómini id
        quód faciás bené.
137 Égo quod bénefecí, maleféci, quía amor mútavít locúm.
138 **St.** Désipiébam méntis cum ílla scrípta míttebám tibí.
139 **Ep.** [*indignantly*] Mén piáculárem opórtet fíeri ob stúltitiám
        tuám,
140 út meum térgum tuaé stultítiae súbdas súccidáneúm?
141 **St.** Quíd istîc?   Vérba fácimus.   Huíc homini [*pointing to
        himself*] ópu'st quadrágintá minís
142 céleritér calidís, danístae quás resólvat ét citó.

143 **Ep.** [*sarcastically*] Díc modô: únde auférre vís me? A quó
     tarpézitá petó?
144 **St.** Únde libét: nam ni ánte sólem occásum e lóculis ádferés,
145 meám domúm ne inbítas—tú te ín pistrínum cónferás.
146 **Ep.** [*bitterly*] Fácile tu ístuc síne períclo et cúrā, córde líberó,
147 fábuláre. Nóvi ego nóstros. Míhi dolét cum ego vápuló.
148 **St.** [*fiercely*] Quíd nunc tú? Patiéri'n út ego me ínterimám?
     Ep. [*with alarm*] Ne fécerís.
149 [*With sudden resolve*] Égo istuc áccedám períclum pótius
     átque audáciám.
150 **St.** [*overjoyed*] Núnc placés. Nunc égo te laúdo. **Ep.** Pá-
     tiar égo istuc—quódlibét.
151 **St.** Quíd illā́ fiet fídicinā́ ígitur? **Ep.** Áliqua rés reperíbi-
     túr . . . [*hesitating*]
152 áliqua ope éxsolvam . . . éxtricábor áliquâ. **St.** Plénus
     cónsilí 's.
153 Nóvi ego te. **Ep.** [*with sudden inspiration*] Ést Eubóicus
     míles lócuples, múlto auró poténs,
154 qui úbi tibi ístam emptam ésse scíbit átque hanc ádductam
     álterám,
155 cóntinuó te orábit últro, ut íllam trámittás sibí.
156 Séd ubi illá 'st quam tu ádduxísti técum? **St.** Iám faxo
     hī́c erít. [*He turns away from* Epidicus.]
157 **Ch.** [*to* Stratippocles] Quíd hîc nunc ágimus? **St.** Eámus
     íntrô huc ád te, ut húnc hodié diém
158 lúculénte habeámus. **Ep.** Íte intrô. [*He pushes them toward*
     Chaeribulus' *house—glad to get rid of them.*] Égo de re
     árgentáriá
159 iám senátum cónvocábo in córde cónsiliáriúm,
160 cuí potíssimum índicátur béllum, unde árgentum aúferám.
161 Épidicé, vide quíd agas: íta res súbito haec óbiectá 'st tibí.
162 Nón enim núnc tibi dórmitándi néque cunctándi cópiá 'st.
163 Ádeundúm 'st. Senem óppugnáre cértum 'st cónsiliúm
     mihí.
164 Ibo íntrô atque ádulescénti dícam, nóstro eríli fílió,
165 ne hínc forás exámbulét neve óbviám veniát sení. [*Exit
     into the house of* Chaeribulus.]

ACT II

Scene 1

This scene is a *canticum*. Its meters are too complex and varied to be indicated here.

[*Enter* Periphanes *from his house with* Apoecides; *they are discussing the former's affairs.*]

166   **Ap.** [*to* Periphanes, *earnestly*] Plerique homines, quos, cum
      nil refert, pudet—
166a ubi pudendum 'st, ibi eos deserit pudor,
167   cum usu'st ut pudeat.
168   Is adeo tu 's.   Quid est quod pudendum siet,
169   genere natam bono pauperem te domum
170   ducere uxorem, praesertim eam, qua ex tibi
171   commemores hanc, quae domi 'st,
172   filiam prognatam?
173   **Pe.** Revereor filium.   **Ap.** At pol ego te credidi
174   uxorem, quam tu extulisti, sine pudore exsequi—
175   cuius quotiens sepulcrum vides, sacrificas
176   ilico Orco hostiis (neque adeo iniuriā),
177   quia licitum 'st eam tibi vincere vivendo.   **Pe.** [*gloomily*]
      Oh!
178   Hercules ego fui, dum illa mecum fuit;
179   neque sexta aerumna acerbior Herculi quam mi illa obiecta
      'st.
180   **Ap.** [*trying to cheer him up*] Pulchra edepol dos pecunia 'st.
      Pe. . . . quae quidem pol non marita 'st.   [*As their conversation grows more confidential, they become completely absorbed and lower their voices to a whisper.*]

Scene 2

The *canticum* continues through l. 189. Then plain dialogue is resumed. Ll. 190–193 and 196–305 are seven-foot trochaics; ll. 194–195, eight-foot iambics.

[*Enter* Epidicus *from* Chaeribulus' *house.*]

181-2 **Ep.** [*motioning to those within to keep quiet*] St! Tacete!
      Habete animum bonum. [*He shuts the door behind him, but remains out of sight and hearing of the old men.*]

183-4 Liquido exeo auspicio foras, avi sinistra.

185 Acutum cultrum habeo, senis qui exenterem marsuppium.
[*He looks about him.*]

186 Sed eccum ipsum ante aedis conspicor

187 cum Apoecide—qualis volo, vetulos duo!

188 Iam ego me convertam in hirudinem atque eorum exsugebo
sanguinem,

189 [*with a sneer*] senati qui columen cluent. [*He tries to over-hear what the old men are saying.*]

190 **Ap.** [*with finality, raising his voice*] Cóntinuo út marítus fíat.
Pe. Laúdo cónsiliúm tuúm.

191 Nam égo illum audívi in amóre haerére apúd nescióquam
fídicinám.

192 Íd ego excrúcior. **Ep.** [*retreating into the doorway and dancing for joy*] Dí me hercle ómnes ádiuvánt, augént, amánt.
[*He gloats over the sudden inspiration* PERIPHANES' *remark has given him.*]

193 Ípsi hi quidém mihi dánt viám, quo pácto ab se árgentum
aúferám. [*He prepares himself for the fray.*]

194 Age núnciam órna te, Épidice, ét pallíolum in cóllum cónicé.

195 Itaque ádsimuláto, quási per úrbem tótam hominém quaesí-verís.

196 Áge, si quíd agis! [*He slips out of the doorway and dashes across stage, pretending not to see* PERIPHANES.] Di ímmortáles! Útinam cónveniám domí

197 Périphaném, quem omném per úrbem súm deféssus quaé-reré . . . [*panting*]

198 pér medicínas, pér tonstrínas, ín gymnásio atque ín foró,

199 pér myropólia ét laniénas círcumque árgentáriás . . .

200 rógitandó sum raúcus fáctus, paéne in cúrsu cóncidí.

201 **Pe.** Épidice! **Ep.** [*pretending to be flustered*] Épidicúm quis
ést qui révocat? **Pe.** Égo sum Périphanés.

202 **Ap.** Ét ego Apoécidés sum. **Ep.** Et quídem ego sum Épidi-cús. Sed, ere, óptimá

203 vós video ópportúnitáte ambo ádveníre. **Pe.** Quíd reí 'st?

204 **Ep.** [*panting more violently*] Máne si's! Síne respírem, quaéso.
Pe. Immo ácquiésce. **Ep.** Animó malé 'st.

205 **Ap.** Récipe ánhelitúm. **Pe.** Cleménter réquiesce. **Ep.**
Ánimadvértité:

206 á legióne omnés remíssi súnt domúm Thebís. **Ap.** Quis
hóc

207 scít factúm? **Ep.** Ego íta factum ésse díco. **Pe.** Scí'n tu
istúc? **Ep.** Sció.

208 **Pe.** Quí tu scís? **Ep.** Quia ego íre vídi mílités plenís viís.

209 Árma réferunt ét iuménta dúcunt. **Pe.** Nímis factúm bené!

210 **Ep.** Túm captívorúm quid dúcunt sécum!—púeros, vír-
ginés—

211 bínos, térnos—álius quínque! Fít concúrsus pér viás.

212 Fíliós suos quísque vísunt. **Pe.** Hércle rém gestám bené!

213 **Ep.** [*letting his imagination run riot*] Túm meretrícum nú-
merus tántus!—quántum in úrbe omní fuít,

214 óbviam órnatae óccurébant suís quaeque ámatóribús.

215 Eós captábant. Íd adeó quí máxime ánimadvérterím—

216 pléraeque eaé sub véstiméntis sécum habébant rétiá.

217 Cum ád portúm venio, átque . . . [*impressively*] ego íllam
illî vídeo praéstoláriér.

218 Ét cum eá tibícinae íbant quáttuór. **Pe.** Quicum, Épidicé?

219 **Ep.** Cúm illa quám tuus gnátus ánnos múltos déamat, déperít,

220 úbi fidémque rémque séque téque próperat pérderé.

221 Éa praestólabátur íllum apud pórtum. **Pe.** [*bitterly*] Vidé'n
venéficám?

222 **Ep.** [*heightening the picture and increasing* PERIPHANES' *fears*]
Séd vestíta, auráta, ornáta ut lépide! ut cóncinne! út
nové!

223 **Pe.** [*overcome by curiosity*] Quíd erat índuta? án regíllam
indúculam án mendículám?

224 **Ep.** [*leading the old man on*] Ímpluviátam—ut ístae fáciunt
véstiméntis nóminá.

225 **Pe.** Útin implúvium indúta fúerit? **Ep.** [*launching into a
diatribe on women's fashions*] Quíd istuc tám mirábilé 'st?

226 Quási non fúndis éxornátae múltae incédant pér viás!

227 Át tribútus cum ímperátus ést, negánt pendí potís.

228 Íllis, quíbus tribútus máior pénditúr, pendí potést.

229 Quíd istae quaé vestí quotánnis nómina ínveniúnt nová!—
230 túnicam rállam, túnicam spíssam, línteolúm caesíciúm,
231 índusiátam, pátagiátam, cáltulam aút crocótulám,
232 súbparum aút subnímium, rícam, básilicum aút exóticúm,
233 cúmatile aút plumátile, cárinum aut gérrinum—gérrae máx-
    imaé!
234 Cáni quoque étiam adémptum 'st nómen. **Pe.** Quî? **Ep.**
    Vocánt Lacónicúm.
235 Haéc vocábula aúctiónes súbigunt út faciánt virós.
236 **Pe.** [*impatiently*] Quín tu, ut óccepísti, lóquere? **Ep.** [*taking
    the hint*] Occépere áliae múlierés
237 duaé sic [*illustrating in mimicry*] póst me fábulári intér se.
    Ego ábscessí sciéns
238 paúlum ab íllis. Díssimulábam earum óperam sérmoní
    daré.
239 Néc satis éxaudíbam, néc sermónis fállebár tamén,
240 quaé loqueréntur. **Pe.** Íd libído 'st scíre. **Ep.** Ibi íllarum
    álterá
241 díxit ílli quícum ipsa íbat . . . [*pausing to think what to say
    next*] **Pe.** Quíd? **Ep.** Tace érgo ut aúdiás.
242 [*Resuming his tale*] . . . póstquam illám sunt cónspicátae,
    quám tuus gnátus déperít,
243 "quám facile ét quam fórtunáte evénit ílli—óbsecró—
244 múlierí, quam líberáre vúlt amátor!" "Quísnam is ést?"
245 ínquit áltera ílli. Ibi ílla nóminát Stratíppoclém,
246 Périphanáï fíliúm. **Pe.** Perii hércle! Quíd ego ex te aúdió?
247 **Ep.** Hóc quod áctum 'st. Égomet póstquam id íllas aúdiví
    loquí,
248 coépi rúrsum vérsum ad íllas paúsillátim accéderé,
249 quási hominúm retrúderét me vís invítum. **Pe.** Intéllegó.
250 **Ep.** Íbi illa intérrogávit íllam, "quî scis? quís id dixít tibí?"
251 "Quía hodie ádlataé tabéllae súnt ad eam á Stratíppoclé:
252 éum argentúm sumpsísse apud Thébas áb danísta fénoré—
253 íd parátum et sése ob eám rem id férre." **Pe.** [*gasping*]
    Cérto ego óccidí!
254 **Ep.** Haéc sic aíbat: sic aúdivísse ex eápse átque epístulá.

255 **Pe.** Quíd ego fáciam? Núnc consílium a te éxpetésso, Apoécidés.

256 **Ap.** Réperiámus áliquid cálidi cónducíbilis cónsilí.

257 Nam ílle quidem aút iam hîc áderit, crédo hercle, aút iam adést. **Ep.** [*slily and with mock humility*] Si aequúm siét

258 mé plus sápere quám vos, déderim vóbis cónsiliúm catúm,

259 quód laudétis, út ego opíno, utérque. . . . **Pe.** [*interrupting him*] Ergo úbi id est, Épidicé?

260 **Ep.** . . . átque ad eám rem cónducíbile. **Ap.** Quíd istuc dúbitas díceré?

261 **Ep.** Vós prióres ésse opórtet, nós postérius díceré,

262 quí plus sápitis. **Pe.** Eía véro! Age, díc! **Ep.** At déridébitís.

263 **Ap.** Nón edepól faciémus. **Ep.** [*to* Periphanes] Ímmo, sí placébit, útitór

264 cónsiliúm; [*to them both*] si nón placébit, réperitóte réctiús.

265 Míhi [*piously*] istîc néc seritúr nec métitur, nísi ea quaé tu vís, voló.

266 **Pe.** Grátiam hábeo. Fác [*ironically*] partícipes nós tuaé sapiéntiaé.

267 **Ep.** [*impressively*] Cóntinuo árbitrétur úxor tuó gnato; átque ut fídicinám

268 íllam, quam ís vult líberáre, quaé illum córrumpít tibí,

269 úlciscáre; atque íta curétur, úsque ad mórtem ut sérviát.

270 **Ap.** [*enthusiastically*] Fíeri opórtet. **Pe.** [*delighted*] Fácere cúpio quídvis, dum íd fiát modô. **Ep.** Hém!

271 Núnc occásió 'st faciéndi, príusquam in úrbem advénerít,

272 sícut crás hîc áderit: hódie nón venít. **Pe.** Quî scís? **Ep.** Sció,

273 quía mihi álius díxit, qui íllinc vénit: máne huc ádforé.

274 **Pe.** Quín tu elóquere, quíd faciémus? **Ep.** Síc faciéndum cénseó,

275 quási tu cúpias líberáre fídicinam ánimi grátiā̃,

276 quásique amés veheménter tu íllam. **Pe.** [*somewhat alarmed*] Quam ád rem istúc rēfért? **Ep.** Rogás?

277 Út enim praéstinés argénto, príusquam véniat fíliús;

278 átque ut eám in líbertátem dícas émere. **Pe.** Intéllegó.

279 **Ep.** Úbi erit émpta, ut áliquô ex úrbe eam ámoveás, nisi quíd tuá 'st

280 sécus senténtia. **Pe.** Ímmo dócte. **Ep.** Quíd tu autem áis, Apoécidés?

281 **Ap.** Quíd ego iám?—nisi té comméntum nímis astúte intéllegó.

282 **Ep.** [*triumphantly*] Iam ígitur ámota éï fúerit ómnis cónsultátió

283 núptiárum, né gravétur quód velís. **Pe.** Vivé sapís,

284 ét placét. **Ep.** Tum tu ígitur cálide, quídquid ácturú's, agé.

285 **Pe.** Rem hércle lóquere. **Ep.** Et répperi, á te quî ábscedát suspíció.

286 **Pe.** Síne me scíre. **Ep.** Scíbis. Aúdi. **Ap.** Sápit hic pléno péctoré.

287 **Ep.** Ópus est hómine, quí illô argéntum déferát pro fídiciná.

288 Nám te nólo, neque ópus fácto 'st. **Pe.** Quíd iam? **Ep.** Né te cénseát

289 fíli caúsā fácere. . . . **Pe.** Dócte! **Ep.** . . . quó illum ab ílla próhibeás,

290 né qua ob eám suspíciónem dífficúltas évenát.

291 **Pe.** Quém hominem ínveniémus ád eam rem útilem? **Ep.** [*designating* APOECIDES, *who swells with pride*] Híc erit óptimús.

292 Híc poterít cavére récte, iúra qui ét legés tenét.

293 **Pe.** [*to* APOECIDES] Épidico hábeas grátiám. **Ep.** [*to* PERIPHANES, *with assumed self-confidence*] Sed ego ístuc fáciam séduló.

294 Égo illum cónveniam átque . . . [*hesitating*] addúcam huc . . . [*to* APOECIDES] ád te, cúia 'st fídiciná. . . .

295 átque [*with a significant glance at* PERIPHANES] argéntum ego cum hóc feram. **Pe.** Íllaec quánti emí minimó potést?

296 **Ep.** Ád quadrágintá fortásse eam pósse emí minimó minís.

297 Vérum sí plus déderis, réferam. Níl in eá re cáptió 'st.

298 Átque id nón decem óccupátum tíbi erit árgentúm diés.

299 **Pe.** Quídum? **Ep.** Quía enim múlierem álius íllam aduléscens déperít,

300 aúro opuléntus, mágnus míles Rhódius, ráptor hóstiúm,

301 glóriósus. Híc emet íllam dé te et dábit aurúm libéns.

302 Fáce modó: 'st lucrum híc tibi ámplum. **Pe.** Deós quidem
óro. **Ep.** Ímpetrás.

303 **Ap.** [*to* Periphanes] Quín tu is íntrô atque huíc argéntum
prómis? Egó visam ád forúm.

304 Épidice, éô vení. **Ep.** Ne abítas, príusquam ego ád te
véneró.

305 **Ap.** Úsque oppériar. [*Exit.*] **Pe.** [*to* Epidicus] Séquere tu
íntrô. **Ep.** [*wishing for a moment to himself in which to
relieve his pent-up feelings*] I, númera.   Níl ego té morór.
[*Exit* Periphanes *into his house.*]

Scene 3

Meter: six-foot iambic

306 **Ep.** [*alone, dancing for joy*] Nullum ésse opínor égo agrum
ín agro Átticó

307 aequé ferácem quam híc est nóster Périphanés.

308 Quin éx occlúso atque óbsignáto armárió

309 decútio argénti tántum, quántum míhi libét.

310 Quod pól ego métuo, sí senéx rescíverít,

311 ne ulmós parasítos fáciat, quae úsque attóndeánt. [*He
knits his brows for a moment.*]

312 Sed me úna túrbat rés ratióque: Apoécidí

313 quam osténdam fídicinam . . . [*deep in thought*] áliquam
cónductíciám.

314 Atque [*he has an inspiration*] íd quoque hábeo: máne mé
iussít senéx

315 condúcere áliquam fídicinám sibi húc domum, út,

316 dum rém divínam fáceret, cántarét sibí.

317 Ea cónducétur, átque ei praémonstrábitúr,

318 quo pácto fíat súbdola ádversúm seném.

319 Ibo íntrô.   Argéntum accípiam ab dámnosó sené. [*Exit
into house.*]

ACT III

Scene 1

A *canticum.*

[*Enter* Stratippocles, *worried and overwrought, from* Chaeri-bulus' *house. He is followed by the phlegmatic* Chaeribulus, *whose calmness only exasperates him.*]

320 **St.** Exspectando exedor miser atque exenteror,
321 quomodo mi Epidici blanda dicta evenant.
322 Nimis diu maceror. Sitne quid, necne sit,
323 scire cupio. **Ch.** Per illam tibi copiam—copiam
324 parare aliam licet. Scivi equidem in principio ilico
325 nullam tibi esse in illo copiam. **St.** Interii hercle ego.
326 **Ch.** [*fatuously*] Absurde facis qui angas te animi. Si hercle ego
327 illum semel prendero, numquam inridere nos
328 illum inultum sinam servum hominem.
329 **St.** [*exploding with wrath*] Quid illum facere vis, qui—tibi cui divitiae sunt maximae—
330 amicis nummum nullum habes, nec sodali tuo in te copia 'st?
331 **Ch.** Si hercle habeam, pollicear libens; [*brightly*] verum ali-quando aliquâ aliquo modo
332 alicunde ab aliqui aliqua tibi spes est fore mecum fortunam.
333 **St.** Vae tibi, muricide homo! **Ch.** [*feeling hurt*] Quî tibi libet mihi male loqui?
334 **St.** Quippe tu mi "aliquid aliquo modo alicunde ab aliqui-bus" blatis—
335 quod nusquam 'st! Neque ego id immitto in auris meas,
336 nec mihi plus adiumenti das, quam ille qui numquam etiam natus est.

Scene 2

The *canticum* continues through l. 340; thereafter the scene is in seven-foot iambics.

[*Enter* Epidicus *from* Periphanes' *house carrying the bag of money.*]

337 **Ep.** [*to* Periphanes *within*] Fecisti iam officium tuum. Me

meum nunc facere oportet. [*He chuckles as he closes the door.*]

338 Per hanc curam quieto tibi licet esse. Hoc quidem iam periit.

339 Ni quid hinc in spem referas tibi: hoc oppido pollinctum 'st.

340 Crede modô tu mihi: sic ego ago, sic egerunt nostri.

341 Pro di ímmortáles! Mihi húnc diém dedístis lúculéntum!

342 Ut fácilem atque ímpetrábilém! Sed [*assuming an important air*] ego hínc migráre césso,

343 ut ímportem ín colóniam húnc meo auspício cómmeátum?

344 Mihi césso, cúm sto. Séd quid hóc? Ante aédis dúo sodáles,

345 erum et Chaéribúlum, cónspicór. [*He approaches them.*] Quid hîc ágitis? [*He bows to* STRATIPPOCLES] Áccipe hóc si's. [*He hands him the moneybag.*]

346 **St.** [*too excited even to thank him*] Quantum hîc inést? **Ep.** [*airily*] Quantúm sat ést, et plús satís. Supérfit.

347 Decém minís plus áttulí, quam tú danístae débes.

348 Dum tíbi ego pláceam atque óbsequár, [*posing as a hero*] meum térgum flócci fácio.

349 **St.** Nam quíd ita? **Ep.** Quía ego tuúm patrém faciám perénticídam.

350 **St.** Quid istúc est vérbi? **Ep.** Níl morór vetera ét vulgáta vérba

351 "perátum dúctare": hódie egó follítum dúctitábo.

352 Nam [*boastfully*] léno omne árgentum ábstulít pro fídicina (égo resólvi!

353 his mánibus dínumerávi!)—patér suam nátam quam ésse crédit.

354 Nunc [*triumphantly*] íterum ut fállatúr patér tibique aúxilium ádparétur,

355 invéni. Nam íta suasí seni (átque hanc hábui óratiónem),

356 ut cúm redísses né tibi éius cópia ésset. **St.** Eúge!

357 **Ep.** Ea iám domí 'st pro fíliá. **St.** Iam téneo. **Ep.** Núnc cautórem

358 dedít mi ad hánc rem Apoécidém (is ápud forúm manét me),

359 quasi qui á me cáveat. **St.** Haúd malé iam ípse caútor
cáptu'st.

360 **Ep.** Ipse ín meo cóllo túus patér crumínam cóllocávit.

361 Is adórnat, . . . [*nonchalantly*] ádveniéns domí extémplo
ut marítus fías.

362 **St.** [*indignantly*] Unó persuádebít modó, si illám quae addúcta 'st mécum

363 mi adémpsit Órcus. **Ep.** Núnc egó astútiam hánc instítui:

364 devéniam ad lénoném domum égomet sólus; eúm docébo

365 (si qui ád eum advéniat) út sibí datum ésse argéntum dícat

366 pro fídicina, árgentí minás se habére quínquagínta—

367 quippe égo quî núdiustértiús meis mánibus dínumerávi

368 pro illá tua amíca, quám patér suam fíliam ésse rétur.

369 Ibi léno scéleratúm capút suum imprúdens ádligábit,

370 quasi pró illa argéntum accéperít, quae técum addúcta núnc
est.

371 **St.** Versútiór es quám rotá figuláris. **Ep.** Iam égo parábo

372 aliquám dolósam fídicinám, nummó condúcta quaé sit,

373 quae se émptam símulet, quaé senés duo dócte lúdificétur.

374 Eam dúcet símul Apoécidés ad tuúm patrem. **St.** Út pa-
ráte!

375 **Ep.** Eam pérmeditátam meís dolís astútiísque onústam

376 mittám. Sed nímis longúm loquór. Diu me éstis démo-
ráti.

377 Haec scítis iam út futúra sínt. Abeó. **St.** Bene ámbuláto.
[*Exit* Epidicus *to the right.*]

378 **Ch.** Nimis dóctus ílle 'st ád malé faciéndum. **St.** Me équidem cérto

379 servávit cónsiliís suís. **Ch.** Abeámus íntrô hinc ád me.

380 **St.** [*somewhat apologetically*] Atque áliquantó libéntiús quam
abs té sum egréssus íntus.

381 Virtúte atque aúspicio Épidicí cum praéda in cástra rédeo.
[*Exeunt.*]

SCENE 3

Meter: six-foot iambic.

[*Enter* Periphanes *from his house; he is very content in the belief
that all his troubles are over.*]

382 **Pe.** [*philosophizing*] Non óris caúsā módô hominés aequúm
     fuít
383 sibi habére spéculum, ubi ós contémplarént suúm,
384-5 sed quí perspícere póssent córdis cópiám;
386 ubi id ínspexíssent, cógitárent pósteá,
387 vitam út vixíssent ólim in ádulescéntiá.
388 Fuit cónducíbile hoc quídem meá senténtiá.
389 Velut égomet dúdum fíli caúsā coéperám
390 animí med éxcruciáre, quási quid fíliús
391 meus déliquísset méd erga—aút non plúrimá
392 malefácta mea éssent sólidă in ádulescéntiá.
393 Profécto délirámus ínterdúm senés. [*He glances down the
     street to the right.*]
     [*Enter* Apoecides *with the music girl whom they both think is*
     Acropolistis.]
394 Sed méus sodális ít cum praéda Apoecidés.
395 [*He calls out merrily to* Apoecides.]   Veníre sálvum mércatórem
     gaúdeó.
396 Quid fít? **Ap.** Di deaéque te ádiuvánt. **Pe.** Omén placét.
397 **Ap.** Quin ómini ómnes súppetúnt res prósperaé.
398 Sed tu ístanc íntrô iúbe si's ábduci. **Pe.** [*calling toward his
     house*] Heús forás
399 exíte huc áliquis. [*Enter a servant from the house.*]   Dúce
     istam íntrô múlierém.
400 Atque aúdi'n? **Se.** Quíd vis? **Pe.** Cáve sirís cum fíliá
401 mea cópulári hanc néque conspícere. Iám tenés?
402 In aédiculam ístanc seórsum cóncludí voló.
403 Divértunt móres vírginí longe ác lupaé.
404 **Ap.** Docte ét sapiénter dícis. Númquam nímis potést
405 pudicítiam quísquam suaé serváre fíliaé.
406 Edepól ne istam hódie témperí gnató tuó
407 sumus praémercáti. **Pe.** Quíd iam? **Ap.** Quía dixít mihí
408 iam dúdum se álius túum vidísse hîc fíliúm.
409 Hanc édepol rem ápparábat. **Pe.** Pláne hercle hóc quidém
     'st.
410 **Ap.** Ne tú habes sérvum gráphicum et quántivís pretí.
411 Non cáru'st aúro cóntra. Ut ílle fídicinám

412 facéte fécit néscire ésse emptám tibí!
413 Ita rídibúndam atque hílaram huc ádduxít simúl.
414 **Pe.** Mirum hóc quî pótuit fíeri. **Ap.** Té pro fílió
415 factúrum díxit rem ésse dívinám domí,
416 quia Thébis sálvus rédierít. **Pe.** Rectam ínstitít.
417 **Ap.** [*recounting the supposed hoax with relish*] Immo ípsus ílli
    díxit cónductam ésse eám,
418 quae hîc ádministráret ád rem dívinám tibí.
420 Ego íllîc me aútem síc adsímulabám; quasí
421 stolidúm combárdum mé faciébam. **Pe.** Immo íta decét.
422 **Ap.** [*regarding this as a compliment and taking his leave with
    an air of great importance*] Res mágna amíci apúd forum
    ágitur. Eí voló
423 ire ádvocátus. **Pe.** Ât, quaeso, úbi erit ótiúm,
424 revértere ád me extémplo. **Ap.** Cóntinuo hîc eró. [*Exit to
    the right.*]
425 **Pe.** [*alone*] Nihil hómini amíco 'st ópportúno amíciús:
426 sine tuó labóre quód velís actúm 'st tamén.
427 Ego si ádlegássem aliquem hóminem ad hóc negótiúm
428 minús quam hunc dóctum mínusque ad hánc rem cállidúm,
429 os súblitum ésset mi átque me álbis déntibús
430 meus déridéret fíliús meritíssimó.
[*Someone is seen approaching from the right.*]
431 Sed quís illic ést quem huc ádveniéntem cónspicór,
432 suám qui undántem chlámydem quássandó facít?

SCENE 4

Meter: six-foot iambic.

[*Enter the Rhodian soldier, admirer of* ACROPOLISTIS. *Note that
he arrives much sooner than* EPIDICUS *had expected. He is accompanied by a servant and inspects the houses intently as he comes
along.*]
433 **Mi.** [*to his servant*] Cave praéterbítas úllas aédis, quín rogés,
434 senex hîc ubi hábitat Périphanés Platéniús.
435 Incértus, tuúm cave ád me réttulerís pedém.
436 **Pe.** [*addressing the soldier*] Aduléscens, si ístunc hóminem,
    quém tu quaéritás,

437 tibi cómmonstrásso, ecquam ábs te iníbo grátiám?
438 **Mi.** [*assuming his usual haughty manner*] Virtúte bélli armá-
     tus prómerui, út mihí
439 omnís mortális ágere déceat grátiás.
440 **Pe.** [*calling his bluff*] Non répperísti, aduléscens, tránquillúm
     locúm,
441 ubi tuás virtútes éxplicés, ut póstulás.
442 Nam strénuióri déteriór si praédicát
443 suas púgnas, de íllius íllae fíunt sórdidaé.
444 Sed istúm quem quaéris Périphaném Platéniúm,
445 ego súm, si quíd vis. **Mi.** [*realizing that he has met his match,
     and resorting to flattery*] Némpe quem in ádulescéntiá
446 memoránt apud réges ármis, árte duéllicá,
447 divítias mágnas índeptum? **Pe.** [*sarcastically*] Ímmo si aú-
     diás
448 meas púgnas, fúgias mánibus dímissís domúm.
449 **Mi.** [*with frankness*] Pol égo magis únum quaéro, meás cui
     praédicém,
450 quam eúm qui mémoret suás mihi. **Pe.** Híc non ést locús.
451 Proin tu álium quaéras, cuí centónes sárciás.
452 Atque [*aside*] haéc stultítia 'st mé illi vítio vérteré,
453 egomét quod fáctitávi in ádulescéntiá,
454 cum mílitábam. Púgnis mémorandís meís
455 erádicábam hominum aúris, quándo occéperám.
456 **Mi.** [*acknowledging his defeat and coming down to business*]
     Animádverte, út, quod ego ád te vénio, intéllegás:
457 meam amícam audívi te ésse mércatum. **Pe.** [*aside*] Áttataé!
458 Nunc démum scío ego hunc quí sit: quém dudum Épidicús
459 mihi praédicávit mílitem. [*To the soldier*] Áduléscéns, itá 'st,
460 ut dícis: émi. **Mi.** [*meekly*] Vólo te vérbis paúculís,
461 si tíbi moléstum nón est. **Pe.** Nón edepól sció,
462 moléstum nécne sít, nisi dícis quíd velís.
463 **Mi.** Mi illam út tramíttas, árgentum áccipiás. [*He shows
     his wallet.*] Adést.
464 Nam quíd ego apúd te véra párcam próloquí?
465 Ego illám volo hódie fácere líbertám meám,
466 mihi cóncubína quaé sit. **Pe.** Te ábsolvám breví.

467 Argénti quínquagínta mihi ílla emptá 'st minís.

468 Si séxagínta míhi dinúmerantúr minaé,

469 tuas [*with a chuckle*] póssidébit múlier fáxo fériás—

470 atque íta profécto, ut eam éx hoc éxonerés agró.

471 **Mi.** Estne émpta mihi ístis légibús? **Pe.** Habeás licét.

472 Concíliavísti púlchre . . . [*calling into the house*] heus, fóras
      edúcité,

473 quam intróduxístis fídicinam . . . [*resuming his remarks to
      the soldier*] átque etiám fidés,

474 ei quae áccessére, tíbi dono áddam grátiís.

[*Enter the music girl who had just arrived with* APOECIDES, *and
whom* PERIPHANES *thought was* ACROPOLISTIS.]

475 Age, áccipe hánc si's. **Mi.** [*angrily, to* PERIPHANES] Quaé
      te intémperiaé tenént?

476 Quas tú mihi ténebras trúdis?   Quín tu fídicinám

477 intús iubés prodúci? **Pe.** Haec érgo 'st fídiciná.

478 Hîc ália núlla 'st. **Mi.** Nón mihi núgarí potés.

479 Quin tu húc prodúcis fídicinam Ácropolístidém?

480 **Pe.** Haec, ínquam, 'st. **Mi.** Nón haec, ínquam, 'st.   Nón
      novísse mé

481 meam rére amícam pósse? **Pe.** Hanc, ínquam, fíliús

482 meus déperíbat fídicinam. **Mi.** Haéc non ést eá.

483 **Pe.** Quid? Nón est? **Mi.** Nón est. **Pe.** Únde haec ígitur
      géntiúm 'st?

484 Equidem hércle argéntum pro hác dedí. **Mi.** Stulté datúm

485 reór, peccátum lárgitér. **Pe.** Immo haéc eá 'st. [*He begins
      to get flustered.*]

486 Nam sérvum mísi, quí illum séctarí solét—

487 meum gnátum: is ípse hanc déstinávit fídicinám.

488 **Mi.** Em istíc homo te árticulátim cóncīdít, senéx—

489 tuus sérvus. **Pe.** Quíd "concídit"? **Mi.** [*shrugging his
      shoulders*] Síc suspíció 'st.

490 Nam pró fidicína haec cérva súpposítá 'st tibí.

491 Senéx, tibi ós est súblitúm plane ét probé.

492 Ego illám requíram iam, úbiubi 'st. **Pe.** [*sarcastically*] Bél-
      latór, valé. [*Exit the soldier;* PERIPHANES *reflects bitterly
      to himself.*]

493   Euge, eúge, Epídice!   Frúgi 's; púgnastí; homó 's—
494   qui mé munxísti múcidúm, minimí pretí.   [*He turns sud-
        denly to the music girl.*]
495   Mercátus te hódie 'st dé lenóne Apoécidés?
496   **Fi.** [*indignantly*] Fando égo istuc nómen númquam audívi
        ante húnc diém,
497   neque mé quidem émere quísquam ullā pecúniā
498   potuít: plus iám quinquénniúm sum líberá.
499   **Pe.** [*angrily*] Quid tíbi negóti 'st meaé domi ígitur?   **Fi.**
        Aúdiés.
500   Condúcta véni ut fídibus cántarém sení,
501   dum rém divínam fáceret.   **Pe.** Fáteor me ómniúm
502   hominum ésse Athénis Átticís minimí pretí.
503   Sed tú novístin fídicinam Ácropolístidém?
504   **Fi.** Tam fácile quám me.   **Pe.** Ubi hábitat?   **Fi.** Póstquam
        líberá 'st,
505   ubi hábitet dícere ádmodum íncerté sció.
506   **Pe.** Eho, an líbera ílla 'st?   Quís eam líberáverít,
507   volo scíre, sí scis.   **Fi.** Íd quod aúdivi, aúdiés.
508   Stratíppoclem áiunt, Périphanáï fíliúm,
509   abséntem cúravísse ut fíeret líberá.
510   **Pe.** Perii hércle, si ístaec véra súnt, planíssimé.
511   Meum exénterávit Épidicús marsúppiúm.
512   **Fi.** [*losing interest*] Haec síc audívi.   Númquid mé vis céte-
        rúm?
513   **Pe.** [*savagely*] Maló cruciátu ut péreas átque abeás citó.
514   **Fi.** Fidés non réddis?   **Pe.** Néque fidés neque tíbiás.
515   Properá si's fúgere hinc, sí te dí amant.   **Fi.** Ábieró.
516   Flagítio cúm maióre póst reddés tamén.   [*Exit.*]
517   **Pe.** [*in a fury*] Quid núnc?   Qui in tántis pósitus súm sen-
        téntiís,
518   eámne ego sínam impúne?   Immo étiam si álterúm
519   tantúm perdéndum 'st, pérdam pótius quám sinám
520   me impúne irrísum esse, hábitum dépeculátuí.
521   Hei! [*bitterly*]   Síc data ésse vérba praésentí palám!
522   Atque [*chuckling*] mé minóris fácio praé illo, qui ómniúm
523   legum átque iúrum fíctor cónditór cluét.

524 Is étiam sése sápere mémorat: málleúm
525 sapiéntiórem vídi—excússo mánubrió. [*He remains deep in thought.*]

ACT IV

Scene 1

Ll. 526–546 form a *canticum;* ll. 547–569 are in seven-foot trochaics.

[*Enter* Philippa *from the left. She has hastily followed the army from Thebes in the hope of tracing her captured daughter,* Telestis. *Unable to locate her in Athens, she is now—as a last resort—looking up her old lover* Periphanes, *to appeal to him for help.*]

526 **Ph.** Si quid est homini miseriarum, quod miserescat, miser ex animo 'st.
527 Id ego experior, cui multa in unum locum
528 confluunt, quae meum pectus pulsant simul.
529 Multiplex aerumna me exercitam habet.
530 Paupertas, pavor territat mentem animi.
531 Neque ubi meas spes collocem, habeo usquam munitum locum:
532 ita gnata mea hostium 'st potita, neque nunc ubi sit scio.
533 **Pe.** [*mildly curious*] Quis illaec est timido pectore, quae peregre adveniens ipsa se
534 miseratur? **Ph.** [*to herself*] In his dictu'st mihi locis habitare Periphanes.
535 **Pe.** Me nominat haec. Credo ego illi hospitio usus venit.
536 **Ph.** Pervelim mercedem dare, qui monstret eum mi hominem aut ubi habitet.
537 **Pe.** [*staring*] Noscito ego hanc? Nam videor nescio ubi vidisse mihi prius.
538 Estne ea an non ea 'st, quam animus retur meus?
539 **Ph.** [*seeing* Periphanes] Di boni! Visitavi hunc ego umquam antidhac?
540 **Pe.** Certo ea 'st, quam in Epidauro pauperculam memini comprimere . . .
541 **Ph.** Plane hic ille est, qui mihi in Epidauro primus pudicitiam pepulit.
542 **Pe.** . . . quae meo compressu peperit filiam—quam domi nunc habeo.

543   Quid si adeam? **Ph.** Hau scio an congrediar. **Pe.** Si haec
      ea 'st! **Ph.** Si is est homo!
544   **Pe.** Sicut anni multi dubia dant . . . ! **Ph.** Longa dies
      meum incertat animum.
545   **Pe.** Sin ea 'st quam incerte autumo, hanc congrediar astu.
546   **Ph.** Muliebris adhibenda mihi malitia nunc est.
547   **Pe.** Cómpellábo. **Ph.** Orátiónis áciem cóntra cónferám.
548   **Pe.** Sálva sís. **Ph.** Salútem accípio mi ét meís. **Pe.** Quid
      céterúm?
549   **Ph.** Sálvus sís: quod crédidísti réddo. **Pe.** Haud áccusó
      fidém.
550   Nóvin égo te? **Ph.** Si égo te nóvi, ánimum indúcam ut
      nóverís.
551   **Pe.** Úbi te vísitávi? **Ph.** Iníque iniúriú's. **Pe.** Quid iám?
      Ph. Quiá
552   tuaé memóriae intérpretári me aéquum cénses. **Pe.** Cóm-
      modé
553   fábuláta 's. **Ph.** Míra mémoras, Périphane. **Pe.** Ém istuc
      réctiús.
554   Méminístin . . . ? **Ph.** Mémini id quód memini. **Pe.**
      . . . ín Epidaúro. . . . **Ph.** Ah, gúttulā
555   péctus árdens mi ádspersísti. **Pe.** . . . vírginí paupérculaé
556   tuaéque mátri mé leváre paúpertátem? **Ph.** Tún is és,
557   quí per volúptatém tuam ín me aerúmnam obsévistí gra-
      vém?
558   **Pe.** Égo sum. Sálve. **Ph.** Sálva súm, quia te ésse sálvum
      séntió.
559   **Pe.** Cédo manum. **Ph.** Áccipe. Aérumnósam et míseri-
      árum cómpotém
560   múlierém retinés. **Pe.** Quid ést quod vúltus túrbatú'st
      tuús?
561   **Ph.** Fíliám, quam ex té suscépi, . . . **Pe.** Quíd eam? **Ph.**
      . . . edúctam pérdidí. [*She bursts into tears.*]
562   Hóstiúm 'st potíta. **Pe.** Habe ánimum lénem et trán-
      quillúm. Tacé.
563   Dómi meae éccam sálvam et sánam. Nám postquam
      aúdivi ílicó

564 éx meo sérvo, illam ésse cáptam, cóntinuo árgentúm dedí,
565 út emerétur. Ílle eam rem ádeo sóbrie ét frugálitér
566 ádcurávit—útut ad álias rés est ímpense ímprobús.
567 **Ph.** [*greatly excited*] Fác videám, si méa—si sálva míhi sit.
Pe. [*calling into his house*] Ého, istinc, Cánthará!
568 Iúbe Teléstidem húc prodíre fíliam ánte aedís meám,
569 út suam vídeat mátrem. **Ph.** [*drying her tears*] Rémigrat
ánimus núnc demúm mihí.

SCENE 2

Meter: seven-foot trochaic.

[*Enter* ACROPOLISTIS *from* PERIPHANES' *house.*]

570 **Ac.** Quíd est, páter, quod me éxcivísti ante aédis? **Pe.**
Út matrém tuám
571 vídeas, ádeas, ádveniénti dés salútem atque ósculúm.
572 **Ac.** [*puzzled*] Quám meam mátrem? **Pe.** [*pointing to* PHIL-
IPPA, *whose gaping astonishment he misinterprets*] Quae
éxanimáta exséquitur ádspectúm tuúm.
573 **Ph.** Quís istaec ést, quam tu ósculúm mihi férre iubés?
Pe. Tua fíliá.
574 **Ph.** Haécine? **Pe.** Haéc. **Ph.** Egone ósculum huíc dem?
Pe. Cúr non, quae éx te náta sít?
575 **Ph.** Tú, homo, insánis. **Pe.** Égone? **Ph.** Tú ne. **Pe.**
Cúr? **Ph.** Quia ego ístanc quaé siét
576 néque sció neque nóvi, néque ego hanc óculis vídi ante
húnc diém.
577-8 **Pe.** Scío quid érres: quía vestítum atque órnatum haéc
habet mútatúm.
579 **Ph.** [*haughtily*] Quía leónis áliter cátuli lónge olént, alitér
sués.
580 Né ego mé nego nósse hanc quaé sit. **Pe.** [*exploding*] Pró
deum átque hominúm fidém!
581 Quód ego lénocínium fácio, quí habeam álienás domí,
582 átque argéntum egúrgitém domo prórsus? Quíd tu [*turning
angrily to* ACROPOLISTIS], quaé patrém
583 tuúm vocás me atque ósculáris—quíd stas stúpida? Quíd
tacés?

584 **Ac.** [*brazenly*] Quíd loquár vis? **Pe.** Haéc negát se túam
esse mátrem. **Ac.** Né fuát,

585 sí non vúlt. Equidem, hác invíta, tamén ero mátris fíliá.

586 Nón med ístanc cógere aéquum 'st méam esse mátrem, sí
nevólt.

587 **Pe.** Cúr me igitúr patrém vocábas? **Ac.** Túa istaec cúlpa
'st, nón meá.

588 Nón patrem égo te nóminem, ubí tu tuám me appélles
fíliám?

589 Hánc quoque étiam, sí me appéllet fíliám, matrém vocém.

590 Négat haec fíliám me súam esse. Nón ergo haéc matér
meá 'st.

591 Póstremo [*growing angrier*] haéc mea cúlpa nón est: quaé
didicí, dixi ómniá.

592 Épidicús mihi fúit magíster. **Pe.** Périi. Plaústrum pér-
culít.

593 **Ac.** Númquid ego íbi, patér, peccávi? **Pe.** Si hércle te
úmquam audíveró

594 mé patrém vocáre, vítam túam ego intérimam. **Ac.** [*coolly*]
Nón vocó.

595 Úbi volés pater ésse, ibi ésto: ubi nóles, né fuerís patér.

596 **Ph.** [*to* PERIPHANES] Quíd? Siób eam rem hánc emísti,
quía tuám gnatám ratú's,

597 quíbus de sígnis ágnoscébas? **Pe.** Núllis. **Ph.** Quáre
fíliam

598 crédidísti nóstram? **Pe.** Sérvus Épidicús dixít mihí.

599 **Ph.** Quíd si sérvo alitér visum ésset, nón poterás nosse,
óbsecró?

600 **Pe.** Quíd ego?—quí illam ut prímum vídi, númquam vídi
pósteá.

601 **Ph.** [*weeping*] Périi mísera! **Pe.** Né fle, múlier. Íntrô abi.
Hábe animúm bonúm.

602 Égo illam réperiam. **Ph.** [*sobbing*] Hínc Athénis cívis eam
émit Atticús.

603 Ádulescéntem equidém dicébant émisse. **Pe.** Ínveniám.
Tacé.

604 Ábi modô ínțrô atque hánc adsérva Círcam, Sólis fíliám.

605 Égo relíctis rébus Épidicum óperam quaérendó dabó.

606 Si ínvenio, éxitiábilem ego flli fáciam hunc út fiát diém.
[PHILIPPA *leads* ACROPOLISTIS *into the house. Exit* PERI-
PHANES *to the right.*]

ACT V

SCENE 1

Meter: seven-foot trochaic.

[*Enter* STRATIPPOCLES *from the house; he is impatiently awaiting
the arrival of* TELESTIS *and the money lender.*]

607 **St.** Mále morígerus míhi 'st danísta, quód a me argéntum
nón petít,

608 néque illam addúcit quae éx praeda émpta 'st. [*Enter*
EPIDICUS *hurriedly from the right, having dodged* PERI-
PHANES.] Séd eccum incédit Épidicús.

609 Quíd illuc ést, quod flli cáperat fróns sevéritúdiné?

610 **Ep.** [*mumbling to himself*] Si úndecím deos praéter sése sécum
addúcat Iúppitér,

611 íta non ómnes éx cruciátu póterunt éximere Épidicúm.

612 Périphanem émere lóra vídi. Ibi áderat únâ Apoécidés.

613 Núnc hominés me quaéritáre crédo. Sénserúnt, sciúnt,

614 síbi data ésse vérba. **St.** [*debonairly, to* EPIDICUS] Quíd
agis, méa commóditas? **Ep.** Quód misér.

615 **St.** Quíd est tibí? **Ep.** Quin tú mi adórnas ád fugám viáti-
cúm,

616 príusquam péreo. Nám per úrbem dúo deflóccatí senés

617 quaéritánt me. In mánibus géstant cópulás secúm simúl.

618 **St.** Hábe bonum ánimum. **Ep.** [*ironically*] Quídni ego, cuí
libértas ín mundó sitá 'st.

619 **St.** Égo te sérvabo. **Ep.** [*laughing sarcastically*] Édepol me
flli mélius, sí nanctí fuánt! [*He looks down the street.*]

620 Séd quis haec ést muliércula et flle grávastéllus quí venít?
[*Enter the money lender and friends, escorting* TELESTIS.]

621 **St.** [*excitedly*] Híc est danísta; haec flla 'st aútem, quám
ego emi éx praeda. **Ep.** Haéciné 'st?

622 **St.** [*proudly*] Haéc est. [*They draw near.*] Éstne ita, út
tibi díxi (adspécta et cóntempla, Épidicé)—

623 úsque ab únguiculo ád capíllum súmmum 'st féstivíssimá?
624 Éstne consímilis, quási cum sígnum píctum púlchre ad-
     spéxerís?
625 **Ep.** Éx tuis vérbis meúm futúrum córium púlchrum praédi-
     cás,
626 quém Apella átque Zeúxis duó pigméntis píngent úlmeís.
627 **St.** [*irritably, to the money lender*] Di ímmortáles! Sícine
     iússi ad me íres?   Pédibus plúmbeís
628 quí perhibétur, príus venísset, quám tu advénistí mihí.
629 **Da.** [*gruffly*] Haéc edepól remoráta méd est. **St.** [*with a
     languishing glance at* Telestis] Sí quidem ístius grátiā
630 íd remorátu's, quód ista vóluit, nímium advénistí citó.
631 **Da.** Age, age, absólve me átque argéntum númera né comi-
     tés morér.
632 **St.** Pérnumerátum 'st. **Da.** [*handing* Stratippocles *an
     empty wallet*] Téne crumínam; huc índe. **St.** Sápientér
     venís.
633 Ópperíre, dum éffero ád te argéntum? **Da.** Máturá. **St.**
     Domí 'st. [*He goes in.*]
634 **Ep.** [*regarding* Telestis *with increasing interest*] Sáti'n ego
     óculis útilitátem obtíneo síncere án parúm?
635 Vídeon égo Teléstidém te, Périphanäï fíliám,
636 é Philíppa mátre nátam Thébis, Épidaurí satám?
637 **Te.** Quís tu homó 's, qui meúm paréntum nómen mémoras
     ét meúm?
638 **Ep.** Nón me nóvistí? **Te.** [*shaking her head*] Quod quídem
     nunc véniat ín mentém mihí.
639 **Ep.** Nón meminísti me aúream ád te adférre nátalí dié
640 lúnulam átque anéllum auréolum in dígitulúm? **Te.** Me-
     miní, mi homó.
641 Tún is és? **Ep.** Ego sum. Ét istic fráter, quí te mér-
     catú'st, tuú'st.
642 **Te.** Hém! Meus fráter ílle ut fíat? **Ep.** Ália mátre, unó
     patré.
643 **Te.** Quíd patér meus? Vívu'st? **Ep.** [*seeing the possibili-
     ties of a rich reward, but careful not to give away his hand
     too soon*] Ánimo líquido et tránquilló 's. Tacé.

644 **Te.** Dí me ex pérditá servátam cúpiunt, sí vera aútumás.

645 **Ep.** Nón habeo úllam occásiónem, ut ápud te fálsa fábulér.

646 **St.** [*returning from within*] Áccipe árgentum hóc, danísta.
Híc súnt quadrágintá minaé.

647 Síquid erít dubium, ímmutábo. **Da.** Béne fecísti. Béne
valé. [*Exeunt money lender and friends.*]

648 **St.** [*embracing* Telestis] Núnc ením tu meá 's. . . . **Te.**
[*holding him off*] . . . sorór quidem édepol—út tu aequé
sciás.

649 Sálve, fráter. **St.** [*to* Epidicus] Sánan haéc est? **Ep.** Sána,
si áppellát suúm.

650 **St.** Quíd? Ego quómodo huíc sum fráter fáctus, dum in-
tróeo atque éxeó?

651 **Ep.** [*mysteriously*] Quód boní 'st, id tácitus táceas túte técum—et gaúdeás.

652 **St.** [*gloomily*] Pérdidísti et répperísti mé, sorór. **Ep.** Stul-
tú's. Tacé.

653 Tíbi quidém, quod amés, domi praésto 'st—fídiciná—operā̃
meā̃.

654 Ét sorórem in líbertátem idem óperā cóncilió meā̃.

655 **St.** [*apologetically*] Épidicé, fateór. . . . **Ep.** [*interrupting
him*] Abi íntrô ac iúbe huic aquám calefíerí.

656 Cétera haéc postérius fáxo scíbis, úbi erit ótiúm.

657 **St.** Séquere mé, soror, hā́c. **Ep.** [*excusing himself from at-
tending them further*] Ego ád vos Théspriónem iússeró

658 húc transíre. Séd [*rapidly formulating plans for dealing with*
Periphanes *and* Apoecides] meménto, sí quid saévibúnt
senés,

659 súppetiás mihi cúm soróre férre. **St.** Fácile istúc erít.
[*Exeunt* Stratippocles *and* Telestis *into the house.*]

660 **Ep.** [*calling in at the door of* Chaeribulus' *house*] Thésprio,
éxi istā́c per hórtum. Abí domum aúxilió mihí.

661 [*He folds his arms with satisfaction.*] Mágna 'st rés. Minóris múlto fácio quám dudúm senés.

662 Rémeabo íntrô ut ádcuréntur ádveniéntes hóspités.

663 Éâdem haec íntus édocébo, quae égo sció, Stratíppoclém.

664 Nón fugió. Domi adésse cértum 'st, néque ille haud óbiciét mihí

665 pédibus sése próvocátum. Abeo íntrô. Nímis longúm loquór. [*Exit into house.*]

SCENE 2

Meter: seven-foot trochaic.

[*Enter* PERIPHANES *and* APOECIDES *from the right, cross and tired. They have searched in vain for* EPIDICUS *and for news of* TELESTIS' *whereabouts.*]

666 **Pe.** [*to* APOECIDES] Sátine illíc homo lúdibrió nos vétulos décrepitós duós

667 hábet? **Ap.** Immo édepol tú quidem míserum méd habés miserís modís.

668 **Pe.** Táce. Siné modô me hóminem apísci. **Ap.** Díco ego tíbi nunc, út sciás:

669 álium té tibi cómitem méliu'st quaérere. Itá, dum té sequór,

670 lássitúdine ínvasérunt mísero in génua fléminá.

671 **Pe.** [*paying no attention to his complaints*] Quót illic hómo hodié me exémplis lúdificátu'st—átque té!

672 Út illic aútem exénterávit míhi opes árgentáriás!

673 **Ap.** Ápage illum á me! Nam ílle quidém Volcáni iráti 'st fíliús:

674 quáquâ tángit, ómne ambúrit; si ástes, aéstu cálefacít.

[*Enter* EPIDICUS *from* PERIPHANES' *house, unobserved.*]

675 **Ep.** [*aside*] Dúodecím dis plús quam in caélo deórum 'st ímmortáliúm

676 míhi nunc aúxilio ádiutóres súnt et mécum mílitánt.

677 Quícquid egó maleféci, auxília mi ét suppétiae súnt domí.

678 Ápolactízo inimícos ómnis. **Pe.** [*to* APOECIDES] Úbi illum quaéram géntiúm?

679 **Ap.** Dúm sine mé quaerás, quaerás meā caúsā vél medio ín marí.

680 **Ep.** [*stepping forward boldly*] Quíd me quaéris? Quíd labóras? Quíd hunc [*pointing to* APOECIDES] sollícitas? Écce mé!

681 Núm te fúgi? Num áb domo ábsum? Num óculis cón-
cessi á tuís?

683[1] Néc tibi súpplicó. Vincíre vís? Em, óstendó manús.

684 Tú habes lóra: ego te émere vídi. Quíd nunc céssas? Cónligá.

685 **Pe.** [*aside, dumbfounded*] Ílicét. Vadimónium últro mi híc
facít. **Ep.** Quin cónligás?

686 **Ap.** Édepol máncipiúm sceléstum! **Ep.** [*sarcastically*] Té
profécto, Apoécidés,

687 níl morór mihi déprecári. **Ap.** Fácile exóras, Épidicé.

688 **Ep.** [*to* PERIPHANES] Écquid agís? **Pe.** Tuon árbitrátu?
Ep. Meo hércle véro atque haú tuó

689 cónligándae haec súnt tibi hódie. **Pe.** At nón libét. Non
cónligó.

690 **Ap.** [*to* PERIPHANES] Trágulam ín te inícere adórnat. Né-
scioquám fabricám facít.

691 **Ep.** [*to* PERIPHANES] Tíbi morám facis, cum égo solútus ásto.
Age, ínquam, cónligá.

692 **Pe.** Át mihi mágis libét solútum té rogitáre. **Ep.** At níl
sciés.

693 **Pe.** [*to* APOECIDES] Quíd ago? **Ap.** Quíd agas? Mós gerá-
tur. **Ep.** [*sarcastically*] Frúgi 's tú homo, Apoécidés.

694 **Pe.** Cédo manús igitúr. [*He ties* EPIDICUS' *hands.*] **Ep.**
Morántur níl—atque árte cónligá.

695 **Pe.** Níhil morór. **Ep.** Obnóxióse! **Pe.** [*tightening the knot*]
Fácto opere, árbitráminó.

696 **Ep.** Béne hoc habét. Age, núnciam éx me exquíre, rógita
quódlibét.

697 **Pe.** Quā fidúciā aúsu's prímum, quae émpta 'st núdiustértiús,

698 fíliám meam dícere ésse? **Ep.** [*defiantly*] Líbuit: éā fidúciā.

699 **Pe.** Ái'n tu? Líbuit? **Ep.** Áio—[*taunting him*] vél da pígnus, ni éa sit fíliá.

700 **Pe.** Quám negát novísse "máter"? **Ep.** [*making fun of him*]
Ni érgo mátris fíliá 'st,

701 ín meum númmum, in tuúm taléntum pígnus da. **Pe.**
[*catching on*] Em ístaec cáptió 'st.

[1] For the omission of l. 682, see Notes (p. 276).

702   Séd quis eá 'st muliér?   **Ep.** [*calmly*] Tui gnáti amíca—ut
ómnem rém sciás.

703   **Pe.** Dédin tibí minás trigínta ob fíliám?   **Ep.** [*coolly*] Fateór
datás—

704   ét eo argénto illám me emísse amícam fíli fídicinám

705   pró tua fília.   Ís te eam ób rem tétigi trígintá minís.

706   **Pe.** Quómodo mé ludós fecísti dé illa cónductíciá

707   fídiciná!   **Ep.** Factum hércle véro et récte fáctum iúdicó.

708   **Pe.** Quíd postrémo argénto fáctum 'st, quód dedí?   **Ep.**
Dicám tibí.

709   Néque malo hómini néque malígno—[*pausing for effect*] tuó
dedí Stratíppoclí.

710   **Pe.** Cúr dare aúsu's?   **Ep.** Quía mi líbitum 'st.   **Pe.** Quae
haéc, malum, ímpudéntiá 'st?

711   **Ep.** [*with sublime effrontery*] Étiam inclámitór quasi sérvus?
Pe. [*ironically*] Cúm tu 's líber gaúdeó.

712   **Ep.** Mérui ut fíerem.   **Pe.** Tú meruísti?   **Ep.** Víse intrô.
Égo faxó sciés

713   hóc ita ésse.   **Pe.** [*puzzled*] Quíd est negóti?   **Ep.** Iam ípsa
rés dicét tibí.

714   Ábi modô íntrô.   **Ap.** [*to* PERIPHANES] I, ílluc non témere
'st.   **Pe.** Adserva ístum, Apoécidés.   [*Exit hurriedly into
the house.*]

715   **Ap.** Quíd illuc, Épidice, ést negóti?   **Ep.** Máximā hércle
iniúriā

716   vínctus ásto, cúius haéc hodie óperā invénta 'st fíliá.

717   **Ap.** Ái'n tu te íllius ínvenísse fíliam?   **Ep.** Ínveni ét domí
'st.

718   Séd ut acérbum 'st, pró benefáctis cúm malí messím metás!

719   **Ap.** Quámne hodié per úrbem utérque súmus deféssi quaé-
reré?

720   **Ep.** Égo sum défessús reperíre, vós deféssi quaéreré.

[*Enter* PERIPHANES *from the house.*]

721   **Pe.** [*speaking to his son and daughter within*] Quíd istî orátis
ópere tánto?   Mé meruísse intéllegó,

722   út liceát merito húius fácere.   [*To* EPIDICUS] Cédo tu, ut
éxsolvám, manús.

723 **Ep.** Ne áttigás. **Pe.** Osténde véro. **Ep.** Nólo. **Pe.** Nón
aequúm facís.

724 **Ep.** Númquam hercle hódie, nísi supplícium míhi das, mé
solví sinám.

725 **Pe.** Óptimum átque aequíssimum óras: sóccos, túnicam,
pálliúm

726 tíbi dabó. **Ep.** Quid deínde pórro? **Pe.** Líbertátem. **Ep.**
At pósteá?

727 Nóvo libérto opus ést, quod páppet. **Pe.** Dábitur: praé-
bebó cibúm.

728 **Ep.** Númquam hercle hódie, nísi me orássis, sólves. **Pe.**
Óro te, Épidicé,

729 míhi ut ignóscas, sí quid imprúdens cúlpā péccaví meā.

730 Át ob eám rem líber ésto. **Ep.** Invítus do hánc veniám
tibí,

731 nísi necéssitáte cógor. Sólve sáne, sí libét.

Grex

732 Híc is homó 'st, qui líbertátem málitiā invenít suā.

733 Plaúdite ét valéte. Lúmbos pórgite átque exsúrgité.

Q. ENNIUS

(Born in 239; active from 204–169 B.C.)

Q. Ennius, the fourth author of this period, was a universal
man-of-letters and a pioneer in several fields. Born in a Greek,
or semi-Greek, town in Calabria, he was probably an Oscan,
and was therefore thoroughly Hellenized before Cato brought him
to Rome, in 204 B.C. Ennius himself said that he had three
minds—Greek, Oscan, and Latin—for he was master of all three
languages; nevertheless, compared with the Greeks, he was dis-
tinctly a "barbarian" and somewhat of a pedant (as the newly-
cultured are inclined to be)—he imbibed more of the learning of
contemporary Greece than he could digest. His works are lost,
save for fragments. Many of these we owe to Cicero, who made
artistic use of quotations from the archaic and rugged verses of
Ennius in his polished prose essays.

Ennius seems to have carried on the established traditions in tragedy and comedy, and very little is known about his miscellanies or "satires" (not satires in the classic sense).   However, the great achievement that earned for Ennius the title "father of Latin literature" was his introduction into Latin of the quantitative hexameter in place of the old Saturnian.   His most important work was an epic in this new meter, the *Annales*, which —like the *Bellum Punicum* of Naevius—treated Roman legend and history.

A survey of the existing fragments of the *Annales* suggests, first of all, the primitive crudeness of Ennius' hexameters.   Occasionally their barbarism is quite "medieval."

[1]

For example, taking too literally the principle of Homeric *tmesis* (i.e., the apparent cutting in two of a word—in reality, only the use of verbs with separable prefixes)—Ennius committed the monstrosity of chopping the noun *cerebrum* in two:

> . . . saxó cere- cómminuít -brum.

[2]

Following a supposed Greek analogy, Ennius took naïve liberties with the principle of *apocope*, or abbreviation, and reduced *domus* to *do:*

> . . . éndo suám do.

[3]

A childish indulgence in alliteration is illustrated by the two following examples:

> Ó Tite túte Tatí tibi tánta tyránne tulísti.
> Máchina múlta mináx minitátur máxima múris.

[4]

Another example of infelicity is the following line, in which there is no overlapping of words and feet—hence the weak rhythmical pattern:

> Spársis hástis lóngis cámpus spléndet et hórret.

[5]

In the following passage the rhythm of the first four lines, reminiscent of the Saturnian, is too monotonous (the poet is describing the chopping of wood for funeral pyres):

Íncedúnt arbústa per álta;   secúribus caédunt;
pércellúnt magnás quercús;   excíditur ílex;
fráxinus frángitur, átque abiés   constérnitur álta;
pínus prócerás pervértunt;   ómne sonábat
árbustúm fremitú silváï fróndosáï.

[6]

Another well-known passage, consisting of two fragments quoted by Cicero (*Brutus* XV, 58), illustrates Ennius' quaint style—a style that charms the sophisticated reader in spite of its shortcomings:

[a] The first fragment conveys with astounding contortions the prosaic information that the golden-tongued orator (*orator suaviloquenti ore*) Marcus Cornelius Marci filius Cethegus (note the pomposity of the full legal name) held the consulship with Tuditanus as his colleague:

Ádditur óratór Cornélius suáviloquénti
óre Cethégus Márcus cónlegaé Tuditáno
Márci fílius. . . .

[b] The second fragment, with its wholly redundant second line, quaintly attests the fame of Cethegus as a speaker:

. . . ís dictú 'st ollís populáribus ólim,
quí tum vívebánt hominés atque aévum agitábant,
flós delíbatús populí suadaéque medúlla.

[7]

Nevertheless, Ennius could and did rise to greater heights. Occasionally he produced rugged and forceful lines, which have the flavor of Elizabethan English:

[a] From the famous eulogy of the Roman Commonwealth:

Móribus ántiquís stat rés Romána virísque.

[b] A tribute to humble worth:

Ílle vir haúd magná cum ré sed plénus fidéï.

[c] From the eulogy of Fabius Maximus, renowned in the Second Punic War for his "Fabian" tactics:

> Únus homó nobís cunctándo réstituít rem;
> noénum rúmorés ponébat ánte salútem;
> érgo póstque magísque virí nunc glória cláret.

[8]

There are also longer passages, which happily contain only the best qualities of Ennius' verse. Such is the stirring reply of Pyrrhus to the Roman envoys, in which he refuses to accept a ransom for his Roman prisoners of war and surrenders them gratis instead:

> Néc mi aurúm poscó, nec mí pretiúm dederítis;
> nón caupónantés bellúm sed bélligerántes,
> férro, nón auró, vitám cernámus utríque.
> Vósne velít an mé regnáre, era quídve ferát Fors,
> 5 vírtute éxperiámur. Et hóc simul áccipe díctum:
> quórum vírtutí bellí Fortúna pepércit,
> eórundém libértatí me párcere cértum 'st.
> Dóno (dúcite!) dóque voléntibus cúm magnís dis.

[9]

Ennius composed the following couplet in the elegiac meter (hexameter plus pentameter) for his own epitaph:

> Némo mé lacrimís decorét nec fúnera flétu
> fáxit. Cúr? Volitó vívus per óra virúm.

* * *

All these contrasting examples display Ennius' imperfect command over a new and extremely difficult medium—difficult particularly in its adaptation to the Latin tongue. Mastery of the Latin hexameter was to require another hundred and fifty years of effort.

M. PORCIUS CATO
(BORN IN 234; ACTIVE FROM 200–149 B.C.)

Cato the Censor, whom tradition has pictured as the bitter opponent of Greek influence in Roman life, was a conservative.

He is regarded as the founder of Roman prose literature, and his greatest work is the history of Rome, the *Origines*.

Whatever may have been the character of his other works, however, his *de Agri Cultura* (the only one of his compositions preserved in full) is so old-fashioned that, although it was published toward the end of the first period of national Roman literature, one might almost take it to be representative of native Latin literature before the period of Greek influence. The style is abrupt, unadorned, monotonous, laconic, and at times condensed to the point of obscurity. The contents vividly portray the hard, shrewd, puritanical Roman landowner; but in comparison with later and far more extensive treatises on the science of agriculture, Cato's pithy compendium might be entitled simply *Advice to the Husbandman*.

The first chapter gives an idea of the work. Its short, matter-of-fact sentences present no difficulty for translation, save where excessive brevity hampers the logic (as in the old Roman laws, see pp. 8–10). While containing much that is *terra incognita* to a beginner, the vocabulary is composed of homely, everyday Latin words.

De Agri Cultura

CHAPTER I: ON BUYING A FARM

1 Praedium cum parare cogitabis, sic in animo habeto: uti
2 ne cupide emas, neve opera tua parcas visere, et ne satis
3 habeas semel circumire. Quotiens ibis, totiens magis place-
4 bit quod bonum erit. Vicini quo pacto niteant, id animad-
5 vertito: in bona regione bene nitere oportebit. Et uti eo
6 introeas et circumspicias, uti inde exire possis.

7 Uti bonum caelum habeat; ne calamitosum siet; solo bono
8 sua virtute valeat. Si poteris, sub radice montis siet; in
9 meridiem spectet, loco salubri; operariorum copia siet bo-
10 numque aquarium; oppidum validum prope siet aut mare
11 aut amnis quâ naves ambulant aut via bona celebrisque.
12 Siet in his agris qui non saepe dominos mutant. Qui in his

13 praedia vendiderint, eos pigeat vendidisse.
14   Uti bene aedificatum siet.   Caveto alienam disciplinam
15 temere contemnas.   De domino, bono colono bonoque aedi-
16 ficatore, melius emetur.
17   Ad villam cum venies, videto vasa torcula et dolia mul-
18 tane sient: ubi non erunt, scito pro ratione fructum esse.
19 Instrumenti ne magni siet, loco bono siet.   Videto, quam
20 minimi instrumenti sumptuosusque ager ne siet.   Scito
21 idem agrum quod hominem: quamvis quaestuosus siet, si
22 sumptuosus erit, relinqui non multum.
23   Praedium quod primum siet, si me rogabis, sic dicam: de
24 omnibus agris optimoque loco iugera agri centum.   Vinea
25 est prima si vino bono vel si vino multo est, secundo loco
26 hortus inriguus, tertio salictum, quarto oletum, quinto pra-
27 tum, sexto campus frumentarius, septimo silva caedua,
28 octavo arbustum, nono glandaria silva.

SECOND PERIOD

(*175–85* B.C.)

THE PERIOD OF APPRENTICESHIP TO CLASSICAL GREEK MODELS OF STYLE

The Second Period

After the popular success of the writers of comedy and the scholarly work of Ennius, the Romans entered upon a new phase of literary production with a dawning appreciation of distinctions of style and the superiority of earlier, or classical, Greek models. Roman literary groups—notably the "Scipionic Circle" [1]—became consciously aloof from the unlettered crowd, and the cleavage between literary and popular, or vulgar, Latin became manifest. Through the careful study of Greek originals, verging often on slavish imitation, devotees of culture began to imbue the literary language with some degree of flexibility and grace—first in verse, and then in prose.

This era of apprenticeship to the Greek masters has suffered more than any other from the ravages of time, for only two of its many authors survive in readable form: Terence, whose comedies belong to the earlier part; and the unknown author of the *Rhetorica ad Herennium,* who may be regarded as the last of that period. It would be difficult to trace the various lines of literary development during this epoch (in so far as they may be deduced from the scanty evidence) and quite beyond the limits of our present survey of extant Roman literature. Eclipsed by the literary giants of the Ciceronian and Augustan eras, most authors of this period passed into an early oblivion, and did not form part of that heritage of classical Roman literature which so deeply influenced the medieval and modern worlds.

P. TERENTIUS AFER

(Born in *185* B.C.; active from *165–159* B.C.)

His Life and Works

Terence, protégé and intimate friend of the cultured nobles of the Scipionic Circle, was a brilliant youthful prodigy, who died

[1] This was a literary coterie that gathered about the patron Scipio Africanus the Younger. It included in its membership the playwright Terence and the satirist Lucilius.

at the age of twenty-six. Despite his extreme youth and the fact that Latin was not his mother tongue, he composed six plays that have always been regarded as models of classic style. According to Suetonius (who wrote in the second century A.D.), Terence was born at Carthage and brought as a child to Rome, where he became a slave of the senator Terentius Lucanus, who soon manumitted him and gave him a liberal education. But these statements of Suetonius only whet our curiosity. Neither the birthplace nor "Roman" name of Terence indicate his nationality. Though born at Carthage, he was not a Phoenician, for he would then have been called P. Terentius *Poenus*—the general term *Afer* (which Terence took as his cognomen) denotes Numidian, Gaetulian, or some other North-African race. Furthermore we do not know his original name, for he did not incorporate it in his adopted Roman name, as did L. Livius *Andronicus* —perhaps it was too outlandish to be Romanized! So the mystery remains. The only other clue is Suetonius' remark that Terence's complexion was swarthy.

The plays of Terence are more polished, academically more "correct"—in short, more bookish—than those of Plautus. They reproduce with greater fidelity the excellence of their Greek originals in plot and characterization; and carry over into the Latin those profound comments on life, that sententious philosophy, which Plautus generally omits from his rollicking farces. The Latin style of Terence is remarkably pure and smooth; and because of his youth and foreign birth he was suspected, even in his own lifetime, of being the mere mouthpiece of some noble Roman playwright who preferred to remain anonymous—a curious anticipation of the Bacon-Shakespeare controversy. There are, however, no real grounds for this gossip concerning Terence. His achievement was remarkable enough, but not superhuman— for it must be remembered that he merely paraphrased from the Greek. Moreover his productions, although polished, lack the native tang and virile genius of Plautus' rough-and-ready adaptations. Caesar was right when he called Terence a "half-Menander," possessing the technical skill, but lacking the originality and insight of his great Greek exemplar.

The Meters of Terence's Plays

Terence is far more subdued, far less exuberant and extravagant than Plautus, in his metrical effects. Dance scenes (*cantica*) are fewer and shorter in his plays than in those of his predecessor. For dialogue he uses the traditional iambic measures (six-, seven-, and eight-foot) and trochaic (seven- and eight-foot). Occasional four-foot iambics or trochaics are of course merely half lines.

Terence differs from Plautus, however, in his indiscriminate use of these dialogue meters; any possible differentiation that may have existed between them in the time of Plautus seems now to have disappeared and been forgotten. In fact—except for the prologue and the exposition, which are always composed entirely in six-foot iambics—Terence purposely mingles all these meters in each and every sense, passing freely from one to another with no appreciable change of effect.

I

Adelphoe (i.e., The Brothers), or The Puritan's Conversion

(ABRIDGED FOR RAPID READING.)

DRAMATIS PERSONAE

(1) Mício \
(2) Démea / : brothers: MICIO, a wealthy bachelor, extravagant, easygoing, genial, and worldly; DEMEA, a closefisted, hard-working farmer, and a strict Puritan and martinet.

(3) Aéschinus \
(4) Ctésipho / : brothers; sons of Demea: AESCHINUS, adopted by Micio and brought up indulgently in the ways of the town; CTESIPHO, kept at home by Demea and reared with old-fashioned severity.

(5) Pármeno \
(6) Syrus / : servants of Aeschinus.

(7) Sánnio: a slave dealer.

(8) Bacchis: a slave girl of the demimonde.

(9) Sóstrata: a poor widow.

(10) Cánthara (or *Wine-Jug*): her old family nurse.

(11) GETA: her faithful manservant.
(12) PÁMPHILA (lit., *beloved of all*): her daughter; secretly betrothed to Aeschinus.
(13) HÉGIO: a highly respected citizen and old family friend of Sostrata.

SCENE

The scene is laid in a street in Athens, on which stand the houses of MICIO and SOSTRATA, facing the audience.

PROLOGUE

1   Postquám poéta sénsit scrípturám suám
2   ab iníquis óbservári et ádversáriós
3   rapere ín peiórem pártem quam ácturí sumús

    .   .   .   .

4   indício dé se ipse érit, vos éritis iúdicés,
5   laudín an vítio dúci id fáctum opórteát.
6   Synápothnescóntes Díphilí comoédiá 'st:
7   eam Cómmoriéntis Plaútus fécit fábulám.
8   In Graéca aduléscens ést, qui lénoni éripít
9   meretrícem in príma fábula: eúm Plautús locúm
10 relíquit íntegrum.   Eum híc locúm sumpsít sibí
11 in Adélphos; vérbum dé verbo éxpressum éxtulít.
12 Eam nós actúri súmus novám: pernóscité
13 furtúmne fáctum exístumétis án locúm
14 reprénsum, quí praetéritus néglegéntiá 'st.
15 Nam quód isti dícunt málivoli, hómines nóbilís
16 hunc ádiutáre adsídueque úná scríberé:
17 quod illí maledíctum véhemens ésse exístimánt,
18 eam laúdem hic dúcit máximám, cum illís placét,
19 qui vóbis únivérsis ét populó placént,
20 quorum ópera in béllo, in ótio, ín negótió
21 suo quísque témpore úsu'st síne supérbiá.
22 Dehinc ne éxpectétis árguméntum fábulaé:
23 senés qui prími vénient, eí partem áperiént,
24 in agéndo pártem osténdent.   Fácite aequánimitás

    .   .   .   .

25 poétae ad scríbendum aúgeát indústriám.

[*Dawn.* *Enter* Micio *from his house.* *He looks apprehensively up and down the street for his adopted son,* Aeschinus— *the apple of his eye—who has failed to return from a dinner party which he attended the night before.*]

1   **Mi.** [*calling loudly and then listening for a reply*] Storáx!
    [*As no one answers, he muses sadly.*]   Non rédiit hác nocte
    á cena Aéschinús.

2   Quibus núnc sollícitor rébus, ne aút ille álserít

[3] aut úspiám cecíderit ósque frégerít!

4   Atque éx me hic nátus nón est, sed éx fratré 'st meó.

5   Dissímili is stúdio 'st iam índe ab ádulescéntiá:

6   ego hánc cleméntem vítam urbánam atque ótiúm

7   secútus sum ét (quod fórtunátum istí putánt)

8   uxórem númquam habui.   Ílle cóntra haec ómniá:

9   ruri ágere vítam; sémper párce ac dúritér

10 se habére; uxórem dúxit; náti fílií

11 duo; índe ego húnc maiórem adóptaví mihí;

12 edúxi a párvulo; hábui, amávi pró meó.

13 Ille út item cóntra me hábeat, fácio séduló:

14 do, praétermítto, nón necésse habeo ómniá

15 pro meó iure ágere; póstremo, álii clánculúm

16 patrés quae fáciunt (quaé fert ádulescéntiá),

17 ea né me célet cónsueféci fíliúm.

18 Pudóre et líberálitáte líberós

19 retinére sátius ésse crédo quám metú.

20 Haec frátri mécum nón convéniunt néque placént.

21 Venit ád me saépe clámans, "Quíd agis, Míció?

22 Cur pérdis ádulescéntem nóbis? Cúr amát?

23 Cur pótat? Cúr tu his rébus súmptum súggerís?

24 Vestítu nímio indúlges. Nímium inéptus és."

25 Nimium ípse 'st dúrus praéter aéquumque ét bonúm;

26 et érrat lónge—meá quidém senténtiá—

27 qui impérium crédat grávius ésse aut stábiliús,

28 vi quód fit, quam íllud quód amicítiā adiúngitúr.

29 Hoc pátrium 'st: pótius cónsuefácere fíliúm

30 sua spónte récte fácere quam álienó metú:

31 hoc páter ac dóminus ínterést.   Hoc quí nequít,
32 fateátur néscire ímperáre líberís.
33 Sed éstne hic ípsus, dé quo agébam?   Et cérte is ést.
[*Enter* DEMEA *from the country.*]
34 Nescióquid trístem vídeo: crédo iam, út solét,
35 iurgábit.   Sálvum te ádveníre, Démeá,
36 gaudémus.   **De.** [*gruffly*] Ehem, ópportúne: te ípsum quaé-
      ritó.
37 **Mi.** Quid trístis és?   **De.** Rogás me (ubi nóbis Aéschinús
38 siét), quid trístis égo sim?   **Mi.** [*to the audience*] Díxin hóc
      foré?
39 [*To* DEMEA] Quid fécit?   **De.** Quíd ille fécerít?—quem néque
      pudét
40 quicquám nec métuit quémquam néque legém putát
41 tenére se úllam.   Nam ílla quae ántehac fácta súnt
42 omítto: módô quid désignávit?   **Mi.** Quídnam id ést?
43 **De.** Forés ecfrégit átque in aédis ínruít
44 aliénas; ípsum dóminum atque ómnem fámiliám
45 mulcávit úsque ad mórtem; erípuit múlierém
46 quam amábat.   Clámant ómnes, índigníssimé
47 factum ésse.   Hoc ádveniénti quót mihi, Mícíó,
48 dixére!   In óre 'st ómni pópulo.   Déniqué,
49 si cónferéndum exémplum 'st, nón fratrém vidét
50 rei dáre operám, ruri ésse párcum ac sóbriúm?
51 Nullum húius símile fáctum.   Haec cum ílli, Mícíó,
52 dicó, tibi díco: tú illum córrumpí sinís.
53 **Mi.** Homine ímperíto númquam quícquam iṇiústiú'st,
54 qui nísi quod ípse fécit níl rectúm putát.
55 **De.** Quorsum ístuc?   **Mi.** Quía tu, Démea, haéc male iúdi-
      cás.
56 Non ést flagítium, míhi crede, ádulescéntulúm
57 scortári—néque potáre (nón est!) néque forés
58 ecfríngere.   Haéc si néque ego néque tu fécimús,
59 non síit egéstas fácere nós.   Tu núnc tibí
60 id laúdi dúcis, quód tum fécisti ínopiấ?
61 Iniúriúm 'st: nam si ésset únde id fíerét,
62 facerémus.   Ét tu illúm tuúm, si essés homó,

63 sinerés nunc fácere, dúm per aétatém licét.
64 **De.** Pro Íuppitér, tu homo ádigis me ád insániám.
65 Non ést flagítium fácere haec ádulescéntulum?   **Mi. Âh,**
66 auscúlta, né me obtúndas de hác re saépiús.
67 Tuum fíliúm dedísti adóptandúm mihí;
68 is méus est fáctus. Sí quid péccat, Démeá,
69 mihi péccat: ego íllî máximám partém feró.
70 Obsónat, pótat, ólet unguénta: dé meó!
71 Amat: dábitur á me argéntum, dúm erit cómmodúm—
72 ubi nón erít, fortásse exclúdetúr forás!
73 Forés ecfrégit: réstituéntur.   Díscidít
74 vestém: resárciétur.   Ét (dis grátiá)
75 est únde haec fíant, ét adhuc nón molésta súnt.
76 **De.** Pater ésse dísce ab íllis, quí veré sciúnt.
77 **Mi.** Natúrā tu ílli páter es, cónsiliís egó.
78 **De.** Tun cónsiliís quicquam?   **Mi.** Âh, si pérgis, ábieró.
79 **De.** Sicíne agis?   **Mi.** Án ego tótiens de éadem re aúdiám?
80 **De.** Curaé 'st mihi.   **Mi.** Ét mihi cúrae 'st.   Vérum, Démeá,
81 curémus aéquam utérque pártem: tu álterúm,
82 ego item álterúm—nam ambós curáre própemodúm
83 repóscere íllum 'st quém dedísti.   **De.** Ah Mício!
84 **Mi.** Mihi síc vidétur.   **De.** Quíd istîc?   Sí tibi istúc placét,
85 profúndat, pérdat, péreat: níl ad me áttinét.   [*Exit to the
   town.*]
86 **Mi.** Non níl molésta haec súnt mihí, sed osténderé
[87] me aegré pati ílli nóluí, quamquam Aéschinús
88 nonnúllam in hác re nóbis fácit iniúriám.
[89] Quam hic nón amávit?   Núper (crédo iam ómniúm
90 taedébat) díxit vélle uxórem dúceré.
91 Sperábam iám deférvisse ádulescéntiám:
92 gaudébam.   Ecce aútem de íntegró!   Nisi, quídquid ést,
93 volo scíre atque hóminem cónveníre, si apúd forúm 'st.
   [*Exit to the town.*]
                    SCENE 2

[*Enter* AESCHINUS *and* PARMENO *from the town, escorting* BAC-
CHIS *and followed by the battered and bandaged* SANNIO.]

94 **Sa.** [*wringing his hands*] Óbsecró, populáres, férte mísero
atque ínnocénti auxílium.

95 súbveníte inopi. **Ae.** [*calming the fears of* BACCHIS] Ótióse:
núnciam ílico hîc consíste.

96 Quíd respéctas? Níl perícli 'st: númquam, dum égo adero,
híc te tánget.

97 **Sa.** Égo istam invítis ómnibús. . . . [*He mutters inaudible
threats.*]

98 **Ae.** Quamquám 'st sceléstus, nón commíttet hódie umquam
íterum ut vápulét.

99 **Sa.** Aéschine, aúdi, né te ignárum fuísse dícas meórum mó-
rum:

[100] léno ego súm. **Ae.** Scio équidem. **Sa.** Créde hoc: égo
meúm ius pérsequár,

101 néque tu vérbis sólves úmquam, quód mihi ré male fécerís.

102 **Ae.** [*to* PARMENO] Ábi praé strenue ác fores áperi. **Sa.**
Céterum hóc nilí facís?

103 **Ae.** [*to* BACCHIS] Î intrô núnciám tu. **Sa.** Enim nón sinam.
[SANNIO *grabs* BACCHIS *by the arm.*] **Ae.** Áccede íllûc,
Pármenó;

104 nímium istûc abísti; hîc própter húnc [*pointing to* SANNIO]
adsíste; em síc voló.

105 Cave núnciam óculos á meis óculis quóquam démoveás
tuós,

106 ne móra sit, si ínnuerím, quin púgnus cóntinuo ín mala
haéreát.

107 **Sa.** Istúc volo érgo ipsum expcríri. **Ae.** [*to* PARMENO] Em
sérva. [*To* SANNIO] Omítte múlierém. [*As* SANNIO *refuses to obey,* AESCHINUS *nods and* PARMENO *strikes him.*]

108 **Sa.** O indígnum fácinus! **Ae.** Nísi cavés, geminábit.
[PARMENO *mistakes this for an order and punches* SANNIO
again.] **Sa.** Heí miseró mihí!

109 **Ae.** [*to* PARMENO] Non ínnuerám; verum ín istam pártem
pótius péccató tamén.

110 [*To* BACCHIS] I núnciám. [*Exeunt* BACCHIS *and* PARMENO
into MICIO's *house.*] **Sa.** Quid hóc rei 'st? Régnumne,
Aéschine, hîc tu póssidés?

111 **Ae.** Si póssidérem, ornátus ésses éx tuís virtútibús.

112 **Sa.** Quid tíbi rei mécum 'st? **Ae.** Níl. **Sa.** Quid? Nóstin
     quí sim? **Ae.** Nón desíderó.

113 **Sa.** Tetigín tui quícquam? **Ae.** Si áttigísses, férres ínfor-
     túniúm.

114 **Sa.** Quî tíbi magís licét meam habére, pró qua ego árgen-
     túm dedí?

[115] **Ae.** Tu sí moléstus pérgis ésse, iam íntrô abrípiere, átque
     ibí

116 usque ád necem óperiére lóris. **Sa.** Lóris líber? **Ae.** Síc
     erít.

117 **Sa.** O hóminem impúrum! Hîcíne libértatem áiunt ésse
     aequam ómnibús?

118 **Ae.** Si sátis iam débacchátus és, leno, aúdi—sí vis—núnc-
     iám.

119 **Sa.** Egon débacchátus sum aútem an tu ín me? **Ae.** Mítte
     ista átque ad rém redí.

120 **Sa.** Quam rém? Quô rédeam? **Ae.** Iámne mé vis dícere
     id quód ad te áttinét?

121 **Sa.** Cupio—aéqui módô aliquíd. **Ae.** Vah! Léno iníqua
     mé non vúlt loquí.

122 Minís vigínti tú illam emísti—quaé res tíbi vertát malé!

123 Argénti tántum dábitur. **Sa.** Quíd si ego tíbi illam nólo
     vénderé?

124 Cogés me? **Ae.** Mínime. **Sa.** Námque id métui. **Ae.**
     Néque vendéndam cénseó,

125 quae líberá 'st; nam ego líberáli illam ádseró causâ manú.

126 Nunc víde utrúm vis, argéntum accípere an caúsam médi-
     tarí tuám.

127 Delíbera hóc, dum ego rédeo, léno. [*Exit into the house.*]
     Sa. Pró supréme Iúppitér.

[*Enter* Syrus *from* Micio's *house.*]

128 **Sy.** [*speaking to* Aeschinus *within*] Tace, égomet cónveniam
     ípsum: cúpide accípiat fáxo atque étiam

129 bene dícat sécum esse áctum. [*Coming forward*] Quíd istuc,
     Sánnio, 'st, quód te aúdió

130 nescióquid cóncertásse cum éro?   **Sa.** Númquam vídi iní-
       quiús

1ﬞ. ﬞ certátiónem cómparátam, quam haéc hodie ínter nós fuít:

132 ego vápulándo, ille vérberándo, usque ámbo défessí sumús.

[133] **Sy.** Tua cúlpa.   [*Glancing down the street, he abruptly deserts*
       Sannio.]   Ctésiphónem vídeo: núnc de amíca laétus ést.

[*Enter* Ctesipho *from the town.   He is overjoyed to hear from*
Sannio *that* Aeschinus *has kidnapped his (i.e.,* Ctesipho's)
sweetheart, Bacchis.]

134 **Ct.** O fráter, fráter, quíd ego núnc te laúdem?   Sátis certó
       scló:

135 numquam íta magnífice quícquam dícam, id vírtus quín
       superét tuá.

136 Itaque únam hanc rém me habére praéter álios praécipuam
       árbitrór:

137 fratrem hómini némini ésse prímarum ártiúm magis prín-
       cipém.

138 **Sy.** O Ctésipho.   **Ct.** Ó Syre, Aéschinús ubi 'st?   **Sy.** Éllum
       te éxspectát domi.   **Ct.** Hém.

139 **Sy.** Quid est?   **Ct.** Quíd sit?   Íllius óperā, Sýre, nunc vívo.
       Féstivúm capút—

140 qui, cum ómniá sibi póst putávit ésse praé meo cómmodó,

141 maledícta—fámam—meúm labórem et péccatum ín se tráns-
       tulít!

142 Nil póte suprá.   [*He starts forward eagerly.*]   Quidnám foris
       crépuit?   **Sy.** Máne, mane: ípse exít forás.

[*Enter* Aeschinus *from the house.*]

143 **Ae.** [*looking for* Sannio] Ubi 'st ílle sácrilegús?   **Sa.** Me
       quaérit.   [*He looks to see if* Aeschinus *has a moneybag in
       his hand.*]   Númquidnam écfert?   Óccidí:

144 nil vídeo.   **Ae.** Ehem, ópportúne: te ípsum quaéro.   [*He
       suddenly sees* Ctesipho *and promptly turns his back on*
       Sannio.]   Quíd fit, Ctésiphó?

145 In túto 'st ómnis rés: omítte véro trístitiém tuám.

146 **Ct.** Ego illam hércle véro omítto, quí quidem te hábeam
       frátrem.   O mi Aéschiné!

147 O mí germáne!   Ah, véreor córam in ós te laúdare ámpliús,

148 ne id ádsentándi mágis, quam quo hábeam grátum, fácere
existimés.

149 **Ae.** Age, inépte, quási nunc nón norímus nós intér nos,
Ctésiphó.

150 Hoc míhi dolét, nos sérô réscisse, ét rem paéne in eúm
locúm

151 redísse, ut, si ómnes cúperent, tíbi nil póssent aúxiliáriér.

152 **Ct.** Pudébat. **Ae.** Áh, stultítia 'st ístaec, nón pudór. Tam
ob párvulám

153 rem paéne e pátria! Túrpe díctu. Deós quaeso ut ístaec
próhibeánt.

[154] Nunc ád forum íbo, ut húnc [*pointing to* SANNIO] absólvam.
Tu i íntrô ad íllam, Ctésiphó.

155 **Sa.** [*to* SYRUS] At ut ómne réddat. **Sy.** Ómne réddet; táce
modô ác sequere hắc. **Sa.** Sequór. [*Exeunt* AESCHINUS,
SANNIO, *and* SYRUS.]

156 **Ct.** [*calling back* SYRUS] Heus heús, Syre. **Sy.** Quíd est?
Ct. Óbsecró te hercle, hóminem istum ímpuríssimúm

157 quam prímum absólvitóte, né, si mágis irrítatús siét,

158 aliquâ ád patrem hóc permánet átque ego túm perpétuo
périerím.

159 **Sy.** Non fíet: bóno animó 's. Tu cum ílla te íntus óblecta
ínterím,

160 et léctulós iube stérni nóbis ét parári céterá.

161 Ego, iám transácta ré, convértam mé domúm cum obsónió.

162 **Ct.** Ita quaéso. Quándo hoc béne succéssit, hílarem hunc
súmamús diém. [*Exit* CTESIPHO *into the house, and*
SYRUS *to the forum.*]

SCENE 3

[*Enter* SOSTRATA *from her house, with* CANTHARA.]

163 **So.** Miserám me! Néminem hábeo. Sólae súmus. Geta
aútem hîc nón adést—

164 néc quem ad óbstetrícem míttam, néc qui arcéssat Aéschinúm.

165 **Ca.** Pól is quidém iam hîc áderit, nám numquam únum in-
térmittít diém,

166 quin sémper véniat. **So.** Sólus meárum míseriárum 'st
     rémediúm.

[*Enter* GETA *from the town, troubled.*]

167 **Ge.** [*muttering to himself*] Nunc íllud ést cum, si ómnia
     ómnes súa consília cónferánt

168 atque huíc maló salútem quaérant, aúxilí nil ádferánt:

169 tot rés repénte círcumvállant se, únde emérgi nón potést—

170 vís egéstas íniustítia sólitúdo infámiá.

171 **So.** Me míseram! Quídnam 'st quód sic vídeo tímidum et
     próperantém Getám?

172 **Ge.** [*hearing her*] Éra. **So.** Quid ést? Quid trépidas? **Ge.**
     Heí mi! **Ca.** Quíd festínas, mí Getá?

173 Ánimam récipe. **Ge.** Prórsus. . . . **So.** Quíd istuc "prór-
     sus" érgo 'st? **Ge.** Périimús.

174 Áctum 'st. **So.** Éloquere, óbsecró te. Quíd fit? **Ge.**
     Iám. . . . **So.** Quid "iám," Getá?

175 **Ge.** Aéschinús . . . **So.** Quid is érgo? **Ge.** . . . aliénus
     ést a nóstra fámilia. **So.** Hém,

176 périi! Quá re? **Ge.** Amáre occépit áliam. **So.** Vaé mise-
     raé mihí!

177 **Ge.** Néque id occúlte fért: a lénone ípsus éripuít palám.

178 **So.** Sáti'n hoc cértum 'st? **Ge.** Cértum: hisce óculis égo-
     met vídi, Sóstrata. **So.** [*sobbing*] Áh,

179 me míseram! Quíd iam crédas, aút cui crédas? Nó-
     strumne Aéschinúm!

180 Nostrám vitam—ómnium! Ín quo nóstrae spés opésque
     omnés sitaé

181 erant! Quí sine hác iurábat se únum númquam vícturúm
     diém!

182 Qui se ín suí gremió positúrum púerum dícebát patrís—

183 ita óbsecráturum, út licéret hánc sibi uxórem dúceré!

184 **Ge.** Era, lácrimas mítte ac pótius quód ad hanc rem ópus
     est pórro próspicé:

185 patiámurne án narrémus cuípiam? **Ca.** Aú au, mí homo,
     sánu'n és?

186 An hoc próferéndum tíbi vidétur úsquam? **Ge.** Mí quidem
     nón placét.

187 Iam prímum, illum álieno ánimo a nóbis ésse, rés ipsa ín-
     dicát.
188 Nunc si hóc palám proférimus, ílle infítias íbit, sát sció:
189 tua fáma et gnátae víta in dúbium véniet. Túm, si máximé
190 fateátur, cúm amet áliam, nón est útile hánc illí darí.
191 Quaprópter quóquo pácto tácito 'st ópus. So. Ah, mínime
     géntiúm!
192 Non fáciam. Ge. Quíd ages? So. Próferam. Ca. Hém,
     mea Sóstratá, vide quám rem agás.
193 So. Peióre rés locó non pótis est ésse quam ín quo núnc
     sitá 'st.
194 Expériar. Ge. Quíd istîc? Cédo, ut mélius dícis. So.
     Tú, quantúm potést,
195 abi atque Hégióni cógnato éius rem énarráto omnem órdiné.
196 Nam is nóstro Símuló fuit súmmus ét nos cóluit máximé.
197 Ge. Nam hercle álius némo réspicít nos. [*Exit to the town.*]
     So. Própere tú, mea Cánthará,
198 curre: óbstetrícem arcésse, ut, cum ópus sit, ne ín morá
     nobís siét. [*Exit* CANTHARA *to the town, and* SOSTRATA
     into the house.]

SCENE 4

[*Enter* DEMEA *from the town, much disturbed.*]

199 De. Dispérii.   Ctésiphónem audívi fíliúm
200 uná fuísse in ráptióne cum Aéschinó.
201 Ubi ego íllum quáeram?   Crédo abdúctum in gáneúm
202 aliquó: persuásit ílle impúrus, sát sció.
203 Sed eccúm Syrum íre vídeo: iam hínc scibo úbi siét.
204 Atque hércle hic dé grege íllo 'st: sí me sénserít
205 eum quáeritáre, númquam dícet cárniféx.
     [*Enter* SYRUS, *returning from the forum with a basketful of pro-
     visions for the feast.*]
206 Non óstendam íd me vélle. Sy. [*to himself*] Omném rem
     módô sení
207 quo pácto habéret, énarrámus órdiné:
208 nil quícquam vídi laétiús. De. Pro Iúppitér,
209 hominís stultítiam! Sy. Cónlaudávit fíliúm.

210 Mihi, qui íd dedíssem cónsilium, égit grátiás.
211 **De.** Disrúmpor! **Sy.** Árgentum ádnumerávit ílicó;
212 dedít praetérea in súmptum dímidiúm minaé;
213 id dístribútum sáne 'st éx senténtia. **De.** [*sarcastically*]
     Hém!
214 Huic mándes, sí quid récte cúratúm velís.
215 **Sy.** Ehem, Démea, haúd aspéxerám te. Quíd agitúr?
216 **De.** Quid agátur? Véstram néqueo mírarí satís
217 ratiónem. **Sy.** [*pretending to agree with* DEMEA] Est hércle
     inépta—né dicám doló,
218 absúrda. [*Aside, to the other servants*] Píscis céterós purgá,
     Dromó;
219 congrum ístum máximum ín aqua sínito lúderé
220 tantísper: úbi ego rédiero, éxossábitúr;
221 prius nólo. **De.** [*continuing his previous reflections*] Haecíne
     flagítia! **Sy.** Mí quidem nón placént,
222 et clámo saépe. [*Aside*] Sálsaménta haec, Stéphanió,
223 fac máceréntur púlchre. **De.** Dí vestrám fidém!
224 Utrúm studióne id síbi habet án laudí putát
225 fore, sí perdíderit gnátum? Vaé miseró mihí!
226 **Sy.** Istúc est sápere, nón quod ánte pedés modô 'st
227 vidére, séd etiam ílla quaé futúra súnt
228 prospícere. **De.** [*ignoring* SYRUS' *philosophizing*] Quíd?
     Istaec iám penés vos psáltriá 'st?
229 **Sy.** Ellam íntus. **De.** Ého, an domí 'st habitúrus? **Sy.**
     [*resuming his pious manner*] Crédo, ut ést
230 deméntia. **De.** Haécin fíeri! **Sy.** Inépta lénitás
231 patris ét facílitas práva. **De.** Frátris mé quidém
232 pudét pigétque. **Sy.** Nímium intér vos, Démeá
233 (non quía ades praésens, díco hoc)—pérnimium ínterést.
234 Tu, quántus quántu's, níl nisi sápiéntiá 's;
235 ille sómniúm. Num síneres véro illúm tuúm
236 facere haéc? **De.** Sinerem íllum? Aut nón sex tótis mén-
     sibús
237 prius ólfecíssem, quám ille quícquam coéperét?
238 **Sy.** Vigilántiám tuam tú mihi nárras? **De.** [*with paternal
     pride*] Síc siét

239 modô, ut núnc est, quaéso.   **Sy.** Ut quísque suúm vult ésse,
     itá'st.

240 **De.** Quid eúm?   Vidístin hódie?   **Sy.** Tuúmne fíliúm?

241 [*Aside*] Abigam húnc rus.   [*To* DEMEA] Iám dudum áliquid
     rúri agere árbitrór.

242 **De.** Sati'n scís ibi ésse?   **Sy.** Oh qui égomet próduxi!   **De.**
     Óptimé 'st.

243 Metuí ne haeréret hî́c.   **Sy.** Atque íratum ádmodúm.

244 **De.** Quid aútem?   **Sy.** Adórtu'st iúrgió fratrem ápud forúm

245 de psáltria ístac.   **De.** [*delighted*] Aí'n vero?   **Sy.** Áh, nil
     réticuít.

·246 Nam, ut númerabátur fórte argéntum, intérvenít

247 homo de ímprovíso: coépit clamáre "O Aéschiné,

248 haecíne flagítia fácere te!   Haéc te admítteré

249 indígna génere nóstro!"   **De.** Oh, lácrimo gaúdió.

250 **Sy.** "Non tu hóc argéntum pérdis, séd vitám tuám."

251 **De.** Salvús sit, spéro: est símilis máiorúm suum.   **Sy.** Huí!

252 **De.** Syre, praéceptórum plénu'st ístorum ílle.   **Sy.** Phý!

253 Domi hábuit únde díscerét.   **De.** Fit séduló.

254 Nil praétermítto; cónsuefácio; déniqué

255 inspícere támquam in spéculum in vítas ómniúm

256 iubeo átque ex áliis súmere éxemplúm sibí:

257 "hoc fácito."   **Sy.** Récte sáne.   **De.** "Hoc fúgito."   **Sy.**
     Cállidé.

258 **De.** "Hoc laúdi 'st."   **Sy.** Ístaec rés est.   **De.** "Hóc vitió
     datúr."

259 **Sy.** Probíssimé.   **De.** Porro aútem. . . .   **Sy.** Nón hercle
     ótiúm 'st

260 nunc mi aúscultándi.   Píscis éx senténtiá

261 nactús sum: ei míhi ne córrumpántur, caútió 'st.

262 Nam id nóbis tám flagítium 'st quam ílla, Démeá,

263 non fácere vóbis, quaé modô díxti; et quód queó,

264 consérvis ád eundem ístunc praécipió modúm:

265 "hoc sálsum 'st"—"hóc adústum 'st"—"hóc lautúm 'st
     parúm"—

266 "illúd recte"—"íterum síc meménto."   Séduló

267 moneó, quae póssum pró meá sapiéntiá:

268 postrémo támquam in spéculum in pátinas, Démeá,
269 inspícere iúbeo et móneo quíd facto úsus sít.
270 Inépta haec ésse, nós quae fácimus, séntió.
271 Verúm quid fácias? Út homo 'st, íta morém gerás.
272 Num quíd vis? De. Méntem vóbis méliorém darí.
273 Sy. Tu rús hinc íbis? De. Réctâ. Sy. [aside] Nám quid
    tu hîc agás,
274 ubi sí quid béne praecípias, némo obtémperét. [Exit into
    the house.]
275 De. [to himself] Ego véro hinc ábeo, quándo is, quam ób
    rem huc vénerám,
276 rus ábiit. Íllum cúro unum; ílle ad me áttinét:
277 quando íta vult fráter, de ístoc ípse víderít.
278 Sed quís illic ést, quem vídeo prócul? Estne Hégió
279 tribúlis nóster? Sí satis cérno, is est hércle; váh,
280 homo amícus nóbis iam índe a púero. O dí boní!
281 Ne illíus modí iam nóbis mágna cíviúm
282 penúriá 'st, antíquā vírtute ác fidé!
283 Oppériar hóminem hîc, út salútem et cónloquár.
[Enter GETA and HEGIO from the town, deep in conversation.]
284 He. Pro di ímmortáles, fácinus índignúm, Getá,
285 quod nárras! Ge. Síc est fáctum. He. Ex íllan fámiliá
286 tam illíberále fácinus ésse ortum! O Aéschiné!
287 De. [aside] De psáltria hác audívit: íd illi núnc dolét
288 aliéno; páter eius níli péndit. Heí mihí,
289 utinam hîc prope adésset álicubi átque audíret haćc.
290 He. Nisi fácient quae íllos aéquum 'st, haúd sic aúferént.
291 Ge. In té spes ómnis, Hégió, nobís sitá 'st:
292 te sólum habémus, tú 's patrónus, tú patér:
293 illé tibi móriens nós comméndavít senéx:
294 si déserís tu, périimús. He. Cave díxerís:
295 neque fáciam néque me sátis pié posse árbitrór.
296 De. [to himself] Adíbo. [To HEGIO] Sálvere Hégiónem plúri-
    múm
297 iubeo. He. Óh, te quaérebam ípsum: sálve, Démeá.
298 De. Quid aútem? He. Máior fíliús tuus, Aéschinús,
299 quem frátri adóptandúm dedísti, néque boní

300 neque líberális fúnctus ófficiúm 'st virí.

301 **De.** Quid istúc est?   **He.** Nóstrum amícum nóras Símulúm

302 aequálem?   **De.** Quíd ni?   **He.** Fíliam éius vírginém

303 vitiávit.   **De.** Hém!   **He.** Mane: nóndum audísti, Démeá,

304 quod ést gravíssimum.   **De.** Án quicquám 'st etiam ám-
plius?

305 **He.** Vero ámpliús.   Nam hoc quídem feréndum aliquó modó
'st:

306 persuásit nóx amór vinum ádulescéntiá:

307 humánum 'st.   Úbi scit fáctum, ad mátrem vírginís

308 venit ípsus últro lácrimans órans óbsecráns

309 fidém dans, iúrans se íllam dúcturúm domúm.

[310] Virgo ílla grávida fácta 'st (ménsis décimus ést):

311 ille bónus vir nóbis psáltriám, si dís placét,

312 parávit, quícum vívat; íllam déserít.

313 **De.** Pro cérton tu ístaec dícis?   **He.** Máter vírginís

314 in médio 'st—ípsa vírgo—rés ipsa—híc Getá

315 praetérea, ut cáptus ést servórum, nón malús.

316 **De.** Pudét: [*aside*] nec quíd agam néque quid huíc respón-
deám

[317] sció.   [*From* Sostrata's *house comes the voice of* Pamphila
crying out in childbirth] **Pa.** Iunó Lucína, sérva me, óbsecró.

318 **He.** Numnam ílla, quaéso, párturít?   **Ge.** Certe, Hégio.
He. Ém,

319 illaéc fidém nunc véstram implórat, Démeá:

320 quod vós ius cógit, íd volúntate ímpetrét.

[321] **De.** Ne tímeas: fíent quaé fieri aéquum 'st ómniá.

322 **He.** Decét te fácere.   Géta, duc me íntrô ad Sóstratám.
[*Exeunt* Geta *and* Hegio *into* Sostrata's *house.*]

323 **De.** [*to himself*] Non me índicénte haec fíunt: útinam híc
sít modó

324 defúnctum.   Vérum nímia illaéc licéntiá

325 profécto evádet ín aliquód magnúm malúm.

326 Ibo ác requíram frátrem, ut ín eum haec évomám.   [*Exit
to the town.*]

[*Enter* HEGIO *from the house, returning from his interview with* SOSTRATA.]

327 **He.** Bono ánimo fác sis, Sóstrata; et ístam, quód potés,
328 fac cónsolére. Ego Míciónem, si ápud forúm 'st,
329 convéniam, atque út res gésta 'st nárrabo órdiné.
330 Si 'st, ís factúrus út sit ófficiúm suúm,
331 faciát; sin áliter de hác re 'st éius senténtiá,
332 respóndeát mi, ut quíd agam quám primúm sciám. [*Exit to the town.*]

SCENE 5

[*Enter* CTESIPHO *and* SYRUS *from* MICIO's *house.*]

333 **Ct.** Aí'n patrem hínc abísse rús? **Sy.** [*not knowing that* DEMEA *had met* HEGIO *and stayed in town*] Iam dúdum.
Ct. Díc sodés. **Sy.** Apud víllam 'st:
334 núnc cum máxime óperis áliquid fácere crédo. **Ct.** Utinám quidém!
335 Quod cúm salúte eius fíat, íta se défetígarít velím,
336 ut tríduo hóc perpétuo prórsum e lécto néqueat súrgeré.
337 **Sy.** Ita fíat, et ístoc, sí quid pótis est, réctiús. **Ct.** Ita; nam húnc diém
338 miseré nimis cúpio, ut coépi, pérpetuum ín laetítia dégeré.
339 Ét illud rús nullā áliā caúsā tám male ódi, nísi quia própe 'st:
340 quód si abésset lóngiús,
341 príus nox óppressísset íllî eum, quam húc revérti pósset íterum.
342 Núnc ubi me íllîc nón vidébit, iam húc recúrret, sát sció:
343 rogitábit mé ubi fúerim: "ego hóc te tóto nón vidí dié."
344 Quid dícam? **Sy.** Nílne in méntem 'st? **Ct.** Númquam quícquam. **Sy.** Tánto néquiór.
345 Cliéns, amícus, hóspes, némo 'st vóbis? **Ct.** Súnt. Quid pósteá?
346 **Sy.** Hisce ópera ut dáta sit. **Ct.** Quaé non dáta sit? Nón potést fierí. **Sy.** Potést.
347 **Ct.** Intérdiús; sed si híc pernócto, caúsae quíd dicám, Syré?
348 **Sy.** Vah, quám vellem étiam nóctu amícis óperam mós essét darí!

349 Quin tu ótiósus ésto: ego illíus sénsum púlchre cálleó:
350 cum férvit máximé, tam plácidum quási ovem réddo. **Ct.**
    Quó modó?
351 **Sy.** Laudári té libénter aúdit: fácio te ápud illúm deúm:
352 virtútes nárro. **Ct.** Meás? **Sy.** Tuás. Homini ílico lácri-
    maé cadúnt
353 quasi púero gaúdio. [*He happens to glance down the street
    and starts with astonishment.*] Ém tibi aútem! **Ct.** Quíd-
    nam est? **Sy.** Lúpus in fábulá.
354 **Ct.** Pater ést? **Sy.** Is ípsus. **Ct.** Sýre, quid ágimus? **Sy.**
    Fúge modô íntrô: ego víderó.
355 **Ct.** Si quíd rogábit, núsquam tú me . . . Audístin? **Sy.**
    Póti'n ut désinás?
    [*Enter* Demea, *returning from his search for* Micio; *he pauses
    at a distance from the latter's house to ruminate.*]
356 **De.** Né ego homó sum infélix: frátrem núsquam invénio
    géntiúm.
357 Praéterea aútem, dum íllum quaéro, a vílla mércennáriúm
358 vídi: is fíliúm negat ésse rúri. Néc quid agám sció.
359 **Ct.** [*opening the door a crack*] Sýre. **Sy.** Quid ést? **Ct.** Men
    quaérit? **Sy.** Vérum. **Ct.** Périi. **Sy.** Quín tu animó
    bonó 's.
360 **De.** [*still unaware of the others' presence*] Núnc redeó: si
    fórte fráter rédierít, visó. **Ct.** Syré,
361 óbsecró, vide ne ílle huc prórsus se ínruát. **Sy.** Etiám tacés?
362 Égo cavébo. **Ct.** Númquam hercle hódie ego ístuc cóm-
    mittám tibí,
363 nám me iam ín cellam áliquam cum ílla cóncludam: íd
    tutíssimúm 'st.
364 **Sy.** Áge, tamén ego hunc ámovébo. [*Exit* Ctesipho.] **De.**
    Séd eccum scéleratúm Syrúm!
365 **Sy.** [*assuming a tone of injured innocence and speaking to
    himself loud enough to be overheard*] Nón hercle híc, qui
    vúlt, duráre quísquam, sí sic fít, potést.
[366] Scíre equidém voló, quot míhi sint dómini. **De.** Quíd rei
    'st? Quíd tibí 'st?

367 **Sy.** Rógitas?   Ctésiphó me púgnis míserum et ístam psáltriám
368 úsque occídit.   **De.** Hém, quid nárras?   **Sy.** Ém, vide ut
díscidít labrúm.
369 **De.** Quam ób rem?   **Sy.** Me ímpulsóre hanc émptam esse
aít.   **De.** Non tu eúm rus hínc modó
370 próduxe aíbas?   **Sy.** Fáctum; vérum vénit póst insániéns.
371 Níl pepércit.   Nón puduísse vérberáre hominém seném!
372 Quem égo modó puerúm tantíllum in mánibus géstaví
meís.
373 **De.** Laúdo: Ctésiphó, patríssas: ábi, virúm te iúdicó.
374 **Sy.** Laúdas?   Né ille cóntinébit pósthac, sí sapiét, manús.
375 **De.** Séd estne fráter íntus?   **Sy.** Nón est.   **De.** Úbi illum
invéniam, cógitó.
376 **Sy.** [*pretending surliness*] Scío ubi sít, verum hódie númquam mónstrabo.   **De.** Hém, quid aís?   **Sy.** Itá.
377 **De.** Dímminuétur tíbi quidém iam cérebrum.   **Sy.** At nómen nésció
378 íllius hóminis, séd locúm novi úbi sit.   **De.** Díc ergó locúm.
379 **Sy.** Nóstin pórticum ápud macéllum hâc deórsum?   **De.**
Quíd ni nóverím?
380 **Sy.** Praéteríto hâc réctā plátéā súrsus: úbi eô vénerís,
381 clívus deórsum vérsus ést: hâc praécipitáto.   Pósteá
382 ést ad hánc manúm sacéllum: ibi ángipórtum própter ést.
383 **De.** Quódnam?   **Sy.** Illî úbi etiám capríficus mágna 'st.
De. Nóvi.   **Sy.** Hâc pérgitó.
384 **De.** Íd quidem ángipórtum nón est pérviúm.   **Sy.** Verum
hércle!   Váh!
385 Cénse'n hóminem me ésse?   Errávi.   In pórticúm rursúm
redí:
386 sáne hâc múlto própius íbis ét minor ést errátió.
387 Scí'n Cratíni huius dítis aédīs?   **De.** Scío.   **Sy.** Ubi eás
praetérierís,
388 ád sinístram hâc réctā plátéā; ubi ád Diánae vénerís,
389 íto ad déxtram.   Príusquam ad pórtam vénias, ápud ipsúm
lacúm

390 ést pistrílla et éxadvérsum fábrica: ibí 'st. **De.** Quid íbi
      facít?

391 **Sy.** [*with a sly twinkle*] Léctulós in sóle ilígnis pédibus fá-
      ciendós dedít.

392 **De.** [*scornfully*] Úbi potétis vós: bene sáne. Séd cesso ád
      eum pérgeré? [*Exit to the town.*]

393 **Sy.** Í sane: égo te exércebo hódie, ut dígnus és, silicérniúm!

394 Aéschinus ódióse céssat; prándiúm corrúmpitúr;

395 Ctésipho aútem in amóre 'st tótus. Égo iam próspiciám
      mihí.

396 Nám iam adíbo atque únum quícquid (quód quidem erít
      bellíssimúm)

397 cárpam et cýathos sórbiláns paulátim hunc próducám diém.
      [*Exit into* Micio's *house.*]

Scene 6

[*Enter* Hegio *and* Micio *from the town, deep in conversation.*]

398 **Mi.** Ego in hác re níl repério, quam ób rem laúder tánto-
      pere, Hégió.

399 Meum offícium fácio. Quód peccátum a nóbis órtum 'st,
      córrigó.

400 **He.** Sed quaéso ut únâ mécum ad mátrem vírginís eas,
      Mício,

401 atque ístaec éadem quaé mihi díxti túte dícas múlierí:

402 suspíciónem hanc própter frátrem eius ésse et íllam psál-
      triám . . .

403 **Mi.** [*interrupting him*] Si ita aéquum cénses aút si ita ópus
      est fácto, eámus. **He.** Béne facís:

404 nam et ílli ita ánimum iám relevábis, quaé dolóre ac míseriá

405 tabéscit, ét tuum offícium fúeris fúnctus. Séd si alitér
      putás,

406 egomét narrábo quaé mihí dixti. **Mi.** Ímmo ego íbo. **He.**
      Béne facís. [*Exeunt into the house of* Sostrata.]

[*Enter* Aeschinus *a moment later, in great agitation; he too is
headed for* Sostrata's *house. Returning from the forum, where
he paid off* Sannio, *he heard everyone talking of his escapade and*

fears that it may have reached the ears of Sostrata, *who will not know that* Bacchis *was kidnapped for* Ctesipho.]

407 **Ae.** Vah, quó modo hác me expédiam túrba?   Tánta núnc
408 suspíció de me íncidít.
409 Haéc adeó meā cúlpā fáteor fíeri.   Nón me hanc rém patrí,
410 útut erát gesta, índicásse!   Exórassem, út eam dúcerém.
411 Núnc hoc prímum 'st: ád illas íbo, ut púrgem me.   Ácce-
       dam ád forés.
412 Périi: horrésco sémper, ubí pultáre hasce óccipió misér.
413 Heús, heus: Aéschinús ego sum.   Áperite áliquis áctutum
       óstiúm.
414 Pródit néscioquís: concédam huc.   [*He steps to one side, as*
       Micio *enters from his interview with* Sostrata.]   **Mi.** Íta
       ut díxi, Sóstratá,
415 fácite.   Ego Aéschinúm convéniam, ut quómodo ácta haec
       sínt sciát.
416 Séd quis óstium hóc pultávit?   **Ae.** [*aside*] Páter hercle ést:
       perii.   **Mi.** Aéschiné.
417 **Ae.** [*aside*] Quid huic hîc negóti 'st?   **Mi.** Túne has pépu-
       listí forés?
418 [*Aside*] Tacet: cúr non lúdo hunc áliquantísper?   Mélius ést,
419 quandóquidem hoc númquam mi ípse vóluit díceré.
420 [*To* Aeschinus] Nil míhi respóndes?   **Ae.** Nón equidem ístas,
       quód sciám.
421 **Mi.** Ita?   Nám mirábar quíd hîc negóti essét tibí.
422 [*Aside*] Erúbuit: sálva rés est.   **Ae.** Díc, sodés, patér,
423 tibi véro quid ístîc ést rëí.   **Mi.** Nil mí quidém.
424 Amícus quídam me á foro ábduxít modó
425 huc ádvocátum síbi.   **Ae.** Quid?   **Mi.** Égo dicám tibí:
426 habitánt hîc quaédam múlierés paupérculaé
427 (ut opínor eás non nósse te—ét certó sció,
428 neque ením diu húc migrárunt).   **Ae.** Quíd tum pósteá?
429 **Mi.** Virgo ést cum mátre.   **Ae.** Pérge.   **Mi.** Haec vírgo
       orbá 'st patré.
430 Hic méus amícus ílli génere 'st próximús.
431 Huic léges cógunt núbere hánc.   **Ae.** [*aside*] Perií?   **Mi.**
       Quid ést?

432 **Ae.** Nil: récte.   Pérge.   **Mi.** Is vénit út secum ávehát,
433 nam habitát Miléti.   **Ae.** Hem, vírginem út secum ávehát?
434 **Mi.** Sic ést.   **Ae.** Milétum usque, óbsecro?   **Mi.** Íta.   **Ae.**
     [*aside*] Animó malé 'st.
435 [*To* Micio] Quid ipsaé?   Quid aíunt?   **Mi.** Quíd illas cénses?
     Níl ením.
436 Comménta máter ést: esse éx alió viró
437 nescióquo púerum nátum, néque eum nóminát;
438 priórem esse íllum, nón opórtere huíc darí.
439 **Ae.** Eho, nónne haec íusta tíbi vidétur pósceré?
440 **Mi.** Non.   **Ae.** Óbsecró, non?   Án illam hinc ábducét,
     patér?
441 **Mi.** Quid illám ni abdúcat?   **Ae.** Fáctum a nóbis dúritér
442 immíserecórditérque atque étiam, sí 'st, patér,
443 dicéndum mágis apérte, illíberálitér.
444 **Mi.** Quam ob rém?   **Ae.** Rogás me?   Quíd illi tándem
     créditís
445 fore ánimi mísero, qui íllā cónsuevít priór?
[446] **Mi.** Verúm quid nóbis cum íllis?   Ábeamús.   Quid ést?
447 Quíd lacrimás?   **Ae.** Pater, óbsecro, aúsculta.   **Mi.** Aé-
     schine, aúdivi ómniá
448 ét sció, nam té amo: quó magis quaé agis cúrae súnt mihí.
[449] **Ae.** Át me tuí pudét.   **Mi.** Credo hércle, nam íngeniúm
     noví tuúm
450 líberále, séd vereór ne indíligéns nimiúm siés.
451 Ín qua cívitáte tándem te árbitráre víveré?
452 Vírginém vitiásti, quám te nón ius fúerat tángeré.
453 Iam íd peccátum prímum mágnum—mágnum, at húma-
     núm tamén:
454 fécere álii saépe itém boni.   At póstquam id évenít, cedó,
455 númquid círcumspéxti?   Aut númquid túte próspextí tibí?
456 Nólim céterárum rérum té socórdem eodém modó.
457 Bóno animó 's; ducés uxórem.   **Ae.** Hem.   **Mi.** Bóno animó
     's, inquám.   **Ae.** Patér,
458 óbsecró, num lúdis tú me?   **Mi.** Égo te?   Quam ób rem?
     Ae. Nésció.
459 Quía tam mísere hoc ésse cúpio vérum, eó vereór magís.

460　**Mi.** Ábi domum ác deos cómprecáre, ut úxorem árcessás:
　　　abí.

461　**Ae.** Quíd?　Iam uxórem?　**Mi.** Iám.　**Ae.** Iam?　**Mi.** Iám,
　　　quantúm potést.　**Ae.** Di mé, patér,

462　ómnes óderínt, ni mágis te quam óculos núnc ego amó meós.

463　**Mi.** Quíd?　Quam illam?　**Ae.** Aéque.　**Mi.** Pérbenígne.
　　　Ae. Quíd?　Ille ubí 'st Milésiús?

464　**Mi.** Périit.　Ábiit.　Návem ascéndit.　Séd cur céssas?
　　　Ae. Ábi, patér,

465　tú potiús deos cómprecáre, nám tibi eós, certó sció,

466　quó vir mélior múlto 's quám ego, obtémperáturós magís.

467　**Mi.** Égo eo intrô, út quae opus súnt paréntur.　Tú fac ut
　　　díxi, sí sapís.　[*Exit into his house.*]

468　**Ae.** Quid hoc ést negóti?　Hoc ést patrem ésse aut hóc est
　　　fílium ésse?

469　Si fráter aút sodális ésset, quí magis mórem géreret?

470　Hic nón amándus?　Hícine nón gestándus ín sinú 'st?
　　　Hem!

471　Itaque ádeo mágnam mi ínicít sua cómmoditáte cúram,

472　ne imprúdens fáciam fórte quód nolít: sciéns cavébo.

473　Sed césso ire íntrô, né moraé meis núptiís egomét sim?
　　　[*Exit into* Micio's *house.*]

Scene 7

[*Enter* Demea, *returning from his wild goose chase.*]

474　**De.** Deféssus sum ámbulándo.　Ut, Sýre, te cúm tuá

475　monstrátióne mágnus pérdat Iúppitér!

476　Perréptavi úsque omne óppidum: ád portam, ád lacúm,

477　quô nón?　Neque íllî fábrica erát nec frátrem homó

478　vidísse se aíbat quísquam.　Núnc veró domí

479　certum óbsidére 'st úsque, dónec rédierít.

[*Enter* Micio *from his house, busy with preparations for the wedding and on his way to* Sostrata's.]

480　**Mi.** [*to himself*] Ibo: íllis dícam núllam esse ín nobís morám.

481　**De.** Sed eccum ípsum.　Té iam dúdum quaéro, Míció.

482　**Mi.** Quidnám?　**De.** Fero ália flágitia ád te ingéntiá

483　boni íllius ádulescéntis.　**Mi.** Écce autém!　**De.** Nová,

484 capitália! **Mi.** Ohé iam! **De.** Néscis quí vir sít. **Mi.**
   [*impatiently*] Sció.

[485] [*He pushes* DEMEA *aside*] Ego hás convénio: póst huc rédeo.
   [*Exit into* SOSTRATA'S *house.*] **De.** O Iúppitér!

486 Hancíne vitam! Hóscin móres! Hánc deméntiám!

487 Uxór sine dóte véniet; íntus psáltriá 'st;

488 domus súmptuósa; aduléscens lúxu pérditús;

489 senéx delírans. Ípsa sí cupiát Salús,

490 serváre prórsus nón potést hanc fámiliám.
   [*Enter* SYRUS *from* MICIO'S *house, tipsy.*]

491 **Sy.** Edepól, Syrísce, té curásti móllitér

492 lautéque múnus ádminístrastí tuúm.

493 Abi. Séd postquam íntus sum ómniúm rerúm satúr,

494 prodeámbuláre huc líbitum 'st. **De.** Íllud, sí's, vidé:

495 exémplum dísciplínae! **Sy.** Écce autem híc adést

496 senex nóster! [*To* DEMEA] Quíd fit? Quíd tu 's trístis?
   De. Óh scelús!

497 **Sy.** Ohe iám! Tu vérba fúndis híc, sapiéntiá!

498 **De.** [*angrily*] Tu sí meus ésses . . . **Sy.** [*interrupting him
   and finishing the sentence for him in a way* DEMEA *did not
   intend*] Dís quidem ésses, Démeá,

499 ac tuám rem cónstabilísses. **De.** [*ignoring the interruption*]
   . . . éxemplo ómnibús

500 curárem ut ésses. **Sy.** Quam ób rem? Quíd fecí? **De.**
   Rogás?

[501] Quasi ré bene gésta, nímium pótastí, scelús.
   [PARMENO *puts his head out at* MICIO'S *door and calls.*]

502 **Pa.** Heus, Sýre, rogát te Ctésipho út redeás. **Sy.** Abí.
   [PARMENO *withdraws.*]

503 **De.** [*startled*] Quid Ctésiphónem hic nárrat? **Sy.** Níl. **De.**
   Eho, cárniféx,

504 est Ctésipho íntus? **Sy.** [*lying*] Nón est. **De.** Cúr hic
   nóminát?

505 **Sy.** Est álius quídam, párasitáster paúlulús:

506 nostín? **De.** Iam scíbo. [*He starts for* MICIO'S *house.*]
   Sy. [*grabbing him*] Quíd agis? Quó abis? **De.** Mítte mé.

507 **Sy.** Noli, ínquam. **De.** Nón manum ábstinés, mastígiá?

508 An tíbi iam mávis cérebrum díspergam híc? [*Exit, breaking away and running, into* Micio's *house.*] **Sy.** Abít.

509 Edepól commíssatórem haud sáne cómmodúm,

510 praesértim Ctésiphóni! Quíd ego núnc agám?

511 Nisi, dum haéc siléscunt túrbae, intérea in ángulúm

512 aliquô ábeam atque édormíscam hoc vílli: síc agám. [*Exit.*]

[*Enter* Micio *from* Sostrata's *house.*]

513 **Mi.** [*starting for home*] Paráta a nóbis súnt, ita ut díxi, Sóstratá:

514 ubi vís . . . [*He hears a commotion in his house.*] Quisnam á me pépulit tám gravitér forés?

[*Enter* Demea, *bursting out of* Micio's *house.*]

515 **De.** Hei míhi! Quid fáciam? Quíd agam? Quíd clamem aút querár?

516 O caélum, o térra, o mária Néptuni! **Mi.** Ém tibí:

517 rescívit ómnem rem: íd nunc clámat scílicét.

518 Parátae lítes: súccurréndum 'st. **De.** Éccum adést

519 commúnis córruptéla nóstrum líberúm.

520 **Mi.** Tandém reprime íracúndiam átque ad té redí.

521 **De.** [*with enforced calm*] Représsi, rédii, mítto máledicta ómniá:

522 rem ipsám putémus. Díctum hoc ínter nós fuít

523 (ex te ádeo 'st órtum), né tu cúrarés meúm

524 neve égo tuúm? Respónde. **Mi.** [*embarrassed*] Fáctum 'st, nón negó.

525 **De.** Cur núnc apúd te pótat? Cúr recipís meúm?

526 Quando égo tuúm non cúro, né curá meúm.

527 **Mi.** [*awkwardly*] Non aéquum dícis. **De.** Nón? **Mi.** [*trying to mollify* Demea] Nam vétus verbum hóc quidém 'st:

528 commúnia ésse amícorum ínter se ómniá.

[529] **De.** [*scornfully*] Facéte! At . . . **Mi.** [*interrupting him jovially*] Mítte iam ístaec; dá te hodié mihí;

530 expórge fróntem. **De.** [*reluctantly*] Scílicét ita témpus fért;

531 faciéndum 'st. [*Sternly*] Céterum egó rus crás cum fílió

532 cum prímo lúci ibo hínc. **Mi.** De nócte, cénseó:

533 hodié modô hílarum fác te. **De.** Et ístam psáltriám

[534] unâ íllûc mécum hinc ábstrahám. **Mi.** Probíssimé.

535 **De.** Atque íbi favíllae pléna, fúmi, ac póllinís
536 coquéndo sít faxo ét moléndo; praéter haéc
537 merídie ípso fáciam ut stípulam cólligát:
538 tam excóctam réddam atque átram quám carbó 'st. **Mi.**
Placét.
539 I ergo íntrô. Et cuí rei 'st, eí rei hunc súmamús diém.
[*Exeunt.*]

SCENE 8

[*Enter* DEMEA *from* MICIO'S *house.*]

540 **De.** [*to himself*] Númquam ita quísquam béne subdúcta
rátione ád vitám fuít,
541 quín res aétas úsus sémper áliquid ádportét noví,
542 áliquid móneat: út illa, quaé te scísse crédas, nésciás,
543 ét quae tíbi putáris príma, in éxperiéndo ut répudiés.
544 Quód nunc mi évenít; nam ego vítam dúram, quám vixi
úsque adhúc,
545 própe iam excúrso spátio, omítto. Id quam ób rem? Re
ípsa répperí,
546 fácilitáte níl esse hómini mélius néque cleméntiā.
547 Íd esse vérum, ex me átque ex frátre cuívis fácile 'st nósceré.
548 Ílle suam égit sémper vítam in ótio, ín convíviís,
549 clémens, plácidus, núlli laédere ós, adrídere ómnibús;
550 síbi vixít, sibi súmptum fécit: ómnes béne dicúnt amánt.
551 Égo ille agréstis, saévus, trístis, párcus, trúculentús, tenáx
552 dúxi uxórem: quam íbi misériam vídi! Náti fílií:
553 ália cúra! Heia aútem, dúm studeo íllis út quam plúrimúm
554 fácerem, cóntrivi ín quaeréndo vítam atque aétatém meám.
555 Núnc, exácta aetáte, hoc frúcti pró labóre ab eís feró:
556 ódium. Ille álter síne labóre pátria pótitur cómmodá.
557 Íllum amánt; me fúgitant. Ílli crédunt cónsilia ómniá;
558 íllum díligúnt; apud íllum súnt ambo: égo desértus súm.
559 Íllum ut vívat óptant; meam aútem mórtem exspéctant
scílicét.
560 Íta eos, méo labóre edúctos máximo, híc fecít suós
561 paúlo súmptu. Míseriam ómnem ego cápio; hic pótitur
gaúdiá.

562 Áge age, núnciam éxperiámur cóntra, ecquíd ego póssiém
563 blánde dícere aút benígne fácere, quándo hoc próvocát.
564 Égo quoque á meís me amári et mágni fíeri póstuló.
565 Si íd fit dándo atque óbsequéndo, nón postériorés ferám.
566 Déerit: íd meā mínime réfert, quí sum nátu máximús.
[*Enter* Syrus *from* Micio's *house.*]
567 **Sy.** Heus, Démea, órat fráter ne ábeas lóngiús.
568 **De.** [*to himself*] Quis homo? [*To* Syrus, *affably*] Ó Syre
    nóster, sálve. Quíd fit? Quíd agitúr?
569 **Sy.** [*astounded*] Recte. **De.** Óptimé 'st. [*Aside*] Iam núnc
    haec tría primum áddidí
570 praetér natúram: "O nóster"—"quíd fit?"—"quíd agitúr?"
571 [*To* Syrus] Servum haúd illíberálem praébes te, ét tibí
572 libéns bene fáxim. **Sy.** [*still nonplused*] Grátiam hábeo.
    De. Atquí, Syré,
573 hoc vérum 'st et ípsa re éxperiére própediém. [*Exit* Syrus.]
[*Enter* Geta, *hurrying out of* Sostrata's *house.*]
574 **Ge.** Era, ego húc ad hós províso, quám mox vírginém
575 arcéssant. Sed éccum Démeám. [*To* Demea, *dutifully*]
    Salvús siés.
576 **De.** [*gushingly*] O quî vocáre? **Ge.** Géta. **De.** Geta, hó-
    minem máximí
577 pretí te esse hódie iúdicávi animó meó;
578 nam is míhi profécto 'st sérvus spéctatús satís,
579 cui dóminus cúrae 'st, íta uti tíbi sensí, Getá;
580 et tíbi ob eám rem, sí quid úsus vénerít,
581 libéns bene fáxim. [*Aside*] Méditor ésse affábilís,
582 et béne procédit. **Ge.** [*much impressed*] Bónus es, cum haéc
    exístimás.
583 **De.** [*aside*] Paulátim plébem prímulúm fació meám. [Geta
    is about to go in when Aeschinus *comes strolling out of*
    Micio's *house; he lingers.*]
584 **Ae.** [*to himself*] Occídunt mé quidem, dúm nimis sánctas
    núptiás
585 student fácere: in ápparándo cónsumúnt diém.
586 **De.** Quid ágitur, Aéschine? **Ae.** Éhem, páter mi, tu hîc
    erás?

587 **De.** Tuus hércle véro et ánimo et náturá patér,
588 qui té amat plús quam hosce óculos! Séd cur nón domúm
589 uxórem arcéssis? **Ae.** Cúpio, vérum hoc míhi moraé 'st:
590 tibícina, ét hymenaéum quí cantént. **De.** Ehó,
591 vi'n tu huíc seni aúscultáre? **Ae.** Quíd? **De.** Missa haéc
      facé
592 —hymenaéum túrbas lámpadás tibícinás—
593 atque hánc in hórto máceriám iube díruí
594 quantúm potést. Hâc tránsfer; únam fác domúm;
595 tradúce et mátrem et fámiliam ómnem ad nós. **Ae.** Placét,
596 patér lepidíssime. **De.** [*to himself*] Eúge, iám lepidús vocór;
597 fratri aédes fíunt pérviaé; turbám domúm
598 addúcet; súmptu amíttet múlta. [*With malicious glee*] Quíd
      meá?
599 [*To* Syrus] Syre, céssas íre ac fácere? **Sy.** Quíd ego? **De.**
      Dírué. [*Exit* Syrus.]
600 [*To* Geta] Tu illás abi ét tradúce. **Ge.** Dí tibi, Démeá,
601 bene fáciant, cúm te vídeo nóstrae fámiliaé
602 tam ex ánimo fáctum vélle. **De.** [*benignly*] Dígnos árbitrór.
      [*Exit* Geta; Demea *turns to* Aeschinus.]
603 Quid tú ais? **Ae.** Síc opínor. **De.** Múlto réctiú'st
604 quam illám puérperam húc nunc dúci pér viám
605 aegrótam. **Ae.** Níl enim vídi mélius, mí patér.
606 **De.** Sic sóleo. Séd eccum Mício égreditúr forás.
[*Enter* Micio, *much excited.*]
607 **Mi.** Iubet fráter? Ubi ís est? [*Seeing* Demea] Tún iubés
      hoc, Démeá?
608 **De.** Ego véro iúbeo et hác re et áliis ómnibús
609 quam máxime únam fácere nós hanc fámiliám,
610 colere, ádiuváre, adiúngere. **Ae.** Ita quaesó, patér.
611 **Mi.** [*tactfully*] Haud áliter cénseo. **De.** Ímmo hercle íta
      nobís decét.
612 Primum [*pointing to* Aeschinus] húius uxóri 'st máter. **Mi.**
      [*curtly*] Ést: quid pósteá?
613 **De.** Proba ét modésta. **Mi.** Ita áiunt. **De.** [*blandly*] Nátu
      grándiór.

614 Nec qui eám respíciat, quísquam 'st: sóla 'st.   **Mi.** Quam
    híc rem agít?

615 **De.** Hanc te aéquum 'st dúcere, ét [*to* Aeschinus] te operam
    út fiát daré.

616 **Mi.** Me dúcere aútem?   **De.** Té.   **Mi.** Me?   **De.** Te ín-
    quam.   **Mi.** Inéptis.   **De.** [*to* Aeschinus] Sí tu sís homó,

617 hic fáciat.   **Ae.** [*coaxingly*] Mí patér!   **Mi.** [*to* Aeschinus]
    Quid tu aútem huic, ásine, auscúltas?   **De.** [*to* Micio]
    Níl agís.

618 Fieri áliter nón potést.   **Mi.** Delíras.   **Ae.** Síne te exórem,
    mí patér.

619 **Mi.** Insánis; aúfer.   **De.** Áge, da véniam fílió.   **Mi.** Sati'n
    sánus és?

620 Ego nóvus marítus ánno démum quínto et séxagésimó

621 fiam, átque anúm decrépitam dúcam?   Idne éstis aúctorés
    mihí?

622 **Ae.** Fac; prómisi ego íllis.   **Mi.** Prómisti aútem?   Dé te
    lárgitór, puér.

623 **De.** Age, quíd si quíd te máius óret?   **Mi.** Quási non hóc sit
    máximúm!

624 **De.** Da véniam.   **Ae.** Né gravére.   **De.** Fác; promítte.
    Mi. Nón omíttitís?

625 **Ae.** Non nísi te exórem.   **Mi.** Vís est haéc quidem.   **De.**
    Áge prolíxe, Míció.

626 **Mi.** Etsi hóc mihi právum inéptum absúrdum atque álienum
    á vitá meá

627 vidétur, sí vos tántopere ístuc vúltis, fíat.   **Ae.** Béne facís.

628 **De.** Meritó te amó.   Verúm. . . .   **Mi.** [*interrupting him*]
    Quid?   **De.** Égo dicam, hóc cum cónfit quód voló.

629 **Mi.** Quid núnc quod réstat?   **De.** Hégió 'st hic hís cognátus
    próximús,

630 adfínis nóbis, paúper: béne nos áliquid fácere illí decét.

631 **Mi.** Quid fácere?   **De.** Agélli 'st híc sub úrbe paúlum, quód
    locitás forás:

632 huic démus, quí fruátur.   **Mi.** Paúlum id aútem 'st?   **De.**
    Sí multúm 'st, tamén

633 faciéndum 'st. Pró patre huíc est, bónus est, nóster ést:
recté datúr.

[634] **Mi.** Quíd istîc? Dábitur. **Ae.** Gaúdeo. [*Enter* SYRUS,
pickax in hand.] **Sy.** Fáctum 'st quód iussísti, Démeá.

635 **De.** Frúgi homó 's. Ergo édepol hódie, meá quidém senténtiá,

636 iúdicó Syrum fíeri esse aéquum líberum. **Mi.** Ístunc líberúm?

637 Quódnam ob fáctum? **De.** Múlta. **Sy.** O nóster Démea,
édepol vír bonú's.

638 Égo istos vóbis úsque a púeris cúravi ámbos séduló.

639 Dócui, mónui, béne praecépi sémper quaé potui ómniá.

[640] **De.** [*drily*] Ápperét: in psáltria ísta eménda hic ádiutór
fuít,

641 híc curávit. Pródesse aéquum 'st. Álii mélliorés erúnt.

642 Dénique híc vult fíeri. **Mi.** [*to* AESCHINUS] Ví'n tu hoc
fíeri? **Ae.** Cúpio. **Mi.** Sí quidém

643 tú vis—Syre, ého accéde huc ád me. Líber ésto. **Sy.**
Béne facís.

644 Ómnibus grátiam hábeo, et seórsum tíbi praetérea, Démeá.

645 **De.** Gaúdeo. **Ae.** Ét ego. **Sy.** Crédo. Utinam hóc per-
pétuum fíat gaúdiúm,

646 Phrýgiam ut úxorém meam únâ mécum vídeam líberám!

647 **De.** Óptimám quidem múlierem! **Sy.** Ét quidem tuó ne-
póti, huius fílió,

648 hódie príma mámmam dédit haec. **De.** Hércle véro sérió,

649 síquidem príma dédit, haud dúbium 'st quín emítti aequúm
siét.

650 **Mi.** Ób eam rem? **De.** Ób eam. Póstremo á me argéntum, quánti 'st, súmitó.

651 **Sy.** Dí tibi, Démea, ómnes sémper ómnia óptata ófferánt.

652 **Mi.** [*sarcastically*] Sýre, procéssisti hódie púlchre. **De.**
[*cheerfully*] Síquidém porro, Mício,

653 tú tuum offícium fácies, átque huic áliquid paúlum praé
manú

654 déderis únde utátur, réddet tíbi citô. **Mi.** [*with mock grati-*
tude] Ístoc víliús!

655   **Ae.** Frúgi homó 'st.   **Sy.** Reddam hércle, dá modô.   **Ae.**
        Áge, patér!   **Mi.** Post cónsulám.

656   **De.** [*cheerfully*] Fáciet.   **Sy.** Ó vir óptime!   **Ae.** Ó patér mi
        féstivíssimé.   [*Exit* Syrus.]

657   **Mi.** [*to* Demea] Quíd istuc?   Quaé res tám repénte móres
        mútavít tuós?

658   Quód prolúbium?   Quaé istaec súbita 'st lárgitás?   **De.**
        Dicám tibí:

659   út id osténderém—quod te ísti fácilem et féstivúm putánt,

660   íd non fíeri ex véra víta néque adeo éx aequo ét bonó,

661   séd ex adséntando, índulgéndo, et lárgiéndo, Mícíó.

662   Núnc adeó si ob eám rem vóbis méa vita ínvisa, Aéschiné,
        'st,

663   quía non iústa iniústa prórsus ómnia ómnino óbsequór,

664   míssa fácio: ecfúndite, émite, fácite quód vobís libét.

665   Séd si id vúltis pótius—quaé vos própter ádulescéntiám

666   mínus vidétis, mágis impénse cúpitis, cónsulitís parúm,

667   haéc reprehéndere ét corrígere me ét secúndare ín locó,

668   écce mé qui id fáciam vóbis.   **Ae.** Tíbi, patér, permíttimús:

669   plús scis quíd facto ópus sit.   Séd de frátre quíd fiét?   **De.**
        Sinó;

670   hábeat; ín istac fínem fáciat.   **Mi.** Ístuc récte.   **Cantor**
        Plaúdité.   [*Exeunt.*]

II

Opening Scene of the Heautontimorúmenos (i.e., The Self-Tormentor), or The Penitent Father

The plays of Terence may seem somewhat conventional after those of Plautus, but they do excel in one respect (not essentially dramatic)—namely, in narration.   This is particularly true of the "exposition" that regularly comprises the first act of a play.   Some of Terence's first acts or scenes are justly famous as pictures of human life and character—stories swiftly and vividly told. Among these perhaps the most celebrated is the first part of the *Heautontimorúmenos*.

The *dramatis personae* in this scene are: MENEDÉMUS, the penitent father; and CHREMES, his neighbor.

Terence's adherence to finer Greek tradition is evidenced by the fact that, at the opening of the play, Menedemus is not a "comic" figure in the modern sense; on the contrary, he is wholly pathetic—even tragic. According to the Greek conception, a "comedy" is a play that deals with humble folk and *ends* happily; a "tragedy," one that deals with gods and heroes and *ends* unhappily. The greatest Greek writer of comedies, Menander, produced plays that "held the mirror up to nature" because they presented human life with laughter and tears commingled. Menedemus is a father who repents bitterly, even fanatically, his severity toward his wayward son. After the son runs away from home, Menedemus imposes upon himself the penance of renouncing all luxury and moves into a humble dwelling (next door to Chremes), where he voluntarily takes up a life of degrading manual drudgery. Chremes, his new neighbor, is an arrant busybody.

The scene represents the adjacent houses of Chremes and Menedemus. Menedemus is discovered toiling in his garden. Chremes, unable longer to contain his curiosity, seeks to elicit from the reticent Menedemus an explanation of all his melancholy toil.

The meter is six-foot iambic.

ACT I

SCENE 1

1 **Ch.** [*approaching* MENEDEMUS *and interrupting his labor*]
    Quamquam haéc intér nos núper nótitia ádmodúm 'st
2 (inde ádeo cum ágrum in próximo híc mercátus és),
3 nec reí fere sáne hoc ámpliús quicquám fuít,
4 tamén vel vírtus túa me vél vicínitás
5 (quod ego ín propínqua párte amícitiaé putó)
6 facit út te audácter móneam et fámiliáritér,

7 quod míhi vidére praéter aétatém tuám
8 facere ét praetér quam rés te adhórtatúr tuá.
9 Nam pró deum átque hominúm fidém, quid vís tibí?
10 Quid quaéris? Ánnos séxagínta nátus és,
11 aut plús eo, út confício. In hís regiónibús
12 meliórem agrúm neque préti maióris némo habét.
13 Servós complúris! Proínde quási nemó siét:
14 ita atténte túte illórum offícia fúngeré.
15 Numquám tam máne egrédior néque tam vésperí
16 domúm revértor, quín te in fúndo cónspicér
17 fodere aút aráre aut áliquid férre. Déniqué
18 nullúm remíttis témpus néque te réspicís.
19 Haec nón voluptáti tibi ésse, sátis certó sció.
20 "Enim" díces "quántum hîc óperis fíat paénitét."
21 Quod in ópere fáciendo óperae cónsumís tuaé,
22 si súmas in íllis éxercéndis, plús agás.
23 **Me.** [*frigidly*] Chremés, tantúmne ab ré tuá 'st otí tibí,
24 aliéna ut cúres éa quae níl ad te áttinént?
25 **Ch.** [*sententiously*] Homó sum: humáni níl a me álienúm
     putó.
26 Vel mé monére hoc vél percóntarí putá:
27 rectúm 'st, ego ut fáciam; nón est, te út detérreám.
28 **Me.** [*wearily*] Mihi síc est úsus; tíbi ut opús factó 'st, facé.
29 **Ch.** [*persisting*] An cuíquam 'st úsus hómini, se út cruciét?
     Me. [*stubbornly*] Mihí!
30 **Ch.** Si quíd labóri 'st, nóllem. Séd quid istúc malí 'st?
31 Quaesó, quid dé te tántum cómmeruísti? **Me.** [*weeping*]
     Eheú!
32 **Ch.** Ne lácruma, atque ístuc quídquid ést fac me út sciám.
33 Ne rétice, né verére, créde inquám mihí:
34 aut cónsolándo aut cónsilio aút re iúveró.
35 **Me.** [*incredulously*] Scire hóc vis? **Ch.** Hác quidem caúsa
     quá dixí tibi.
36 **Me.** Dicétur. [*He starts to resume his work while talking.*]
     Ch. At ístos rástros íntereá tamén
37 adpóne; né labóra. **Me.** Mínime. **Ch.** [*astonished*] Quám
     rem agís?

38 **Me.** Sine mé, vocívum témpus né quod dém mihí
39 labóris. **Ch.** [*taking the mattock away from him*] Nón sinam,
    ínquam. **Me.** Ah, nón aequúm facís.
40 **Ch.** [*hefting the mattock*] Hui, tám gravís hos quaéso? **Me.**
    Síc meritúm 'st meúm.
41 **Ch.** Nunc lóquere. **Me.** [*wearily*] Fílium únicum ádules-
    céntulúm
42 habeo. [*Groaning*] Áh quid díxi? Habére me? Ímmo
    habuí, Chremés:
43 nunc hábeam nécne incértum 'st. **Ch.** Quíd ita istúc?
    Me. Sciés.
44 Est é Coríntho hîc ádvena anús paupérculá.
45 Eius fíliam ílle amáre coépit pérdité,
46 prope út pro uxóre habéret: haéc clam me ómniá.
47 Ubi rém rescívi, coépi nón humánitús
48 neque ut ánimum décuit aégrotum ádulescéntulí
49 tractáre, séd vi et víā pervúlgatā patrúm.
50 Cottídie áccusábam: "Hem tíbine haec díutiús
51 licére spéras fácere, mé vivó patré,
52 amícam ut hábeas própe iam in úxorís locó?
53 Errás, si id crédis, ét me ignóras, Clíniá.
54 Ego té meum ésse díci tántispér voló,
55 dum quód te dígnum 'st fácies; séd si id nón facís,
56 ego quód me in té sit fácere dígnum invéneró.
57 Nulla ádeo ex re ístuc fít nisi éx nimio ótió.
58 Ego istúc aetátis nón amóri operám dabám,
59 sed in Ásiam hinc ábii própter paúperiem átque ibí
60 simúl rem et glóriam ármis bélli répperí."
61 Postrémo adeó res rédiit: ádulescéntulús
62 saepe éadem et gráviter aúdiéndo víctus ést.
63 Aetáte mé putávit ét sapiéntiā
64 plus scíre et próvidére quám se ipsúm sibí.
65 In Ásiam ad régem mílitátum abiít, Chremés.
66 **Ch.** [*shocked*] Quid aís? **Me.** Clam mé proféctus ménsis trís
    abést.
67 **Ch.** [*judiciously*] Ambo áccusándi; etsi íllud ínceptúm tamén
68 animí 'st pudéntis sígnum et nón instrénuí.

69 **Me.** [*sadly*] Ubi cómperi éx eis, quí fuére ei cónscií,
70 domúm revértor maéstus átque animó feré
71 pertúrbato átque incérto prae aégritúdiné.
72 Adsído; accúrrunt sérvi; sóccos détrahúnt;
73 video álios féstináre léctos stérneré,
74 cenam ápparáre; pró se quísque séduló
75 faciébant, quo íllam míhi lenírent míseriám.
76 Ubi vídeo, haec coépi cógitáre: "Hem, tót meā́
77 solíus sollíciti súnt causā̄, út me unum éxpleánt?
78 Ancíllae tót me véstiánt?   Sumptús domí
79 tantós ego sólus fáciam?   Séd gnatum únicúm,
80 quem páriter úti his décuit aút etiam ámpliús,
81 quod illa aétas mágis ad haéc uténda idóneá 'st,
82 eum ego hínc eiéci míserum iniústitiā́ meā́!
83 Maló quidém me quóvis dígnum députém,
84 si id fáciam.   Nam úsque dum flle vítam illám colét
85 inopém, caréns patriam ób meás iniúriás,
86 intérea usque ílli dé me súppliciúm dabó
87 labórans, párcens, quaérens, ílli sérviéns."
88 Ita fácio prórsus.   Níl relínquo in aédibús,
89 nec vás nec véstiméntum.   Cónrasi ómniá.
90 Ancíllas, sérvos, nísi eos qui ópere rústicó
91 faciéndo fácile súmptum exércerént suúm,
92 omnís prodúxi ac véndidi.   Ínscripsi ílicó
93 aedís mercéde.   Quási talénta ad quíndecím
94 coégi.   Agrum húnc mercátus sum.   Hĭ́c me exérceo.
95 Decrévi tántispér me mínus iniúriaé,
96 Chremés, meo gnáto fácere, dúm fiám misér;
97 nec fás esse úllā̄ mé volúptate hĭ́c fruí,
98 nisi ubi ílle huc sálvus rédierít meus párticéps.
99 **Ch.** Ingénio te ésse in líberós lení putó,
100 et illum óbsequéntem, sí quis récte aut cómmodé
101 tractáret.   Vérum néc tu illúm satis nóverás,
102 nec te ílle: hoc quód fit, úbi non vére vívitúr.
103 Tu illúm numquam óstendísti quánti pénderés,
104 nec tíbi ille 'st crédere aúsus quaé 'st aequúm patrí.
105 Quod si ésset fáctum, haec númquam evénissént tibí.

106 **Me.** [*sadly*] Ita rés est, fáteor: péccatum á me máximúm
'st.

107 **Ch.** [*more cheerfully*] Menedéme, at pórro récte spéro, et
illúm tibí

108 salvum ádfutúrum esse híc confído própediém.

109 **Me.** Utinam íta di fáxint! **Ch.** Fácient. Núnc si cómmodúm 'st,

110 Dionýsia híc sunt hódie: apúd me sís voló.

111 **Me.** Non póssum. **Ch.** Cúr non? Quaéso tándem aliquán-
tulúm

112 tibi párce: idem ábsens fácere te hóc vult fíliús.

113 **Me.** Non cónvenít, cui illum ád labórem hinc pépulerím,

114 nunc me ípsum fúgere. **Ch.** Sícine 'st senténtiá?

115 **Me.** Sic. **Ch.** Béne vale. **Me.** Ét tu. [*Exit into his own
house.*] **Ch.** [*shaking his head, sadly*] Lácrimas éxcussít
mihí.

PLOT

In the remainder of the play, the plot takes a turn for the comic.
CLINIA, MENEDEMUS' son, returns. Ignorant of his father's grief and
repentance, he takes refuge from anticipated parental ire with CLI-
TIPHO, son of CHREMES. CHREMES now undertakes to manage everyone's affairs: he persuades MENEDEMUS to teach CLINIA a belated
lesson by *pretending* to refuse a reconciliation, but meanwhile to keep
him supplied with funds (through CHREMES) and to allow him clan-
destinely to marry his sweetheart. CHREMES improves the occasion
by preaching the folly of CLINIA to his own son—not knowing, however, that CLITIPHO also has a sweetheart. Meanwhile the two young
men have "cooked up" a plot to *share* the funds that come from
MENEDEMUS, to pass off CLITIPHO's sweetheart as CLINIA's (thus
gaining access for her to CLITIPHO's house), and to disguise CLINIA's
sweetheart as the other girl's maid. The plot is successfully and
ludicrously carried out, and when finally the truth is discovered,
MENEDEMUS has the laugh on CHREMES. Naturally the young men
are forgiven and live happily ever after.

III

Opening Scene of the Andria, or The Woman Of Andros

The first act of the *Andria* is a clever piece of "exposition" and a charming romantic story.   Mr. Thornton Wilder has taken it as the basis of his novel, *The Woman of Andros*.

A successful play, whether modern or ancient, is an extraordinary piece of condensation.   The action begins at the moment of impending climax, following a long series of preliminary events; and the dramatist must therefore carry us both forward and backward, so to speak.   He spreads a panorama before our eyes, beginning at the *middle* and unrolling it at both ends.   As neither dramatist nor audience can do two things at once, the processes must naturally alternate; but the dramatist must keep them both in view: he must reveal to the audience the series of events that preceded the action of a play and, at the same time, carry the action swiftly forward to its dénouement.   The account of what has already happened comes first, and is called the "exposition."

The simplest and crudest form of exposition is the soliloquy. This may even be distinct from the play proper—i.e., it may constitute the prologue—and the audience be thus unceremoniously informed of preceding events in the story.   But the Greek writers of comedy of manners had already achieved a more artistic technique of exposition by casting it in dialogue form, incorporating it in the play proper, and giving it some simple natural motivation and action of its own.   Combining in this play the *Andria* and *Perinthia* of Menander, Terence produced a lively exposition of this sort.

The characters are: SIMO, an elderly citizen of Athens, who is burdened with a problem of parental authority; and SOSIA, his faithful (if not obsequious) freedman and confidant, who now occupies the position of steward or cook in Simo's household. An interesting development rivets one's attention at the very start.   Enter (on the customary scene) Simo, deferentially attended by Sosia and followed by slaves, carrying a sumptuous assortment of provisions for a feast. The feast, as we soon learn, is intended for the wedding of Simo's son.

Note the care with which the characterization of Simo and Sosia (and their mutual relation) is carried out. Thus this first act, or exposition, may almost be regarded as a play within a play—for Sosia appears only in this scene; there is no further use for him in the rest of the play. A character that serves only to motivate the exposition and then disappears was called by the ancient critics a "protatic," or preliminary, character.

ACT I

Scene 1

1 **Si.** [*to the slaves carrying the provisions*] Vos ístaec íntrô auférte. Abíte. [*Exeunt slaves into* Simo's *house;* Simo *detains* Sosia.] Sósiá,

2 adés dum: paúcis té voló. **So.** [*briskly*] Dictúm putá:

3 nempe út curéntur récte haec? **Si.** Ímmo aliúd. **So.** Quid ést

4 quod tíbi mea árs effícere hoc póssit ámpliús?

5 **Si.** [*solemnly*] Nil ístac ópus est árte ad hánc rem quám paró,

6 sed eís quas sémper ín te intéllexí sitás—

7 fide ét tacitúrnitáte. **So.** [*very curious*] Exspécto quíd velís.

8 **Si.** [*impressively*] Ego póstquam te émi, a párvulo út sempér tibí

9 apúd me iústa et clémens fúerit sérvitús

10 scis. Féci ex sérvo ut ésses líbertús mihí,

11 proptérea quód servíbas líberálitér:

12 quod hábui súmmum prétium pérsolví tibí.

13 **So.** [*taken aback*] In mémoria hábeo. **Si.** Haud múto fáctum. **So.** [*concealing his uneasiness*] Gaúdeó,

14 si tíbi quid féci aut fácio quód placeát, Simó;

15 et id grátum fuísse advérsum te, hábeo grátiám.

16 Sed hóc mihi moléstum 'st: nam ístaec cómmemorátió

17 quasi éxprobrátió 'st immémori béneficí.

18 Quin tu úno vérbo díc, quid ést quod mé velís?
19 **Si.** Ita fáciam.   Hoc prímum in hác re praédicó tibí:
20 quas crédis ésse has nón sunt vérae núptiaé.
21 **So.** Cur símulas ígitur?   **Si.** Rem ómnem a príncipio aúdiés:
22 eo pácto et gnáti vítam et cónsiliúm meúm
23 cognósces ét quid fácere in hác re té velím.
24 Nam is póstquam excéssit éx ephébis, Sósia, ét
25 libérius vivéndi fuít potéstas (nam ánteá
26 quî scíre pósses aút ingénium nósceré,
27 dum aetás metús magíster próhibebánt?   **So.** Itá 'st.)
28 **Si.** . . . quod plérique ómnes fáciunt ádulescéntulí,
29 ut ánimum ad áliquod stúdium adiúngant (aút equós
30 alere aút canés ad vénandi aút ad phílosophós),
31 horum ílle níl egrégie praéter céterá
32 studébat—ét tamen ómnia haéc medíocritér.
33 Gaudébam.   **So.** Nón iniúriā; nam id árbitrór
34 adpríme in víta esse útile, út "ne quíd nimís."
35 **Si.** Sic víta erát: facile ómnis pérferre ác patí;
36 cum quíbus erát cumque únâ, eis sése déderé;
37 eórum stúdiis óbsequi; advérsus néminí;
38 numquám praepónens se íllis—íta ut facíllimé
39 sine invídia laúdem invénias ét amicós parés.
40 **So.** Sapiénter vítam instítuit; námque hoc témporé
41 obséquium amícos, véritás odiúm parít.
42 **Si.** Intérea múlier quaédam abhínc triénniúm
43 ex Ándro cómmigrávit húc vicíniám,
44 inópiā et cógnatórum néglegéntiā
45 coácta, egrégiā fórmā atque aétate íntegrā̂.
46 **So.** Hei, véreor né quid Ándria ádportét malí!
47 **Si.** Primo haéc pudíce vítam párce ac dúritér
48 agébat, lánā ac télā víctum quaéritáns;
49 sed póstquam amáns accéssit prétium póllicéns
50 unús et item álter, íta ut ingénium 'st ómniúm
51 hominum áb labóre próclive ád libídiném,
52 accépit cóndiciónem, deín quaestum óccipít.
53 Qui tum íllam amábant fórte, ita út fit, fíliúm
54 perdúxēre íllûc, sécum ut únâ essét, meúm.

55 Egomét contínuo mécum, "cérte cáptus ést:
56 habet." Óbservábam máne illórum sérvulós
57 veniéntis aút abeúntis: rógitabam, "heús puér,
58 dic sódes, quís heri Chrýsidem hábuit?"—nam Ándriaé
59 illi íd erat nómen. **So.** Téneo. **Si.** Phaédrum aut Clíniám
60 dicébant aút Nicératum. Hí tres túm simúl
61 amábant. "Ého, quid Pámphilús?" "Quid? Sýmbolám
62 dedít, cenávit." Gaúdebam. Ítem alió dié
63 quaerébam: cómperíbam níl ad Pámphilúm
64 quicquam áttinére. Enim véro spéctatúm satís
65 putábam et mágnum exémplum cóntinéntiaé;
66 nam quí cum ingéniis cónflictátur éius modí
67 neque cómmovétur ánimus ín ea ré tamén,
68 scias pósse habére iam ípsum suaé vitaé modúm.
69 Cum id míhi placébat, tum úno ore ómnes ómniá
70 bona dícere ét laudáre fórtunás meás,
71 qui gnátum habérem táli ingénio praéditúm.
72 Quid vérbis ópus est? Hác fama ímpulsús Chremés
73 ultro ád me vénit, únicám gnatám suám
74 cum dóte súmma fílio úxorem út darét.
75 Placuít: despóndi. Hic núptiís dictú'st diés.
76 **So.** Quid ígitur óbstat cúr non fíant? **Si.** Aúdiés.
77 Fere ín diébus paúcis quíbus haec ácta súnt
78 Chrysís vicína haec móritur. **So.** Ó factúm bené!
79 Beásti: hei, métui a Chrýside. **Si.** Íbi tum fíliús
80 cum illís qui amárant Chrýsidem únâ aderát frequéns;
81 curábat únâ fúnus; trístis ínterím,
82 nonnúmquam cónlacrimábat. Plácuit tum íd mihí.
83 Sic cógitábam: "Hic párvae cónsuetúdinís
84 causā húius mórtem tám fert fámiliáritér.
85 Quid si ípse amásset? Quíd hic mihí faciét patrí?"
86 Haec égo putábam esse ómnia húmani íngení
87 mansuétique ánimi offícia. Quíd multís morór?
88 Egomét quoque éius caúsā in fúnus pródeó,
89 nil étiam súspicáns mali. **So.** Hém, quid is ést? **Si.** Sciés.
90 Ecfértur; ímus. Ínterea ínter múlierés,
91 quae ibi áderant, fórte unam áspicio ádulescéntulám,

92 formā . . . **So.** . . . bonā fortásse. **Si.** . . . et vúltu, Sósiá,
93 adeó modésto, adeó venústo, ut níl suprá.
94 Quae cúm mihi lámentári praéter céterás
95 visá 'st, et quía erat fórmā praéter céterás
96 honéstā ac líberáli, accédo ad pédisequás;
97 quae sít rogó.   Sorórem esse áiunt Chrýsidís.
98 Percússit ílico ánimum: "Āttat, hoc íllud ést;
99 hinc íllae lácrimae; haec ílla 'st mísericórdiá."
100 **So.** Quam tímeo quórsum evádas!   **Si.** Fúnus ínterím
101 procédit; séquimur; ád sepúlcrum vénimús;
102 in ígnem impósita 'st; flétur.   Ínterea haéc sorór
103 quam díxi ad flámmam accéssit ímprudéntiús,
104 satis cúm perículo.   Ibi tum éxanimátus Pámphilús
105 bene díssimulátum amórem et célatum índicát:
106 adcúrrit; médiam múlierém compléctitúr;
107 "mea Glýcerium" ínquit "quíd agis? Cúr te is pérditúm?"
108 Tum illa, út consuétum fácile amórem cérnerés,
109 reiécit se ín eum, fléns quam fámiliáritér!
110 **So.** Quid aís?   **Si.** Redeo índe irátus átque aegré feréns—
111 nec sátis ad óbiurgándum caúsae.   Dícerét:
112 "Quid féci?   Quíd commérui aut péccaví, patér?
113 Quae sése in ígnem inícere vóluit, próhibuí,
114 servávi."   Honésta orátió 'st.   **So.** Recté putás;
115 nam si íllum obiúrges, vítae qui aúxiliúm tulít,
116 quid fácias ílli, déderit quí damnum aút malúm?
117 **Si.** Venít Chremés postrídie ád me clámitáns,
118 "indígnum fácinus"; cómperísse Pámphilúm
119 pro uxóre habére hanc péregrinam.   Égo illud séduló
120 negáre fáctum.   Ille ínstat fáctum.   Déniqué
121 ita túm discédo ab íllo, ut quí se fíliám
122 negét datúrum.   **So.** Nón tu ibi gnátum . . . ?   **Si.** Ne
   haéc quidém
123 satis vémens caúsa ad óbiurgándum.   **So.** Quí?   Cědó.
124 **Si.** "Tute ípse his rébus fínem praéscriptí, patér;
125 prope adést cum aliéno móre vívendúm 'st mihí;
126 sine núnc meó me vívere íntereá modó."

127 **So.** Qui igitúr relíctus ést obiúrgandí locús?
128 **Si.** Si própter amórem uxórem nólet dúceré,
129 ea prímum ab íllo animádverténda iniúriá 'st.
130 Et núnc id óperam do, út per fálsas núptiás
131 vera óbiurgándi caúsa sít, si dénegét;
132 simúl scelerátus Dávus, sí quid cónsilí
133 habet, út consúmat núnc, cum níl obsínt dolí—
134 quem ego crédo mánibus pédibusque óbnixe ómniá
135 factúrum, mágis id ádeo, míhi ut incómmodét,
136 quam ut óbsequátur gnáto. **So.** Quáproptér? **Si.** Rogás?
137 Mala méns malus ánimus. Quém quidem egó si sén-
         seró . . .
138 Sed quíd opu'st vérbis? Sín evéniat quód voló,
139 in Pámphilo út nil sít moraé, restát Chremés
140 qui mi éxorándus ést: et spéro cónforé.
141 Nunc tuúm 'st offícium, has béne ut adsímules núptiás,
142 pertérrefácias Dávum, obsérves fíliúm,
143 quid agát, quid cum íllo cónsilí captét. **So.** Sat ést:
144 curábo. **Si.** Eámus núnciam íntrô: i praé, sequór.

PLOT

The remaining action of the play moves rapidly to its climax and revolves about a conflict of wits between DAVUS, the intriguing slave, and SIMO. Seeing through SIMO's plans, DAVUS gives the former's son, PAMPHILUS, cunning advice—namely, to *assent* unconditionally to the mock wedding and thus embarrass his father—for SIMO will have no one for him to marry. In the nick of time SIMO then obtains CHREMES' consent to the immediate marriage of his daughter PHILU-MENA with PAMPHILUS, as originally planned. Thus the tables are turned on DAVUS; but he counters by producing the newborn child of PAMPHILUS and GLYCERIUM. And so on, with other complications, until ultimately it is discovered (of course) that GLYCERIUM too is CHREMES' daughter—his long-lost daughter, supposedly shipwrecked in infancy but actually saved and brought up in Andros. Thus the much-disputed wedding takes place after all—but between PAMPHILUS and GLYCERIUM!

Rhetorica Ad Herennium

(PUBLISHED IN *86* B.C.; AUTHOR UNKNOWN.)

The so-called *Rhetorica ad Herennium* owes its preservation to the glamor of a great name, for at the beginning of the Dark Ages it was ascribed to Cicero, inasmuch as it resembles (and occasionally reproduces almost word for word) his genuine rhetorical treatise, *De Inventione*.[1] The author of the *Rhetorica ad Herennium*, whoever he may have been (some claim that he was Cornificius), was a cultured man of affairs. His treatise, written about 86 B.C., is a protest against academic theory. It is sound and practical, with flashes of genius. The author's aims are admirably set forth in a concise and unostentatious preface, as follows:

PREFACE

1 Etsi, negotiis familiaribus impediti, vix satis otium studio
2 suppeditare possumus, et id ipsum quod datur otii libentius
3 in philosophia consumere consuevimus, tamen tua nos, C.
4 Herenni, voluntas commovit, ut de ratione dicendi con-
5 scriberemus, ne aut tuā causā noluisse aut fugisse nos labo-
6 rem putares. Et eo studiosius hoc negotium suscepimus,
7 quod te non sine causa velle cognoscere rhetoricam intelle-
8 gebamus. Non enim in se parum fructūs habet copia
9 dicendi et commoditas orationis, si rectā intellegentiā et
10 definitā moderatione animi gubernetur. Quas ob res illa,
11 quae Graeci scriptores inanis arrogantiae causā sibi ad-
12 sumpserunt, reliquimus: nam illi, ne parum multa scisse
13 viderentur, ea conquisiverunt, quae nihil attinebant, ut ars
14 difficilior cognitu putaretur. Nos ea, quae videbantur ad
15 rationem dicendi pertinere, sumpsimus, non enim, spe
16 quaestūs aut gloriā commoti, venimus ad scribendum, quem-
17 admodum ceteri; sed ut industriā nostrā tuae morem
18 geramus voluntati. Nunc ne nimium longa sumatur ora-
19 tio, de re dicere incipiemus, si te unum illud monuerimus,
20 artem sine assiduitate dicendi non multum iuvare, ut in-

[1] See p. 182 for a discussion of this work.

21 tellegas hanc rationem praeceptionis ad exercitationem ac-
22 comodari oportere.

SELECTIONS FROM BOOK IV

The treatise itself is in four books. The first three books deal chiefly with "invention" (i.e., the planning of one's case); this is followed by brief chapters on "disposition" (i.e., the presentation of one's case), on voice and gesture, and on memory systems (identical with those in vogue today). The fourth book, which is the most interesting part of the work, treats of style.

[1]

The Three Styles

An interesting feature of the fourth book is the exposition of the three generic types of style (*figurae*): the "formal" or "lofty" (*gravis*), the "medium" (*mediocris*), and the "informal" or "colloquial" (*extenuata*). The author has the temerity to illustrate these three styles by sample compositions of his own—a procedure that horrified the timid pedants who wrote in Greek and drew their examples religiously from the classic masters, chiefly from Demosthenes:

1 Sunt igitur tria genera, quae genera nos figuras appella-
2 mus, in quibus omnis oratio non vitiosa consumitur: unam
3 gravem, alteram mediocrem, tertiam extenuatam vocamus.
4 Gravis est, quae constat ex verborum gravium et lēvi et
5 ornatā constructione. Mediocris est, quae constat ex
6 humiliore neque tamen ex infima et pervulgatissima verb-
7 orum dignitate. Attenuata est, quae demissa est usque ad
8 usitatissimam puri consuetudinem sermonis.

[a] Example of the formal, or lofty, style—appropriate to emotional appeals:

THE TRAITOR

[*The traitor is beyond the pale; he deserves no mercy.*]

1 "Nam quis est vestrum, iudices, qui satis idoneam possit in
2 eum poenam cogitare, qui prodere hostibus patriam cogi-

3 tarit? Quod maleficium cum hoc scelere comparari, quod
4 huic maleficio dignum supplicium potest inveniri? In iis,
5 qui violassent ingenuum, matrem familias constuprassent,
6 maxima supplicia maiores consumpserunt: huic truculentis-
7 simo ac nefario facinori singularem poenam non reliquerunt.
8 Atque in aliis maleficiis ad singulos aut ad paucos ex alieno
9 peccato iniuria pervenit: huius sceleris qui sunt adfines, uno
10 consilio universis civibus atrocissimas calamitates machinan-
11 tur. O feros animos! O crudeles cogitatiónes! O derelictos
12 homines ab humanitate! qui id agere ausi sunt aut cogitare
13 potuerunt, quo pacto hostes, revulsis maiorum sepulcris,
14 deiectis moenibus, ovantes inruerent in civitatem; quo modo,
15 deūm templis spoliatis, optimatibus trucidatis, aliis abreptis
16 in servitutem, matribus familias et ingenuis sub hostilem
17 libidinem subiectis, urbs acerbissimo concidat incendio con-
18 flagrata; qui se non putant id, quod voluerint, ad exitum
19 perduxisse, nisi sanctissimae patriae miserandum scelerati
20 viderint cinerem. Nequeo verbis consequi, iudices, in-
21 dignitatem rei, sed neglegentius id fero, quia vos mei non
22 egetis. Vester enim vos animus amantissimus rei publicae
23 facile edocet, ut eum, qui fortunas omnium voluerit prodere,
24 praecipitem proturbetis ex ea civitate, quam iste hostium
25 spurcissimorum dominatu nefario voluit obruere."

[b] Example of the medium style—appropriate to logical
argumentation:

THE REVOLT OF THE FREGELLANI

[*Fregellae, a small allied town, has risen in revolt against the vast
territory of Rome. The speaker argues that this revolt must have
been instigated by more powerful and unknown foes.*]

1   " Quibuscum bellum gerimus, iudices, videtis: cum sociis!
2 qui pro nobis pugnare et imperium nostrum nobiscum simul
3 virtute et industriā conservare soliti sunt. Hi cum se et
4 suas opes et copiam necessario norunt; tum vero nihilo
5 minus propter propinquitatem et omnium rerum societatem,

6 quid omnibus rebus populus Romanus posset, scire et
7 existimare poterant. Hi cum deliberassent nobiscum bel-
8 lum gerere, quaeso, quae res erat, qua freti bellum suscipere
9 conarentur, cum multo maximam partem sociorum in offi-
10 cio manere intellegerent, cum sibi non multitudinem mili-
11 tum, non idoneos imperatores, non pecuniam publicam
12 praesto esse viderent, non denique ullam rem, quae res
13 pertineret ad bellum administrandum? Si cum finitimis de
14 finibus bellum gererent, si totum certamen in uno proelio
15 positum putarent, tamen omnibus rebus instructiores et ap-
16 paratiores venirent; nedum illi imperium orbis terrae—cui
17 imperio omnes gentes reges nationes partim vi partim volun-
18 tate concesserunt, cum aut armis aut liberalitate a populo
19 Romano superati essent—ad se transferre tantulis viribus
20 conarentur. Quaeret aliquis: 'Quid? Fregellani non sua
21 sponte conati sunt?' Eo quidem isti minus facile conaren-
22 tur, quod, illi quemadmodum discessissent, videbant. Nam
23 rerum imperiti, qui unius cuiusque rei de rebus ante gestis
24 exempla petere non possunt, ii per imprudentiam facillime
25 deducuntur in fraudem; at ii, qui sciunt quid aliis acciderit,
26 facile ex aliorum eventis suis rationibus possunt providere.
27 Nulla igitur re inducti, nulla spe freti arma sustulerunt?
28 Quis hoc credet, tantam amentiam quemquam tenuisse, ut
29 imperium populi Romani temptare auderet nullis copiis
30 fretus? Ergo aliquid fuisse necessum est. Quid aliud, nisi
31 id, quod dico, potest esse?"

[c] Example of the informal, or colloquial, style—appropriate
to narrative of everyday events:

THE BATHHOUSE BRAWLER

*[The lawyer for the defense describes his client's encounter with a
bathhouse brawler.]*

1   "Nam ut forte hic in balneas venit, coepit, postquam per-
2 fusus est, defricari; deinde, ubi visum est ut in alveum
3 descenderet, ecce tibi iste de transverso: 'Heus' inquit

4 'adulescens, pueri tui modô me pulsarunt; satisfacias
5 oportet.' Hic, qui id aetatis ab ignoto praeter consuetud-
6 inem appellatus esset, erubuit.   Iste clarius et eadem et alia
7 dicere coepit.   Hic vix 'tamen' inquit 'sine me consider-
8 are.'   Tum vero iste clamare voce ista, quae vel rabulae
9 cuivis rubores elicere potest. . . . Conturbatus est adules-
10 cens; nec mirum—cui etiam nunc paedagogi lites ad
11 auriculas versarentur, imperito huiusmodi conviciorum.
12 Ubi enim vidisset scurram exhausto rubore, qui se putaret
13 nihil habere quod de existimatione perderet, omnia sine
14 famae detrimento facere posse?''

[2]

What to Avoid in the Three Styles

In conclusion, the author presents some brief examples of what
the speaker should *avoid*—i.e., bombast, incoherence, and dullness.

[a] Bombast: Est autem cavendum, ne, dum haec
2 genera consectemur, in finitima et propinqua vitia veniamus.
3 Nam gravi figurae, quae laudanda est, propinqua est ea
4 quae fugienda; quae recte videbitur appellari, si "sufflata"
5 nominabitur: nam ita ut corporis bonam habitudinem tumor
6 imitatur saepe, item gravis oratio saepe imperitis videtur ea
7 quae turget et inflata est, cum aut novis aut priscis verbis
8 aut duriter aliunde translatis aut gravioribus quam res
9 postulat aliquid dicitur, hoc modo:

(THE TRAITOR)

10 "Nam qui perduellionibus venditat patriam, non satis
11 supplicii dederit, si praeceps in Neptunias depulsus erit
12 lacunas: poenite igitur istum, qui montes belli fabricatus est,
13 campos sustulit pacis."

14 In hoc genus plerique cum declinantur, specie gravitatis
15 falluntur nec perspicere possunt orationis tumorem.

[b] Incoherence: Qui in mediocre genus orationis profecti
2 sunt, si pervenire eo non potuerunt, errantes perveniunt ad
3 confine genus eius generis, quod appellamus "dissolutum,"

4 eo quod fluctuat huc et illûc nec potest confirmate neque
5 viriliter sese expedire. Id est huiusmodi:

(THE REVOLT OF THE FREGELLANI)

6 "Socii nostri, cum belligerare nobiscum vellent, profecto
7 ratiocinati essent etiam atque etiam, quid possent facere, si
8 quidem sua sponte facerent et non haberent hinc adiutores
9 multos, malos homines et audaces: solent enim diu cogitare
10 omnes, qui magna negotia volunt agere."

11 Non potest huiusmodi sermo tenere attentum auditorem;
12 diffluit enim totus neque quicquam comprehendens per-
13 fectis verbis amplectitur.

[c] Dullness: Qui non possunt in illa facetissima verb-
2 orum attenuatione commode versari, veniunt ad aridum et
3 exsangue genus orationis, quod non alienum est "exile"
4 nominari, cuiusmodi est hoc:

(THE BATHHOUSE BRAWLER)

5 "Nam istic in balineis accessit ad hunc; postea dicit 'hic
6 tuus servus me pulsavit.' Postea dicit hic illi 'considera-
7 bo.' Post ille convicium fecit et magis magisque praesente
8 multis clamavit."

9 Frivolus hic quidem iam et illiberalis est sermo; non enim
10 est adeptus id quod habet attenuata figura: puris et electis
11 verbis compositam orationem.

[3]

Definitions and Examples of Familiar Themes

Most of these definitions are rather technical and the illustra-
tive examples of the briefest, but in a few instances the author has
developed his theme more fully and has produced a picture or a
story quite capable of standing by itself—e.g.:

[a] *Notatio*, or depiction of a type of character: Here our
author introduces a complete essay—patterned after the fascinating and witty character sketches of Theophrastus:[1]

---

[1] The Greek philosopher Theophrastus, originator of this type of sketch,
died about two hundred years before the *Rhetorica ad Herennium* was written.
His work, entitled *Characters*, was very popular in the XVII century and was
imitated by English and French writers—notably La Bruyère. Other ramifications of the art of character-sketching lie in comedy and satire.

1   Notatio est cum alicuius natura certis describitur signis,
2   quae, sicuti notae quaedam, naturae sunt attributa: ut si
3   velis non divitem, sed ostentatorem pecuniosi, describere:

THE SIMULATOR OF WEALTH, OR THE SHAM MILLIONAIRE

4   "Iste," inquias, "iudices, qui se dici divitem putat esse
5   praeclarum, primum nunc videte, quo vultu nos intueatur.
6   Nonne vobis videtur dicere, 'darem, si mihi molesti non
7   essetis'?   Cum vero sinistrā mentum sublevavit, existimat
8   se gemmae nitore et auri splendore aspectus omnium per-
9   stringere.
10   "Cum puerum respicit hunc unum, quem ego novi—vos
11   non arbitror—, alio nomine appellat, deinde alio atque alio.
12   'Tu' inquit 'veni, Sannio, ne quid isti barbari turbent'; ut
13   ignoti, qui audiunt, unum putent selegi de multis.   Ei
14   dicit in aurem, ut aut domi lectuli sternantur, aut ab
15   avunculo rogetur Aethiops qui ad balneas veniat, aut
16   asturconi locus ante ostium suum detur, aut aliquid falso
17   gloriae comparetur.   Deinde exclamat, ut omnes audiant:
18   'videto, ut diligenter numerentur, si potest, ante noctem.'
19   Puer, qui iam bene naturam novit, 'tu plures mittas opor-
20   tet,' inquit, 'si hodie vis transnumerari.'   'Age,' inquit,
21   'duc tecum Libanum et Sosiam.'   'Sane.'
22   "Deinde casu veniunt hospites homini, quos iste, dum
23   splendide peregrinatur, invitarat.   Ex ea re homo hercule
24   sane conturbatur, sed tamen a vitio naturae non recedit:
25   'bene' inquit 'facitis, cum venitis, sed rectius fecissetis, si
26   ad me domum rectâ abissetis.'   'Id fecissemus,' inquiunt, 'si
27   domum novissemus.'   'At istud quidem facile fuit undelibet
28   invenire; verum ite mecum.'   Sequuntur illi.   Sermo in-
29   terea huius consumitur omnis in ostentatione.   Quaerit, in
30   agris frumenta cuiusmodi sint; negat se, quia villae incensae
31   sint, accedere posse nec aedificare etiamnunc audere; 'tam-
32   etsi in Tusculano quidem coepi insanire et in isdem funda-
33   mentis aedificare.'   Dum haec loquitur, venit in aedes
34   quasdam, in quibus sodalitium erat eodem die futurum,
35   quô iste, pro notitia domini aedium, ingreditur cum hospiti-
36   bus.   'Hîc' inquit 'habito.'   Perspicit argentum, quod erat

37 expositum; visit triclinium stratum; probat. Accedit servu-
38 lus; dicit homini clare, dominum iam venturum, si velit exire.
39 'Itane?' inquit. 'Eamus, hospites; frater venit ex Falerno;
40 ego illi obviam pergam; vos huc decimā venitote.' Hospites
41 discedunt. Iste se raptim domum suam conicit; illi decimā,
42 quô iussi erant, veniunt. Quaerunt hunc; reperiunt, domus
43 cuia sit; in diversorium, derisi, conferunt sese.
44 "Vident hominem postridie, narrant, expostulant, ac-
45 cusant. Ait iste, eos, similitudine loci deceptos, angiporto
46 deerrasse; contra valetudinem suam ad noctem multam ex-
47 spectasse. Sannioni puero negotium dederat, ut vasa,
48 vestimenta, pueros rogaret. Servulus non inurbanus satis
49 strenue et concinne compararat. Iste hospites domum
50 deducit; ait se aedes maximas cuidam amico ad nuptias
51 commodasse. Nuntiat puer, argentum repeti: pertimuerat
52 enim qui commodarat. 'Apage,' inquit, 'aedes commodavi,
53 familiam dedi: argentum quoque vult? Tametsi hospites
54 habeo, tamen utatur licet; nos Samiis delectabimur.' —
55 Quid ego, quae deinde efficeret, narrem? Eiusmodi est
56 hominis natura, ut, quae singulis diebus efficiat gloriā atque
57 ostentatione, ea vix annuo sermone enarrare possim."
58 Huiusmodi notationes, quae describunt, quid consentan-
59 eum sit cuiusque naturae, vehementer habent magnam de-
60 lectationem, totam enim naturam cuiuspiam ponunt ante
61 oculos: aut gloriosi (ut nos exempli causā coeperamus) aut
62 invidi aut timidi aut avari, ambitiosi, amatoris, luxuriosi,
63 furis, quadruplatoris; denique cuiusvis studium protrahi
64 potest in medium tali notatione.

[b] *Sermocinatio,* or dramatic dialogue: Sermocinatio est,
2 cum alicui personae sermo attribuitur, et is exponitur cum
3 ratione dignitatis, hoc modo:

THE PITILESS MURDERER

[*The murderer is a hard-boiled army officer; the victim, a saintly
philosopher. Knowing that escape is impossible, the latter is
resigned to his fate and dies like a Christian martyr. We may imagine that such a scene took place during the civil wars and proscrip-*

*tions of Marius and Sulla, when private grudges were avenged and
the wealthy ruthlessly plundered.   The orator or lawyer here appeals
to the sympathy of the jury by his vivid dramatic description, in
which he makes effective use of dialogue.*]

4   "Cum militibus urbs redundaret, et omnes, timore op-
5   pressi, domi continerentur, venit iste cum sago, gladio suc-
6   cinctus, tenens iaculum; tres adulescentes homines simili
7   .ornatu subsequuntur. Inrupit in aedes subito; deinde
8   magnā voce 'ubi est iste beatus' inquit 'aedium dominus?
9   Quin mihi praesto fuit? Quid tacetis?' Hîc alii omnes,
10   stupidi timore, obmutuerunt; uxor illius infelicissimi cum
11   maximo fletu ad istius pedes abiecit sese; 'parce' inquit 'et
12   per quae tibi dulcissima sunt in vita, miserere nostri;
13   noli exstinguere exstinctos; fer mansuete fortunam; nos
14   quoque fuimus beati: nosce te esse hominem.' 'Quin illum
15   mihi datis, ac vos auribus meis opplorare desinitis? Non
16   abibat.' Illi nuntiatur interea venisse istum et clamore
17   maximo mortem minari. Quod simul ut audivit, 'heus'
18   inquit 'Gorgia, absconde pueros; defende; fac ut incolumis
19   sit adulescentia.' Vix haec dixerat, cum ecce iste praesto!
20   'Sedes,' inquit 'audax? Non vox mea tibi vitam ademit?
21   Exple meas inimicitias, et iracundiam satura tuo sanguine.'
22   Ille cum magno spiritu 'verebar' inquit 'ne plane victus
23   essem. Nunc video. Tu mecum contendere non vis, ubi
24   superari turpissimum et superare pulcherrimum est: inter-
25   ficere vis. Occidar equidem, sed victus non peribo.' 'Tu
26   in extremo vitae tempore es et sententias eloqueris, neque ei,
27   quem vides dominari, vis supplicare?' Tum mulier: 'immo
28   iste quidem rogat et supplicat; sed tu, quaeso, commovere;
29   et tu per deos' inquit 'hunc amplexare: dominus est.   Vicit
30   hic te: vince tu nunc animum.' 'Quid non desinis,' inquit,
31   'uxor, loqui quae me digna non sint? Tace, et quae curanda
32   sunt, cura. Tu cessas, mihi vitam, tibi omnem bene vivendi
33   spem meā morte eripere?' Iste mulierem reppulit ab se
34   lamentantem; illi nescioquid incipienti dicere, quod dignum
35   videlicet illius virtute esset, gladium in latere defixit."

36   Puto in hoc exemplo datos esse uni cuique sermones ad
37   dignitatem accomodatos; id quod oportet in hoc genere
38   conservare.

THIRD PERIOD

(*85*–43 B.C.)

The Ciceronian Era. Chief extant authors:
Caesar, Cicero, Lucretius, and Catullus.

The Third Period

HAVING passed through childhood and youthful apprenticeship, Roman literature had now reached maturity—a maturity whose vigor was to endure for some two hundred years, as long as the Latin race dominated the world. In their consciousness of power, the Romans gave full and untrammeled expression to national ideals and exploits. The study and imitation of Greek masterpieces did not cease—it was intensified, if anything; but the pupils had so nearly attained the stature of their masters, that the inspiration of the older literature bore fruit in genuine (if not very original) works of art. Thus the Romans created an immortal literature, far greater than their own unguided efforts could ever have achieved.

The Ciceronian era comprised roughly the first half-century of this long period of mature achievement. These same years were also the *last* half-century of the so-called "Republic," when the Roman Commonwealth was endeavoring to administer a great over-sea empire through the medium of a superannuated system of local government. The hectic political and social life of this ill-adjusted period encouraged rather than repressed the rapid extension of culture. Artistic taste became widespread among the aristocracy; and Greek philosophy replaced an outworn national religion among the educated. Freedom of thought and laxity of moral standards characterized society more than at any other time in Roman history. Poetry reached its zenith of spontaneity; prose literature, influenced by existing political conditions, bore the constant impress of the spoken word—of parliamentary debate, or of forensic and military harangue. For the most part, literature was *of* and *for* the present—a cross section of contemporary life.

C. JULIUS CAESAR

(Born in 100 B.C.; active from *80*–44.)

His Works

C. Julius Caesar was a man of extraordinary gifts in many fields. His political prominence he owed primarily to his greatness as an orator; unfortunately none of his speeches are preserved. He was noted for his purity of style, and a single illuminating sentence on this point has been preserved from his theoretical treatise on style (*de Analogia, ad Marcum Tullium Ciceronem, libri duo*)—, which he found time to compose while crossing the Alps in the midst of his Gallic campaigns: *Habe semper in memoria atque in pectore, ut tamquam scopulum sic fugias inauditum atque insolens verbum.*

The few extant letters of Caesar, incidentally preserved by Cicero, are well worth reading. There are six of them, all dealing with events that occurred in March and April of the year 49 B.C.

Caesar's fame as a writer now rests on his *Commentaries: de Bello Gallico* and *de Bello Civili.* These masterpieces belonged ostensibly to a type of literature often produced at Rome—namely, memoirs. Many men of affairs who played important parts in the last century of the Republic published autobiographical memoirs, from which the historian might quarry—by correcting, supplementing, and discounting! But as Cicero says, Caesar's *Commentaries* were history itself, clarified in his own mind before it was recorded in matchless form and style. He alone combined the functions of doer and recorder.

I

Letters

[1]

Written in March, 49 B.C.; an open letter to Oppius and Balbus, his agents in Rome. Caesar had captured Domitius and his army at Corfinium, and had treated them with clemency:

1 CAESAR OPPIO CORNELIO SAL. Gaudeo mehercule vos
2 significare litteris, quam valde probetis ea, quae apud

3 Corfinium sunt gesta. Consilio vestro utar libenter—et hoc
4 libentius, quod mea sponte facere constitueram ut quam
5 lenissimum me praeberem, et Pompeium darem operam ut
6 reconciliarem. Temptemus, hoc modo si possumus omnium
7 voluntates recuperare et diuturnā victoriā uti, quoniam
8 reliqui crudelitate odium effugere non potuerunt neque
9 victoriam diutius tenere, praeter unum L. Sullam—quem
10 imitaturus non sum. Haec nova sit ratio vincendi, ut
11 misericordia et liberalitate nos muniamus. Id quemad-
12 modum fieri possit, nonnulla mihi in mentem veniunt et
13 multa reperiri possunt. De his rebus rogo vos ut cogita-
14 tionem suscipiatis. N. Magium, Pompeii praefectum, de-
15 prehendi. Scilicet meo instituto usus sum et eum statim
16 missum feci. Iam duo praefecti fabrum Pompeii in meam
17 potestatem venerunt et a me missi sunt. Si volent grati esse,
18 debebunt Pompeium hortari, ut malit mihi esse amicus
19 quam iis, qui et illi et mihi semper fuerunt inimicissimi,
20 quorum artificiis effectum est ut res publica in hunc statum
21 perveniret.

[2]

Written early in March, 49 B.C., to Cicero:

1 CAESAR IMP. S. D. CICERONI IMP. Cum Furnium nos-
2 trum tantum vidissem neque loqui neque audire meo com-
3 modo potuissem, properarem atque essem in itinere prae-
4 missis iam legionibus, praeterire tamen non potui, quin et
5 scriberem ad te et illum mitterem gratiasque agerem, etsi
6 hoc et feci saepe et saepius mihi facturus videor. Ita de me
7 mereris. Imprimis a te peto, quoniam confido me celeriter
8 ad Urbem venturum, ut te ibi videam, ut tuo consilio, gratia,
9 dignitate, ope omnium rerum uti possim. Ad propositum
10 revertar; festinationi meae brevitatique litterarum ignosces.
11 Reliqua ex Furnio cognosces.

[3]

Written in March, 49 B.C., and sent by Cicero to Atticus:

1 CICERO ATTICO SAL. Cum quod scriberem ad te, nihil
2 haberem, tamen, ne quem diem intermitterem, has dedi

3 litteras. A. d. VI K. Caesarem Sinuessae mansurum nun-
4 tiabant. Ab eo mihi litterae redditae sunt a. d. VII K.,
5 quibus iam "opes" meas, non ut superioribus litteris "opem"
6 exspectat. Cum eius clementiam Corfiniensem illam per
7 litteras collaudavissem, rescripsit, hoc exemplo:

8   "CAESAR IMP. CICERONI IMP. SAL. DIC. Recte auguraris
9 de me—bene enim tibi cognitus sum—nihil a me abesse
10 longius crudelitate. Atque ego cum ex ipsa re magnam
11 capio voluptatem, tum meum factum probari abs te trium-
12 pho gaudio. Neque illud me movet, quod ii, qui a me
13 dimissi sunt, discessisse dicuntur, ut mihi rursus bellum in-
14 ferrent. Nihil enim malo quam et me mei similem esse et
15 illos sui. Tu velim mihi ad Urbem praesto sis, ut tuis con-
16 siliis atque opibus, ut consuevi, in omnibus rebus utar.
17 Dolabellā tuo nihil scito mihi esse iucundius. Hanc adeo
18 habebo gratiam illi; neque enim aliter facere poterit. Tanta
19 eius humanitas; is sensus, ea in me est benevolentia."

[4]

Written on April 16, 49 B.C., on his way to Spain; a plea to
Cicero to remain neutral:

1   CAESAR IMP. SAL. D. CICERONI IMP. Etsi te nihil temere,
2 nihil imprudenter facturum iudicaram, tamen permotus
3 hominum famā scribendum ad te existimavi et pro nostra
4 benevolentia petendum, ne quô progredereris proclinatā iam
5 re, quô integrā etiam progrediendum tibi non existimares.
6 Namque et amicitiae graviorem iniuriam feceris et tibi
7 minus commode consulueris, si non fortunae obsecutus
8 videbere (omnia enim secundissima nobis, adversissima illis
9 accidisse videntur), nec causam secutus (eadem enim tum
10 fuit, cum ab eorum consiliis abesse iudicasti), sed meum
11 aliquod factum condemnavisse; quo mihi gravius abs te nil
12 accidere potest. Quod ne facias, pro iure nostrae amicitiae
13 a te peto. Postremo quid viro bono et quieto et bono civi
14 magis convenit quam abesse a civilibus controversiis?
15 Quod nonnulli cum probarent, periculi causā sequi non

16 potuerunt; tu explorato et vitae meae testimonio et ami-
17 citiae iudicio neque tutius neque honestius reperies quic-
18 quam quam ab omni contentione abesse. XV Kal.
19 Maias ex itinere.

II

De Bello Gallico

CAESAR'S CONFERENCE WITH ARIOVISTUS

[*Invited across the Rhine by the Sequanian faction of the Gauls,
the Germans, under Ariovistus, had enslaved the Sequanians and
were threatening to overrun the country. Caesar espoused the cause
of the Aeduan faction, over which the Romans had already exercised
a protectorate for three years, and posed as the deliverer of all the
Gauls.*]

1 Planities erat magna et in ea tumulus terrenus satis
2 grandis. Hic locus aequo fere spatio a castris utriusque
3 aberat. Eô, ut erat dictum, ad conloquium venerunt.
4 Legionem Caesar, quam equis devexerat, passibus CC ab eo
5 tumulo constituit; item equites Ariovisti pari intervallo
6 constiterunt. Ariovistus, ex equis ut conloquerentur et
7 praeter se denos ut ad conloquium adducerent, postulavit.
8 Ubi eô ventum est, Caesar initio orationis sua senatusque in
9 eum beneficia commemoravit, quod rex appellatus esset ab
10 senatu, quod amicus, quod munera amplissima missa; quam
11 rem et paucis contigisse et ab Romanis pro maximis
12 hominum officiis consuesse tribui docebat; illum, cum
13 neque aditum neque causam postulandi iustam haberet,
14 beneficio ac liberalitate sua ac senatus ea praemia consecu-
15 tum. Docebat etiam, quam veteres quamque iustae
16 causae necessitudinis ipsis cum Aeduis intercederent, quae
17 senatus consulta quotiens quamque honorifica in eos facta
18 essent, ut omni tempore totius Galliae principatum Aedui
19 tenuissent, prius etiam quam nostram amicitiam adpetis-
20 sent. Populi Romani hanc esse consuetudinem, ut socios
21 atque amicos non modo sui nihil deperdere, sed gratia,

22 dignitate, honore auctiores velit esse; quod vero ad amici-
23 tiam populi Romani attulissent, id iis eripi quis pati posset?
24 Postulavit deinde eadem, quae legatis in mandatis dederat:
25 ne aut Aeduis aut eorum sociis bellum inferret; obsides red-
26 deret; si nullam partem Germanorum domum remittere
27 posset, at ne quos amplius Rhenum transire pateretur.
28 Ariovistus ad postulata Caesaris pauca respondit, de
29 suis virtutibus multa praedicavit: Transisse Rhenum sese
30 non sua sponte, sed rogatum et arcessitum a Gallis; non
31 sine magna spe magnisque praemiis domum propinquosque
32 reliquisse; sedes habere in Gallia ab ipsis concessas, obsides
33 ipsorum voluntate datos; stipendium capere iure belli,
34 quod victores victis imponere consuerint. Non sese Gallis,
35 sed Gallos sibi bellum intulisse: omnes Galliae civitates
36 ad se oppugnandum venisse ac contra se castra habuisse;
37 eas omnes copias a se uno proelio pulsas ac superatas esse.
38 Si iterum experiri velint, se iterum paratum esse decertare;
39 si pace uti velint, iniquum esse de stipendio recusare,
40 quod sua voluntate ad id tempus dependerint. Amicitiam
41 populi Romani sibi ornamento et praesidio, non detrimento
42 esse oportere, atque se hac spe petisse. Si per populum
43 Romanum stipendium remittatur et dediticii subtrahantur,
44 non minus libenter sese recusaturum populi Romani amici-
45 tiam, quam adpetierit. Quod multitudinem Germanorum
46 in Galliam traducat, id se sui muniendi, non Galliae im-
47 pugnandae causā facere: eius rei testimonio esse, quod
48 nisi rogatus non venerit et quod bellum non intulerit, sed
49 defenderit. Se prius in Galliam venisse quam populum
50 Romanum. Numquam ante hoc tempus exercitum populi
51 Romani Galliae provinciae finibus egressum. Quid sibi
52 vellet? Cur in suas possessiones venerit? Provinciam
53 suam hanc esse Galliam, sicut illam nostram. Ut ipsi
54 concedi non oporteret, si in nostros fines impetum faceret,
55 sic item nos esse iniquos, quod in suo iure se interpel-
56 laremus. Quod fratres Aeduos appellatos diceret, non se
57 tam barbarum neque tam imperitum esse rerum, ut non
58 sciret neque bello Allobrogum proximo Aeduos Romanis

59 auxilium tulisse neque ipsos in his contentionibus, quas
60 Aedui secum et cum Sequanis habuissent, auxilio populi
61 Romani usos esse. Debere se suspicari, simulatā Caesarem
62 amicitiā, quod exercitum in Gallia habeat, sui opprimendi
63 causā habere. Qui nisi decedat atque exercitum deducat ex
64 his regionibus, sese illum non pro amico, sed pro hoste
65 habiturum. Quod si eum interfecerit, multis sese nobilibus
66 principibusque populi Romani gratum esse facturum: id se
67 ab ipsis per eorum nuntios compertum habere, quorum
68 omnium gratiam atque amicitiam eius morte redimere
69 posset. Quod si discessisset et liberam possessionem Galliae
70 sibi tradidisset, magno se illum praemio remuneraturum et,
71 quaecumque bella geri vellet, sine ullo eius labore et
72 periculo confecturum.

73   Multa a Caesare in eam sententiam dicta sunt, quare
74 negotio desistere non posset: neque suam neque populi
75 Romani consuetudinem pati, uti optime merentes socios
76 desereret, neque se iudicare Galliam potius esse Ariovisti
77 quam populi Romani. Bello superatos esse Arvernos et
78 Rutenos a Q. Fabio Maximo, quibus populus Romanus
79 ignovisset neque in provinciam redegisset neque stipendium
80 imposuisset. Quod si antiquissimum quodque tempus
81 spectari oporteret, populi Romani iustissimum esse in Gallia
82 imperium; si iudicium senatus observari oporteret, liberam
83 debere esse Galliam, quam bello victam suis legibus uti
84 voluisset.

85   Dum haec in conloquio geruntur, Caesari nuntiatum est
86 equites Ariovisti propius tumulum accedere et ad nostros
87 adequitare, lapides telaque in nostros conicere. Caesar
88 loquendi finem fecit seque ad suos recepit suisque imperavit,
89 ne quod omnino telum in hostes reicerent. Nam etsi sine
90 ullo periculo legionis delectae cum equitatu proelium fore
91 videbat, tamen committendum non putabat, ut pulsis
92 hostibus dici posset eos a se per fidem in conloquio circum-
93 ventos. Posteaquam in vulgus militum elatum est, qua
94 arrogantia in conloquio Ariovistus usus omni Gallia Romanis
95 interdixisset impetumque in nostros eius equites fecissent,

96 eaque res conloquium ut diremisset, multo maior alacritas
97 studiumque pugnandi maius exercitui iniectum est.
98   Biduo post Ariovistus ad Caesarem legatos misit: Velle
99 se de his rebus, quae inter eos agi coeptae neque perfectae
100 essent, agere cum eo: uti aut iterum conloquio diem consti-
101 tueret aut, si id minus vellet, ex suis legatis aliquem ad se
102 mitteret.   Conloquendi Caesari causa visa non est, et eo
103 magis, quod pridie eius diei Germani retineri non potuerant,
104 quin in nostros tela conicerent.   Legatum ex suis sese magno
105 cum periculo ad eum missurum et hominibus feris obiectu-
106 rum existimabat.   Commodissimum visum est C. Valerium
107 Procillum, C. Valeri Caburi filium, summa virtute et
108 humanitate adulescentem, cuius pater a C. Valerio Flacco
109 civitate donatus erat, et propter fidem et propter linguae
110 Gallicae scientiam, qua multa iam Ariovistus longinqua
111 consuetudine utebatur, et quod in eo peccandi Germanis
112 causa non esset, ad eum mittere et unâ M. Metium, qui
113 hospitio Ariovisti utebatur. His mandavit, ut, quae
114 diceret Ariovistus, cognoscerent et ad se referrent.   Quos
115 cum apud se in castris Ariovistus conspexisset, exercitu suo
116 praesente conclamavit: Quid ad se venirent? an speculandi
117 causâ?   Conantes dicere prohibuit et in catenas coniecit.

M. TULLIUS CICERO

(Born in 106 B.C.; active from 85–43.)

His Character and Achievements

M. Tullius Cicero was a fully Hellenized Roman, endowed
with a brilliant mind, a retentive memory, and a fluent command
of language. As a youth he was devoted to enthusiastic and
ardent study—even to the detriment of his health—in all fields
of Greek and Roman learning. By his absorption of Greek culture and the ability to express his thoughts in eloquent prose,
Cicero became a founder of intellectual life in the western world.
No less deeply imbued with the philosophical and political ideal-
ism of the Greeks, he became the querulous leader of the lost
cause of Roman democracy. The weak point in his nature

(fostered by a quick rise to political power) was his personal vanity—a trait that may be abundantly paralleled in Greek history.

As an orator Cicero was supreme; as a letter writer he was fluent and indefatigable, bequeathing to posterity a mirror of his times; as a poet he was uninspired; as an essayist he commanded a prose style that has become a landmark of the world's literature—a model of fluency, clarity, and volubility. Words issue from him in a torrent that is never beyond control, representing the ultimate development of this type of prose style. A century after his death, when prose style had developed along entirely different lines, Cicero was criticised for his fulsomeness. His style was found to be lacking in delicate chiseling, in epigrammatic finesse—one could not cull exquisite gems of thought from every paragraph! But on the whole, posterity has deemed Cicero's rich and fluent prose a more sane and helpful model than that of the Empire, with its "pointed" style, its preciosity, its rhetorical and romantic coloring.

I

Letters

Cicero is the only great figure of the ancient world—Greek or Roman—whose private correspondence was published *in extenso*. About half survives, thanks to the enthusiasm of fifteenth-century Italian humanists. Most of the groups or collections of Cicero's letters were edited by his faithful secretary, Tiro. Indiscreet hero worship obviously prompted this, for Cicero's revelation of his own character is not always flattering; posterity has learned from his letters more of Cicero's weakness than of his strength. They are an amazing record and belong on the whole rather to political history than to literature, although naturally of infinite variety. Reading them, we wonder increasingly at Cicero's perfect command of the written, as well as the spoken, word. The following letters are selected from the *Epistolae ad Atticum* [1] and from the *Epistolae ad Familiares*, or *Letters to Various Friends*. [2]

[1] T. Pomponius Atticus, publisher and litterateur, was Cicero's lifelong friend. He himself published this group of letters.

[2] These were edited by Tiro.

[1]

Letters Written From 65–50 B.C.

[a] Written in the summer or autumn of 65 B.C., when Cicero was already planning his campaign for the consulship of 63:

1 CICERO ATTICO SAL. L. Iulio Caesare C. Marcio Figulo
2 consulibus filiolo me auctum scito salvā Terentiā. Abs te
3 tam diu nihil litterarum! Ego de meis ad te rationibus
4 scripsi antea diligenter. Hoc tempore Catilinam, competi-
5 torem nostrum, defendere cogitamus. Iudices habemus,
6 quos voluimus, summa accusatoris voluntate. Spero, si
7 absolutus erit, coniunctiorem illum nobis fore in ratione
8 petitionis; sin aliter acciderit, humaniter feremus. Tuo ad-
9 ventu nobis opus est maturo; nam prorsus summa hominum
10 est opinio tuos familiares, nobiles homines, adversarios
11 honori nostro fore. Ad eorum voluntatem mihi concilian-
12 dam maximo te mihi usui fore video. Qua re Ianuario
13 mense, ut constituisti, cura ut Romae sis.

[b] Written on April 29, 58 B.C., from Brundisium, his port of departure for Greece, on his way into exile:

1 TULLIUS S. D. TERENTIAE ET TULLIOLAE ET CICERONI
2 SUIS. Ego minus saepe do ad vos litteras quam possum,
3 propterea quod cum omnia mihi tempora sunt misera, tum
4 vero, cum aut scribo ad vos aut vestras lego, conficior lacri-
5 mis sic, ut ferre non possim. Quod utinam minus vitae
6 cupidi fuissemus! Certe nihil aut non multum in vita mali
7 vidissemus. Quod si nos ad aliquam alicuius commodi
8 aliquando reciperandi spem fortuna reservavit, minus est er-
9 ratum a nobis: si haec mala fixa sunt, ego vero te quam
10 primum, mea vita, cupio videre et in tuo complexu emori,
11 quando neque di, quos tu castissime coluisti, neque homines,
12 quibus ego semper servivi, nobis gratiam rettulerunt.
13 Nos Brundisi apud M. Laenium Flaccum dies XIII
14 fuimus, virum optimum, qui periculum fortunarum et
15 capitis sui prae mea salute neglexit neque legis improbissi-
16 mae poena deductus est quominus hospitii et amicitiae ius

17 officiumque praestaret. Huic utinam aliquando gratiam
18 referre possimus! Habebimus quidem semper. Brundisio
19 profecti sumus a. d. II. Kalendas Maias: per Macedoniam
20 Cyzicum petebamus. O me perditum! O adflictum! Quid
21 enim? Rogem te ut venias? Mulierem aegram et corpore
22 et animo confectam? Non rogem? Sine te igitur sim?
23 Opinor, sic agam: si est spes nostri reditus, eam confirmes et
24 rem adiuves; sin, ut ego metuo, transactum est, quoquo
25 modo potes, ad me fac venias. Unum hoc scito: si te habe-
26 bo, non mihi videbor plane perisse. Sed quid Tulliolā meā
27 fiet? Iam id vos videte: mihi deest consilium. Sed certe,
28 quoquo modo se res habebit, illius misellae et matrimonio et
29 famae serviendum est. Quid? Cicero meus quid aget?
30 Iste vero sit in sinu semper et complexu meo. Non queo
31 plura iam scribere: impedit maeror. Tu quid egeris nescio:
32 utrum aliquid teneas an (quod metuo) plane sis spoliata.
33 Pisonem, ut scribis, spero fore semper nostrum.
34   De familia liberata nihil est quod te moveat. Primum
35 tuis ita promissum est: te facturam esse, ut quisque esset
36 meritus. Est autem in officio adhuc Orpheus: praeterea
37 magnopere nemo. Ceterorum servorum ea causa est, ut, si
38 res a nobis abisset, liberti nostri essent, si obtinere potuis-
39 sent: sin ad nos pertineret, servirent, praeterquam oppido
40 pauci. Sed haec minora sunt.
41   Tu quod me hortaris, ut animo sim magno et spem habeam
42 reciperandae salutis, id velim sit eiusmodi, ut recte sperare
43 possimus. Nunc miser quando tuas iam litteras accipiam?
44 Quis ad me perferet? Quas ego exspectassem Brundisi, si
45 esset licitum per nautas, qui tempestatem praetermittere
46 noluerunt. Quod reliquum est, sustenta te, mea Terentia,
47 ut potes, honestissime. Viximus; floruimus; non vitium
48 nostrum, sed virtus nostra nos adflixit. Peccatum est nul-
49 lum, nisi quod non unâ animam cum ornamentis amisimus.
50 Sed si hoc fuit liberis nostris gratius, nos vivere, cetera,
51 quamquam ferenda non sunt, feramus. Atqui ego, qui te
52 confirmo, ipse me non possum.
53   Clodium Philhetaerum, quod valetudine oculorum im-

54 pediebatur, hominem fidelem, remisi. Sallustius officio
55 vincet omnes. Pescennius est perbenevolus nobis, quem
56 semper spero tui fore observantem. Sica dixerat se mecum
57 fore, sed Brundisio discessit.

58   Cura, quod potes, ut valeas; et sic existimes, me vehe-
59 mentius tua miseria quam mea commoveri. Mea Terentia,
60 fidissima atque optima uxor, et mea carissima filiola et spes
61 reliqua nostra, Cicero, valete. Pridie Kalendas Maias
62 Brundisio.

[c] Written during the first week in May, 51 B.C., from Min-
turnae, a town on the Appian Way, about seventy-five miles south
of Rome. Cicero had left Rome and parted from his old friend
Atticus about May 1, and was now on his way to assume the
governorship of his oriental province:

1   CICERO ATTICO SAL. Ego vero et tuum in discessu vidi
2 animum et meo sum ipse testis. Quo magis erit tibi viden-
3 dum, ne quid novi decernatur, ut hoc nostrum desiderium
4 ne plus sit annuum. . . .

5   Nunc venio ad transversum illum extremae epistulae tuae
6 versiculum, in quo me admones de sorore. Quae res se sic
7 habet. Ut veni in Arpinas, cum ad me frater venisset, im-
8 primis nobis sermo—isque multus—de te fuit. Ex quo ego
9 veni ad ea, quae fueramus ego et tu inter nos de sorore in
10 Tusculano locuti. Nihil tam vidi mite, nihil tam placatum,
11 quam tum meus frater erat in sororem tuam, ut, etiam si qua
12 fuerat ex ratione sumptus offensio, non appareret. Ille sic
13 dies. Postridie ex Arpinati profecti sumus. Ut in Arcano
14 Quintus maneret, dies fecit; ego Aquini; sed prandimus in
15 Arcano. Nosti hunc fundum. Quô ut venimus, humanis-
16 sime Quintus "Pomponia" inquit "tu invita mulieres, ego
17 accivero viros." Nihil potuit (mihi quidem ut visum est)
18 dulcius—idque cum verbis tum etiam animo ac vultu. At
19 illa audientibus nobis "Ego ipsa sum" inquit "hîc hospita,"
20 id autem ex eo (ut opinor) quod antecesserat Statius, ut
21 prandium nobis videret. Tum Quintus "En" inquit mihi

22 "haec ego patior cotidie." Dices: "quid, quaeso, istuc
23 erat?" Magnum! Itaque me ipsum commoverat: sic
24 absurde et aspere verbis vultuque responderat. Dissimu-
25 lavi dolens. Discubuimus omnes praeter illam, cui tamen
26 Quintus de mensa misit. Illa reiecit. Quid multa? Nihil
27 meo fratre lenius, nihil asperius tua sorore mihi visum est.
28 Et multa praetereo, quae tum mihi maiori stomacho quam
29 ipsi Quinto fuerunt. Ego inde Aquinum. Quintus in
30 Arcano remansit, et Aquinum ad me postridie mane venit
31 mihique narravit, nec secum illam dormire voluisse, et cum
32 discessura esset fuisse eiusmodi, qualem ego vidissem. Quid
33 quaeris? Vel ipsi hoc dicas licet, humanitatem ei meo
34 iudicio illo die defuisse.
35   Haec ad te scripsi fortasse pluribus, quam necesse fuit, ut
36 videres tuas quoque esse partes instituendi et monendi.
37 Reliquum est, ut, antequam proficiscare, mandata nostra
38 exhaurias, scribas ad me omnia. . . . Cum profectus eris,
39 cures ut sciam. Sic habeas: nihil mehercule te mihi nec
40 carius esse nec suavius. A. Torquatum amantissime dimisi
41 Minturnis, optimum virum—cui me ad te scripsisse aliquid,
42 in sermone significes velim.

[d] Written on April 4, 50 B.C., from Laodicéa, capital of
Cicero's province:

1   M. Cicero Imp. S. D. M. Caelio Aed. Cur. Putaresne
2 umquam accidere posse ut mihi verba deessent, neque solum
3 ista vestra oratoria, sed haec etiam levia nostratia? Desunt
4 autem propter hanc causam, quod mirifice sum sollicitus
5 quidnam de provinciis decernatur. Mirum me desiderium
6 tenet Urbis, incredibile meorum atque imprimis tui, satietas
7 autem provinciae, vel quia videmur eam famam consecuti,
8 ut non tam accessio quaerenda quam fortuna metuenda sit,
9 vel quia totum negotium non est dignum viribus nostris, qui
10 maiora onera in re publica sustinere et possimus et soleamus,
11 vel quia belli magni timor impendet, quod videmur effugere,
12 si ad constitutam diem decedemus.

13 De pantheris per eos, qui venari solent, agitur mandatu
14 meo diligenter, sed mira paucitas est, et eas, quae sunt,
15 valde aiunt queri, quod nihil cuiquam insidiarum in mea
16 provincia nisi sibi fiat, itaque constituisse dicuntur in Ca-
17 riam ex nostra provincia decedere.   Sed tamen sedulo fit et
18 imprimis a Patisco.   Quidquid erit, tibi erit, sed quid esset,
19 plane nesciebamus.   Mihi mehercule magnae curae est
20 aedilitas tua—ipse dies me admonebat: scripsi enim haec
21 ipsis Megalensibus.   Tu velim ad me de omni rei publicae
22 statu quam diligentissime perscribas: ea enim certissima
23 putabo, quae ex te cognoro.

[2]

Letters Written Early in 49 B.C.

[a] Written on January 12, from some place near Rome, to his
faithful secretary, Tiro.   Because of illness, the latter had been
left behind in Greece when Cicero returned from his province.
Cicero reached Rome on January 4; but he has now been waiting
for eight days outside the city walls, in the hope that the senate
may grant him a triumph and not require him to relinquish the
military power he had exercised in his province.   Meanwhile
Caesar had crossed the Rubicon on January 10, and was now
marching on Rome:

1   TULLIUS ET CICERO, TERENTIA, TULLIA, Q. Q. TIRONI S.
2   PLUR. DIC. Etsi opportunitatem operae tuae omnibus
3   locis desidero, tamen non tam meā quam tuā causā doleo te
4   non valere; sed quoniam in quartanam conversa vis est
5   morbi—sic enim scribit Curius—spero te diligentiā adhibitā
6   iam firmiorem fore; modô fac (id quod est humanitatis tuae)
7   ne quid aliud cures hoc tempore, nisi ut quam commodis-
8   sime convalescas.   Non ignoro, quantum ex desiderio
9   labores; sed erunt omnia facilia, si valebis.   Festinare te
10 nolo, ne nauseae molestiam suscipias aeger et periculose
11 hieme naviges.
12 Ego ad Urbem accessi pr. Non. Ian.   Obviam mihi
13 sic est proditum, ut nihil possit fieri ornatius; sed incĭdi

14 in ipsam flammam civilis discordiae vel potius belli. Cui
15 cum cuperem mederi et, ut arbitror, possem, cupiditates
16 certorum hominum—nam ex utraque parte sunt qui
17 pugnare cupiant—impedimento mihi fuerunt. Omnino et
18 ipse Caesar, amicus noster, minacis ad senatum et acer-
19 bas litteras miserat et erat adhuc impudens, qui exercitum
20 et provinciam invito senatu teneret, et Curio meus illum
21 incitabat; Antonius quidem noster et Q. Cassius, nulla vi
22 expulsi, ad Caesarem cum Curione profecti erant, postea-
23 quam senatus consulibus, pr., tr. pl. et nobis, qui pro cos.
24 sumus, negotium dederat, ut curaremus, ne quid res p.
25 detrimenti caperet. Numquam maiore in periculo civitas
26 fuit, numquam improbi cives habuerunt paratiorem ducem.
27 Omnino ex hac quoque parte diligentissime comparatur.
28 Id fit auctoritate et studio Pompei nostri, qui Caesarem serô
29 coepit timere.

30 Nobis inter has turbas senatus tamen frequens flagitavit
31 triumphum; sed Lentulus consul, quo maius suum benefi-
32 cium faceret, simul atque expedisset, quae essent necessaria
33 de re p., dixit se relaturum. Nos agimus nihil cupide,
34 eoque est nostra pluris auctoritas. Italiae regiones di-
35 scriptae sunt, quam quisque partem tueretur. Nos Capuam
36 sumpsimus.

37 Haec te scire volui. Tu etiam atque etiam cura, ut
38 valeas litterasque ad me mittas, quotienscumque habebis,
39 cui des. Etiam atque etiam vale. D. pr. Idus Ian.

[b] Written on January 18, six days after the previous letter
and presumably from the same place. After waiting two weeks
outside of Rome, Cicero has given up hope; his proposed triumph
has been completely lost sight of in the general panic caused by
Caesar and his approaching armies. Pompey and his supporters,
including practically all the magistrates, have left Rome and
withdrawn to Southern Italy. Cicero now follows suit—a lukewarm member of the Pompeian party:

1 CICERO ATTICO SAL.   Subito consilium cepi, ut, antequam
2 luceret exirem, ne qui conspectus fieret aut sermo, lictoribus

3 praesertim laureatis. De reliquo neque hercule quid agam
4 nec quid acturus sim scio: ita sum perturbatus temeritate
5 nostri amentissimi consilii. Tibi vero quid suadeam, cuius
6 ipse consilium exspecto? Gnaeus noster quid consilii
7 ceperit capiatve, nescio, adhuc in oppidis coartatus et
8 stupens. Omnes, si in Italia consistet, erimus unâ; sin
9 cedet, consilii res est. Adhuc certe (nisi ego insanio) stulte
10 omnia et incaute. Tu, quaeso, crebro ad me scribe vel quod
11 in buccam venerit.

[c] Written on January 24, from Formiae,[1] to his wife and
daughter. The latter were still in Rome, and Cicero was anxious
for their safety:

1   TULLIUS TERENTIAE SUAE ET PATER SUAVISSIMAE FILIAE,
2   CICERO MATRI ET SORORI S. D. P. Considerandum vobis
3 etiam atque etiam, animae meae, diligenter puto, quid
4 faciatis, Romaene sitis an mecum an aliquo tuto loco; id non
5 solum meum consilium est, sed etiam vestrum. Mihi ve-
6 niunt in mentem haec: Romae vos esse tuto posse per Dola-
7 bellam, eamque rem posse nobis adiumento esse, si quae vis
8 aut si quae rapinae fieri coeperint. Sed rursus illud me
9 movet, quod video omnis bonos abesse Romā et eos mulieres
10 suas secum habere. Haec autem regio, in qua ego sum,
11 nostrorum est cum oppidorum tum etiam praediorum, ut et
12 multum esse mecum, et cum abieritis, commode et in nostris
13 esse possitis. Mihi plane non satis constat adhuc, utrum
14 sit melius. Vos videte, quid aliae faciant isto loco feminae,
15 et ne, cum velitis, exire non liceat. Id velim diligenter
16 etiam atque etiam vobiscum et cum amicis consideretis.
17 Domus ut propugnacula et praesidium habeat, Philotimo
18 dicetis; et velim tabellarios instituatis certos, ut cotidie
19 aliquas a vobis litteras accipiam; maxime autem date
20 operam, ut valeatis, si nos vultis valere. VIIII. K. Formiis.

[1] Formiae is situated on the coast of Italy near Capua, south of Rome.

[d] Written on February 23 or 24, from Formiae:

1 CICERO ATTICO SAL. Unum etiam restat amico nostro
2 ad omne dedecus, ut Domitio non subveniat. "At nemo
3 dubitat quin subsidio venturus sit." Ego non puto.
4 "Deseret igitur talem civem et eos, quos unâ scis esse, cum
5 habeat praesertim et ipse cohortes XXX?" Nisi me omnia
6 fallunt, deseret. Incredibiliter pertimuit. Nihil spectat
7 nisi fugam, cui tu—video enim quid sentias—me comitem
8 putas debere esse. Ego vero quem fugiam habeo; quem se-
9 quar non habeo. Quod enim tu meum laudas et memo-
10 randum dicis, "malle" quod dixerim "me cum Pompeio vinci
11 quam cum istis vincere," ego vero malo, sed cum illo Pom-
12 peio, qui tum erat aut qui mihi esse videbatur; cum hoc
13 vero, qui ante fugit quam scit aut quem fugiat aut quô, qui
14 nostra tradidit, qui patriam reliquit, Italiam relinquit—si
15 malui, contigit: victus sum. Quod superest, nec ista videre
16 possum, quae numquam timui ne viderem, nec mehercule
17 istum, propter quem mihi non modô meis, sed memet ipso
18 carendum est. . . .

[e] Written on March 1, from Formiae:

1 CICERO ATTICO SAL. Lippitudinis meae signum tibi sit
2 librarii manus et eadem causa brevitatis; etsi nunc quidem,
3 quod scriberem, nihil erat. Omnis exspectatio nostra erat
4 in nuntiis Brundisinis. Si nactus hic esset Gnaeum
5 nostrum, spes dubia pacis; sin ille ante tramisisset, exitiosi
6 belli metus. Sed videsne, in quem hominem incĭderit res
7 publica, quam acutum, quam vigilantem, quam paratum?
8 Si mehercule neminem occĭderit, nec cuiquam quicquam
9 ademerit, ab iis, qui eum maxime timuerant, maxime
10 diligetur. Multum mecum municipales homines loquuntur,
11 multum rusticani; nihil prorsus aliud curant nisi agros, nisi
12 villulas, nisi nummulos suos. Et vide, quam conversa res
13 sit; illum, quo antea confidebant, metuunt; hunc amant,
14 quem timebant. Id quantis nostris peccatis vitiisque
15 evenerit, non possum sine molestia cogitare. Quae autem

16 impendere putarem, scripseram ad te et iam tuas litteras
17 exspectabam.

[3]

Letter Written After Caesar's Assassination

Written in May, 43 B.C., from Rome, to Decimus Brutus,
commander of the army at Mutina, in Northern Italy:

1   M. Cicero S. D. D. Bruto Imp. Cos. Des.   Tres uno
2   die a te accepi epistulas: unam brevem, quam Flacco
3   Volumnio dederas; duas pleniores, quarum alteram tabel-
4   larius T. Vibii attulit, alteram ad me misit Lupus.   Ex tuis
5   litteris et ex Graeceii oratione non modo non restinctum
6   bellum, sed etiam inflammatum videtur.   Non dubito autem
7   pro tua singulari prudentia quin perspicias, si aliquid firmi-
8   tatis nactus sit Antonius, omnia tua illa praeclara in rem
9   publicam merita ad nihilum esse ventura; ita enim Romam
10 erat nuntiatum, ita persuasum omnibus: cum paucis inermis,
11 perterritis metu, fracto animo fugisse Antonium.   Qui si ita
12 se habet, ut (quemadmodum audiebam de Graeceio) confligi
13 cum eo sine periculo non possit, non ille mihi fugisse a
14 Mutina videtur, sed locum belli gerendi mutasse.   Itaque
15 homines alii facti sunt.   Nonnulli etiam queruntur, quod
16 persecuti non sitis: opprimi potuisse, si celeritas adhibita
17 esset, existimant.   Omnino est hoc populi maximeque nostri,
18 in eo potissimum abuti libertate, per quem eam consecutus
19 sit.   Sed tamen providendum est, ne quae iusta querela
20 esse possit.   Res se sic habet: is bellum confecerit, qui An-
21 tonium oppresserit.   Hoc quam vim habeat te existimare
22 mālo quam me apertius scribere.

II

Essays

With one slight exception—which we shall consider presently—
Cicero's score or more of essays were the product of the last twelve

years of his life. Since his first love had always been oratory, writing books was at best only a substitute for making speeches. Nevertheless, embittered by his enforced retirement from political life, Cicero found consolation for a wounded spirit and occupation for a restless mind by resuming the scholarly pursuits of his youth. After several essays on oratory and government, combining practical experience with theoretical speculation, he conceived the bolder idea of interpreting *Greek philosophy* in a series of popular essays. He was thus the first of a group of transmitters (ancient, medieval, and modern) who have brought the message of Greek speculative thinking to the western world. His "library of Greek philosophy" began with the essay entitled *Hortensius* (now lost), on the value of Greek philosophy in general; then came the *Academica,* advocating his own chosen school of thought, the "New Academy"; third, *de Finibus Bonorum et Malorum,* outlining the tenets of the chief schools with respect to the pivotal problem of what constitutes ultimate good and evil; fourth, the *Tusculan Disputations,* discussing popular problems of moral philosophy; fifth, *de Natura Deorum,* on the basic concepts of religion; sixth, *de Divinatione (On Prophecy);* seventh, *de Fato;* eighth, *de Officiis (On Duty);* and finally, *de Gloria* and *de Virtutibus* (both now lost). There were also four popular essays that did not enter into this expository scheme, but may be regarded as by-products of his philosophical studies: *de Consolatione* (now lost), written after the death of his daughter, Tullia; *Cato Maior,* or *de Senectute; Laelius,* or *de Amicitia;* and *Cato Minor,* or *Eulogy of Cato the Younger* (now lost). As his life drew to a close and the number and importance of his essays increased, Cicero professed to see in them all— rhetorical, political, and theoretical alike—a single unifying element: Greek philosophy! Like Plato and Aristotle, he—M. Tullius Cicero—had subjected all human faith and knowledge to the test of a philosophic mind and had selected that which he deemed worthy of bequeathing to posterity. Thus Cicero ultimately fulfilled his mission as apostle of Greek culture to his countrymen. But let us now return to the very beginning of his career.

[1]

Essays on Oratory [1]

[a] DE INVENTIONE

The first work ever published by Cicero—antedating by many years his important orations and essays—was a treatise, or text-book, on the art of oratory. It was produced when Cicero was *adulescentulus*—i.e., probably less than twenty years old. Only that portion of the work has been preserved to us which deals with the first department of the art of oratory—namely "invention," or the planning of a speech. The exposition of the subject is clear, though wholly technical; oddly enough, it closely resembles the anonymous *Rhetorica ad Herennium*—some passages are even identical. Which author was the plagiarist? Perhaps neither—for both may simply have edited an older hand-book, whose author had been forgotten or ignored because of the pedagogical and non-literary character of his work. Although it is impossible to say which came first—the *Rhetorica ad Herennium* or the *de Inventione*—, a conscious rivalry is evident between them. Cicero's exposition of the subject is somewhat more logical than that of his older contemporary, whose occasional discursiveness is quaint, but less scholarly.

However that may be, it is not the treatise itself which interests us, but its brief preface. This is Cicero's *first* essay—an extraordinary prelude to his later and maturer work. Awkward though some of its paragraphs are, it indicates that the precocious young student was already preoccupied with the philosophical speculation which ripened thirty years later, and that beliefs and theories for which he argued with consummate skill in maturity, were already firm convictions in his youth.

This brief essay deals with the "idealistic," as contrasted with the "practical," conception of the art of oratory. Cicero always held to Cato's famous definition of the orator—*vir bonus, dicendi peritus*—, which places ideals of character above mere technical skill:

---

[1] These are often called by their technical name, "rhetorical" essays.

The Faculty of Eloquence—A Blessing or a Curse to Mankind?

1 Saepe et multum hoc mecum cogitavi: bonine an mali plus
2 attulerit hominibus et civitatibus copia dicendi ac summum
3 eloquentiae studium. Nam cum et nostrae rei publicae
4 detrimenta considero, et maximarum civitatum veteres
5 animo calamitates colligo, non minimam video per disertis-
6 simos homines invectam partem incommodorum; cum
7 autem res ab nostra memoria propter vetustatem remotas ex
8 litterarum monumentis repetere instituo, multas urbes con-
9 stitutas, plurima bella restincta, firmissimas societates,
10 sanctissimas amicitias intellego cum animi ratione tum
11 facilius eloquentiā comparatas. Ac me quidem diu cogi-
12 tantem ratio ipsa in hanc potissimum sententiam ducit, ut
13 existimem sapientiam sine eloquentia parum prodesse civita-
14 tibus, eloquentiam vero sine sapientia nimium obesse ple-
15 rumque, prodesse numquam. Quare, si quis, omissis rectis-
16 simis atque honestissimis studiis rationis et officii, consumit
17 omnem operam in exercitatione dicendi, is inutilis sibi,
18 perniciosus patriae civis alitur; qui vero ita sese armat elo-
19 quentiā, ut non oppugnare commoda patriae, sed pro his
20 propugnare possit, is mihi vir et suis et publicis rationibus
21 utilissimus atque amicissimus civis fore videtur.

Oratory—The Chief Civilizer of the Human Race

1 Ac si volumus huius rei quae vocatur eloquentia—sive
2 artis, sive studii, sive exercitationis cuiusdam, sive facultatis
3 ab natura profectae—considerare principium, reperiemus id
4 ex honestissimis causis natum atque ab optimis rationibus
5 profectum. Nam fuit quoddam tempus, cum in agris
6 homines passim bestiarum modo vagabantur, et sibi victu
7 fero vitam propagabant, nec ratione animi quicquam, sed
8 pleraque viribus corporis administrabant; nondum divinae
9 religionis, non humani officii ratio colebatur; nemo nuptias
10 viderat legitimas, non certos quisquam aspexerat liberos;
11 non, ius aequabile quid utilitatis haberet, acceperat. Ita
12 propter errorem atque inscientiam, caeca ac temeraria
13 dominatrix animi—cupiditas—ad se explendam viribus

14 corporis abutebatur, perniciosissimis satellitibus. Quo
15 tempore quidam magnus videlicet vir et sapiens cognovit,
16 quae materia et quanta ad maximas res opportunitas in ani-
17 mis inesset hominum, si quis eam posset elicere et praeci-
18 piendo meliorem reddere; qui dispersos homines in agros, et
19 in tectis silvestribus abditos, ratione quadam compulit
20 unum in locum et congregavit; et eos in unam quamque rem
21 inducens utilem atque honestam, primo propter insolentiam
22 reclamantes, deinde propter rationem atque orationem
23 studiosius audientes, ex feris et immanibus mites reddidit et
24 mansuetos. Ac mihi quidem videtur hoc nec tacita nec
25 inops dicendi sapientia perficere potuisse, ut homines a con-
26 suetudine subito converteret et ad diversas rationes vitae
27 traduceret. Age vero, urbibus constitutis, ut fidem colere
28 et iustitiam retinere discerent, et aliis parēre sua voluntate
29 consuescerent, ac non modo labores excipiendos communis
30 commodi causā, sed etiam vitam amittendam existimarent,
31 quî tandem fieri potuit, nisi homines ea, quae ratione in-
32 venissent, eloquentiā persuadere potuissent? Profecto
33 nemo, nisi gravi ac suavi commotus oratione, cum viribus
34 plurimum posset, ad ius voluisset sine vi descendere; ut inter
35 quos posset excellere, cum iis se pateretur aequari, et sua
36 voluntate a iucundissima consuetudine recederet, quae
37 praesertim iam naturae vim obtineret propter vetustatem.
38 Ac primo quidem sic et nata et progressa longius eloquentia
39 videtur, et item postea maximis in rebus pacis et belli cum
40 summis hominum utilitatibus esse versata; postquam vero
41 commoditas quaedam, prava virtutis imitatrix, sine ratione
42 officii, dicendi copiam consecuta est, tum ingenio freta
43 malitia pervertere urbes et vitas hominum labefactare ad-
44 suevit. Atque huius quoque exordium mali, quoniam
45 principium boni diximus, explicemus.

The Decline of Oratory—Causes

*[In the beginning the nobler type of oratory—the parliamentary—
was distinct from the baser—the forensic; then, compelled by circumstances to defend their friends from unjust attacks, statesmen were*

*drawn into controversy with pettifoggers. In these controversies men
of high ideals were often defeated by clever and unprincipled casuists,
who won first the applause and then the suffrage of the superficial
masses. Becoming demagogues, these wrecked the state; whereupon
the people, with hasty judgment, damned statesmen and demagogues
alike; and the art of oratory, having thus fallen into disrepute, was
abandoned by men of ability for other and less opprobrious or
hazardous pursuits.*]

1 Verisimillimum mihi videtur, quodam tempore neque in
2 publicis rebus infantes et insipientes homines solitos esse
3 versari, nec vero ad privatas causas magnos ac disertos
4 homines accedere; sed cum a summis viris maximae res
5 administrarentur, arbitror alios fuisse non incallidos
6 homines, qui ad parvas controversias privatorum acceder-
7 ent. Quibus in controversiis cum saepe a mendacio contra
8 verum stare hominés consuescerent, dicendi assiduitas in-
9 duit audaciam, ut necessario superiores illi propter iniurias
10 civium resistere audacibus, et opitulari suis quisque neces-
11 sariis cogeretur. Itaque cum in dicendo saepe par, non-
12 numquam etiam superior, visus esset is qui, omisso studio
13 sapientiae, nihil sibi praeter eloquentiam comparasset,
14 fiebat, ut et multitudinis et suo iudicio dignus, qui rem
15 publicam gereret, videretur. Hinc nimirum, cum ad
16 gubernacula rei publicae temerarii atque audaces homines
17 accesserant, maxima ac miserrima naufragia fiebant.
18 Quibus rebus tantum odii atque invidiae suscepit eloquen-
19 tia, ut homines ingeniosissimi, quasi ex aliqua turbida
20 tempestate in portum, sic ex seditiosa ac tumultuosa vita se
21 in studium aliquod traderent quietum. Quare mihi viden-
22 tur postea cetera studia recta atque honesta, per otium
23 concelebrata ab optimis, enituisse; hoc vero, a plerisque
24 eorum desertum, obsolevisse tempore quo multo vehemen-
25 tius erat retinendum et studiosius adaugendum.

Nobler Ideals of Oratory—The Need for Fostering Them

1 Nam quo indignius rem honestissimam et rectissimam
2 violabat stultorum et improborum temeritas et audacia—

3 summo cum rei publicae detrimento—, eo studiosius et illis
4 resistendum fuit et rei publicae consulendum. Quod nos-
5 trum illum non fugit Catonem neque Laelium neque eorum
6 (ut vere dicam) discipulum Africanum neque Gracchos
7 (Africani nepotes): quibus in hominibus erat summa virtus
8 et summa virtute amplificata auctoritas et (quae et his
9 rebus ornamento et rei publicae praesidio esset) eloquentia!
10 Quare, meo quidem animo, nihilo minus eloquentiae studen-
11 dum est, etsi eā quidam et privatim et publice abutuntur,
12 sed eo quidem vehementius, ne mali, magno cum detrimento
13 bonorum et communi omnium pernicie, plurimum possint;
14 cum praesertim hoc sit unum, quod ad omnes res et privatas
15 et publicas maxime pertineat; hoc tuta, hoc honesta, hoc il-
16 lustris, hoc eodem vita iucunda fiat. Nam hinc ad rem
17 publicam plurima commoda veniunt, si moderatrix omnium
18 rerum praesto est—sapientia; hinc ad ipsos, qui eam adepti
19 sunt, laus, honos, dignitas confluit; hinc amicis quoque eo-
20 rum certissimum et tutissimum praesidium comparatur.
21 Ac mihi quidem videntur homines, cum multis rebus humili-
22 ores et infirmiores sint, hac re maxime bestiis praestare, quod
23 loqui possunt. Quare praeclarum mihi quiddam videtur
24 adeptus is qui, qua re homines bestiis praestent, ea in re
25 hominibus ipsis antecellat.

[b] De Oratore

In 55 B.C., some thirty years after the publication of his *de Inventione*, Cicero wrote his first great dialogue in the grand Platonic manner. This dialogue, the *de Oratore*, was an essay on training the orator or statesman. Cicero now scorned conventional textbooks on the art of oratory (including his own youthful "indiscretion"), with their narrow pedagogical limitations and their emphasis on mechanical features. His mind now dwelt on ideas expressed in the preface of his boyish work, treating the *philosophy* of oratory—a subject even broader than its name would seem to imply, for the Latin meaning of "eloquence" included all literary style—the power of the written as well as the spoken word. Though purely a fiction of Cicero's imagination, this dialogue—

like Plato's *Symposium* and other famous treatises—is given a realistic setting. It purports to record a discussion or friendly debate on the art of oratory between two giants of the previous generation, L. Crassus and M. Antonius (grandfather of the famous·Marc Antony). The discussion takes place amid pleasant surroundings and in the presence of congenial friends, at the Tusculan villa of Crassus.

Selection From Book II

After some introductory paragraphs, Book II opens with an interesting and characteristic passage:

1   Postero igitur die, . . . horā fere secundā, cum etiam tum
2 in lecto Crassus esset et apud eum Sulpicius sederet, An-
3 tonius autem inambularet cum Cotta in porticu, repente eô
4 Q. Catulus senex cum C. Iulio fratre venit. Quod ubi
5 audivit, commotus Crassus surrexit, omnesque (admirati)
6 maiorem aliquam esse causam eorum adventus suspicati
7 sunt.
8   Qui cum inter se, ut ipsorum usus ferebat, amicissime
9 consalutassent, "quid vos tandem?" Crassus "numquid-
10 nam" inquit "novi?"
11   "Nihil sane" inquit Catulus; "etenim vides esse ludos.
12 Sed (vel tu nos ineptos licet" inquit "vel molestos putes)
13 cum ad me in Tusculanum" inquit "heri vesperi venisset
14 Caesar de Tusculano suo, dixit mihi, a se Scaevolam hinc
15 euntem esse conventum; ex quo mira quaedam se audisse
16 dicebat—te, quem ego totiens omni ratione temptans ad dis-
17 putandum elicere non potuissem, permulta de eloquentia
18 cum Antonio disseruisse, et tamquam in schola prope ad
19 Graecorum consuetudinem disputasse. Ita me frater
20 exoravit (ne ipsum quidem a studio audiendi nimis abhor-
21 rentem, sed mehercule verentem ne molesti vobis interven-
22 iremus), ut huc secum venirem. Etenim Scaevolam ita
23 dicere aiebat: bonam partem sermonis in hunc diem esse
24 dilatam. Hoc tu, si cupidius factum existimas, Caesari at-
25 tribues; si familiarius, utrique nostrum. Nos quidem, nisi
26 forte molesti intervenimus, venisse delectat."

27   Tum Crassus: "Equidem, quaecumque vos causa huc at-
28   tulisset, laetarer, cum apud me viderem homines mihi
29   carissimos et amicissimos; sed tamen (vere dicam) quaevis
30   causa mallem fuisset quam ista, quam dicis.   Ego enim—ut
31   quemadmodum sentio loquar—numquam mihi minus quam
32   hesterno die placui (magis adeo id facilitate quam aliā ullā
33   culpā meā contigit), qui, dum obsequor adulescentibus,
34   me senem esse sum oblitus; fecique id quod ne adulescens
35   quidem feceram, ut iis de rebus, quae doctrinā aliquā con-
36   tinerentur, disputarem.   Sed hoc tamen cecĭdit mihi perop-
37   portune, quod, transactis iam meis partibus, ad Antonium
38   audiendum venistis."
39   Tum Caesar "equidem" inquit "Crasse, et ita sum cupi-
40   dus in illa longiore te ac perpetua disputatione audiendi, ut,
41   si id mihi minus contingat, vel hoc sim cotidiano tuo
42   sermone contentus.   Itaque experiar equidem (ut ne Sul-
43   picius familiaris meus aut Cotta plus quam ego apud te
44   valere videatur) et te exorabo profecto, ut mihi quoque et
45   Catulo tuae suavitatis aliquid impertias.   Sin tibi id minus
46   licebit, non te urgebo, neque committam, ut, dum vereare
47   tu ne sis ineptus, me esse iudices."
48   Tum ille "ego mehercle," inquit "Caesar, ex omnibus
49   Latinis verbis huius verbi vim vel maximam semper putavi.
50   Quem enim nos 'ineptum' vocamus, is mihi videtur ab hoc
51   nomen habere ductum, quod non sit aptus, idque in ser-
52   monis nostri consuetudine perlate patet.   Nam qui aut
53   tempus quid postulet non videt aut plura loquitur aut se
54   ostentat aut eorum, quibuscum est, vel dignitatis vel com-
55   modi rationem non habet aut denique in aliquo genere aut
56   inconcinnus aut multus est, is ineptus esse dicitur.   Hoc
57   vitio cumulata est eruditissima illa Graecorum natio.
58   Itaque quod vim huius mali Graeci non vident, ne nomen
59   quidem ei vitio imposuerunt.   Ut enim quaeras omnia,
60   quomodo Graeci 'ineptum' appellent non reperies.   Om-
61   nium autem ineptiarum, quae sunt innumerabiles, haud
62   sciam an nulla sit maior, quam (ut illi solent), quocumque in
63   loco, quoscumque inter homines visum est, de rebus aut

64 difficillimis aut non necessariis argutissime disputare. Hoc
65 nos ab istis adulescentibus facere, inviti et recusantes, heri
66 coacti sumus."
67 Tum Catulus "ne Graeci quidem," inquit "Crasse, qui in
68 civitatibus suis clari et magni fuerunt sicuti tu es nosque
69 omnes in nostra re publica volumus esse, horum Graecorum,
70 qui se inculcant auribus nostris, similes fuerunt; nec in
71 otio sermones huiusmodi disputationesque fugiebant. Ac
72 si tibi videntur qui temporis, qui loci, qui hominum ra-
73 tionem non habent 'inepti' (sicut debent videri), num tan-
74 dem aut locus hic non idoneus videtur?—in quo porticus
75 haec ipsa, ubi nunc ambulamus, et palaestra et tot locis
76 sessiones gymnasiorum et Graecorum disputationum me-
77 moriam quodam modo commovent; aut num importunum
78 tempus in tanto otio?—quod et raro datur et nunc perop-
79 tato nobis datum est; aut homines ab hoc genere disputa-
80 tionis alieni?—qui omnes ii sumus, ut sine iis studiis vitam
81 nullam esse ducamus."
82 "Omnia ista" inquit Crassus "ego alio modo interpretor,
83 qui primum palaestram et sedis et porticus etiam ipsos,
84 Catule, Graecos exercitationis causā invenisse arbitror; nam
85 et saeculis multis ante gymnasia inventa sunt, quam in iis
86 philosophi garrire coeperunt, et hoc ipso tempore, cum omnia
87 gymnasia philosophi teneant, tamen eorum auditores discum
88 audire quam philosophum malunt; qui simul ut increpuit,
89 in media oratione de maximis rebus et gravissimis disputan-
90 tem philosophum omnes unctionis causā relinquunt: ita
91 levissimam delectationem gravissimae (ut ipsi ferunt) utili-
92 tati anteponunt. Otium autem quod dicis esse, assentior.
93 Verum otii fructus est animi non contentio sed relaxatio—
94 saepe ex socero meo audivi, cum is diceret socerum suum
95 Laelium semper fere cum Scipione solitum rusticari, eosque
96 incredibiliter repuerescere esse solitos, cum rus ex urbe
97 tamquam e vinclis evolavissent: non audeo dicere de talibus
98 viris, sed tamen ita solet narrare Scaevola, conchas eos et
99 umbilicos ad Caietam et ad Laurentum legere consuesse et
100 ad omnem animi remissionem ludumque descendere. Sic

101 enim res sese habet, ut, quemadmodum volucris videmus
102 procreationis atque utilitatis suae causā effingere et con-
103 struere nidos, easdem autem, cum aliquid effecerint, levandi
104 laboris sui causā passim ac libere, solutas opere, volitare, sic
105 nostri animi, negotiis forensibus atque urbano opere defessi,
106 gestiant ac volitare cupiant vacui curā ac labore. Itaque
107 illud ego, quod in causa Curiana Scaevolae dixi, non dixi
108 secus ac sentiebam:

109   'Nam si,' inquam 'Scaevola, nullum erit testamen-
110   tum recte factum, nisi quod tu scripseris, omnes ad
111   te cives cum tabulis veniemus; omnium testamenta
112   tu scribes unus. Quid igitur?' inquam. 'Quando
113   ages negotium publicum? quando amicorum? quan-
114   do tuum? Quando denique nihil ages?' Tum
115   illud addidi: 'mihi enim liber esse non videtur qui
116   non aliquando nihil agit.'

117 In qua permaneo, Catule, sententia, meque, cum huc veni,
118 hoc ipsum nihil agere et plane cessare delectat. Nam, quod
119 addidisti tertium (vos esse eos qui vitam insuavem sine his
120 studiis putaretis), id me non modô non hortatur ad dispu-
121 tandum, sed etiam deterret. Nam ut C. Lucilius, homo et
122 doctus et perurbanus, dicere solebat, neque se ab indoctissi-
123 mis neque a doctissimis legi velle, quod alteri nihil intelle-
124 gerent, alteri plus fortasse quam ipse—de quo etiam scripsit
125 'Pérsiúm non cúro légere,' (hic fuit enim, ut noramus, omnium
126 fere nostrorum hominum doctissimus) 'Laéliúm Decimúm
127 voló' (quem cognovimús virum bonum et non illitteratum,
128 sed nihil ad Persium)—; sic ego, si iam mihi disputandum
129 sit de his nostris studiis, nolim equidem apud rusticos, sed
130 multo minus apud vos. Mālo enim non intellegi orationem
131 meam quam reprehendi."

132   Tum Caesar "equidem," inquit "Catule, iam mihi videor
133 navasse operam, quod huc venerim. Nam haec ipsa recusa-
134 tio disputationis disputatio quaedam fuit mihi quidem
135 periucunda. Sed cur impedimus Antonium?—cuius audio
136 esse partīs, ut de tota eloquentia disserat; quemque iam
137 dudum et Cotta et Sulpicius expectat."

138   "Ego vero" inquit Crassus "neque Antonium verbum

139 facere patiar et ipse obmutescam, nisi prius a vobis im-
140 petraro. . . ."
141   "Quidnam?" inquit Catulus.
142   ". . . ut hîc sitis hodie.'
143   Tum, cum ille dubitaret, quod ad fratrem promiserat,
144 "ego" inquit Iulius "pro utroque respondeo: sic faciemus.
145 Atque ista quidem condicione, vel ut verbum nullum faceres,
146 me teneres."
147   Hîc Catulus adrisit, et simul "praecisa" inquit "mihi
148 quidem est dubitatio, quoniam neque domi imperaram, et
149 hic, apud quem eram futurus, sine mea sententia tam facile
150 promisit."
151   Tum omnes oculos in Antonium coniecerunt. Et ille
152 "audite vero, audite" inquit; "hominem enim audietis de
153 schola atque a magistro et Graecis litteris eruditum. Et eo
154 quidem loquar confidentius, quod Catulus auditor accessit,
155 cui non solum nos Latini sermonis, sed etiam Graeci ipsi
156 solent suae linguae subtilitatem elegantiamque concedere.
157 Sed quia tamen hoc totum (quicquid est—sive artificium sive
158 studium dicendi), nisi accessit os, nullum potest esse, docebo
159 vos, discipuli, id quod ipse non didici, quid de omni genere
160 sentiam." Hîc posteaquam adriserunt, "res mihi videtur
161 esse" inquit "facultate praeclară, arte mediocris. Ars
162 enim earum rerum est quae sciuntur, oratoris autem omnis
163 actio opinionibus, non scientiā, continetur. Nam et apud
164 eos dicimus qui nesciunt, et ea dicimus quae nescimus ipsi.
165 Itaque et illi alias aliud isdem de rebus et sentiunt et iudi-
166 cant, et nos contrarias saepe causas dicimus, non modo ut
167 Crassus contra me dicat aliquando aut ego contra Crassum,
168 cum alterutri necesse sit falsum dicere, sed etiam ut uterque
169 nostrum eadem de re alias aliud defendat, cum plus uno ve-
170 rum esse non possit. Ut igitur in eiusmodi re, quae menda-
171 cio nixa sit, quae ad scientiam non saepe perveniat, quae
172 opiniones hominum et saepe errores aucupetur, ita dicam—
173 si causam putatis esse, cur audiatis."
174   "Nos vero et valde quidem" Catulus inquit "putamus,
175 atque eo magis, quod nullā mihi ostentatione vidēris esse

176 usurus.   Exorsus es enim non gloriose—magis a veritate, ut
177 tu putas, quam nescioqua dignitate."
178   "Ut igitur de ipso genere sum confessus," inquit An-
179 tonius, "artem esse non maximam, sic illud adfirmo,
180 praecepta posse quaedam dari peracuta ad pertractandos
181 animos hominum et ad excipiendas eorum voluntates.
182 Huius rei scientiam si quis volet magnam quandam artem
183 esse dicere, non repugnabo."

[2]

Philosophical Essays

We have already noted (see p. 180) the larger scheme and
general purpose that lay behind Cicero's numerous essays.
Let us turn now to a brief consideration of the nature and appeal
of Greek philosophy, whose adoption by the Romans was a factor
in occidental civilization no less far-reaching than the subsequent
adoption of Christianity.

"Philosophy" and "philosopher" are words that cover a wide
range of meaning, or rather of application.   For if philosophy
means "love of wisdom," what then is wisdom?   To the ancient
Orientals, wisdom meant either patriarchal sagacity or mystical
reverie—the fruit of *experience;* to the Greeks, it meant scientific
speculation (beyond the realm of human experience)—enlarging
the scope and systematizing the details of human knowledge.
The earliest Greek thinkers (who did not call themselves philosophers, but were later so named) were pure scientists, whose
speculations took them into realms now identified as astronomy,
chemistry, and physics. The range of their interests grew, but
continued predominantly scientific until Socrates revolted from
abstract science and turned to the study of man's mind and soul.

After Socrates the old and the new realms of knowledge were
cultivated side by side, and complete "philosophies of life"
evolved, embracing theories of God, of the physical universe, and
of the whole duty of man.   Ultimately there were two such
philosophies, the Epicurean and the Stoic; and what were these
but religions?   Their founders and followers gave faith and adherence to a complete system of belief.   In the growing com-

plexity of civilized life during the century before the Christian
era, such systems of belief met the needs of an ever-increasing
number of people.

THE TUSCULAN DISPUTATIONS—BOOK V

It is not surprising to find the ideal philosopher akin to the
saint: each despises and rejects both the pleasures and the tribula-
tions of this transitory world. In Book V of the *Tusculan
Disputations* Cicero presents, in attractive popular form, the ideal
of the philosopher-saint.

[a] On the fifth day of this discussion (or *schola*) at Cicero's
Tusculan villa, the dialogue begins in the conventional manner
between the master (*magister*) and his disciple (*auditor*):

1 Quinto die, cum eodem in loco consedissemus, sic est
2 propositum de quo disputaremus:
3 **Au.** Non mihi videtur ad beate vivendum satis posse
4 virtutem.
5 **Ma.** At hercule Bruto meo videtur, cuius ego iudicium
6 (pace tuā dixerim) longe antepono tuo!
7 **Au.** Non dubito; nec id nunc agitur, tu illum quantum
8 ames, sed hoc, quod mihi dixi videri quale sit—de quo a te
9 disputari volo.
10 **Ma.** Nempe negas ad beate vivendum satis posse vir-
11 tutem?
12 **Au.** Prorsus nego.
13 **Ma.** Quid?   Ad recte, honeste, laudabiliter, postremo ad
14 bene vivendum satisne est praesidii in virtute?
15 **Au.** Certe satis.
16 **Ma.** Potes igitur aut, qui male vivat, non eum miserum
17 dicere, aut, quem bene fateare, eum negare beate vivere?
18 **Au.** Quidni possim?   Nam etiam in tormentis recte,
19 honeste, laudabiliter—et ob eam rem, bene—vivi potest,
20 dummodo intellegas, quid nunc dicam "bene."   Dico enim
21 constanter, graviter, sapienter, fortiter.   Haec etiam in
22 eculeum coniciuntur, quô vita non adspirat beata.
23 **Ma.** Quid igitur?   Solane beata vita, quaeso, relinquitur
24 extra ostium limenque carceris, cum constantia, gravitas,

25 fortitudo, sapientia, reliquaeque virtutes rapiantur ad tor-
26 torem nullumque recusent nec supplicium nec dolorem?
27   **Au.** Tu, si quid es facturus, nova aliqua conquiras opor-
28 tet; ista me minime movent, non solum quia pervulgata
29 sunt, sed multo magis quia, tamquam levia quaedam vina
30 nihil valent in aqua, sic Stoicorum ista magis gustata quam
31 potata delectant. . . . . Cum autem animum ab ista pictura
32 imaginibusque virtutum ad rem veritatemque traduxeris,
33 hoc nudum relinquitur, possitne quis beatus esse, quamdiu
34 torqueatur.   Quam ob rem hoc nunc quaeramus. . . .
35   **Ma.** Facile patior te isto modo agere, etsi iniquum est
36 praescribere mihi te, quemadmodum a me disputari velis.
37 Sed quaero utrum aliquid actum superioribus diebus an
38 nihil arbitremur.
39   **Au.** Actum vero, et aliquantum quidem.
40   **Ma.** Atqui, si ita est, profligata iam haec et paene ad
41 exitum adducta quaestio est.
42   **Au.** Quo tandem modo?
43   **Ma.** Quia motus turbulenti iactationesque animorum inci-
44 tatae et impetu inconsiderato elatae, rationem omnem
45 repellentes, vitae beatae nullam partem relinquunt.   Quis
46 enim potest, mortem aut dolorem metuens (quorum alterum
47 saepe adest, alterum semper impendet), esse non miser?
48 Quid si idem (quod plerumque fit) paupertatem, igno-
49 miniam, infamiam timet—si debilitatem, caecitatem—si
50 denique (quod non singulis hominibus, sed potentibus
51 populis saepe contigit) servitutem?   Potest, ea timens, esse
52 quisquam beatus?   Quid qui non modô ea futura timet, verum
53 etiam fert sustinetque praesentia?   Adde eôdem exsilia,
54 luctus, orbitates: qui (rebus his fractus) aegritudine eliditur,
55 potest tandem esse non miserrimus?   Quid vero?   Illum
56 quem libidinibus inflammatum et furentem videmus (omnia
57 rabide appetentem cum inexplebili cupiditate; quoque af-
58 fluentius voluptates undique hauriat, eo gravius ardentius-
59 que sitientem), nonne recte miserrimum dixeris?   Quid?
60 Elatus ille levitate inanique laetitiâ exultans et temere
61 gestiens nonne tanto miserior, quanto sibi videtur beatior?

62 Ergo, ut hi miseri, sic contra illi beati, quos nulli metus
63 terrent, nullae aegritudines exedunt, nullae libidines inci-
64 tant, nullae futtiles laetitiae exultantes languidis lique-
65 faciunt voluptatibus. Ut maris igitur tranquillitas intellegi-
66 tur nullā ne minimā quidem aurā fluctus commovente, sic
67 animi quietus et placatus status cernitur, cum perturbatio
68 nulla est, qua moveri queat.   Quodsi est, qui vim fortunae,
69 qui omnia humana quae cuique accidere possunt tolerabilia
70 ducat (ex quo nec timor eum nec angor attingat), idemque si
71 nihil concupiscat, nullā ecferatur animi inani voluptate,
72 quid est cur is non beatus sit?   Et si haec virtute efficiuntur,
73 quid est cur virtus ipsa per se non efficiat beatos?

[b] When the debate proves rather one-sided, the master delivers a lengthy sermon, full of popular anecdotes and examples,
on characteristics of the true philosopher—a fitting conclusion to
five whole days of discussion.   The following excerpts are from
the master's sermon:

[i] Which Was the Happier—The Despot Dionysius
or the Mathematician Archimedes? [1]

1   Duodequadraginta annos tyrannus Syracusanorum fuit
2 Dionysius, cum quinque et viginti natus annos dominatum
3 occupavisset.   Qua pulchritudine urbem, quibus autem
4 opibus praeditam servitute oppressam tenuit civitatem!
5 Atqui de hoc homine a bonis auctoribus sic scriptum accepi-
6 mus: summam fuisse eius in victu temperantiam, in rebusque
7 gerendis virum acrem et industrium—eundem tamen malefi-
8 cum naturā et iniustum.   Ex quo omnibus bene veritatem
9 intuentibus videri necesse est miserrimum.   Ea enim ipsa
10 quae concupierat, ne tum quidem, cum omnia se posse
11 censebat, consequebatur.   Qui cum esset bonis parentibus
12 atque honesto loco natus (etsi id quidem alius alio modo
13 tradidit) abundaretque et aequalium familiaritatibus et con-
14 suetudine propinquorum, . . . credebat eorum nemini, sed
15 iis, quos ex familiis locupletium servos delegerat (quibus
16 nomen servitutis ipse detraxerat) et quibusdam convenis et

[1] Both men were famous Syracusans.

17 feris barbaris corporis custodiam committebat.   Ita propter
18 iniustam dominatus cupiditatem in carcerem quodam modo
19 ipse se incluserat.
20   Quin etiam, ne tonsori collum committeret, tondere filias
21 suas docuit.   Ita sordido ancillarique artificio regiae vir-
22 gines, ut tonstriculae, tondebant barbam et capillum patris.
23 Et tamen ab his ipsis, cum iam essent adultae, ferrum
24 removit, instituitque ut candentibus iuglandium putamini-
25 bus barbam sibi et capillum adurerent.
26   Cumque duas uxores haberet (Aristomachen, civem suam,
27 Doridem autem Locrensem) sic noctu ad eas ventitabat, ut
28 omnia specularetur et perscrutaretur ante.   Et cum fossam
29 latam cubiculari lecto circumdedisset eiusque fossae transi-
30 tum ponticulo ligneo coniunxisset, eum ipsum, cum forem
31 cubiculi clauserat, detorquebat.   Idemque cum in com-
32 munibus suggestis consistere non auderet, contionari ex turri
33 altā solebat.   Atque is cum pilā ludere vellet (studiose enim
34 id factitabat) tunicamque poneret, adulescentulo, quem
35 amabat, tradidisse gladium dicitur.   Hîc cum quidam
36 familiaris iocans dixisset "huic quidem certe vitam tuam
37 committis" adrisissetque adulescens, utrumque iussit inter-
38 fici, alterum, quia viam demonstravisset interimendi sui,
39 alterum, quia dictum id risu approbavisset.   Atque eo facto
40 sic doluit, nihil ut tulerit gravius in vita; quem enim vehe-
41 menter amarat, occiderat.   Sic distrahuntur in contrarias
42 partis impotentium cupiditates. . . .
43   Quamquam hic quidem tyrannus ipse iudicavit, quam
44 esset beatus.   Nam cum quidam ex eius adsentatoribus,
45 Damocles, commemmoraret in sermone copias eius, opes,
46 maiestatem dominatus, rerum abundantiam, magnificen-
47 tiam aedium regiarum, negaretque umquam beatiorem
48 quemquam fuisse, "visne igitur," inquit, "O Damocle,
49 quoniam te haec vita delectat, ipse eam degustare et fortu-
50 nam experiri meam?"   Cum se ille cupere dixisset, conlo-
51 cari iussit hominem in aureo lecto, . . . abacosque complu-
52 ris ornavit argento auroque caelato.   Tum ad mensam

53 eximiā formā pueros delectos iussit consistere, eosque, nutum
54 illius intuentīs, diligenter ministrare. Aderant unguenta,
55 coronae; incendebantur odores; mensae conquisitissimis
56 epulis exstruebantur. Fortunatus sibi Damocles videbatur.
57 In hoc medio apparatu fulgentem gladium e lacunari, saetā
58 equinā aptum, demitti iussit, ut impenderet illius beati
59 cervicibus. Itaque nec pulchros illos ministratores aspicie-
60 bat nec plenum artis argentum, nec manum porrigebat in
61 mensam; iam ipsae defluebant coronae; denique exoravit
62 tyrannum, ut abire liceret, quod iam beatus nollet esse.
63 Satisne videtur declarasse Dionysius, nihil esse ei beatum,
64 cui semper aliqui terror impendeat? Atque ei ne integrum
65 quidem erat ut ad iustitiam remigraret, civibus libertatem
66 et iura redderet; iis enim se adulescens improvidā aetate
67 inretierat erratis eaque commiserat, ut salvus esse non
68 posset, si sanus esse coepisset.
69 Quantopere vero amicitias desideraret, quarum infidelita-
70 tem extimescebat, declaravit in Pythagoriis duobus illis,
71 quorum cum alterum vadem mortis accepisset, alter, ut
72 vadem suum liberaret, praesto fuisset ad horam mortis de-
73 stinatam, "utinam ego" inquit "tertius vobis amicus adscri-
74 berer!" Quam huic erat miserum carere consuetudine ami-
75 corum, societate victus, sermone omnino familiari—homini
76 praesertim docto a puero et artibus ingenuis erudito! Musi-
77 corum vero perstudiosum, poetam etiam tragicum—quam
78 bonum, nihil ad rem; in hoc enim genere nescioquo pacto,
79 magis quam in aliis, suum cuique pulchrum est; adhuc
80 neminem cognovi poetam (et mihi fuit cum Aquinio amici-
81 tia), qui sibi non optimus videretur; sic se res habet: te tua,
82 me delectant mea—sed ut ad Dionysium redeamus, omni
83 cultu et victu humano carebat; vivebat cum fugitivis, cum
84 facinerosis, cum barbaris; neminem, qui aut libertate dignus
85 esset aut vellet omnino liber esse, sibi amicum arbitrabatur.
86 Non ego iam cum huius vitā (qua taetrius, miserius,
87 detestabilius excogitare nihil possum) Platonis aut Archytae
88 vitam comparabo, doctorum hominum et plane sapientium;

89 ex eadem urbe humilem homunculum a pulvere et radio
90 excitabo, qui multis annis post fuit, Archimedem. Cuius
91 ego, quaestor, ignoratum ab Syracusanis (cum esse omnino
92 negarent), saeptum undique et vestitum vepribus et dumetis
93 indagavi sepulchrum. Tenebam enim quosdam senariolos,
94 quos in eius monumento esse inscriptos acceperam, qui
95 declarabant in summo sepulchro sphaeram esse positam cum
96 cylindro. Ego autem cum omnia conlustrarem oculis (est
97 enim ad portas Agragentinas magna frequentia sepulchro-
98 rum), animadverti columellam non multum e dumis eminen-
99 tem, in qua inerat sphaerae figura et cylindri. Atque ego statim
100 Syracusanis (erant autem principes mecum) dixi me illud
101 ipsum arbitrari esse, quod quaererem. Immissi cum falci-
102 bus multi purgarunt et aperuerunt locum. Quô cum pate-
103 factus esset aditus, ad adversam basim accessimus. Ap-
104 parebat epigramma, exesis posterioribus partibus versicu-
105 lorum—dimidiatis fere. Ita nobilissima Graeciae civitas,
106 quondam vero etiam doctissima, sui civis unius acutissimi
107 monumentum ignorasset, nisi ab homine Arpinate didi-
108 cisset.

109   Sed redeat, unde aberravit oratio. Quis est omnium, qui
110 modô cum Musis (id est cum humanitate et cum doctrina)
111 habeat aliquod commercium, qui se non hunc mathematicum
112 malit quam illum tyrannum? Si vitae modum actionemque
113 quaerimus, alterius mens rationibus agitandis exquirendis-
114 que alebatur cum oblectatione sollertiae (qui est unus
115 suavissimus pastus animorum), alterius in caede et iniuriis
116 cum et diurno et nocturno metu. Age confer Democritum,
117 Pythagoram, Anaxagoram: quae regna, quas opes studiis
118 eorum et delectationibus antepones? Etenim, quae pars
119 optima est in homine, in ea situm esse necesse est illud, quod
120 quaeris, optimum. Quid est autem in homine sagaci ac
121 bona mente melius? Eius bono fruendum est igitur, si beati
122 esse volumus; bonum autem mentis est virtus; ergo hac
123 beatam vitam contineri necesse est. Hinc omnia quae pul-
124 chra, honesta, praeclara sunt, ut supra dixi—sed dicendum

125 idem illud paulo uberius videtur—plena gaudiorum sunt.
126 Ex perpetuis autem plenisque gaudiis cum perspicuum sit
127 vitam beatam existere, sequitur ut ea existat ex honestate.

[*ii*] Socrates, Xenocrates, and Diogenes—Despisers of
Wealth and Power

1 Socrates, in pompa cum magna vis auri argentique ferre-
2 tur, "quam multa non desidero" inquit. Xenocrates, cum
3 legati ab Alexandro quinquaginta ei talenta attulissent
4 (quae erat pecunia temporibus illis, Athenis praesertim,
5 maxima), abduxit legatos ad cenam in Academiam; iis ap-
6 posuit tantum quod satis esset, nullo apparatu. Cum pos-
7 tridie rogarent eum, cui numerari iuberet, "quid? vos
8 hesternā" inquit "cenulā non intellexistis, me pecuniā non
9 egere?" Quos cum tristiores vidisset, triginta minas ac-
10 cepit, ne aspernari regis liberalitatem videretur. At vero
11 Diogenes liberius (ut Cynicus) Alexandro, roganti ut diceret,
12 si quid opus esset, "nunc quidem paululum" inquit "a sole":
13 offecerat videlicet apricanti. Et hic quidem disputare sole-
14 bat, quanto regem Persarum vitā fortunāque superaret; sibi
15 nihil deesse, illi nihil satis umquam fore; se eius voluptates
16 non desiderare, quibus numquam satiari ille posset—suas
17 eum consequi nullo modo posse.

[*iii*] Simplicity—The Source of True Happiness

1 Darius in fuga cum aquam turbidam et cadaveribus in-
2 quinatam bibisset, negavit umquam se bibisse iucundius.
3 Numquam videlicet sitiens biberat. Nec esuriens Ptolo-
4 maeus ederat, cui cum, peragranti Aegyptum (comitibus
5 non consecutis), cibarius in casa panis datus esset, nihil
6 visum est illo pane iucundius.
7 Socraten ferunt, cum usque ad vesperum contentius
8 ambularet, quaesitumque esset ex eo quare id faceret, re-
9 spondisse se, quo melius cenaret, obsonare ambulando
10 famem.
11 Quid? Victum Lacedaemoniorum in philitiis nonne
12 videmus? Ubi cum tyrannus cenavisset Dionysius, negavit

se iure illo nigro, quod cenae caput erat, delectatum.   Tum
is, qui illa coxerat: "minime mirum!—condimenta enim
defuerunt." "Quae tandem?" inquit ille. "Labor in
venatu, sudor, cursus ad Eurotam, fames, sitis: his enim
rebus Lacedaemoniorum epulae condiuntur."

Atque hoc non ex hominum more solum, sed etiam ex
bestiis intellegi potest, quae, ut quicquid obiectum est quod
modô a natura non sit alienum, eo contentae non quaerunt
amplius. . . .

Timotheum, clarum hominem Athenis et principem
civitatis, ferunt, cum cenavisset apud Platonem eoque con-
vivio admodum delectatus esset vidissetque eum postridie,
dixisse: "vestrae quidem cenae non solum in praesentia, sed
etiam postero die iucundae sunt."

Quid quod ne mente quidem recte uti possumus, multo
cibo et potione completi?   Est praeclara epistula Platonis
ad Dionis propinquos, in qua scriptum est his fere verbis:
"quô cum venissem, vita illa beata (quae ferebatur), plena
Italicarum Syracusiarumque mensarum, nullo modo mihi
placuit—bis in die saturum fieri, nec umquam pernoctare
solum, ceteraque quae comitantur huic vitae; in qua sapiens
nemo efficietur umquam, moderatus vero multo minus.
Quae enim natura tam mirabiliter temperari potest?"

Quo modo igitur iucunda vita potest esse, a qua absit
prudentia, absit moderatio?   Ex quo Sardanapalli, opu-
lentissimi Syriae regis, error agnoscitur, qui incîdi iussit in
busto:

"Haec habeo quae edi, quaeque exsaturata libido
hausit; at illa iacent multa et praeclara relicta."

"Quid aliud" inquit Aristoteles "in bovis, non in regis,
sepulchro inscriberes?   Haec habere se mortuum dicit,
quae ne vivus quidem diutius habebat quam fruebatur."

Cur igitur divitiae desiderentur, aut ubi paupertas beatos
esse non sinit? . . . Dies deficiat, si velim paupertatis
causam defendere.   Aperta enim res est—et cotidie nos ipsa
Natura admonet, quam paucis, quam parvis rebus egeat,
quam vilibus.

T. LUCRETIUS CARUS

(Born in *99* B.C.; active from *70–55*)

His Life and Works

Lucretius was one of the world's great philosophic poets.   He was an Epicurean and, following the tradition of the great Greek philosopher-scientists (Xenócrates, Empédocles, and Parménides), embodied his philosophy in a didactic poem of some 7000 lines, contained in six books.   The style of the poem is essentially epic— i.e., Lucretius consciously endeavored to impart to his language and style the grandeur and dignity associated with epic poetry. He succeeded so well that the *de Rerum Natura* is a landmark in the evolution of Latin hexameter verse, a milestone in its course of development from the crude beginnings of Ennius to the perfection of Vergil—for Lucretius had genuine poetic genius and power. But only certain passages of the long didactic poem reflect this power; the rest, although sometimes ingenious and sometimes profound, is no more poetic than versified physics, chemistry, and astronomy would be in any language or era.   Had he lived elsewhere and at some other time, Lucretius might have found literary models more suited—from our point of view—to his needs; as a philosophical scientist and a Roman, however, he cannot be blamed for following his great Greek predecessors.   Thus he created a monumental work of human thought, permeated with poetic genius.   The uneven quality of his work Lucretius shares with all other philosophic poets—Dante and Goethe included; it is not possible to be wholly philosophic and wholly poetic at the same time.

Not even Plato treats of more compelling and fundamental human problems.   To be sure, Lucretius presents the physical side of the atomic theory—with its explanations of matter, energy, and mind—more or less perfunctorily; but he argues with prophetic zeal and passionate earnestness for the moral inferences of this system—namely, the materialistic conception of the universe, the mortality of the soul, and atheism.   For him contemporary religions held only empty formalism and superstitious terrors. Although he denounced religion, his enthusiasm rose to such heights that he unwittingly promulgated a "religion of science." As an apostle of Epicureanism, Lucretius was as religious as any poet-teacher that ever lived.

The only sketch of the life of Lucretius that has survived from ancient times happens to come from the *Chronological Tables* of St. Jerome. The following entry appears under the year 95 B.C.[1]: "T. Lucretius the poet was born, who afterwards was made insane by a love potion, and when, in the intervals of his madness, he had written several books, which Cicero corrected, he killed himself by his own hand in the forty-fourth year of his age." Hardly anything more derogatory to the great poet could be said or implied; in other words Lucretius was anathema to the Christian fathers. It is safe to conclude that whatever truth there may be in St. Jerome's account has been considerably colored. On the whole this biographical item tells us almost nothing worth while about Lucretius—it is pure scandal!

Nevertheless St. Jerome does give *one* interesting fact—namely, that Cicero edited the *de Rerum Natura*. This is really surprising, as Cicero opposed the Epicurean philosophy and mentions Lucretius only once, in a letter to his brother—a brief reference, obscure in part, but indicating that Cicero recognized the other man's greatness.

Epicureanism and Stoicism were the two great schools of Greek philosophy in the Roman period. But nothing could be more misleading than to call them "philosophies" in the modern sense, for inasmuch as they supplied adherents with a complete faith— i.e., an explanation of the universe and man's place therein, a code of morals, and a philosophy of life—, they were essentially religions. Stoicism, which had many tenets in common with Christianity, appealed more strongly to the Romans than Epicureanism, which always suffered from misinterpretation. Because Epicurus taught that the chief good in life is pleasure and the chief evil pain, and that there is neither a hereafter nor a personal God, he became the patron saint of every roué and voluptuary and gave to modern languages the word *epicure*.

[1] St. Jerome made a technical error in the date.

We know, however, that the historical Epicurus was a man of blameless life:

> Him not the splintered lightenings, nor the roll
> Of thunders daunted. Undismayed his soul
> Rose, and outsoared the thunder, plumbed the abyss,
> And scanned the wheeling worlds from pole to pole;

> And from the abyss brought back for you and me
> The secret that alone can set men free.
> He showed us how the worlds and worlds began,
> And what things can, and what things cannot be.[1]

Lucretius represented the nobler interpretation of Epicureanism, not the false philosophy of the voluptuary.

De Rerum Natura

SELECTIONS FROM BOOK I

[1]

INVOCATION

[Lucretius appeals for poetic inspiration not to the Muses, but to Venus! In deference to mythological tradition, he depicts her as the mundane goddess of love; but in his philosophy she symbolizes something higher—the universal regenerative power that transcends all other forces of nature. There is little, if any, inconsistency in the invocation of a goddess by a reputed atheist, for Lucretius was that in name only; in spirit he was a devout and reverent worshipper of the mystery of the universe. Moreover the Epicureans did not deny the existence of the gods, but denied only their interest and intervention in human affairs and in the immutable laws of nature. It is therefore appropriate for Lucretius, the philosopher and poet, to invoke Venus, the spirit of Life and of Peace.]

1   Aeneadum genetrix, hominum divomque voluptas,
2 alma Venus, caeli subter labentia signa
3 quae mare navigerum, quae terras frugiferentis

---

[1] W. H. Mallock, *Lucretius on Life and Death*, II, vi–viii, p. 9; Portland, Maine, 1919.

4 concelebras, per te quoniam genus omne animantum
5 concipitur visitque exortum lumina solis,

. . . .

6 te sociam studeo scribendis versibus esse,
7 quos ego de rerum natura pangere conor
8 Memmiadae nostro, quem tu, dea, tempore in omni
9 omnibus ornatum voluisti excellere rebus.
10 Quo magis aeternum da dictis, diva, leporem.
11 Effice ut interea fera moenera militiaï
12 per maria ac terras omnis sopita quiescant.
13 Nam tu sola potes tranquillā pace iuvare
14 mortalis, quoniam belli fera moenera Mavors
15 armipotens regit, in gremium qui saepe tuum se
16 reicit, aeterno devictus vulnere amoris.

. . . .

17 Nam neque nos agere hoc patriaï tempore iniquo
18 possumus aequo animo nec Memmi clara propago
19 talibus in rebus communi desse saluti.

[2]

THE MISSION OF EPICURUS

1   Humana ante oculos foede cum vita iaceret
2 in terris, oppressa gravi sub Religione,
3 quae caput a caeli regionibus ostendebat
4 horribili super aspectu mortalibus instans,
5 primum Graius, homo mortalis, tollere contra
6 est oculos ausus primusque obsistere contra,
7 quem neque fama deum nec fulmina nec minitanti
8 murmure compressit caelum, sed eo magis acrem
9 inritat animi virtutem, effringere ut arta
10 naturae primus portarum claustra cupiret.
11 Ergo vivida vis animi pervicit et extra
12 processit longe flammantia moenia mundi
13 atque omne immensum peragravit mente animoque;
14 unde refert nobis victor, quid possit oriri,
15 quid nequeat, finita potestas denique cuique

16 quanam sit ratione atque alte terminus haerens.
17 Quare Religio pedibus subiecta vicissim
18 obteritur; nos exaequat victoria caelo.

[3]

RELIGION, WHAT CRIMES ARE COMMITTED IN THY NAME!

[Lucretius proves his point by a famous story from Greek mythology: When the Greeks assembled at Aulis in Boeotia to embark on the Trojan War, their fleet was long held by adverse winds, until the seer Calchas declared that the gods could be appeased only by the sacrifice of Iphigenía (or Iphianassa), eldest daughter of Agamemnon. On the pretext that she was to marry Achilles, Iphigenia was lured to Aulis and there sacrified to Diana. A less savage version has it that as the knife fell, a hart was miraculously substituted for the victim and she herself snatched away by the goddess and transported to Tauris.[1]

Lucretius' description of Iphigenia's sacrifice may be compared with Tennyson's, in the latter's *Dream of Fair Women*. Iphigenia speaks:

> I was cut off from hope in that sad place,
>   Which yet to name my spirit loathes and fears:
> My father held his hand upon his face;
>   I, blinded, with my tears,
>
> Still strove to speak: my voice was thick with sighs
>   As in a dream. Dimly I could descry
> The stern black-bearded kings with wolfish eyes,
>   Waiting to see me die.
>
> The high masts flickered as they lay afloat;
>   The crowds, the temples, waver'd, and the shore;
> The bright death quiver'd at the victim's throat,
>   Touch'd; and I knew no more.

Lucretius might well have used examples from Roman history— e.g., the burying alive of four human victims in Rome during the panic that followed the battle of Cannae, in 216 B.C.—about a century and a half before he wrote. Had he lived in medieval or

---

[1] Cf. Abraham and Isaac.

modern times, he might have instanced many wars of religious
persecution, but of such wholesale crimes in the name of religion
he was happily ignorant.]

1   Illud in his rebus vereor, ne forte rearis
2   impia te rationis inire elementa viamque
3   indugredi sceleris.   Quod contra saepius illa
4   Religio peperit scelerosa atque impia facta:
5   Aulide quo pacto Triviaï virginis aram
6   Iphianassaï turparunt sanguine foede
7   ductores Danaum delecti, prima virorum.
8   Cui simul infula, virgineos circumdata comptus,
9   ex utraque pari mālarum parte profusa 'st,
10   et maestum simul ante aras adstare parentem
11   sensit et hunc propter ferrum celare ministros
12   aspectuque suo lacrimas effundere civis,
13   muta metu terram genibus summissa petebat.
14   Nec miserae prodesse in tali tempore quibat
15   quod patrio princeps donarat nomine regem.
16   Nam sublata virum manibus tremibundaque ad aras
17   deducta est, non ut, sollemni more sacrorum
18   perfecto, posset claro comitari hymenaeo;
19   sed casta inceste, nubendi tempore in ipso,
20   hostia concǐderet, mactatu maesta parentis,
21   exitus ut classi felix faustusque daretur.
22   Tantum Religio potuit suadere malorum!

[4]

The Difficulty of Lucretius' Task

1   Nec me animi fallit Graiorum obscura reperta
2   difficile illustrare Latinis versibus esse,
3   multa novis verbis praesertim cum sit agendum
4   propter egestatem linguae et rerum novitatem;
5   sed tua me virtus tamen et sperata voluptas
6   suavis amicitiae quemvis sufferre laborem
7   suadet et inducit noctes vigilare serenas
8   quaerentem, dictis quibus et quo carmine demum

9 clara tuae possim praepandere lumina menti,
10 res quibus occultas penitus convisere possis.

[5]

THE TWO BASIC LAWS OF NATURE

[Not religion, but science, is man's solace. We live in a universe based on immutable law. Miracles, the caprice of the gods, and divine vengeance are impossible in an ordered universe. Religion is but the reflex of man's ignorant fears.

According to Lucretius the two basic laws of nature are: (1) that nothing ever comes from nothing, and (2) that nothing is ever reduced to nothing.   Here he has vaguely foreshadowed the doctrines of the Conservation of Energy and the Indestructibility of Atomic Matter, although the proofs which he adduces would seem superficial to modern experimental science.]

1   Hunc igitur terrorem animi tenebrasque necesse est
2   non radii solis neque lucida tela diei
3   discutiant, sed naturae species ratioque.
4   Principium cuius hinc nobis exordia sumet:
5   NULLAM REM E NILO GIGNI DIVINITUS UMQUAM.
6   Quippe ita formido mortalīs continet omnīs,
7   quod multa in terris fieri caeloque tuentur,
8   quorum operum causas nulla ratione videre
9   possunt, ac fieri divino numine rentur.
10 Quas ob res ubi viderimus nil posse creari
11 de nilo, tum quod sequimur iam rectius inde
12 perspiciemus, et unde queat res quaeque creari
13 et quo quaeque modo fiant operā sine divum.

  .   .   .   .

[14]   Praeterea HAUD REDIT AD NILUM RES ULLA, sed omnes
15 discidio redeunt in corpora materiaï.
[16] Quapropter pereunt imbres, ubi eos pater aether
17 in gremium matris terraï praecipitavit;
18 at nitidae surgunt fruges ramique virescunt
19 arboribus, crescunt ipsae fetuque gravantur;
20 hinc alitur porro nostrum genus atque ferarum;

21 hinc laetas urbes pueris florere videmus
22 frondiferasque novis avibus canere undique silvas;
23 hinc fessae pecudes pingui per pabula laeta
24 corpora deponunt, et candens lacteus umor
25 uberibus manat distentis; hinc nova proles
26 artubus infirmis teneras lasciva per herbas
27 ludit, lacte mero mentes perculsa novellas.
28 Haud igitur penitus pereunt quaecumque videntur,
29 quando alid ex alio reficit natura nec ullam
30 rem gigni patitur, nisi morte adiuta alienā.

[6]

The Composition of Matter

[Lucretius contends that matter is not composed of atoms solidly packed; there is void in all things.   He adduces two proofs of his contention: (1) the permeability of matter (ll. 4–11); and (2) the relative density, or specific gravity, of different substances (ll. 12–21).]

1   Nec tamen undique corporeā stipata tenentur
2 omnia naturā; namque est in rebus inane.
3 Quod tibi cognosse in multis erit utile rebus.

. . . .

4   Dissipat in corpus sese cibus omne animantum.
5 Crescunt arbusta et fetus in tempore fundunt,
6 quod cibus in totas usque ab radicibus imis
7 per truncos ac per ramos diffunditur omnis.
8 Inter saepta meant voces et clausa domorum
9 transvolitant.   Rigidum permanat frigus ad ossa.
10 Quod, nisi inania sint, quâ possint corpora quaeque
11 transire, haud ulla fieri ratione videres.
12   Denique cur alias aliis praestare videmus
13 pondere res rebus, nilo maiore figurā?
14 Nam si tantundem est in lanae glomere quantum
15 corporis in plumbo est, tantundem pendere par est,
16 corporis officium est quoniam premere omnia deorsum,

17 contra autem natura manet sine pondere inanis.
18 Ergo quod magnum est aeque leviusque videtur,
19 nimirum plus esse sibi declarat inanis;
20 at contra gravius plus in se corporis esse
21 dedicat et multo vacui minus intus habere.
22   Est igitur nimirum (id quod ratione sagaci
23 quaerimus) admixtum rebus, quod inane vocamus.

C. VALERIUS CATULLUS

(BORN IN *84* B.C.; ACTIVE FROM *66–54*)

His Character and Achievements

Catullus is the most versatile and original genius of all the
Latin poets. Although he died at about thirty years of age,
Catullus produced a remarkable variety of verse in the dozen
years of his literary career and, by virtue of a few masterpieces,
ranks among the great lyric poets of the world.   Nevertheless
he is not generally regarded as the greatest of Roman poets,
"originality" not being the criterion in classical literature it is in
modern.   His is rather an exotic quality, lacking the depth and
maturity of character of both Vergil and Horace.   But in the first
twelve years of their literary careers neither Vergil nor Horace
could match even the technical skill of Catullus; nor did they ever
equal his spontaneity.   One can only conjecture what Catullus
might have accomplished, had he lived his full span of life.

Catullus was both gifted and studious   His poems include, on
the one hand, the most simple and natural verses in the Latin
language, and on the other, some of the most elaborate and artificial of metrical compositions.   Because of the rigidity and complexity of the meters of Greek and Latin verse, Catullus achieved
an extraordinary feat in mastering so many different verse forms;
in this respect he is Horace's peer, if not his superior.   Employing
about a dozen different metrical forms, he showed himself a facile
epigrammatist, a trenchant satirist, a charming and witty writer
of *vers de société*, an elegist tenderly serious or mockingly trivial as
the occasion demanded, and a lyric poet unsurpassed.

For modern readers the term "lyric" requires a word of explanation. It is a term that is very loosely and vaguely used in modern times to cover a multitude of sins! In literature it is generally applied to short poems that are subjective expressions of a poet's moods and feelings, and defines the spirit rather than the form of a composition. In Greek and Latin literature, however, the term merely denotes verses written in those meters and stanzas which the Greeks originally designed for song, as contrasted with recitation; it is therefore a definition of metrical form. Now Catullus wrote comparatively few poems that were lyric in form (i.e., in the Greek sense), but many that were lyric in spirit (i.e., in the modern sense). His modern fame as a lyric poet is based therefore on the spirit of his poetry and on the expression of his emotional nature, regardless of the verse forms he used. To the Romans he was renowned chiefly as an elegist and an epigrammatist.

Catullus was born of a wealthy family, in the town of Verona. Thus, descended from Roman colonists, he nevertheless grew up in a land of Celtic traditions—Cisalpine Gaul. His poetic career began in Verona, though he went to live in Rome when hardly more than a stripling. He followed no career save that of a gentleman of leisure and a poet.

The verses of this brilliant young poet reveal to us a stratum of Roman society in which Greek culture and Greek morals are supreme. The old sturdy puritanical Roman character has completely vanished from this "high" society. The rapidity with which Roman morals had become corrupted is amazing. Catullus led the life of an aesthete and a Bohemian; he is no more representative of traditional Roman character than Lord Byron or Oscar Wilde are of the British.

I

Preliminary Brief Selections

(TO FAMILIARIZE THE STUDENT WITH THE METERS OF CATULLUS.)

[1]

The Non-Lyric Meters

[a] HEXAMETER

The Greek hexameter was the traditional meter of stately epic narrative. When, in the sixth century B.C., epics ceased to be written by the Greeks, the hexameter was not discarded; it was adapted, in style and technique, to other uses—to familiar verse, to the pastoral, and even to song.

After a lapse of three or four centuries—in the Hellenistic or Alexandrian period of Greek literature—, the epic was revived. The metrical technique of the "new" epic hexameter was more refined and mannered, and the length of poems greatly reduced. Apollonius of Rhodes with his *Argonautica* in four books was regarded as an extremist in lengthy composition; most poets cultivated the *epyllion*—a mere scene or single episode in epic style, generally briefer than a single book of Homer.

Catullus showed his versatility in the two hexameter poems that are included in his collected works. One is a song, the other an *epyllion*.

[i] The idyllic wedding song, in which youths and maidens sing in antiphonal chorus, begins as follows:

1 Vesper adest; iuvenes, consurgite; Vesper Olympo,
2 exspectata diu, vix tandem lumina tollit.
3 Surgere iam tempus, iam pinguīs linquere mensas;
4 iam veniet virgo; iam dicetur hymenaeus:
5 Hýmēn, ó Hўmĕnaé', Hymén ades, ó Hymenaée.

And in praise of maidenhood the maidens sing:

6 Ut flos in saeptis secretus nascitur hortis,
7 ignotus pecori, nullo convulsus aratro,
8 quem mulcent aurae, firmat sol, educat imber;
9 multi illum pueri, multae optavēre puellae;

10 idem cum tenui carptus defloruit ungui,
11 nulli illum pueri, nullae optavēre puellae:
12 sic virgo, dum intacta manet, dum cara suis est;
13 cum castum amisit polluto corpore florem,
14 nec pueris iucunda manet nec cara puellis.
15 Hýmen ó Hymenaé', Hymén ades ó Hymenaée.

The youths reply:

16 Ut vidua in nudo vitis quae nascitur arvo
17 numquam se extollit, numquam mitem educat uvam,
18 sed tenerum prono deflectens pondere corpus
19 iam iam contingit summum radice flagellum;
20 hanc nulli agricolae, nulli accoluēre iuvenci;
21 at si forte eadem est ulmo coniuncta marito,
22 multi illam agricolae, multi accoluēre iuvenci:
23 sic virgo, dum intacta manet, dum inculta senescit;
24 cum par conubium maturo tempore adepta est,
25 cara viro magis et minus est invisa parenti.

[*ii*] Very different is the stately measure of his precise and learned *epyllion* on the marriage of Peleus and Thetis, which opens as follows, telling how the *Argo* carried a band of youths to fetch the Golden Fleece:

1 Peliaco quondam prognatae vertice pinus
2 dicuntur liquidas Neptuni nasse per undas
3 Phásidos ád fluctús et fínes Aéetaéos,
4 cum lecti iuvenes, Argivae robora pubis,
5 auratam optantes Colchīs avertere pellem,
6 ausi sunt vada salsa citā decurrere puppi,
7 caerula verrentes abiegnis aequora palmis.

[b] ELEGIAC

The elegiac couplet was a very ancient Greek variant of the straight hexameter—i.e., every other verse was a pentameter. Actually this is a misnomer, for the pentameter has *six* feet, or bars—musically speaking; but in the third and sixth bars a "rest," or pause, is substituted for the unaccented half of the foot:

Hexameter   ∠ ˇˇ   ∠ ˇˇ   ∠ ˇˇ   ∠ ˇˇ   ∠ ˇˇ   ∠ ˍ

Pentameter   ∠ ˇˇ   ∠ ˇˇ   ∠   ∠ ˇˇ   ∠ ˇˇ   ∠

Subtracting two half-feet from six feet, theoretically one gets five; therefore the shorter line is called a "pentameter."

Originally the Greeks used the elegiac couplet for that very important form of primitive emotional poetry, the dirge. As Greek literature developed, elegiacs came to be used for reflective and didactic verse, love poetry, brief narrative, *vers de société*, and epigrams—in other words, for everything but the epic. Catullus uses the elegiac couplet chiefly for epigrams (some of which would be called lyrics today) and for two or three longer poems. Two of the epigrams follow:

[*i*] Misplaced *H*'s

[Arrius—a startling anticipation of the cockney *'Arry*—affects a Greek accent and bungles.]

1 "Chommoda" dicebat, si quando "commoda" vellet
2   dicere; et "insidias" Arrius "hinsidias,"
3 et tum mirifice sperabat se esse locutum,
4   cum, quantum poterat, dixerat "h-hinsidias."
5 Credo, sic mater, sic liber avunculus eius,
6   sic maternus avus dixerat atque avia.
7 Hoc misso in Syriam, requierant omnibus aures:
8   audibant eadem haec leniter et leviter;
9 nec sibi postillā metuebant talia verba,
10   cum subito affertur nuntius horribilis:
11 Ionios fluctus, postquam illûc Arrius isset,
12   iam non Ionios esse, sed "Hionios."

[*ii*] A Curt Rebuff to Julius Caesar

[The occasion for this poem is unknown.]

1 Nil nimium studeo, Caesar, tibi velle placere;
2   nec scire utrum sis albus an ater homo.

[c] LIMPING IAMBIC

The Greek satiric poet Hippónax (sixth century B.C.) invented a meter whose taunting drawl just suited the insolence of his nature. The "limping" iambic—called variously the choliambic, or scazon—became a traditional meter for satire, and is so used by Catullus. The limp comes at the end—i.e., it is a six-foot iambic with a *trochee* in the last foot:

‿ ∠   ‿ ∠   ‿ ∠   ‿ ∠   ‿ ∠   ∠ ‿

To avoid monotony, other feet are substituted for the pure iambs—though far less freely than in the iambic verses of comic dialogue.　For instance, Catullus generally uses spondees in the first and third feet, as in line 11 of the epigram on Suffenus:

$$- \; \acute{} \quad \cup \; \acute{} \quad - \; \acute{} \quad \cup \; \acute{} \quad \cup \; \acute{} \quad \acute{} \; \cup$$

Nimir'　id'om　nesfall　imur　neque'st　quisquam.

Other substitutions are rare, the only example occurring in line 12 of this same epigram:

$$- \; \acute{} \quad \cup \; \acute{} \; \cup \quad - \; \acute{} \quad \cup \; \acute{} \quad \cup \; \acute{} \quad \acute{} \; \cup$$

quemnon　inali　quare　vide　resuf　fenum.

On the One Failing of Suffenus

1 Suffenus iste, Vare, quem probe nosti,
2 homo est venustus et dicax et urbanus,
3 idemque longe plurimos facit versus!
4 Puto esse ego illi milia aut decem aut plura.
. . . .
5 Haec cum legas tu, bellus ille et urbanus
6 Suffenus unus caprimulgus aut fossor
7 rursus videtur—tantum abhorret ac mutat!
8 . . . . Neque idem umquam
9 aeque est beatus, ac poema cum scribit:
10 tam gaudet in se tamque se ipse miratur.
11 Nimirum idem omnes fallimur, neque est quisquam
12 quem non in aliqua re videre Suffenum
13 possis.　Suus cuique attributus est error,
14 sed non videmus manticae quod in tergo est.

There is more to be said, however, about Catullus' use of the choliambic.　No better proof of his originality could be found than the successful use of this meter, in defiance of its traditional connotation, to express deep and tender sentiment.　Catullus could and did employ the choliambic for lyrics (in the modern sense), as we shall see later.

[d] REGULAR IAMBIC

In addition to the three meters already discussed (the hexameter, elegiac, and limping iambic)—all frequently used by Catullus—, there are three varieties of the regular iambic—viz., the six- and seven-foot iambic with free substitutions, as in

comedy; and the "pure" six-foot.   These meters are used spar-
ingly.   The infrequency of the iambic with substitutions in
Catullus is probably due to its being regarded as unliterary and
unpolished for brief epigrams—fit only for popular extemporaneous satire.   The " pure " iambic on the other hand, because of
its difficulty, was used but once by Catullus.

[i] Six-Foot Iambic With Substitutions

This meter occurs in a political epigram—a jibe at the Caesarian party:

The World is Going to the Dogs!

1 Quid ést, Catúlle?   Quíd moráris émorí?
2 Sellā ín curúli strúma Nóniús sedét.
3 Per cónsulátum périerát Vatíniús.
4 Quid ést, Catúlle?   Quíd moráris émorí.

[ii] " Seven-Foot "[1] Iambic With Substitutions

This meter is used in a poem of personal invective:

To a Light-Fingered and Effeminate Dandy

1 Remítte pálliúm mihí meúm, quod ínvolásti,
2 sudáriúmque Saétabúm catágraphósque Thýnos,
3 inépte, quaé palám solés habére támquam avíta.
4 Quae núnc tuís ab únguibús reglútina ét remítte,
5 ne láneúm latúsculúm manúsque móllicéllas,
6 inústa túrpitér tibí, flagélla cónscribíllent,
7 et ínsolénter aéstués, velút minúta mágno
8 deprénsa návis ín marí, vesániénte vénto.

[iii] "Pure" Iambic

The "pure" iambic—every foot a pure iamb, with no substitutions—was an experiment.   In discussing Plautus, we have already contrasted this meter with the loose rhythms of comedy
(see p. 29).   Catullus used it for the dainty and playful verses
on his sailboat:

The Yacht's Epitaph

1 Phasellus ille quem videtis, hospites,
2 ait fuisse navium celerrimus.

         . . . .

[1] There are really seven and a half feet to a line.

3 Amastri Pontica et Cytore buxifer,
4 tibi haec fuisse et esse cognitissima
5 ait phasellus; ultimā ex origine
6 tuo stetisse dicit in cacumine,
7 deinde tot per impotentia freta
8 erum tulisse (laeva sive dextera
9 vocaret aura, sive utrumque Iuppiter
10 simul secundus incidisset in pedem),
11 neque ulla vota litoralibus deis
12 sibi esse facta, cum veniret a mari
13 novissime hunc ad usque limpidum lacum.
14 Sed haec prius fuere; nunc recondita
15 senet quiete seque dedicat tibi,
16 gemelle Castor et gemelle Castoris.

[e] GALLIAMBIC

Finally there is the most unusual of all of Catullus' experiments—his *Attis*, a poem of almost one hundred lines in the wild galliambic meter. This meter is too difficult and uncertain, however, for beginners to discuss.

[2]
The Lyric Meters

Lyric meters—i.e., song meters, in the technical Greek sense—exhibit greater complexity of rhythmical structure, combined with greater rigidity; in other words, lines and stanzas are uniform—they do not vary as in the epic chant and the stage dialogue. Although the metrical pattern may be more complex, it is strictly adhered to; consequently lyric meters (as contrasted with those of comedy) are difficult to compose but easy to "scan," for almost no variations or alternatives occur.

[a] HENDECASYLLABIC

The full flower of lyric melody is found only in the poems composed in strophes, or stanzas; but first—as a natural transition from the non-lyric to the lyric—we should consider the measure that was semi-lyric in spirit—Catullus' most distinctive and original verse form: the eleven-syllable (hendecasyllabic) line, or

Phalaecéan.[1] With masterly touch, Catullus used this meter
chiefly for epigrams and occasionally for what we would call
lyrics. The non-lyric affinities of the meter prevailed in subsequent Latin literature, although the form was made slightly more
rigid. It became one of the three traditional meters—all established by Catullus—that were used for the satiric epigram (viz.,
the elegiac, the choliambic, and the hendecasyllabic).[2]

The scheme of Catullus' hendecasyllabics is as follows:[3]

$$\left.\begin{array}{c} \angle\ x \\ \cup\ - \end{array}\right\} \qquad \angle\ \cup\ \cup \qquad \angle\ \cup \qquad \angle\ \cup \qquad \angle\ x$$

There are always eleven syllables in the spoken line—i.e., after
elisions have been made. The three different forms of the first
foot are found in lines 4–6 of the first selection:

$\angle\ \cup$	$\angle\ \cup\ \cup$	$\angle\ \cup$	$\angle\ \cup$	$\angle\ \cup$
grati	astibi	maxi	masca	tullus
$\cup\ -$	$\angle\ \cup\ \cup$	$\angle\ \cup$	$\angle\ \cup$	$\angle\ \cup$
agit	pessimus	omni	umpo	eta
$\angle\ -$	$\angle\ \cup\ \cup$	$\angle\ \cup$	$\angle\ \cup$	$\angle\ \cup$
tánto	pessimus	omni	umpo	eta.

Catullus uses this meter with an ease and simplicity of style that
is unmatched in all Latin literature.

[i] Humble Thanks to Cicero

[The occasion for this poem is unknown.]

1 Disertissime Romuli nepotum,
2 quot sunt quotque fuēre, Marce Tulli,
3 quotque post aliis erunt in annis,
4 gratias tibi maximas Catullus
5 agit, pessimus omnium poeta:
6 tanto pessimus omnium poeta,
7 quanto tu optimus omnium patronus.

[1] Like all Greek lyric measures, this was named for the poet who composed
or established it—i.e., Phalaécus.

[2] These three meters occur later in the epigrams of Martial.

[3] The long and short syllables are denoted in the usual way for this verse
form, but the sign x is now introduced to indicate a variable syllable.
It must be remembered that in any one line the variable syllable is either long
or short—not both! In *all* kinds of verse—epic and dramatic, as well as lyric—
the final syllable in a line is variable, since it is associated with the pause coming at the end of that line.

[ii] To Julius Caesar

[On hearing that his verses had stung Caesar to the quick.]

1 Irascēre iterum meis iambis
2 immerentibus, unice "imperator"!

[iii] Overheard in the Crowd

[How C. Licinius Calvus, famous orator and poet, was called an *eloquent runt*.]

1 Risi nescioquem modô e corona,
2 qui, cum mirifice Vatiniana
3 meus crimina Calvus explicasset,
4 admirans ait haec—manusque tollens:
5 "Di magni! SALAPUTIUM DISERTUM!"

[iv] Ill Winds

1 Furi, villula nostra non ad Austri
2 flatus opposita est neque ad Favoni
3 nec saevi Boreae aut Apheliotae,
4 verum ad milia quindecim et ducentos.
5 O ventum horribilem atque pestilentem!

[v] An Invitation to a Barmecide Feast

1 Cenabis bene, mi Fabulle, apud me
2 paucis—si tibi di favent—diebus,
3 si tecum attuleris bonam atque magnam
4 cenam, non sine candida puella
5 et vino et sale et omnibus cachinnis.
6 Haec si, inquam, attuleris, venuste noster,
7 cenabis bene: nam tui Catulli
8 plenus sacculus est aranearum.
9 Sed contra accipies "Meros Amores"
10 (seu quid suavius elegantiusve est),
11 nam unguentum dabo, quod meae puellae
12 donarunt Veneres Cupidinesque.
13 Quod tu cum olfacies, deos rogabis
14 totum ut te faciant, Fabulle, nasum.

[*vi*] *Cherchez la Femme* [1]

[To Camerius on his mysterious disappearance—Catullus suspects him of having eloped!]

1 Oramus, si forte non molestum est,
2 demonstres ubi sint tuae tenebrae.
3 Te in Campo quaesivimus Minore,
4 te in Circo, te in omnibus libellis,
5 te in templo summi Jovis sacrato.
6 In Magni simul Ambulatione
7 femellas omnes, amice, prendi,
8 quas vultu vidi tamen serenas.
9 Avens te, sic usque flagitabam:
10 "Cámeriúm mihi, péssimaé puéllae".

. . . .
11 Sed te iam ferre Herculi labos est:

. . . .
12 tanto ten fastu negas, amice?
13 Dic nobis ubi sis futurus; ēde
14 audacter; committe; crede luci.
15 Nunc te lacteolae tenent puellae?
16 Si linguam clauso tenes in ore,
17 fructus proicies amoris omnes.
18 Verbosā gaudet Venus loquellā.

[b] LYRIC STROPHES

Catullus also experimented with the composition of lyric strophes, or stanzas. His poems of this sort are few but notable. The credit for establishing lyric stanzas as a stereotyped form of Latin verse belongs to Horace—a generation later; but had Catullus lived, it is doubtful whether Horace would ever have composed his *Odes*. The lyric stanzas of Catullus have a freshness and, above all, an ease and simplicity that Horace never attained.

[*i*] The Sapphic stanza (later conventionalized by Horace) is a quatrain in which the scheme of the first three lines is:

　∠ ◡　　　∠ x　　　∠ ◡ ◡　　　∠ ◡　　　∠ x

---

[1] The meter of this poem is a unique type of hendecasyllabic, in that many of the lines (e.g., 1, 3, 4, 5, 7, 8, 9, 11, 12, 14, 16, and 18) are *deca*syllabic—i.e., a spondee (or trochee) is substituted for the dactyl in the second foot. Had Catullus written more poems in this meter, the Phalaecean would never have been nicknamed the *hendeca*syllabic.

and that of the last line, which is much shorter:

$$\acute{-} \cup \cup \qquad \acute{-} \, \mathrm{x}$$

Catullus' two poems in Sapphics will be found in a later section (see pp. 239, 249).

[*ii*] Another stanza, which he used twice (it had no popular name), consisted of either three or four so-called "second glyconics":

$$\left.\begin{matrix} \acute{-} \, \mathrm{x} \\ \smile \, - \end{matrix}\right\} \qquad \acute{-} \cup \cup \qquad \acute{-} \cup \qquad \acute{\mathrm{x}}$$

followed by one "second pherecratic":

$$\left.\begin{matrix} \acute{-} \, \mathrm{x} \\ \smile \, - \end{matrix}\right\} \qquad \acute{-} \cup \cup \qquad \acute{-} \qquad \acute{\mathrm{x}}$$

The resulting five-line stanza is used in the marriage song for Torquatus, which will be read later (see p. 231). The four-line stanza is used in the following hymn:

A Festal Hymn to Diana

1	Dianae sumus in fide		13	tu Lucina dolentibus
2	puellae et pueri integri;		14	Iuno dicta puerperis,
3	Dianam pueri integri		15	tu potens Trivia, et notho es
4	puellaeque canamus.		16	dicta lumine Luna.
5	O Latonia, maximi		17	Tu cursu, dea, menstruo
6	magna progenies Iovis,		18	metiens iter annuum,
7	quam mater prope Deliam		19	rustica agricolae bonis
8	deposivit olivam,		20	tecta frugibus exples.
9	montium domina ut fores		21	Sis quocumque tibi placet
10	silvarumque virentium		22	sancta nomine; Romulique,
11	saltuumque reconditorum		23	antique ut solita es, bonā
12	amniumque sonantum,		24	sospites ope gentem.

[c] Lyric Long-Lines

Lyric long-lines—having one or more caesuras, or pauses—, may properly be classed with lyric stanzas. Although traditionally written as long-lines (and in Catullus occasionally *without* the caesuras), their effect is that of a short-line *stanza*. For instance, combining the two lines discussed in the previous paragraph into couplets:

$$\text{∠ x} \qquad \text{∠ ∪ ∪} \qquad \text{∠ ∪} \qquad \text{x́}$$
$$\qquad \text{∠ x} \qquad \text{∠ ∪ ∪} \qquad \text{∠ x}$$

gives us the exact equivalent of the Priapéan long-line:

$$\text{∠ x} \quad \text{∠ ∪ ∪} \quad \text{∠ ∪} \quad \text{∠} \quad \text{∠ x} \quad \text{∠ ∪ ∪} \quad \text{∠ x}$$

of which the following verses in honor of Priapus, god of Lampsacus (on the Hellespont), are an example:

1 Hunc lucum tibi dedico consecroque, Priape,
2 quâ domus tua Lampsací est quâque silva, Priape.
3 Nam te praecipue in suis urbibus colit ora
4 Hellespontia, ceteris ostriosior oris.

Similarly the "greater Asclepiadéan" line (see p. 246):

$$\text{∠} \quad \text{–} \quad \text{∠} \quad \text{∪ ∪ ∠} \quad \text{∠ ∪} \quad \text{∪∠} \quad \text{∠ ∪} \quad \text{∪ ∠ ∪ ∠}$$
iam te nil miseret dure tui dulcis amiculi

might just as well be written:

$$\text{∠} \quad \text{–} \quad \text{∠} \quad \text{∪ ∪ ∠}$$
iam te nil miseret
$$\text{∠ ∪} \quad \text{∪∠}$$
dure tui
$$\text{∠ ∪} \quad \text{∪ ∠ ∪ ∠}$$
dulcis amiculi.

II

The Carmina

The collection of Catullus' poems that we possess today was published posthumously and entitled simply *Carmina*. In accordance with a literary custom of the Greeks and Romans (which seems very strange to us), epigrams, lyrics, and other short poems were never given individual titles and were collected more or less haphazardly—neither in strict chronological order nor grouped according to subject matter, but generally arranged to contrast form and content. The editor of Catullus' poems (whoever he may have been) divided his material into three groups: (a) some sixty short poems in *various* meters; (b) nine longer poems; (c) forty-eight short poems in elegiac couplets. The modern reader will acquire a more sympathetic understanding of Catullus if the *Carmina* are rearranged in modern categories and supplied with modern titles.

[1]

Vers de Société

As a writer of graceful occasional verse, sometimes perhaps extemporaneous, Catullus was unequalled.   In fact he was unique among Latin poets—and in this respect appeals particularly to the modern reader—in his choice of homely everyday themes and his ability to treat them with genuine wit and humor. It is interesting to note that these satiric but genial verses differ greatly in tone from his political lampoons and virulent invectives.

To the category of *vers de société* belong some of the poems we have already read in the preliminary selections—viz., the elegiac couplets on Arrius' misplaced *h*'s; the limping iambics on Suffenus the poetaster; and above all, the hendecasyllabics—the meter most used by Catullus for this type of verse.

[a] On Presenting a De Luxe Edition of His Verses to Cornelius Nepos [1]

1 Cui dono lepidum novum libellum,
2 arido modô pumice expolitum?
3 Corneli, tibi; namque tu solebas
4 meas esse aliquid putare nugas,
5 iam tum cum ausus es unus Italorum
6 omne aevum tribus explicare chartis,
7 doctis—Iuppiter!—et laboriosis.
8 Quare habe tibi quicquid hoc libelli
9 qualecumque: quod, o patrona virgo,
10 plus uno maneat perenne saeclo.

[b] After a Merry Evening

1 Hesterno, Licini, die otiosi
2 multum lusimus in meis tabellis,
3 ut convenerat esse delicatos.
4 Scribens versiculos uterque nostrum

[1] This is the famous Nepos, scholar, historian and author of the *Lives*. The edition of Catullus' poems here mentioned is not the posthumous collection which has come down to us, but an earlier publication of a limited number of the poems.

5 ludebat numero modô hoc modô illoc,
6 reddens mutua per iocum atque vinum;
7 atque illinc abii tuo lepore
8 incensus, Licini, facetiisque,
9 ut nec me miserum cibus iuvaret
10 nec somnus tegeret quiete ocellos,
11 sed toto, indomitus furore, lecto
12 versarer, cupiens videre lucem,
13 ut tecum loquerer simulque ut essem.
14 At defessa labore membra postquam
15 semimortua lectulo iacebant,
16 hoc, iucunde, tibi poema feci,
17 ex quo perspiceres meum dolorem.
18 Nunc audax cave sis, precesque nostras
19 (oramus) cave despuas, ocelle,
20 ne poenas Nemesis reposcat a te.
21 Est vemens dea: laedere hanc caveto.

[c] I'LL GET EVEN WITH YOU YET!

[How Calvus played a practical joke on Catullus by sending him
an anthology not of the best, but of the *worst*, Greek poets for a
Saturnalia—i.e., a Christmas present.]

1 Ni te plus oculis meis amarem,
2 iucundissime Calve, munere isto
3 odissem te odio Vatiniano:
4 nam quid feci ego quidve sum locutus,
5 cur me tot male perderes poetis?
6 Isti di mala multa dent clienti,
7 qui tantum tibi misit impiorum.
8 Quod si, ut suspicor, hoc novum ac repertum
9 munus dat tibi Sulla litterator,
10 non est mi male, sed bene ac beate,
11 quod non dispereunt tui labores.
12 Di magni!   Horribilem et sacrum libellum!
13 quem tu scilicet ad tuum Catullum
14 misti, continuo ut die periret,
15 Saturnalibus, optimo dierum.

16　Non non hoc tibi, salse, sic abibit:
17　nam, si luxerit, ad librariorum
18　curram scrinia—Caesios, Aquinos,
19　Suffenum, omnia colligam venena,
20　ac te his suppliciis remunerabor.
21　Vos hinc interea valete, abite
22　illûc, unde malum pedem attulistis,
23　saecli incommoda, pessimi poetae.

[d] An Epistle

[Caecilius is asked to leave his love nest on Lake Como and visit his fellow poet at Verona, on a little matter of business.]

1　Poetae tenero, meo sodali,
2　velim, Caecilio, papyre, dicas
3　Veronam veniat, Novi relinquens
4　Comi moenia Lariumque litus:
5　nam quasdam volo cogitationes
6　amici accipiat sui meique.
7　Quare, si sapiet, viam vorabit—
8　quamvis candida miliens puella
9　euntem revocet manusque collo
10　ambas iniciens roget morari;
11　quae nunc, si mihi vera nuntiantur,
12　illum deperit impotente amore;
13　nam quo tempore legit incohatam
14　"Dindymi dominam," ex eo misellae
15　ignes interiorem edunt medullam.
16　Ignosco tibi, Sapphicā puella
17　Musā doctior: est enim venuste
18　"Magna" Caecilio incohata "Mater."

[e] Absent-Minded!

[A humorous anecdote at Catullus' own expense, describing how, on his return from Bithynia, he had put on airs and his bluff had been called! Catullus had gone to Bithynia as a hanger-on in the retinue of the governor, hoping for a share of the graft; but the governor had double-crossed him and pocketed all the boodle

himself. Obviously Catullus' political ideas were somewhat im-
perialistic! The urbanity of the following verses is unsurpassed.
The rather profane, but delightfully witty, dialogue on which
they are based is between Catullus, Varus, and a lady (the latter's
mistress); it may be reconstructed as follows:

Va. Well, how did you make out in Bithynia? Anything doing?

Ca. Not a blamed thing! But what could one expect from such a
blankety-blank governor?

Va. Yes, but surely you managed to bring back some chairmen? [1]

Ca. (*with an eye on* VARUS' *pretty mistress*) Oh, of course I managed
that all right! I brought home eight of them, in fact.

La. Won't you lend them to me, my dear Catullus? I'm going to
the Temple of Serapis.[2]

Ca. (*overcome by embarrassment*) Hold on! I didn't mean that.
It's my friend Cinna who has them, but of course I use them just as if
they were mine. (*His confusion changes to chagrin as he sees them
laughing at him. To the lady*) But look here, you little minx, can't a
gentleman be a bit airy without your holding him down to facts?
(VARUS *and the lady both laugh, and Catullus has to join in.*)]

1 Varus me meus ad suos amores
2 visum duxerat e foro otiosum,
3 scortillum, ut mihi tum repente visum est,
4 non sane illepidum nec invenustum.
5 Huc ut venimus, incĭdēre nobis
6 sermones varii, in quibus, quid esset
7 iam Bithynia, quo modo se haberet,
8 et quonam mihi profuisset aere.
9 Respondi (id quod erat), nihil neque ipsis,
10 hoc praetore, fuisse—nec cohorti,
11 cur quisquam caput unctius referret;
12 praesertim quibus esset irrumator
13 praetor, nec faceret pili cohortem.
14 "At certe tamen" inquiunt "quod illĭc
15 natum dicitur esse, comparasti
16 ad lecticam homines." Ego, ut puellae
17 unum me facerem beatiorem,

1 I.e., slaves who carried sedan chairs.

2 The cult of Serapis was very popular with the women.

18 "non" inquam "mihi tam fuit maligne,
19 ut, provincia quod mala incĭdisset,
20 non possem octo homines parare rectos."
21 (At mi nullus erat neque hîc neque illîc,
22 fractum qui veteris pedem grabati
23 in collo sibi collocare posset.)
24 Hîc illa, ut decuit cinaediorem,
25 "quaeso" inquit "mihi, mi Catulle, paulum
26 istos commoda, nam volo ad Serapim
27 déferrí." "Mănĕ" ínquií puéllae,
28 "istud quod modô dixeram, 'me habere,'
29 —fūgit me ratio.—Meus sodalis
30 —Cínna est—Gáĭŭs—ís sibí parávit.
31 Vérum, utrum íllius án meí, quid ád me?
32 Utor tam bene quam mihi pararim.
33 Sed tu insulsa male et molesta vivis,
34 per quam non licet esse neglegentem."

[f] FAREWELL TO MY VILLA

[Catullus, who had wittily invited Fabullus to a Barmecide feast (see p. 218), was now invited to dinner by a certain Sestius, an orator famous for his lavish entertainments. But before the dinner party, Sestius sent Catullus a copy of his latest speech—a bitter invective against a certain Antius. Taking the hint, Catullus dutifully read the speech, but was so chilled by its *frigid* style that he caught cold (so he says), missed the party, and even had to go to his villa at Tibur to recuperate! He wrote these verses when he was finally cured and about to return to Rome.]

1 O funde noster seu Sabine seu Tiburs
2 (nam te esse Tiburtem autumant, quibus non est
3 cordi Catullum laedere; at quibus cordi est,
4 quovis Sabinum pignore esse contendunt)
5 —sed seu Sabine sive verius Tiburs,
6 fui libenter in tua suburbana
7 villa malamque pectore expuli tussim,
8 non immerenti quam mihi meus venter,
9 dum sumptuosas appeto, dedit, cenas.

10 Nam Sestianus dum volo esse conviva,
11 orationem in Antium petitorem
12 plenam veneni et pestilentiae legi.
13 Hîc, me gravedo frigida et frequens tussis
14 quassavit, usque dum in tuum sinum fugi
15 et me recuravi otioque et urticā.
16 Quare refectus maximas tibi grates
17 ago, meum quod non es ulta peccatum.
18 Nec deprecor iam (si nefaria scripta
19 Sesti recepso), quin gravedinem et tussim
20 —non mi, sed ipsi Sestio ferat frigus,
21 qui tunc vocat me cum malum librum legi.

[g] "Come, Landlord, Fill the Flowing Bowl"

1 Minister vetuli puer Falerni,
2 inger mi calices amariores,
3 ut lex Postumiae iubet magistrae,
4 ebrioso acino ebriosioris.
5 At vos quôlibet hinc abite, lymphae,
6 vini pernicies, et ad severos
7 migrate: hîc merus est Thyonianus.

[h] To Marrucinus Asinius

[Asinius is here exposed as a cleptomaniac.]

1 Marrucine Asini, manu sinistra
2 non belle uteris in ioco atque vino:
3 tollis lintea neglegentiorum.
4 Hoc salsum esse putas? Fugit te, inepte.
5 Quamvis sordida res et invenusta est.
6 Non credis mihi? Crede Pollioni
7 fratri, qui tua furta vel talento
8 mutari velit: est enim leporum
9 disertus puer ac facetiarum.
10 Quare aut hendecasyllabos trecentos
11 expecta aut mihi linteum remitte;
12 quod me non movet aestimatione,
13 verum est mnemosynum mei sodalis.

14 Nam sudaria Saetaba ex Hiberis
15 miserunt mihi muneri Fabullus
16 et Veranius: haec amem necesse est,
17 ut Veraniolum meum et Fabullum.

[i] ADVICE TO EGNATIUS

[Egnatius, the Spaniard with the perpetual grin, is advised to stop advertising his Spanish tooth wash.]

1 Egnatius, quod candidos habet dentes,
2 renidet usque quâque. Si ad rei ventum est
3 subsellium, cum orator excitat fletum,
4 renidet ille. Si ad pii rogum fili
5 lugetur, orba cum flet unicum mater,
6 renidet ille. Quicquid est, ubicumque est,
7 quodcumque agit, renidet. Hunc habet morbum
8 neque elegantem, ut arbitror, neque urbanum.
9 Quare monendum est te mihi, bone Egnati:
10 si Urbanus esses aut Sabinus aut Tiburs,
11 aut parcus Umber, aut obesus Etruscus,
12 aut Lanuvinus ater atque dentatus,
13 aut Transpadanus (ut meos quoque attingam!),
14 aut quilibet qui PURITER lavit dentes,
15 tamen renidere usque quâque te nollem!—
16 nam risu inepto res ineptior nulla est.
17 Nunc Celtiber es: Celtiberia in terra,
18 quod quisque minxit, hoc sibi solet mane
19 dentem atque russam defricare gingivam,
20 ut, quo iste vester expolitior dens est,
21 hoc te amplius bibisse praedicet loti.

[j] SCURVY POLITICIANS

[Even as Catullus had come back empty-handed from Bithynia, so his boon companians, Veranius and Fabullus, were disappointed in Macedonia. There the governor, L. Calpurnius Piso, unduly favored his baser henchmen, Porcius and Socration. The two young aristocrats are now hanging about town with nothing

to do but pick up dinner invitations.   Catullus expresses his in-
dignation at their undeserved misfortune.]

1 Porci et Socration, duae sinistrae
2 Pisonis, scabies famesque mundi,
3 vos Veraniolo meo et Fabullo
4 verpus praeposuit Priapus ille?
5 Vos convivia lauta sumptuose
6 de die facitis?   Mei sodales
7 quaerunt in trivio vocationes?

[k] Welcome to the Wanderer
[On the return of his friend Veranius from Spain.]

1 Verani, omnibus e meis amicis
2 antistans mihi milibus trecentis,
3 venistine domum ad tuos penates
4 fratresque unanimos anumque matrem?
5 Venisti!   O mihi nuntii beati!
6 Visam te incolumem audiamque Hiberum
7 narrantem loca, facta, nationes,
8 ut mos est tuus; applicansque collum,
9 iucundum os oculosque saviabor.
10 O quantum est hominum beatiorum,
11 quid me laetius est beatiusve?

[l] Homeward Bound
[On leaving the retinue of Memmius, Governor of Bithynia.]

1 Iam ver egelidos refert tepores;
2 iam caeli furor aequinoctialis
3 iucundis Zephyri silescit auris.
4 Linquantur Phrygii, Catulle, campi
5 Nicaeaeque ager uber aestuosae;
6 ad claras Asiae volemus urbes.
7 Iam mens praetrepidans avet vagari;
8 iam laeti studio pedes vigescunt.
9 O dulces comitum valete coetus,
10 longe quos simul a domo profectos
11 diversae variae viae reportant.

[m] Home Again

[On returning to his villa in Sirmio, on Lake Garda.]

1 Paene insularum, Sirmio, insularumque
2 ocelle (quascumque in liquentibus stagnis
3 marique vasto fert uterque Neptunus),
4 quam te libenter quamque laetus inviso,
5 vix mi ipse credens Thyniam atque Bithynos
6 liquisse campos et videre te in tuto.
7 O quid solutis est beatius curis,
8 cum mens onus reponit, ac peregrino
9 labore fessi venimus larem ad nostrum
10 desideratoque adquiescimus lecto?
11 Hoc est quod unum est pro laboribus tantis.
12 Salve, o venusta Sirmio, atque ero gaude;
13 gaudete vosque, o Lydiae lacus undae;
14 ridete quicquid est domi cachinnorum.

[n] When Cupid Sneezes

[Sneezing is a sign of good luck.]

1 Acmen Septimius, suos amores,
2 tenens in gremio, "mea" inquit "Acme,
3 ni te perdite amo, atque amare porro
4 omnes sum assidue paratus annos
5 (quantum qui pote plurimum perire),
6 solus in Libya Indiaque tosta
7 caesio veniam obvius leoni."
8 Hoc ut dixit, Amor sinistrā, ut ante
9 dextrā, sternuit approbationem.
10 At Acme, leviter caput reflectens
11 et dulcis pueri ebrios ocellos
12 illo purpureo ore saviata,
13 "sic" inquit "mea vita, Septimille,
14 huic uni domino usque serviamus,
15 ut multo mihi maior acriorque
16 ignis mollibus ardet in medullis."
17 Hoc ut dixit, Amor, sinistrā ut ante,

18 dextrā sternuit approbationem.
19 Nunc, ab auspicio bono profecti,
20 mutuis animis amant amantur;
21 unam Septimius misellus Acmen
22 mavult quam Syrias Britanniasque;
23 uno in Septimio fidelis Acme
24 facit delicias libidinesque.
25 Quis ullos homines beatiores
26 vidit, quis Venerem auspicatiorem?

[2]

Epithalamia, or Wedding Songs

The poems of Catullus include three epithalamia. One is the song of the Fates, at the marriage of Peleus and Thetis (ll. 323–381 of the *epyllion*, see p. 212); another, the idyllic wedding chorus of youths and maidens (see p. 211). In contrast with these two—which deal with imaginary characters and adhere closely in style and form to the true Greek epithalamium—is the quasi-epithalamium, or ode to Hymen, in honor of two friends of Catullus'. This charming poem was the poet's wedding gift to Manlius Torquatus and Vinia Aurunculeia. It is not a true epithalamium in the Greek sense—i.e., a choral ode actually sung to the bride and groom by the wedding party—, but more comprehensive and imaginative—a highly idealized and dramatic account of all the wedding festivities from the spectator's point of view. Beginning with an invocation of the god of marriage and ending with blessings on the bridal pair, it portrays a romantic blend of Greek and Roman customs and ceremonies. The poem is composed in lyric strophes, or stanzas, identical with those of the *Hymn to Diana* (see preliminary selections, p. 220), except that four—instead of three—glyconics precede the final pherecratic.

FOR MANLIUS TORQUATUS AND HIS BRIDE

1 Collis O Heliconii
2 cultor, Uraniae genus,
3 qui rapis teneram ad virum

4 vírginem, ó Hymenaée Hymén,
5 ó Hymén Hymenaée,

6 cinge tempora floribus
7 suave olentis amarici;
8 flammeum cape; laetus huc,
9 huc věni, niveo gerens
10 luteum pede soccum;

11 excitusque hilari die,
12 nuptialia concinens
13 voce carmina tinnulā,
14 pelle humum pedibus; manu
15 pineam quate taedam.

16 Namque Vinia Manlio,
17 qualis Idalium colens
18 venit ad Phrygium Venus
19 iudicem, bona cum bonā
20 nubet alite virgo,

21 floridis velut enitens
22 myrtus Asia ramulis,
23 quos hamadryades deae
24 ludicrum sibi rosido
25 nútriúnt umóre.

26 Quare age, huc aditum ferens,
27 perge linquere Thespiae
28 rúpis Áoniós specús,
29 nympha quos super irrigat
30 frigerans Aganippe;

31 ac domum dominam voca,
32 coniugis cupidam novi,
33 mentem amore revinciens,
34 ut tenax hedera huc et huc
35 arborem implicat errans.

36 Vosque item simul, integrae
37 virgines, quibus advenit
38 par dies, agite, in modum
39 dicite "ó hymenaée Hymén,
40 ó Hymén Hymenaée,"

41 ut libentius, audiens
42 se citarier ad suum
43 munus, huc aditum ferat
44 dux bonae Veneris, boni
45 coniugator amoris.

    · · · · · ·

46 Claustra pandite ianuae:
47 virgo adest.   Viden ut faces
48 splendidas quatiunt comas?

    · · · · · ·

49 Flere desine.   Non tibi, Au-
50 runculeia, periculum est
51 ne qua femina pulchrior
52 clarum ab Oceano diem
53 viderit venientem.

54 Talis in vario solet
55 divitis domini hortulo
56 stare flos hyacinthinus.
57 Sed moraris, abit dies:
58 prodeas, nova nupta.

59 Prodeas, nova nupta, si
60 iam videtur, et audias
61 nostra verba.   Vide ut faces
62 aureas quatiunt comas:
63 prodeas, nova nupta.

    · · · · · ·

64 Tollite, o pueri, faces:
65 flammeum video venire.
66 Ite, concinite in modum
67 "ó Hymén Hymenaée ió,

68   ó Hymén Hymenaée."

.   .   .   .   .   .

69   En tibi domus ut potens
70   et beata viri tui!
71   Quae tibi sine serviat
72   (o Hymen Hymenaee io,
73   o Hymen Hymenaee),

74   usque dum tremulum movens
75   cana tempus anilitas
76   omnia omnibus adnuit.
77   O Hymen Hymenaee io,
78   o Hymen Hymenaee.

79   Transfer omine cum bono
80   limen aureolos pedes,
81   rasilemque subi forem.
82   O Hymen Hymenaee io,
83   o Hymen Hymenaee.

.   .   .   .   .   .

84   Mitte bracchiolum teres,
85   praetextate, puellulae:
86   iam cubile adeat viri.
87   O Hymen Hymenaee io,
88   o Hymen Hymenaee.

89   Vos bonae senibus viris
90   cognitae bene feminae,
91   collocate puellulam.
92   O Hymen Hymenaee io,
93   o Hymen Hymeneee.

94   Iam licet venias, marite:
95   uxor in thalamo tibi est,
96   ore floridulo nitens,
97   alba parthenice velut
98   luteumve papaver.

99 At, marite, (ita me iuvent
100 caelites) nihilo minus
101 pulcher es, neque te Venus
102 neglegit.   Sed abit dies:
103 perge, ne remorare.

104 Non diu remoratus es.
105 Iam venis.   Bona te Venus
106 iuverit, quoniam palam
107 quod cupis cupis et bonum
108 non abscondis amorem.
        . . . . . .
109 Ludite ut libet, et brevi
110 liberos date.   Non decet
111 tam vetus sine liberis
112 nomen esse, sed indidem
113 semper ingenerari.

114 Torquatus volo parvulus,
115 matris e gremio suae
116 porrigens teneras manus
117 dulce rideat ad patrem
118 semihiante labello.

119 Sit suo similis patri
120 Manlio, et facile insciis
121 noscitetur ab omnibus,
122 et pudicitiam suae
123 matris indicet ore.

124 Talis illius a bonā
125 matre laus genus approbet,
126 qualis unica ab optimā
127 matre Telemacho manet
128 fama Penelopeo.

129 Claudite ostia, virgines:
130 lusimus satis.   At, boni

131 coniuges, bene vivite et
132 munere adsiduo valentem
133 exercete iuventam.

[3]

Elegies

[a] ON THE DEATH OF HIS BROTHER

Nothing is known of Catullus' brother and of the manner of
his death save that, from the Roman point of view, his loss was
peculiarly tragic, because he died and was buried far from home
and kindred, in the Troad, in Asia Minor.   Catullus made a pious
pilgrimage to his grave, over which he performed the belated
last rites.

[i] From an Epistle to Manlius

[Having lost his young wife, Manlius requested some consola-
tory verses from Catullus.   Because of his own bereavement,
however, Catullus regrets that he cannot comply with the request.]

1 Quod mihi, fortunā casuque oppressus acerbo,
2   conscriptum hoc lacrimis mittis epistolium,
3 (naufragum ut eiectum spumantibus aequoris undis
4   sublevem et a mortis limine restituam,
5 quem neque sancta Venus molli requiescere somno
6   desertum in lecto caelibe perpetitur,
7 nec veterum dulci scriptorum carmine Musae
8   oblectant, cum mens anxia pervigilat),
9 id gratum est mihi, me quoniam tibi dicis amicum,
10   muneraque et Musarum hinc petis et Veneris:
11 sed tibi ne mea sint ignota incommoda, Manli,
12   neu me odisse putes hospitis officium,
13 accipe, quīs merser fortunae fluctibus ipse,
14   ne amplius a misero dona beata petas.
15 Tempore quo primum vestis mihi tradita pura est,
16   iucundum cum aetas florida ver ageret,
17 multa satis lusi: non est dea nescia nostri,
18   quae dulcem curis miscet amaritiem.

19 Sed totum hoc studium luctu fraterna mihi mors
20   abstulit.   O misero frater adempte mihi!
21 Tu mea tu moriens fregisti commoda, frater;
22   tecum unâ tota est nostra sepulta domus;
23 omnia tecum unâ perierunt gaudia nostra,
24   quae tuus in vita dulcis alebat amor—
25 cuius ego interitu tota de mente fugavi
26   haec studia atque omnes delicias animi.

[*ii*] From an Epistle to Allius

1 Troia (nefas!) commune sepulchrum Asiae Europaeque!
2   Troia virum et virtutum omnium acerba cinis,
3 quaene etiam nostro letum miserabile fratri
4   attulit!   Hei misero frater adempte mihi!
5 Hei misero fratri iucundum lumen ademptum!
6   Tecum unâ tota est nostra sepulta domus.
7 Omnia tecum unâ perierunt gaudia nostra,
8   quae tuus in vita dulcis alebat amor.
9 Quem nunc tam longe, non inter nota sepulchra
10   nec prope cognatos compositum cineres,
11 sed Troiā obscenā, Troiā infelice sepultum,
12   detinet extremo terra aliena solo.

[*iii*] At His Brother's Tomb in the Troad

[It was probably when Catullus went to Bithynia in the retinue
of the new governor, Memmius, that he took advantage of the opportunity to visit his brother's grave and to perform the important burial service, so intimately connected with family worship.]

1 Multas per gentes et multa per aequora vectus,
2   advenio has miseras, frater, ad inferias,
3 ut te postremo donarem munere mortis
4   et mutam nequiquam adloquerer cinerem,
5 quandoquidem Fortuna mihi tete abstulit ipsum,
6   heu miser indignē frater ademptĕ mihi,
7 Nunc tamen interea haec, prisco quae more parentum
8   tradita sunt tristi munere ad inferias,

9 accipe fraterno multum manantia fletu,
10   atque in perpetuum, frater, ave atque vale.

The above poem and the one on Sirmio (p. 230) inspired Tenny-
son to write his famous *Frater Ave Atque Vale*, when he visited
the ruins of Catullus' villa—near the modern Desenzáno—, on the
Lake of Garda.   In reading Tennyson's poem, pronounce the
Latin phrases in mid-Victorian style—i.e., as though they were
English prose: *Fráter áve átque vále* (not *Fráter av' átque valé*):

> Row us out to Desenzáno, to your Sirmióne row!
> So they rowed, and there we landed—"O venusta Sirmio"!
> There to me through all the groves of olive in the summer
> glow,
> There beneath the Roman ruin where the purple flowers
> grow,
> Came that "áve átque vále," of the poet's hopeless woe,
> Tenderest of Roman poets, nineteen hundred years ago,
> "Fráter áve átque vále"—as we wandered to and fro,
> Gazing at the Lydian laughter of the Garda Lake below,
> Sweet Catullus' all-but-island, olive-silvery Sirmio!

[b] To CALVUS—ON THE DEATH OF HIS WIFE, QUINTILIA

1 Si quicquam mutis gratum acceptumve sepulchris
2   accidere a nostro, Calve, dolore potest
3 (quo desiderio veteres renovamus amores
4   atque olim missas flemus amicitias),
5 certe non tanto mors immatura dolori est
6   Quintiliae, quantum gaudet amore tuo.

[4]

Poems to Lesbia

Scattered haphazard among the published poems of Catullus
are those dealing with his "grand passion"—his love affair with
Clodia, sister of the notorious P. Clodius Pulcher (who was
murdered by the henchmen of Milo) and wife of Q. Caecilius
Metellus Celer.   Following the romantic tradition, Catullus gave
to Clodia, in the verses she inspired, a metrically equivalent

pseudonym; he called her *Lesbia*, the Lesbian—i.e., Sappho! She was a fascinating, beautiful, and dissolute woman—idealized by Catullus, but unflatteringly portrayed by Cicero in his oration *Pro Caelio*.

In the society of that time liaisons were expected; they were even governed by their own code of honor, to which Catullus, genuinely in love, adhered. But Clodia was in reality on a lower moral plane than her youthful lover; she was the final product of a decadent society—the well-born harlot. The blow of this discovery almost cost Catullus his sanity.

The poems inspired by this deep experience are unique in Roman literature for their intensity and variety of expression. By any *modern* test of literary power they would entitle Catullus to the first place among Roman poets. They have been grouped here in their probable chronological order:

[a] INNAMORAMENTO

A Declaration of Jealous Passion

[A masterly translation, in the original meter (see p. 219), of one of the most famous love lyrics of Greek literature, Sappho's *Ode to Anactoria*. In his treatise *On the Sublime*, Longinus has preserved the Greek original for us, quoting it as an example of sublime simplicity.]

1 Ille mi par esse deo videtur;
2 ille, si fas est, superare divos,
3 qui, sedens adversus, identidem te
4   spectat et audit

5 dulce ridentem, misero quod omnīs
6 eripit sensus mihi; nam simul te,
7 Lesbia, aspexi, nihil est super mi
8   vocis in ore,

9 lingua sed torpet; tenuis sub artus
10 flamma demanat; sonitu suopte
11 tintinant aures; gemina teguntur
12   lumina nocte.

[b] Symptoms

[*i*] Telltale Irritability

1 Lesbia mi, praesente viro, mala plurima dicit:
2 　haec illi fatuo maxima laetitia est.
3 Mule, nihil sentis.　Si nostri oblita taceret,
4 　sana esset: nunc quod gannit et obloquitur,
5 non solum meminit, sed, quae multo acrior est res,
6 　irata est: hoc est, uritur et loquitur.

[*ii*] Telltale Garrulity

1 Lesbia mi dicit semper male nec tacet umquam
2 　de me: Lesbia me dispeream nisi amat.
3 Quo signo?　Quia sunt totidem mea: deprecor illam
4 　adsidue, verum dispeream nisi amo.

[c] The Heyday of Love

[*i*] Life is Short

1 Vivamus, mea Lesbia, atque amemus,
2 rumoresque senum severiorum
3 omnes unius aestimemus assis.
4 Soles occidere et redire possunt:
5 nobis cum semel occidit brevis lux,
6 nox est perpetua una dormienda.
7 Da mi basia mille, deinde centum,
8 dein mille altera, dein secunda centum,
9 deinde usque altera mille, deinde centum;
10 dein, cum milia multa fecerīmus,
11 conturbabimus illa, ne sciamus,
12 aut ne quis malus invidere possit,
13 cum tantum sciat esse basiorum.

[*ii*] How Many Kisses?

1 Quaeris quot mihi basiationes
2 tuae, Lesbia, sint satis superque.
3 Quam magnus numerus Libyssae harenae
4 láserpíciferís iacét Cyrénis,

5 oraclum Iovis inter aestuosi
6 et Batti veteris sacrum sepulcrum;
7 aut quam sidera multa, cum tacet nox,
8 furtivos hominum vident amores;
9 tam te basia multa basiare
10 vesano satis et super Catullo est,
11 quae nec pernumerare curiosi
12 possint nec mala fascinare lingua.

[*iii*] Enviable Sparrow!

[In this and the following poem, the sentimental idealization of Lesbia reaches its height. Catullus actually pictures her as an ingénue!]

1 Passer, deliciae meae puellae
2 (quicum ludere, quem in sinu tenere,
3 cui primum digitum dare appetenti
4 et acrīs solet incitare morsus,
5 cum desiderio meo nitenti
6 carum nescioquid libet iocari),
7 et solaciolum sui doloris
8 (credo, ut tum gravis acquiescat ardor)—
9 tecum ludere sicut ipsa possem
10 et tristis animi levare curas!

[*iv*] The Sparrow Is Dead!

1 Lugete, O Veneres Cupidinesque
2 et quantum est hominum venustiorum:
3 passer mortuus est meae puellae,
4 passer, deliciae meae puellae,
5 quem plus illa oculis suis amabat;
6 nam mellitus erat suamque norat
7 ipsam tam bene quam puella matrem,
8 nec sese a gremio íllĭus movebat,
9 sed circumsiliens modô huc modô illûc
10 ad solam dominam usque pipiabat.
11 Qui nunc it per iter tenebricosum
12 illûc unde negant redire quemquam.

13 At vobis male sit, malae tenebrae
14 Orci, quae omnia bella devoratis:
15 tam bellum mihi passerem abstulistis!
16 Vae factum male!   Vae miselle passer!
17 Tuā nunc operā meae puellae
18 flendo turgiduli rubent ocelli.

[v] Quintia Is Fair, But Lesbia Is Charming

1 Quintia formosa est multis: mihi candida, longa,
2   recta est.   Haec ego sic singula confiteor.
3 Totum illud "formosa" nego.   Nam nulla venustas,
4   nulla in tam magno est corpore mica salis.
5 Lesbia formosa est, quae cum pulcherrima tota est,
6   tum omnibus una omnis surripuit Veneres.

[vi] To Ameána—Who Claimed to Be As Fair As Lesbia

1 Salve, nec minimo puella naso
2 nec bello pede nec nigris ocellis
3 nec longis digitis nec ore sicco
4 nec sane nimis elegante lingua,
5 decoctoris amica Formiani.
6 Ten Provincia narrat esse bellam?
7 Tecum Lesbia nostra comparatur?
8 O saeclum insapiens et infacetum!

[vii] Warning to a Would-Be Rival

1 Quaenam te mala mens, miselle Ravide,
2 agit praecipitem in meos iambos?
3 Quis deus tibi non bene advocatus
4 vecordem parat excitare rixam?
5 An ut pervenias in ora vulgi?
6 Quid vis?   Quâlibet esse notus optas?
7 Eris, quandoquidem meos amores
8 cum longa voluisti amare poena.

[c] A Falling-Out
Regrets Are Vain

1 Miser Catulle, desinas ineptire,
2 et quod vides perisse, perditum ducas.

3 Fulsere quondam candidi tibi soles,
4 cum ventitabas quô puella ducebat,
5 amata nobis, quantum amabitur nulla.
6 Ibi illa multa tum iocosa fiebant,
7 quae tu volebas nec puella nolebat.
8 Fulsere vere candidi tibi soles.
9 Nunc iam illa non vult: tu quoque, impotens, noli
10 —nec quae fugit, sectare—nec miser vive—
11 sed obstinata mente perfer—obdura!
12 Vale, puella! Iam Catullus obdurat,
13 nec te requiret nec rogabit invitam:
14 at tu dolebis, cum rogaberis nulla.
15 Scelesta, vae te! Quae tibi manet vita!
16 Quis nunc te adibit? Cui videberis bella?
17 Quem nunc amabis? Cuius esse diceris?
18 Quem basiabis? Cui labella mordebis?—
19 At tu, Catulle, destinatus obdura!

[d] RECONCILIATION

Unhoped-For Joy

1 Si cui quid cupido optantique obtigit umquam
2   insperanti, hoc est gratum animo proprie.
3 Quare hoc est gratum nobis quoque, carior auro,
4   quod te restituis, Lesbia, mi cupido.
5 Restituis cupido atque insperanti, ipsa refers te
6   nobis: o lucem candidiore notā!
7 Quis me uno vivit felicior, aut magis hac rem
8   optandam in vita dicere quis poterit?

[e] DOUBTS

[i] All Things are Fleeting

1 Iucundum, mea vita, mihi proponis amorem
2   hunc nostrum inter nos perpetuumque fore.
3 Di magni, facite ut vere promittere possit,
4   atque id sincere dicat et ex animo,
5 ut liceat nobis totā perducere vitā
6   aeternum hoc sanctae foedus amicitiae.

[*ii*] Writ in Water

1 Nulli se dicit mulier mea nubere malle
2 quam mihi, non si se Iuppiter ipse petat.
3 Dicit: sed mulier cupido quod dicit amanti
4 in vento et rapidā scribere oportet aquā.

[f] STEADFAST DEVOTION
[*i*] To a Scandalmonger

1 Credis me potuisse meae maledicere vitae,
2 ambobus mihi quae carior est oculis?
3 Non potui, nec si possem tam perdite amarem:
4 sed tu cum Tappone omnia monstra facis.

[*ii*] To Allius—In Memory of Happier Days

[Allius had opened his house to Catullus and Lesbia for their
first rapturous secret meetings. These lines are from an elegy.]

1 Non possum reticere, deae, qua me Allius in re
2 iuverit aut quantis iuverit officiis,

. . . .

3 cum tantum arderem quantum Trinacria rupes
4 lymphaque in Oetaeis Mālia Thermopylis,
5 maesta neque adsiduo tabescere lumina fletu
6 cessarent tristique imbre madere genae.

. . . .

7 Is clausum lato patefecit limite campum,
8 isque domum nobis isque dedit dominae,
9 ad quam communes exerceremus amores.
10 Quô mea se molli candida diva pede
11 intulit, et, trito fulgentem in limine plantam
12 innixa, argutā constituit soleā—
13 coniugis ut quondam flagrans advenit amore
14 Prótesiláëám Láodamía domúm.

. . . .

15 Aut nihil aut paulo cui tum concedere digna,
16 lux mea se nostrum contulit in gremium,
17 quam circumcursans hinc illinc saepe Cupido
18 fulgebat crocina candidus in tunica.
19 Quae tamenetsi uno non est contenta Catullo,

20   rara verecundae furta feremus erae,
21 ne nimium simus stultorum more molesti:
22   saepe etiam Juno, maxima caelicolum,
23 coniugis in culpa flagrantem cóncoquit íram,
24   noscens omnivoli plurima furta Iovis.

. . . .
25 Nec tamen illa mihi, dextrā deducta paternā,
26   fragrantem Assyrio venit odore domum,
27 sed furtiva dedit mirā munuscula nocte,
28   ipsius ex ipso dempta viri gremio.
29 Quare illud satis est, si nobis is datur unis,
30   quem lapide illǎ diem candidiore notat.
31 Hoc tibi, quod potui, confectum carmine, munus
32   pro multis, Alli, redditur officiis.

. . . .
33 Sitis felices et tu simul et tua vita
34   et domus (in qua nos lusimus et domina)

. . . .
35 et longe ante omnes mihi quae me carior ipso est,
36   lux mea, quā vivā vivere dulce mihi est.

[g] BITTERNESS AND PAIN

[i] Successful Rivals

[a] 1 Quinti, si tibi vis oculos debere Catullum
     2   (aut aliud si quid carius est oculis),
     3 eripere ei noli multo quod carius illi
     4   est oculis—seu quid carius est oculis.

[b] 1 Rufe, mihi frustra ac nequiquam creditě amicě
     2   (frustra?—immo magno cum pretio atque malo),
     3 sicine subrepsti mi, atque (intestina perurens)
     4   hei misero eripuisti omnia nostra bona?
     5 Eripuisti eheu—nostrae crudele venenum
     6   vitae, eheu!—nostrae pestis amicitiae!

[ii] Unsympathetic Friends

[a] 1 Mále est, Córnificí, tuó Catúllo;
     2 mále est (me hércule) ei—ét labórióse,

3 et magis magis in dies et horas:
4 quem tu (quod minimum facillimumque est)
5 qua solatus es adlocutione?
6 Irascor tibi.   Sic meos amores?
7 Paulum quidlibet adlocutionis,
8 maestius lacrimis Simonidéïs!

[b] 1 Alfene, immemor atque unanimis falsĕ sodalibus,
2 iam te nil miseret, durĕ, tui dulcis amiculi?
3 Iam me prodere, iam non dubitas fallere, perfidĕ?
4 Num facta impia fallacum hominum caelicolis placent?
5 —quae tu neglegis, ac me miserum deseris in malis.
6 Eheu, quid faciant (dic!) homines, cuive habeant fidem?
7 Certe tute iubebas animam tradere, iniquĕ, me—
8 inducens in amorem, quasi tuta omnia mi forent.
9 Idem nunc retrahis te, ac tua dicta omnia factaque
10 ventos irrita ferre ac nebulas aërias sinis.
11 Si tu oblitus es, at di meminerunt, meminit Fides,
12 quae te ut paeniteat postmodo facti faciet tui.

[c] 1 Num te leaena montibus Libystīnis
2 aut Scylla latrans infimā inguinum parte
3 tam mente durā procreavit ac taetrā,
4 ut supplicis vocem in novissimo casu
5 contemptam haberes, ah nimis fero corde?

[d] 1 Desine de quoquam quicquam bene velle mereri
2   aut aliquem fieri posse putare pium.
3 Omnia sunt ingrata; nihil fecisse benigne—
4   immo etiam taedet—taedet obestque magis:
5 ut mihi, quem nemo gravius nec acerbius urget
6   quám modô quí me unum átque únicum amícum habuít.

[iii] Despair

[From the elegy to Manlius.]
1 . . . Quod scribis "Veronae turpe, Catulle,
2   esse, quod hîc quisquis de meliore notā est
3 frigida deserto tepefecit membra cubili,"
4   id, Manli, non est turpe, magis miserum est.

[*iv*] Disillusionment

1 Dicebas quondam solum te nosse Catullum,
2   Lesbia, nec prae me velle tenere Iovem.
3 Dilexi tum te, non tantum ut vulgus amicam,
4   sed pater ut gnatos diligit et generos.
5 Nunc te cognovi: quare etsi impensius uror,
6   multo mihi tamen es vilior et lĕvior.
7 "Quî potis est?" inquis.   Quod amantem iniuria talis
8   cogit amare magis, se bene velle minus.

[h] STRUGGLE AND SELF-MASTERY

[*i*] Hate and Love

1 Odi et amo.   Quare id faciam, fortasse requiris.
2   Nescio, sed fieri sentio et excrucior.

[*ii*] Reproach

1 Nulla potest mulier tantum se dicere amatam
2   vere, quantum a me, Lesbia, amata, mea, es.
3 Nulla fides ullo fuit umquam foedere tanta,
4   quanta in amore tuo ex parte reperta mea est.

[*iii*] Impasse

1 Huc est mens deducta tuā, mea Lesbia, culpā
2   (atque ita se officio perdidit ipsa suo),
3 ut iam nec bene velle queat tibi, si optima fias;
4   nec desistere amare, omnia si facias.

[*iv*] *Apologia Pro Amore Suo*

1 Si qua, recordanti benefacta priora, voluptas
2   est homini, cum se cogitat esse pium,
3 nec sanctam violasse fidem, nec foedere in ullo
4   divum ad fallendos numine abusum homines,
5 multa parata manent in longa aetate, Catulle,
6   ex hoc ingrato gaudia amore tibi;
7 nam quaecumque homines bene cuiquam aut dicere possunt
8   aut facere, haec a te dictaque factaque sunt:
9 omnia quae ingratae perierunt credita menti.

10   Quare cur tu te iam amplius excrucies?
11   Quin tu animum offirmas, atque istinc teque reducis
12   et dis invitis desinis esse miser?
13   Difficile est longum subito deponere amorem.
14   Difficile est, verum hoc quâlibet efficias.
15   Una salus haec est; hoc est tibi pervincendum;
16   hoc facias, sive id non pote sive pote.
17   O di, si vestrum est misereri, aut si quibus umquam
18   extremam iam ipsa in morte tulistis opem,
19   me miserum aspicite et, si vitam puriter egi,
20   eripite hanc pestem perniciemque mihi.
21   Heu, mihi subrepens imos ut torpor in artus,
22   expulit ex omni pectore laetitias!
23   Non iam illud quaero, contra me ut diligat illa,
24   aut, quod non potis est, esse pudica velit:
25   ipse valere opto et taetrum hunc deponere morbum.
26   O di, reddite mi hoc pro pietate mea.

[i] LOATHING

[i] To M. Caelius Rufus

[Rufus was first the friend, then the rival, and now again the friend of Catullus.]

1   Caeli, Lesbia nostra—Lesbia illa
2   —illa Lesbia, quam Catullus unam
3   plus quam se atque suos amavit omnes,
4   nunc in quadriviis et angiportis
5   glubit magnanimi Remi nepotes.

[ii] Clodia and Clodius

[In which Catullus hints at incestuous relations between Clodia and her brother, P. Clodius Pulcher.]

1   Lesbius est pulcher: quid ni?—quem Lesbia malit
2   quam te cum totâ gente, Catulle, tuâ.
3   Sed tamen hic Pulcher vendat cum gente Catullum,
4   si tria notorum savia reppererit.

[j] SCORN

The Final Word

[Catullus repulses Lesbia's offers of reconciliation.   With deep irony, Catullus wrote this last poem to Lesbia in Sapphic strophes —which he had not used since his first poem to her, the translation of Sappho's *Ode to Anactoria*.]

1 Furi et Aureli, comites Catulli,
2 sive in extremos penetrabit Indos,
3 litus ut longe resonante Eoā
4   tunditur undā,

5 sive in Hyrcanos Arabasve molles,
6 seu Sagas sagittiferosque Parthos,
7 sive quae septemgeminus colorat
8   aequora Nilus,

. . . .
9 omnia haec, quaecumque feret voluntas
10 caelitum, temptare simul parati—
11 pauca nuntiate meae puellae
12   non bona dicta:

13 cum suis vivat valeatque moechis,
14 quos simul complexa tenet trecentos,
15 nullum amans vere, sed identidem omnium
16   ilia rumpens;

17 nec meum respectet, ut ante, amorem,
18 qui illĭús culpá cecidít velút prati
19 ultimi flos, praetereunte postquam
20   tactus aratro est.

Epilogue

If Catullus' obscenity is occasionally offensive to modern taste, it must be remembered that literature in his day did not circulate so indiscriminately as in the modern era of the printing press and the newspaper; moreover fashions change.   Even English literature has the ribaldry of the Elizabethan and Restoration poets. In modern times no poet has shown a vein of genius so similar to

that of Catullus as Robert Burns, who could write the purest
and tenderest of lyrics and at the same time shock his contemporaries by saying:

> The kirk and state may join, and tell
> To do such things I maunna:
> The kirk and state may gae to hell,
> And I'll gae to my Anna.

To be outspoken was the fad in the society in which Catullus
moved.   Catullus himself—if one may venture to piece together a
fragment and an excerpt—has left us an apology for his naught-
iness:

> 1 Si qui forte mearum ineptiarum
> 2 lectores eritis manusque vestras
> 3 non horrebitis admovere nobis,
> 4 *num* me ex versiculis *putabitis* (*quod*
> 5 *hi* sunt molliculi) parum pudicum?
> 6 Pol castum esse decet pium poetam
> 7 ipsum, versiculos nihil necesse est!

Or, as Walter Savage Landor wrote:

> Tell me not what too well I know
> About the bard of Sirmio.
> Yes, in Thalia's son
> Such stains there are—as when a Grace
> Sprinkles another's laughing face
> With nectar, and runs on.

Notes

EXPLANATIONS

Boldface indicates lemmata—i.e., words or phrases commented on. Where no lemma occurs, a note is on the entire passage or line.

Italic indicates: (1) English translations; (2) Latin synonyms and equivalents—e.g., *Miles*, l. 33: **vivere,** *esse;* (3) Latin and other foreign words in English sentences; and (4) titles of literary works.

Leaders indicate: (1) correlatives—e.g.: **cum ... tum,** *not only ... but also;* (2) tmesis—i.e., the separation of parts of a compound word by the intervention of one or more words, —e.g.: **qui ... cumque,** *quicumque;* and (3) words included within a lemma—e.g., *Miles*, 1. 1: **Ubi ... est, Ubi Artotrogus nunc est.**

Square brackets indicate words supplied to expand or complete a phrase—e.g., *Miles*, l. 4: *ad tuas* [*virtutes*].

Notes

PLAUTUS

MILES GLORIOSUS

Induction

Like Shakespeare's *Taming of the Shrew*, the *Miles Gloriosus* has an induction, or preliminary tableau, unconnected with the plot and even preceding the prologue.

[1] A bracketed number indicates a line abridged or otherwise adapted to the purposes of this edition.

2. formā regiā, ablative of description, *of royal mien.*

3. tum, in the enumerative sense, *furthermore, also.* **ausit,** equivalent to *audeat.* **discere,** *mention,* supply *virtutes* as object.

4. aequiperare, *aequare.*

5. Quemne, *the one whom?* **servavi,** i.e., spared his life. **campi Curculionii,** a comic invention. *Curculio* means *weevil* (for which we might use a more familiar equivalent—e.g., *cockroach* or *cootie*).

6. Bumbo–mach–ides Clyto–mestori–dysarch–ides, a bombastic mock-heroic Greek name meaning approximately: *Buzz-battle-son Famed-wise-misleader-son.*

8. nempe, *of course.*

9. spiritu, *breath.*

10. Vel, *for instance.* The connection is intentionally vague, for Artotrogus' flattery is quite *à propos* of nothing.

10-11. elephanto, dative of possession, modifies *bracchium* (l. 11): lit., *the arm to the elephant*—i.e., *the elephant's arm.* **ei bracchium,** *its arm.* English would render the entire sentence as follows: *For example, that elephant in India!—how you broke its arm.*

11. pactum, the same as *modus* in such phrases as: *quomodo, nullo modo* (l. 415). **pugno** (from *pugnus*), *fist.* **prae-fregisti,** from *prae-fringo.*

12. femur, *thigh.*

13. īceram, from *īco* (cf. the more familiar participle *ictus*). **pol** (or *edepol*), a mild oath or byword originally meaning *by Pollux* (cf. *me-castor* and *e-castor, by Castor;* and *mehercle* and *hercle, by Hercules*).

14. con-nixus (from *con-nitor*), emphatic *nitor* (*strive*). **corium,** *hide.*

15. os, *bone* (or *bones*). **transmineret,** *pierce* (cf. the more familiar *e-minēre*).

16. istaec, *ista,* neuter plural; **hasce,** *has.* Compare *istaec* with the form *haec, istanc* (l. 284) with *hanc,* and *istuc* (l. 105) with *hoc.* The full suffix *-ce* appears in *has-ce* and *istis-ce* (l. 194) and originally meant *here* (cf. vulgar English *this-here*). **aerumnas,** *woes.* **venter,** i.e., *my hunger.*

17. 'st, *est.* For *est* and *es* (but for no other forms of the verb *to be*) the usual rule of elision is reversed—i.e., the final syllable of the preceding word remains intact, and the *e* of *est* or *es* is dropped. **adsentandum 'st,** lit., *must be assented to.* **mentibitur,** *mentietur, say falsely, tell a lie.*

18. tabellas, *writing tablets.*

19. facete, *cleverly.*

20. meditate, adverb, *by heart.*

21. prae-olat mihi, impersonal, equivalent to *prae-olfaciam, I smell in advance, I get a whiff* (or *an inkling*) *of.*

22. Ecquid, interrogative, *anything.*

23. Scytho-latronia, an imaginary country, *Scytho-mercenaria* (see note on l. 50).

25. tu, metrical hiatus because of the dramatic pause.

26. istaec, *ista,* nominative singular feminine (see note on l. 16). **summa,** noun. **rationem,** *reckoning, calculation.*

29. memoriā optimā, emphasized by hiatus, ablative of description. **'s,** *es* (see note on l. 17). **offae,** *morsels,* a humorous word, like our *grub.*

30. ĕdes, *eat* (not from *ē-do*).

31. te, accusative. The more logical thing to say would have been *communicabo mensam meam tecum,* but Pyrgopolinices reverses the personal and impersonal objects of the verb—as though his food were more important than his guest: *I'll present you to my food.*

32. Quid, *why?* **quod,** *what.*

33. vivere, *esse.*

34. Ablatives of specification.

35. ted, *te.* **iniuriā,** *wrongly* (opposite of *iure*).

36. here, *heri,* adverb. **pallium,** *mantle* (see p. 264, column 2).

38. hic-i-ne, for *hic-ci-ne,* lit., *this-here man?* The suffix *-ci* is the same as *-ce* (see note on l. 16). **inquit mihi,** *says one to me* (not logical after the plural *rogitabant,* but amusingly colloquial).

39. Immo, *no.* In l. 44 it means *yes;* the reader must judge by the context.

41. liberalis, *noble, aristocratic.* **caesaries** (singular), *hair, locks.* **quam,** *how.*

42. Quae-n, *quae-ne* (cf. *tu-n,* l 167); **obsecraverint,** subjunctive in a relative clause of cause. The equivalent English idiom would be: *What! When they begged me?*

43. Pyrgopolinices is a host in himself, a whole parade, a one-man circus. **illā,** adverb, *by that route* (or *way*).

44. nimius-a-um, nimis, (in Plautus) *much, very, etc.* (not *too much, too, etc.*).

46. arcesso, -ĕre, also spelled *accerso.*

47. ut, result. **dare operam,** more often *operam dare* or *operámdare, attend to.*

49. Seleucus, a name to conjure with—as if one should say: *my boss, Napoleon.* **opere maximo,** *maximopere* (superlative of *magnopere*), *maxime.*

50. latrones, *mercenaries.* It was not until Cicero's time that the word quite deservedly came to mean *brigands.* **cogerem,** *gather.*

51. Age, *come* (exclamatory).

Prologue

52. Erus (or *herus*), *master* (of a slave only).

53. sese, *him,* object of the infinitive. **sectarier,** *sectari.* This longer form of the present passive infinitive is found in all conjugations.

54. quaquā, *by whatever way, whereever*—hardly different from *quoquô, whithersoever.*

55. hau, *haud* (not the exclamation *hau* or *au*). **diu servio,** the equivalent English idiom requires the perfect tense. **servitutem servio,** cognate accusative—i.e., *be a slave.*

58. erus, Pleusicles.

59. mulierem, Philocomasium.

60. He was envoy of Athens to Naupactus (situated on the Gulf of Corinth).

61. forte, *by chance.*

63. ubi, *when.* **amicam,** *sweetheart.* **erilem,** *master's. Erilis-e* is the possessive adjective derived from *erus.*

64. vivus, *lively, quick.* **quantum possum,** *quam maxime.*

66. altum, *mare* (Latin), *the deep.*
volunt, *decree.*

67. ubi, *where, in which.*

68. *dono (for a gift) dat me huic militi.*

71. contra, *in turn.* **aspexit,** the subject is *she.*

75. sese, subject of *amare* and *odisse* (l. 76).

77. quoniam, *when, after.*

78. clan-culum, adverb, *clam.*

82. in proximo, *next door.* **devertitur,** *lodges.*

83. lepidum, *pleasant, jolly.*

85. intus, adverb; *within, indoors.* **machinas** (cf. English *machinations*), *trick, scheme.* There are many other colloquial and witty terms used to designate the stratagems that are a favorite feature of the comedy of manners—e.g., *astutia* (l. 108), *commentum* (l. 112), *dolus* (l. 118), *sycophantia* (l. 282), and *fabricae* (l. 286).

86. quî, *whereby.* Here it introduces a purpose clause (cf. the use of *quo* with certain purpose clauses). **amantis,** noun, *lovers.* **unâ,** lit., *together.* **inter se convenas,** *accessible to each other.*

87. conclave, *room.*

88. eapse, *ipsa.*

90. commeatus, *passage.* **hinc huc,** *to and fro.*

91. sene, Periplectomenus.

92. foris concrepuit, *the door creaked (rattled, was kicked,* or whatever stage business traditionally preceded an entrance). **hinc a vicino,** lit., *hence from our neighbor's.* The English idiom requires the locative—i.e., *here at our neighbor's.*

Act I, scene 1

94. quid agis, *how are you?* **occisi sumus** (slang), *we are ruined.*

95. negoti, *trouble.* **tegulae,** *tiles—* i.e., *roof.*

96. modô, adverb, *just now.* **ves-**

trum, *vestrorum.* **familiarium,** lit., *housemates*—i.e., *some one from your house.*

97. im-pluvium, lit., *rainhole.* **hospitem,** *my friend* (or *guest*), Pleusicles.

100. periisse (slang), *occisum esse* (see note on l. 94). **heus** (*not heu*), *hey!* **quid agis** (not as in l. 94), lit., *what are you doing?*

101. sectari, *sequi.* **simiam,** *monkey.*

102. hîc-i-ne (see note on l. 38), *here?*

103. si's, *si vis, if you will*—i.e., *please.* **iube,** supply *her.* **transire,** i.e., *through the hole in the wall.* **quantum possit,** *quam primum, quam celerrime* (l. 64). **se,** *her.*

104. familiares, *the household* (cf. l. 96). The servants could testify that they had seen her at home, where she belonged.

105. dicito, *dic.*

106. The *ut*-clause indicates that *dicito* connotes *command.* **ut verbis vincat,** *that she convince.* **se** (both times), *her.* **ne,** metrical hiatus emphasizes the negative.

107. si quidem, *etsi.* **infitias eat,** lit., *go to denial;* equivalent to the simple verb *infitiari, deny.*

108. incipisso, *incipio.* **astutiam,** see note on l. 85.

109. Philocomasium will pretend to be twins. This is just the opposite of the *Comedy of Errors.*

110. If *cum* were elided, it would make an iambic foot.

111. lacte, nominative, *lac.* **eos,** the supposed twin sister and her lover. **devertier,** see note on l. 53.

112. euge (or *eu*), Greek for *bene.* **commentum,** see note on l. 85.

113. ut . . . , a clause of purpose. *illic, he,* the *conservus* (l. 98 ff). **adversum,** preposition, *to.*

114. hanc, Philocomasium, object of *vidisse.* This is indirect discourse, depending on *concriminatus.*

115. alteram, the supposed twin sister.

116. exquiret, compound of *quaero*

117. titubo, *totter, falter*—i.e., *err.*

118. Nimis, see note on l. 44. **doctum,** *clever.*

122. prandet, *she is lunching.* **operae non est,** *she's not at leisure.*

123. istî, *there, "chez vous."*

124. dice, *dic.*

125. docte perdoctam, *cleverly coached.*

129. illic, *ille* (see note on l. 16). **custos,** *jailer*—i.e., Sceledrus, to whom Pyrgopolinices had assigned the task of keeping an eye on Philocomasium.

Act I, scene 2

131. proximae viciniae, locative case, *in the very near neighborhood*—i.e., *at our next-door neighbor's.*

132. malam rem (slang), *trouble.*

133. quantum, *as far as.*

135. volup est [*mihi*], *I am glad. Volup* is an adverb (cf. *bene est mihi*). **fac sciam,** *fac ut sciam, let me know.*

137. forte fortunâ, colloquial redundancy, *just by chance.*

140. Tu-ti-n, *tu,* with emphatic suffix *-ti* (or *-te;* cf. *tu-te,* l. 144) and interrogative suffix *-n* (or *-ne*). The whole word means therefore. *What! You?*

142. pergi'n, *continue,* supply *haec dicere.* The form is a colloquial contraction of *pergis-ne* (cf. *iube'n,* l. 147; *vi'n,* l. 155; *sci'n,* l. 157; and *audi'n,* l. 408). **vis dicam,** *vis* (from *volo*) *ut dicam.*

143. Quin etiam, emphatic, *but still!* **'st,** *she is.* **Eho,** exclamation of surprise.

144. vise, from *viso.* **tu-te,** see note on l. 140. **postulo,** *expect* (older meaning of the word.)

145. certum 'st (colloquial), *I am resolved.* **opperiar,** *await.*

146. te, ablative of comparison.

147. Iube'n, *iubes-ne,* colloquial use of the present for the future. **tibi,** equivalent to *tuos.* **nusquam 'st,** i.e., *does not exist.* Sceledrus must be seeing things!

148. eccam, *ecce eam* (cf. *ecc-um,* l. 262; *ecc-os,* l. 593; *ecc-illam* l. 296).

150. îlico, derived from *in loco* (cf. *Johnny on the spot*), *right there* (or *here*).

151. nihil est quâ, *there is no way by which* (cf. *nihil est ubi, nihil est cur,* etc.).

152. suscitant, *madden.*

155. Vi'n, *vis-ne,* verb. **uti,** *ut.*

156. corde, *animo,* need not be translated. **uti,** from *utor.*

157. nullum commeatum, Palaestrio is bluffing. There is no apparent reason for the hiatus after *commeatum.*

159. dignu'n, *dignus-ne.* **verberibus,** from *verber.*

161. Pede, *on the hoof, in the flesh!*

Act I, scene 3

163. Quid ais tu, the conventional phrase to attract a person's attention —e.g., *look here!, hey there!* **Hanc rem gero** (idiom), *I'm busy.*

164. Respice-dum, if translated at all, the suffix *-dum* means *just.*

165. probrum, adjective used as noun, *wickedness.*

166. em (not *hem*), *ecce, here you are!*

167. tu-n, *tu-ne.*

168. hercle, see note on l. 13.

169. carebis, supply *istis oculis.*

170. qui, *which*—i.e., eyes.

171. víderím, emphasized by hiatus. **mora,** *foolish* (cf. *sopho-more*), supply *sum.* **multum,** *very.* **capitis perdam,** *I'll have his life* (comic exaggeration).

175. exit, *exiit.*

176. facinus, verbal noun from *facio; happening, fact, thing.* In Plautus' time it had not yet come to mean *crime.*

177. domi, i.e., at Pyrgopolinices' house. **'st,** *she is.* **certa res est,** *certum est* [*mihi*]. (See note on l. 145).

180. Ne (sometimes spelled *nae*), a positive particle used only in combination with personal pronouns, need not be translated. **serô,** *too late.*

181. resipisces, *recover your senses.* **si prius,** *cum primum.*

182. experior, *I realize.* **caliginem,** *a mist.*

185. con-ticiscam, derived from *taceo.*

Act I, scene 4

186. Inde, imperative of the verb *in-do* (not the adverb *thence*). **gratis,** *gratias.*

187. templis, in its original meaning of *regions.* This is a mock-heroic description of the stormy sea.

188. servavit, the indicative in a *cum*-causal clause is common in early Latin.

191. See l. 176.

192. quidem, *really.* **eam esse hanc,** *hanc* (i.e., *the woman we see*) *esse eam* (Philocomasium).

193. quid istuc est (colloquial), expresses remonstrance.

194. quid tibi debetur (idiom), *what's your business?*

195. tu-te, supply *loqueris.*

196. viti, from *vitium.*

197. quicum, *quocum.*

199. Quin, *why not?*

200. odiosu's, *odiosus es,* a common contraction.

202. enim, *why* (non-interrogative). **nos, nos-met,** subject and object respectively of *perdiderimus* (*have lost*).

203. intemperiae, *distemper, madness.*

204. perperam, adverb, *wrongly.*

206. Tu-ne, here the *positive* particle -*ne* echoes the interrogative. **quae,** i.e., *I who.* As she is a stranger

in Ephesus, Sceledrus can know nothing about her name.

208. ind-audivi, *in-audivi.* **quaesitum,** supine.

210. manifestaria, *caught in the act.*

211. altrinsecus, adverb, *on the other side*—i.e., *by the other arm.*

212. nil moror (idiom), *I don't care to* (with complementary infinitive), *I don't care for* (with direct object). **quî,** *how* (see l. 86 and note).

213. atque, *but*—i.e., not Philocomasium, but another like her. **siet,** *sit* (so also *siem, sies,* etc.).

215. nusquam, emphatic negative. **firmatam fidem,** *oath, word of honor.*

216. cogis, an oath given under compulsion is not binding.

218. fide, *sense of honor* (nonexistent in a woman!).

220. machaeram, the national Greek weapon, a kind of bowie knife. **intus,** means *from within* as well as *within.* **eâ,** *with it.*

221. rectâ, adverb, *straight.* **quemque,** *quemcumque.*

224. faxo, old future perfect of *facio,* *I'll see to it* (or *warrant*).

225. opu'st, *opus est,* a common contraction. **Eccam,** Philocomasium. **lecto,** *bed.*

226. ne, a positive particle (see note on l. 180).

228. faciet quin, *convince that . . . not*—i.e., *prevent her from being . . . .*

229. istaec, eam, Dicea. **huius,** Philocomasium.

230. propius, *surer,* lit., *nearer.*

231. ero, dative of *erus.* In ll. 234–235 *ero* is the future of *sum.*

232. mussitabis, *keep mum.*

233. consili, *consilii,* partitive genitive with *quid.*

234. hunc, Periplectomenus.

Act I, scene 5

236. Tun, *tu-ne.*

237. ludificavisti, *mocked, insulted.* **hospitam,** Dicea.

238. ausculta, *listen.*

239. Purgare, *exculpate.*

241. Licet-ne, supply *loqui.* me di . . . , equivalent to our phrase *so help me God.*

242. virgarum, *rods, switches*—i.e., *unless I get the revenge of having you flogged by your master.*

246. nosträi, the old genitive form— i.e., *ista tua est ita similis huius nostrae.*

247. me, i.e., *my house.*

257. complexam, agrees with *illam,* but refers to *hospitem* as well (cf. variations of the same phrase in ll. 97–98, 138, and 149). osculantem, emphasized by hiatus. Ea-ne, Philocomasium.

259. iam (with the future), *soon, immediately.* It is emphatic here and is therefore not elided.

260. ludificarier, *fooled.*

261. miris modis, *wonderfully.*

266. ex-cors, *brainless.*

267. furci-fer, lit., *wearer of a frame*—i.e., *condemned criminal, rogue, rascal.*

268. vincam . . . , *I shall control myself.*

271. comprimes, future indicative, equivalent to a command (so also the future perfects, *nesciveris* and *videris,* in ll. 271–272).

Act II, scene 1

276. Cohibete, *keep.*

278. sterilis, *empty.* platea, *plaza, street.*

280. bonis, *good men.*

282. nam, were this elided, it would make an iambic foot. sycophantiam, see note on l. 85.

283. quî, see note on 86. admutiletur, *be trimmed.*

284. dari, i.e., *be told.* rationem, *plan.*

285. anulus, *finger ring.*

286. igitur, *then.* fabricarum, see note on l. 85.

288. ut, *as,* correlative with *ita.*

290. praedicat, *predicates, states*— viz., that his beauty exceeds the beauty of Alexander (i.e., the Homeric Paris, whose other name was Alexander).

291. se, object of *sectari.* memorat, *states.*

292. potis, adjective, *able,* supply *es.*

293. facetiarum, *drollery.*

294. ingenuam, agrees with *mulierem* (l. 292). aequi facio (idiom), *it's all the same to me.*

297. usus, noun, *opus* (cf. l. 301).

298. crinis comptos, matron's headdress.

299. Erro . . . , idiomatic or proverbial phrase (cf. the English: *I don't follow you, I don't get what you're driving at*).

300. ancilla, *maidservant.* illi, *to her*—i.e., *has she?* cata, *clever.*

302. de-perire (slang), *be smitten* (or *dead in love*) *with.*

303. quasi, depends on *simulet;* colloquial, as in the English *pretend as if.* favea, *ancilla.* porro, *deinde.* mihi, supply *dederit.*

304. interpres, *go-between.*

305. potuit, supply *Sol.* Nothing is hidden from the sun!

306. The fifth foot is a tribrach (*quăm ĕgŏ*), therefore no elision is possible.

309. nomines [*eam*], *call her.*

311. face, see note on l. 135.

Act II, scene 2

313. salvum, supply *te.* ornatus, *attended.*

314. obviam es, *you are met.*

315. ornatu, *guise.* Eu, *bravo,* see note on l. 112. noster, *meus,* colloquial phrase, *my friend forever.*

316. amabo (colloquial), *please.*

318. ecquid, mere interrogative particle.

319. meditatam, *trained, coached, rehearsed.*

321. populi odium, *quem populus odit*—i.e., *quem omnes oderunt, the most unpopular man in town, the universal "bête noire."* **cincinnatum,** *curlyheaded.*

322. nam, interrogative particle.

323. illum, Pyrgopolinices.

325. datum, the subject is *the ring.* de-perire (see note on l. 302), the subject is *eam;* the object, *illum.*

326. cum extemplo, *cum primum.*

327. cura, imperative of the verb.

328. Vos, object of *curate.* **modô,** *just, only.* **oneratum** (slang), *stuffed, loaded*—i.e., *fooled.*

329. meditate, adverb, *carefully.*

Act II, scene 3

332. quod . . . , *si id quod agas.*

333. Seleucum, see ll. 49–50. **parasitum,** Artotrogus.

335. dum fieret, purpose is implied—i.e., *that meanwhile.*

336. rem, *affairs.*

337. condicio, *amour, match.* **luculenta,** *high-toned.*

339. -dum, see note on l. 164. **auceps,** *snarer,* (with *sermoni*) *eavesdropper.*

340. hoc (with partitive genitive), *this bit of.* **clandestino,** adverb.

341. arrabo, *token, pledge.*

342. *Quid* [*est*] *hic* [*arrabo*]? **luculenta,** note the hiatus.

343. expetessit, *expetit.*

344. *nunc porro ancilla mi dedit eius* (her) *anulum, ut deferrem ad te.*

345. Nupta-ne . . . , *married or single? Vidua* is emphasized by hiatus. **potis,** supply *est* (see note on l. 292).

350. de-moritur (slang), see note on l. 302.

351. muliere, Philocomasium (for the idiom see note on l. 220 for *ea*).

352. Quin, *just.* **sicut,** *in as much as.*

355. occasionem, accusative of exclamation.

356. cĕ-do, old imperative of *dare* with prefix *-ce, here* (see note on l. 16), *give, out with!* This is not to be confused with *cēdo, I yield.*

357. actutum, *at once.* **per gratiam,** *with good grace, with no ill will.*

358. adfatim, *satis.*

359. mulieri, having been attracted into the relative clause, this is made to agree with *illi*—i.e., *iube mulierem habere sibi dono aurum . . .* **sibi dono habere,** *have as a gift for herself, take and keep.* **instruxti,** *instruxisti, bestowed.*

362. delicatu(s e)s, *you're joking.* **quae,** *since she* (relative clause of cause).

365. bellula, sentimental diminutive of *bellus-a-um, pretty.* **pithecium,** *ape.* **prae illā,** *compared to her* (the lady). **spinturnicium,** call it *rain crow.*

Act II, scene 4

366. hos, the object of *videam* and the subject of *esse.*

369. sati'n, *satis-ne,* used as a mere interrogative particle. **haec,** Milphidippa.

370. subigit, *impels.*

371. nihil amassis (colloquial), *ne amaveris,* prohibition. **illa,** the lady.

372. hanc, the lady's maid.

374. evenat, *eveniat.*

375. *ubi sit id quod quaeris.*

377. cedo, *cĕ-do.* **horunc,** from *horum-ce.*

378. multae, supply *faciunt.*

379. numquis, covertly alluding to Pyrgopolinices. **cĕ-do . . . ,** *a word with you alone!* **solae,** *soli.*

381. tantisper, *tam diu* (cf. *paulisper*).

381. hac, *mea.*

382. tibi, *for you.* **Properando,** lit., *hurrying*—i.e., *hurry up.* The word is used for the sake of the pun, *operámdo* (colloquial pronunciation) and *(pr)operando*. Note the hiatus.

383. pede-temptim, *step by step, cautiously.*   **mercis** (from *merx*), *wares.*

384. concinnum, *commodum, convenient, agreeable.*   **hoc,** ablative, *than he.*

385. teneo, *I know, I haven't forgotten.* She knows her part in the plot all right, but wants a hint as to how she may approach Pyrgopolinices *now*.

387. illaec, Milphidippa.

388. illam, the lady, her mistress.

389. tis, genitive of *tu.*   **missa,** the subject is Milphidippa.

391. non libeat [*tibi*], i.e., *nolis*, supply *illam ducere uxorem.*   **inclamato,** imperative, *scold.*

392. Voco-ne, interrogative.

394. Pyrgopolinices jestingly lays claim to the famous Roman cognomen *Pulcher*, or *Prettyman*.

395. liceat, Milphidippa would have added some such phrase as: *era mea orat*—i.e., *my lady begs that she may spend her life with you;* but thinking she has finished, Pyrgopolinices gives her words the meaning: *that I may spend my life with you.*

399. illaec, the maidservant.   **illa,** the lady.

400. Qua ab, *a qua.*

402. ab tui (genitive) **cupienti** (ablative), *from one desirous* (or *a lover*) *of you.*

403. quae, *who,* the antecedent is *eam.*

404. illi, *to her.*   **suppetias,** *auxilium.*

406. Exprome, *display.*

407. Eu, sarcastic.   **verbero** (*-onis*), *one who gets flogged*—i.e., *villain, rascal.*

408. condicionem, see note on l. 337.

409. eampse, *ipsam,* the lady.

414. istic, *at your house.*

415. pacto, *modo* (see note on l. 11).

416. recipi, *be welcomed.* **amiserim,** *dimiserim.*

420. domum, i.e., *to Athens.*

426. cubare, *be sick-a-bed.* **lippam,** *sore-eyed.*

427. nauclérus (Greek), *skipper*—i.e., Pleusicles in disguise.

430. Quî potius quam, lit., *how rather than?*—i.e., *why not* (*quin*)?

431. ducere, *marry.*

432. cognatos, *your relatives.*

433. Quid ego ni, *what can I do but?, how can I help?, why shouldn't I?*

435. illaec, Acroteleutium.

436. extrudam, *expellam.*

437. faxis, perfect subjunctive, *feceris* (see note on l. 224).

438. illaec, *those things*—i.e., her clothing and jewelry.

440. usu'st, *usus* (*opus*) *est ut Acroteleutium ad me veniat.*

443. arbiter, *witness.*

444. conventum, colloquial construction, the past participle instead of a complementary infinitive.   **Et ego vos,** supply *conventos volo.*

445. date . . . (colloquial), *just pay attention.*   **id,** *for that reason, that's why.*   **si,** *in case.*

447. differri, *distraught.*

448. istius, Pyrgopolinices.

449. abierim, i.e., *I have divorced my husband.* **istius nuptiarum,** *marriage with him*—i.e., Pyrgopolinices. **ordine** (colloquial), *in due order, correct.*

450. dotalis, adjective, *belonging to your dowry*—i.e., *your own property.*

451. hinc, i.e., *from the house.* **senem,** Periplectomenus in the rôle of her divorced husband.   **postquam,** *now that.*

452. ille, Pyrgopolinices.   **alienam,** *another man's.*

453. discito, imperative of *disco, learn, hear.*

454. abierit, i.e., after her tryst with Pyrgopolinices.   gubernator, nauclerus (see l. 427).

455. verbis, *in the name of.*

457. siquid, *quicquid, whatever.*

458. soluturum, *cast off, set sail.* operam dare, *serves, is favorable.*

459. ille, Pyrgopolinices.

461. illi, Philocomasium.   dicam, *bid* (see note on l. 106).   onus, i.e., *her luggage.*

462. adeo, *moreover.*

463. prorsum, adverb of place, *straight to;* protinam, adverb of time, *straightway.*

464. triduum, *tris dies.*   quin liber sis, *without your being free*—rather illogical, but typically colloquial.

465. numquid . . . , (question) *Numquid aliud vis?*, (answer) *Volo ut haec memineris.*

466. illum, Pyrgopolinices.

467. commodum, adverb, *just in time, pat.*

Act II, scene 7

469. ei, *to her.*

470. 's, *es,* imperative.

471. te, ablative.   *Ero optimo* stands in apposition.

472. cum, *since, that.*   concilio, verb.

474. gestio, *I long for her.*   modice, supply *gestire.*

Act II, scene 8

475. ipsum, Pyrgopolinices.

476. Ut, *how.*

477. te, the subject, supply *eum* as the object.

478. adiri eum, *he is approached*—i.e., by those who would present their credentials.

479. copia, *opportunity.*

480. inclitu's, *are famous* (or *renowned*).

482. Two wishes: (1) *ut Pyrgopolinices benignus sit,* (2) *ne gravetur* (*be not vexed at*) *id quod cupiam.*

486. mutent, i.e., *cause him to change.*

488. praedicatio, *statement, description.*

489. opinione illius, *than his expectation*—i.e., *than he expected.*

490. ducere, emphasized by hiatus.

491. quibo, from *queo* (*possum*).

493. vilem, *cheap.*

494. Sine [*ut*], *let her.*

495. obtigisse, *contigisse.*

496. Phaoni, Phaon of Lesbos, for whom—according to legend—Sappho died of unrequited love. se, *him*—i.e., *ut mulier se tam amaret.*

497. Eo, verb, present tense equivalent to future.

499. ec-fringam, from *ec* (*ex*) and *frango*—i.e., pull them off their hinges.

500. Tene, verb.

501. animus defit, *my senses leave me.*

501. per oculos, the eyes are the windows of the soul.

503. mea (colloquial), *my dear.*   si, *if only.*

504. ut, *when, as soon as.*

505. nescio, supply *whether.*

506. Ut, *how.*

507. te, emphasized by hiatus.

511. mulierem, supply *istuc facere.*

512. se, *her.*   eas, verb.

514. Quin, *nay.*   virum, emphatic —hence no elision.

515. dotales, *belonging to her dower*—i.e., *her own personal property.* huius, Acroteleutium.

516. in exspectatione, *late.*

517. animi, locative case.   Non ero, supply *in exspectatione.*

519. thalassico (Greek), *nautical.*

520. hanc, Philocomasium.

Act II, scene 10

529. Quid modi, lit., *what of end?*— i.e., *when will you stop?* Quid ego ni, see note on l. 433.

530. ubi, *where*.

531. Audi'n, peremptory, *look here!*

532. isti, *to her*—i.e., Philocomasium.

535. explicent, *unfurl*—i.e., *set sail*.

536. See l. 426. venissent, supply *mother and sister* as subject.

539. attinēre, *attinuēre, attinuerunt, have touched.* animum, *heart*.

541. complecti, the object *te* would naturally be understood, but Philocomasium means Pleusicles.

543. affligatur, *be hurt*.

543-544. animo . . . huic, *she's had a spell* (or *turn*).

545. moror, see note on l. 212. mālo, verb—i.e., *mālo ut quiescat*.

546. nexa (from *necto*), *closely joined.* his-ce, old nominative plural masculine plus the suffix *-ce*.

548. Temptabam, *I was trying to find out.* spirarent, the subject is *lips*. admotam oportuit, *you ought to have applied*.

549. magis vis, *mavis*.

550. resipisti, *resipivisti*.

551. apud me, *in my senses*.

553. cum ero, *with my master*.

555. rerum omnium, genitive of cause.

561. dicant, *people would say*.

565. factum, noun.

Act II, scene 11

571. duo . . . , *quem duo di*.

572. obsecrat, the subject is *she*.

574. fer opem, cf. *fers suppetias* (l. 404).

Act II, scene 12

576. sublimem, *aloft*—i.e., *on your shoulders*.

577. inter . . . , like the accursed Sinis of Greek fable.

579. numerô, *too soon*.

580. subigitare, *make advances to.* Note the hiatus.

581. ventum 'st ad me, impersonal, equivalent to *I was approached*.

585. non de nihilo, *not without reason*.

587. Iura, verb. non homini nemini, colloquial redundance, *not a single soul*.

589. Venerium nepotulum, see l. 505.

590. Mavortem, *Martem*.

591. vapularim, active verb with passive meaning, *be beaten* (or *flogged*). iure, *rightly*.

595. lanam, *patch* (see l. 517).

597. porta, i.e., the city gate.

599. Verba . . . esse, *I have been cheated.* scelus viri, genitive, *vir scelestus*.

600. illexit (from *in-licio*), *enticed.* fraudem, *misdeed.* ad me, *home*.

POENULUS

Act V

1. quae, in grammatical agreement with the feminine noun *avis*, but to be translated by *who*. tunicis (from *tunica*), a Semitic costume—a long flowing garment, unbelted, with no cape (*pallium*) over the shoulders (see note on l. 1 of *Epidicus*, p. 264).

2. num-nam, interrogative particle. circumductu'st, *was he cheated out of?*—i.e., is it because someone stole his clothes at the bath, that he appears in a bathrobe—so to speak?

3. 'st, *est* (see note on l. 17, p. 253). Gugga, the meaning of this word is unknown.

5. Quî, *how?* Vide'n, *vides-ne* (see note on l. 142, p. 256). sarcinatos, *burdened*—i.e., *bent* (like old men).

7. Quia . . . , lit., *because they walk with ringed ears*—i.e., *because they wear rings in their ears.* This was a thing no Greek or Roman would do, unless he were prevented from wearing finger rings by lack of fingers!

8. hos-ce, see note on l. 16, p. 253. **punice,** adverb, *in the Punic language.*

11. commeministi, English requires the addition of the complementary infinitive *to speak.*

13. illim, adverb, *illinc, from there.* This is redundant with *Carthagine,* but colloquial. **perierim,** *was lost.*

14. ad, expresses manner. English uses *in* or *after.* **illunc,** see note on l. 16, p. 253.

15. pueri, *children* (of both sexes). Hanno is thinking of his kidnapped daughters.

16. Vi'n, *vis-ne,* supply *ut.*

17. scis, i.e., to talk Punic.

19. cuiatis, nominative singular, *of what nationality?*

20. parseris, from *parco.* **Avo,** a Punic greeting. This happens (quite accidentally) to be so similar to the Latin **ave,** that any Roman could easily *guess* its meaning. Of course it is inconsistent for Milphio to switch to Latin after the first word, but just a word or two of Punic is enough for dramatic effect; besides the *audience* must understand what Milphio says. *Avo* is probably the one Punic phrase that the rascally Milphio really knows—all the rest is bluff.

21. byn, *son of,* like the Hebrew *ben* and similar forms in all Semitic languages.

24. Donni . . . doni, here Milphio's extremely meager knowledge of Punic fails him, and he begins to pun. **Doni vult . . . ,** *hic* (Hanno) *vult dare tibi nescioquid doni.*

25. pollicitarier, *pollicitari* (see note on l. 53, p. 254). *Pollicitor* has the same meaning as *polliceor.*

26. verbis meis (idiom), *in my name, for me.*

27. Avo donnim, the clever bluffer puts together the only two Punic words that he has heard so far from Hanno.

28. Mehar bocca . . . , this and all the other Punic is mere gibberish, so far as the play is concerned. It would contribute nothing to the thought even if it did make sense, for its sole purpose is to give Milphio an opportunity to pun and bluff. **sit,** a wish.

29. miseram buccam, *sore jaw.*

30. arbitrarier, narrative infinitive, equivalent to *arbitratur.*

31. nega . . . , *nega [nos] esse [medicos].*

34. Tu, although he is addressing Hanno, Milphio includes Hanno's followers in his questions (*venistis* and *quaeritis* being plural). **zonam,** *belt.*

36. Quid venit, *why has he come?* Agorastocles assumes that Hanno is answering the questions.

37. mures (from *mus*), *mice.*

38. dare . . . , *give to the aediles for a procession at the games.*

40. Ligulas, canalis, nuces, *shoe straps, water pipes, and nuts.*

41. operam . . . sibi, *to help him.* **veneant** (from *ven-eo*), *be sold.*

42. Assam . . . Arvinam, whatever *assam* may mean in Carthaginian, it happens also to mean *roast* in Latin (adjective, *assus-a-um*), and Milphio immediately answers: . . . *yes, suet.*

44. Palas et mergas, *spades and pitchforks.* **datas** [*esse*], infinitive in indirect discourse. **vendendas,** *to be sold, for sale.*

45. messis, noun, *harvest.*

46. metĕre, verb, *harvest.*

49. si's, *si vis, if you please.*

51. ut . . . , [*orat*] *ut iubeas te supponi.* **cratis,** *hurdle* in the old English sense—i.e., a piece of woven wickerwork, large enough to be set up as a fence and jumped over on horseback. To be drowned, crushed, or suffocated under such a hurdle (placed flat and weighted down with stones) was a very ancient form of execution. For one to **request** such treatment, is of course absurd. eô, adverb, *thereon, on it.*

56. nequam, indeclinable adjective, *wicked.*

57. hominem . . . , *qui hominem . . . inrideas.* **peregrinum,** *foreign.*

59. captatum, supine to express purpose. **migdilix,** the meaning of this word is unknown.

60. bisulci, *forked.*

61. compescas face, *fac [ut] compescas.*

67. popularitatis, *our common nationality.*

69. Antidamäi, genitive.

71-72. tessera hospitalis, *a friendship token*—e.g., a large coin broken in half, or two pieces of metal engraved with the same inscription. Friends long parted, or sons of friends, proved their identity by matching tokens.

73. Est par, *it matches.*

74-75. mi tuus . . . , *tuus pater Antidamas fuit mihi hospes.*

77. praebebitur, supply *tibi* or *vobis.*

80. uti, *ut.*

81. Aetolum, *Aetolian.* Calydon was in Aetolia.

84. tuum, *tuorum.*

85. Memora-dum, *just tell me.*

86. novi [*eos*], verb.

88. Patrem . . . , Hanno starts to say: *patrem amisisti,* or some such statement—but wishing to break the news more gently, he changes the construction of his sentence and concludes: *vellem [ut] viverent tibi.*

89. Factum, *it is a fact.*

90. sobrina, *cousin on the mother's side.*

91. frater patruelis, *cousin on the father's side.*

93. quo privatum . . . mortuo, somewhat redundant, *deprived of him dead.* **med,** accusative, subject of *privatum* [*esse*].

94. ita 'st, ut, *is true that.*

96. puero [*tibi*], i.e., *when you were a boy.*

EPIDICUS

Dramatis Personae

Thesprio, a typical slave's name, denotes foreign birth, but is of no significance as regards his character. **Apoecides** should mean *Emigrant* or *Colonist;* but as the character represents an influential citizen, and not a foreigner, his name can have no significance for the Latin play— whatever it may have suggested in Plautus' Greek original.

Act I, scene 1

1. pallium, the national Greek costume—viz., a short cape, worn over a tunic—,very different from the Roman toga. Because the comedies of Plautus and Terence, presented **Greek** characters in **Greek** costume, they were called *fabulae palliatae.*

2. odio, *a nuisance,* dative of the noun, equivalent to the adjective *odiosus.* **'s,** *es.* **nimium** (and **nimis**), *very* in the Latin of Plautus' day (not *too much*).

7. Venire . . . gaudeo, conventional greeting to a returned traveler. **Quid,** *what about?* **eô,** *thereto.* **ad-solet,** lit., *is customary in addition.*

8. Cena, *dinner.* **Spondeo,** *promise.*

9. Ut, lit., *how?* **Exemplum,** *proof.* **Eu-ge-pae** (Greek), *bravo.*

10. vidēre, *vidēris.* **habitior,** *more portly.* **gratia,** *thanks to.*

11. Quam, i.e., his left hand.

12. furti-ficus, *furtum faciens.* **rapio,** *rob* (as highwaymen do).

13. Ut, *how.*

14. ut, *when.*

15. modô, *just now.* **Scurra,** *town chap*—i.e., *weakling.*

16. quamvis audacter, [*tam*] *audacter quam vis.*

17. perpetue-n, the suffix *-ne.*

17-18. The joke lies in the pun on *varie: How's your health been since I left?* asks Epidicus. *Chequered (varie)!* answers Thesprio. *I don't like "chequered" men;* replies Epidicus, *they remind me of goats (capreae) or panthers*—i.e., their backs are chequered from flogging.

19. vis, *vis* [*ut*] *dicam.* **Ut illae res,** *how were things there?*

20. erilis, adjective. (*H*)*erilis noster filius* (Stratippocles) is equivalent to *filius nostri* (*h*)*eri.* **pugilice,** *athletice,* Greek words with Latin terminations having the same meaning as their English derivatives.

22. 'st, *est.* is, Stratippocles. **nisi si,** *perhaps.* The second *si* is superfluous. **vidulus,** *traveling bag.* **melina,** *marten skin*—i.e., *knapsack* (made waterproof by the cheap marten fur).

23. Te volo, the expected retort to *Di te perdant,* would be: *Te volo perditum*—but Epidicus does not dare say it to Thesprio. He therefore pauses and adds: . . . *percontari* (or *percunctari*) . . . *to ask you a question.*

24. operam da, *pay attention, listen.* **opera reddetur,** *deinde ego operam dabo tibi.*

25. Ius dicis, a pun meaning either: *you say what is fair and just (aequum dicis),* or: *you interpret the law*—i.e., *you are a judge (praetor).* **praeturam geris,** *hold the praetorship, are praetor.*

26. hoc, i.e., *than me.*

28. Thesprio implies that the elm rods would be used **on,** not **by,** Epidicus.

31. Mulciber, Vulcan.

32. travolaverunt, *flew across.* Vulcan (the Greek Hephaestus) could

make all sorts of magic appliances—even mechanical men or robots! **prognatu'st** (*prognatus est*) . . . , *son of Thetis*—i.e., Achilles. Heaven knows, Stratippocles is no Achilles; he is more of a Paris!

33. Sine, *sine* [*ut*] *perdat* [*arma*]. **Nerei filiae,** daughters of Nereus, sea nymphs. In the *Iliad* Thetis and her nymphs brought Achilles a new suit of armor after the death of Patroclus.

35. Plautus (or Menander) may have had others in mind, but at least we know that the Greek poets Archilochus and Alcaeus lost their shields in battle and boasted of it.

36. honori, dative of the noun, equivalent to the adjective *honorabile.* **fuit,** *fuit* [*honori*].

37. scutarius, *shield maker, armorer.*

38. in singulis stipendiis, *in quoque stipendio, in every campaign.* **dabit,** the subject is *he* (Stratippocles).

42. nevolt, *non vult.*

45. Animi causā, *because of affection, for love.* And Epidicus retorts: *How many loves has he?*

47. leno, *slave dealer.* **fidicina,** *music girl.*

48. id . . . , lit., *I have rendered that accomplished for him*—i.e., *it is a "fait accompli."*

49. A proverb—i.e., *one trims one's sails to suit the wind.*

51. Quid, *what about?*

52. mina, Latin corruption of the Greek *mna.* Call it *silver piece,* rather than any exact sum in dollars and cents.

53. adeo, *moreover.* **danista,** *money lender.*

54. In dies . . . , *at the rate of a nummus (farthing) for each silver piece per day*—i.e., at least one—perhaps even two—percent per day. This is usury with a vengeance! **Papae, an** exclamation.

55. qui, the antecedent is *danista,* not *eo* (Stratippocles).

56. basilice, Greek word with Latin ending, *royally.* As we would say: *It's better to be hanged for a sheep than a goat.*

57. epistulas, i.e., the letters reminding Epidicus to secure Acropolistis (!) at any cost.

59. plus . . . , lit., *to know more than say.* The English idiom would be: *to know more than he says.*

60. servum hominem, the subject of *scire* and *loqui* (l. 59).

61. timidu's, *timidus es.*

62. vidēre, *vidēris.* **commeruisse in te aliquid mali,** *to have committed some crime.*

63. poti'n, *potis-ne* [*es*]. **astare,** *ad-stare.*

65. de-agetur corium, *the hide will be removed.*

66. amat, supply *her* as object.

68. iussit, *iussit* [*me ire*].

71. dinumerare, *count out, pay in full.*

72. res turbulentas, accusative of exclamation.

73. Haec-i-ne, *haec*+*ce* (*herc*) +*ne* (indicating exclamation).

74. puppis, *my stern.*

78. benevolens cum benevolente, *amicus cum amico*—i.e., *we'll stand by each other to the bitter end.*

83. suffulcis, Epidicus is like a man in a nightmare—he seems to see a cliff tottering above his head and tries vainly to hold it up (*suffulcire*) with his hand.

84. itaque montes mali, *such mountains of disaster.*

88. senem, Periphanes. **censeret . . . ,** i.e., he thought he was buying (and freeing from slavery) his long-lost daughter, Telestis, when actually he was getting his son's sweetheart, Acropolistis.

90. fidicinam, Acropolistis. **ille,** the son. **quam . . . ,** *quam abiens* [*emendam*] *mandavit mihi, whom he* (Stratippocles), *on his departure, commissioned me to buy for him.*

93. verba dare alicui (idiom), *to deceive someone.*

95. bat, a meaningless comic word echoing *at.* English translators have rendered the echo variously by: *o but, o tut; o well, o hell;* etc.

96. Nequam, indeclinable adjective, *worthless.*

97. Quî, *why?* **libido** [*tibi*] **est,** *tibi libet.* **loqui,** *loqui* [*tibi*].

99. dare mutua (idiom), *loan.* **consilia,** *good suggestions.*

100. obviam, *to meet.*

101. adulescenti, Stratippocles. **illîc est,** *adest.*

103. orationem, *sermonem, talk, conversation.*

Act I, scene 2

104. admodum, *fully,* with *edictavi.*

105. summam, noun.

106. praeter . . . es, a parody of the familiar phrase: *you are wise beyond your years.* This is witty, but not strictly logical; for it really means: *you are stupider than the average of your age and profession*—being both very young and a soldier!

108. vitio . . . , *qui id tibi vitio-vertat.* **vitio vertere** (idiom), *blame.*

109. Qui . . . , [*eos*] *omnes, qui* [*mihi*] *invident, inimicos . . .*

110. vim nec vitium, *violence nor damage.* This is redundant, but Stratippocles wants to make it emphatic.

111. istoc, *for that reason.*

112. agit, *accomplishes.*

112-113. verbis [*iuvat*], **re iuvat,** these are contrasted.

114. tibi, *for you.*

115. quod, *which amount.*

116. Nam quid, *quid-nam?* **te,** the subject of *esse* (not the object of the impersonal verb *rē-tulit*).

117. ad rem, attributive phrase, modifies *auxilium,* **practical** *help.*

118. clamor, collective noun; *claim-*

ants, creditors, duns. **differor,** *am distracted.*

119. istiusmodi, *of your type, like you.* **furno mersos quam foro,** a pun that cannot be exactly reproduced in English. The picturesque phrase *foro mergi* (*to be sunk in the forum*) means *to be bankrupt;* the phrase *furno mergi* suggests *to be thrown into the oven.*

120. operam, *help.* **pretio pretioso,** *even at a costly price*—therefore *at any price.*

121. irrigatum plagis, *drenched with blows*—i.e., *bloody.* **pistori,** *to the miller*—i e., to work in the *pistrinum* as a penalty.

122. comparassit, equivalent to *comparaverit* (future perfect). **prius,** with *quam* (l. 124).

124. promittit, servabit, the subject is *he* (Stratippocles).

125. scapulis, *for my shoulders* (or *back*)—i.e., that part where the flogging is administered.

126. symbolae, equivalent to *picnic* (or *party*).

127. Impertit salute, a ridiculously pompous phrase for *salutat.*

128. Salvum . . . huc [*gaudeo*], the usual conventional phrase, less pompous than the expression employed in ll. 126–127.

131. Quod . . . impetratum 'st, means the same as *quod . . . curavi* (l. 130). Epidicus repeats the idea because he hopes to trap Stratippocles and make him admit his fickleness. **quod,** *the matter about which.*

132. missiculo, *send often,* frequentative verb derived from *mitto.* **operam,** *efforts.*

133. placet, the subject is *she.*

135. illam, Acropolistis. **cura,** *fancy* (noun), *love*—i.e., Telestis, the captive maiden.

136. quî, an untranslatable particle attached to *hercle.* **id quod facias bene,** *beneficium.* **ingratum homini,** i.e., *unwelcome to the recipient.*

138. mentis, practically the locative case. **scripta,** *epistolas.*

139. Men, *me-ne?* **piacularem,** *a scapegoat.*

140. subdas succidaneum, *offer as a substitute.*

141. Quid istîc, *come now* (expressing impatience).

142. calidis (slang), *hot off the griddle.*

143. tarpezita, *banker.*

144. loculi (plural), *moneybox.*

145. ne in-bitas, *ne in-eas,* prohibition.

147. fabulare, *fabularis.* **nostros,** *my fellow slaves* (especially those who did the flogging). **mihi,** emphatic.

148. Patiĕri'n, *patiĕris-ne.*

149. audaciam, *bold emprise.*

150. istuc, i.e., the danger (or hardship). **quodlibet,** he corrects *istuc* (*that*) to *quodlibet* (*anything*).

151. illa fidicina, Acropolistis. **res,** *means, solution.*

152. aliqua ope exsolvam, *by some means I'll fulfill my promise.*

154. tibi, *for you.* **istam,** Acropolistis. **hanc,** Telestis, the prisoner of war.

155. continuo, *on the spot.* **ultro,** *of his own accord.*

156. erit, the subject is *she.*

157. hunc hodie diem, colloquial redundance.

158. luculente habeamus, *spend merrily.*

159. senatum, *meeting of the senate.* **consiliarium,** adjective, *deliberative.* We would say: *a meeting of the senate to consider.* The question to be considered is: *On whom shall I declare war in order to get the money?* (l. 160), and is decided in l. 163—viz., to tackle the old man, Periphanes.

Act II, scene 1

166. quos pudet, *who are reluctant, who hesitate* (not quite so strong as *who are ashamed*).

166-167. A loosely constructed and redundant sentence. The subject nominative, *plerique homines*, is left hanging in the air. Apoecides might have said: *plerique homines . . . amittunt pudorem, most men* **lose** *their reluctance;* instead of that he changes the construction to: *most men—their reluctance leaves them.*

168. Is adeo tu 's, *that's you, you're an example.*

168-177. In ll. 168–172 Apoecides proves his first point—viz., that Periphanes now hesitates when there is no need to hesitate; in ll. 173–177 he proves his second point—viz., that formerly, when Periphanes buried his wife, he did not show quite the reluctance he should have shown.

169-170. genere . . . uxorem, the subject is *te;* the verb, *domum-ducere* (*marry*); and the object, *uxorem*—modified by *genere-natam-bono* and *pauperem.*

170. qua ex, *e qua.* tibi, with *prognatam.*

172. filiam, quae domi 'st, Periphanes thinks it is his daughter Telestis whom he has in his house, but it is really Acropolistis.

173-174. te credidi exsequi, *I thought you buried.*

174. extulisti, *carried to the grave*, practically a synonym of *exsequi.*

175. sacrificas ilico Orco, exaggerated of course.

176. iniuriā, adverb, *sine iure.*

177. tibi, with *licitum 'st.* eam vincere vivendo, *outlive* (*eam* is the object), *ei superstitem esse.*

179. aerumna, *labor* (one of the twelve labors of Hercules). There seems to be nothing particularly appropriate about the sixth.

180. Pulchra . . . , *pecunia est pulchra dos.* Quae . . . , English would use an *if*-clause—e.g., *yes, if it's not married* (i.e., *if it comes without*

a wife)—an impossibility of course, but pleasant to imagine.

Act II, scene 2

183. liquido, *clear*, modifies *auspicio.*

184. avi sinistra, *with favorable omen* (lit., *bird*).

185. qui, ablative neuter, *quo.* The antecedent is *cultrum, knife.* ex-entero, *disembowel.* marsuppium, *purse.*

186. ipsum, *my master.* vetulos, *dotards.*

187. hirudo, *bloodsucker* (not to be confused with *hirundo*).

189. qui, the antecedent is *eorum.* cluent, *are reputed.* The form is active, but the meaning passive. senati, genitive singular. columen, English uses the plural, *pillars*, when speaking of two individuals.

190. As is often the case, the unsupported *ut*-clause expresses a suggestion: *let him get married*—i.e., *get him a wife.* During his confidential whisperings with Periphanes, Apoecides has evidently suggested that this is the best way to overcome any opposition on Stratippocles' part to his father's remarrying. Observe Periphanes' last previous remark on the subject (l. 173): *Revereor filium.*

191. nescioquam, Periphanes little knows that his son's sweetheart is the girl whom Epidicus has already palmed off on him as his own daughter.

193. pactum, equivalent to *modus* (in all such phrases as *quomodo, eo modo, etc*).

194. orna te, *dress yourself for the part* (see l. 195). palliolum, equivalent to *pallium* (see note on l. 1). in collum conice, i.e., in order to seem to be running. *Con-ice* comes from *con-icio*, which in turn comes from *iacio.*

196. Age . . . agis, self-encouragement.

199. per myropolia et lanienas, *at all the perfumers and butcher shops.*

204. animo male 'st, *I feel faint.*

208. plenis, i.e., *full of people.*

209. arma et iumenta, i.e., *booty.*

210. captivorum quid, *quot et quales captivos.*

212. quisque visunt, the usual colloquial construction, equivalent to *omnes visunt* or *quisque visit.*

214. meretrix, *harlot.* **numerus tantus . . . quantum,** the logical equivalent of *tantum . . . quantum* or *tot . . . quot.*

215. quî, *how.*

216. retia, *nets.*

217. atque, *lo!* **illam,** emphatic, *her.* **praestolor,** *wait.*

218. tibicina, *flute player* (cf. *fidicina*). **Quicum,** *quacum.*

219-220. Epidicus cleverly plays on Periphanes' fears, expressed in ll. 191-192. **de-amat, de-perit** (synonyms), *loves madly.*

221. veneficam, *poisoner, sorceress.*

222. ut lepide, *how charmingly.* **ut concinne,** *how elegantly.*

223. an . . . , *in a "princess" or "gypsy" dress?*

224. Impluviatam . . . , *in a "skylight" dress—just an example of the names they give to women's clothes nowadays!*

225. Uti-n(e), *how?*

226. fundis, *farms*—i.e., dresses worth as much as farms.

227. tributus, *taxes.* **negant,** supply *people* as the subject—i.e., (for the most part) the husbands of extravagant wives. **pendi,** *be paid,* supply *tributum* as the subject. **potis** [*esse*], *posse.*

228. Illis . . . , lit., *to those women for whom* (or *whose support*) *a larger "tax" is paid, it can be paid!*

229. Quid istae, *how about those?*

230-233. This list of queer and extraordinary words for women's fashions is of course full of puns and

local hits, which it would be mere pedantry to reproduce exactly—anyone may make a similar list for today. The approximate meaning of the Latin terms is as follows: (l. 230) *loose-woven, close-woven, cut-linen;* (l. 231) *skin-tight, gold-fringed, marigold or buttercup;* (l. 232) *scanty* (with a pun on *supparus,* a sort of tunic) *or not-quite, mantilla, royal or exotic;* (l. 233) *wavy* or *plumy, waxen or flaxen(?)—all flummery!*

234. Cani . . . , *they've even borrowed the name of* (*a certain breed of*) *dog.* **Laconicum,** cf. Shakespeare's: *Hounds bred out of the Spartan kind.*

235. auctiones . . . , *subigunt viros ut faciant auctiones, bring husbands to bankruptcy.*

236. Quin . . . , *get back to your story.* **oc-cepisti,** *in-cepisti.*

237. abscessi, from *abs-cedo.* **sciens,** *purposely.*

238. dissimulabam dare, *simulabam non dare.*

239. satis, *fully.*

240. libido 'st, [*mihi*] *libet.*

242. sunt conspicatae, the subject is *mulieres duae* (ll. 236-237).

244. Supply some such phrase as: *said one to the other.*

245. illi, *to her.*

246. Periphanaî, genitive.

248. rursum accedere, *to back.* **versum ad,** *towards.*

249. hominum vis, *the crowd.* **retruderet,** *were shoving.*

253. Id paratum [*esse*], *that it was got*—i.e., *that he had actually got the cash.*

254. eapse, *her.*

256. aliquid, *some sort of* (followed by the genitive). **calidi conducibilis,** *prompt and profitable.*

257. ille, Stratippocles.

258. catum, *clever.*

263. utitor, imperative.

264. rectius, *a better plan.*

265. mihi, dative of agent. Said

in the passive the statement is more modest and humble, but it would mean the same in the active: *ego istîc nec sero nec meto (reap)*. **nisi,** *only*.

267. arbitretur, not deponent here, *be determined* (or *decided on*). This recommendation—viz., *get your son a wife*—is only a blind. Epidicus is merely seconding Periphanes' own desires. **atque ut,** *and I advise that*.

269. curetur, impersonal passive, *cura* (or *cures*) *ut.* **serviat,** i.e., remain a slave. This second recommendation—viz., to get even with the music girl by keeping her in slavery—is the more important item in Epidicus' plan. As a matter of fact the real music girl, Acropolistis, has already been freed and is in Periphanes' house, masquerading as his daughter. **fiat,** *be accomplished*.

271. Nunc, emphatic. **advenerit,** the subject is *he* (Stratippocles).

273. alius, another soldier.

275. animi gratiā, *for your own pleasure*.

276. Quam . . . , *what's the advantage of that?*

277. prae-stino, *buy first,* supply *her* as the object.

278. ut . . . , *ut dicas te eam emere in libertatem.* **dicas,** *claim*—contrary to his real intentions.

279. ut, *I advise that*.

280. Immo, docte, *no, no! well done!*

281. te commentum [*esse*], from *comminiscor, that you have contrived*.

282. amota ei fuerit, *there will be removed from him*—i.e., *he will have no chance for*.

282-283. omnis consultatio nuptiarum, *any discussion of his marriage*—i.e., *a discussion on his part as to whether or not he will marry*. Thus the first recommendation can be carried out without hindrance. With the disappearance of his demimonde

sweetheart, Stratippocles will have no decent excuse for refusing to marry any girl his father may select for him.

283. ne gravetur, *lest he dissent from, that he may assent to.* **vive,** adverb.

285. rem loquere, *verum dicis.* **repperi . . . ,** *repperi quî suspicio abscedat a te*.

287. homine, *someone.* **illô,** *thither* —i.e., *to him* (the slave dealer who owns the music girl).

289. fili causā, *on your son's account* (not *for the sake of*).

289-290. This is merely a pretext to keep Periphanes in the background; the real reason is to prevent Periphanes from questioning the slave dealer or from discovering the hoax in any other way. Instead of Periphanes' going to the slave dealer, the slave dealer will be brought to the go-between, Apoecides.

290. evenat, *eveniat.*

292. tenet, *comprehendit.*

293. habeas, subjunctive expressing obligation, *you ought to*.

294. illum, the slave dealer. **cuiusa-um,** *whose.* Here *illum* is the antecedent of *cuia*.

295. hoc, Apoecides. As there is no time to spare (for supposedly everything must be done before Stratippocles arrives), Epidicus gives Periphanes this broad hint: *with him* (Apoecides) *I'll take the money* (to the slave dealer), *please.* **quanti, minimo,** the genitive of indefinite, and the ablative of definite, price.

296. posse, a complementary infinitive, depends on *fortasse* (*it may be that*). **Ad quadraginta . . . minis,** it would be more grammatical to say: *ad quadraginta minas, for about forty silver pieces;* but *minis* (ablative of price) is added as an afterthought.

297. referam, *I'll bring back the change.* **captio,** *trap*.

298. occupatum, *tied up.* **non decem dies,**—*less than ten days, ten days at the most.*

302. impetras (colloquial), *you get your wish.*

303. huic, Epidicus. **visam,** *I'll look in at, I'll run down to.*

304. eô veni, *meet me there.* **a-bitas,** *ab-eas.*

305. *I* [*intrô*], *numera* [*argentum*].

Act II, scene 3

307. feracem, i.e., Periphanes is a rich field to work.

310. Quod, *but.*

311. ulmos . . . , i.e., make the lash stick to him and fleece him like a parasite.

313. Quam, interrogative, with *fidicinam.*

314. mane, *this morning.*

315-316. The same music girls played secular music for gay parties and sacred music for religious rites just as a musician today may play for dances on week days and in church on Sundays.

317. ei praemonstrabitur, impersonal; *it shall be shown to her, she shall be coached.* It will not be necessary therefore for Epidicus to bring any slave dealer to Apoecides, as he had reluctantly anticipated (l. 294). By merely doing what he was asked to (namely, hire a music girl for a sacrificial rite) he will fool Apoecides, who will think this is Epidicus' ruse for getting the girl away from her owner and into the hands of Periphanes.

317-318. Epidicus takes it for granted that the girl who is hired for sacred music will be quite willing to connive at an amorous intrigue.

318. fiat subdola adversum, *be deceptive to.*

319. damnoso, *spendthrift* (unintentionally, of course).

Act III, scene 1

320. exedor, *I am consumed.* **exenteror,** *I am tormented.*

323. Per, *in regard to.* **illam copiam,** *that resource*—i.e., Epidicus.

324. parare licet (colloquial), *you might as well get.*

325. illo, *him.*

329. qui, with *habes* (l. 330). The antecedent is *tu,* subject of *vis.* **tibi cui** (idiom), *tu cui,* repeats the subject of *vis* for emphasis.

332. aliqui, *aliquo, someone.* **tibi mecum,** *for you with* (i.e., *and*) *me.*

333. muri-cîdus, lit., *mouse-killer.*

Act III, scene 2

338. Per hanc curam, *as regards this matter.*

338, 339. hoc, the money.

339. ni, *ne.* **oppido,** *utterly, quite.* This has nothing to do with *oppidum, town.* **pollinctum,** *ready for burial.*

340. Crede, said to an imaginary listener. **nostri,** *my family.*

343. commeatum, *caravan.* He will carry the money to its destination, like a captain convoying a caravan.

344. mihi, *to my own cost, it's my own loss.*

346. plus satis, *plus* [*quam*] *satis.*

348. flocci facio, *make light of.*

349. Nam quid, *quidnam, why?* **perenticîda** (from *pera*+*enti*+*caedo*), a comic word coined by Plautus, perhaps meaning *cutpurse.*

350. nil moror, *I don't care for.*

351. peratum ductare, *take a purseful.* **follitum,** *a sackful.*

352. omne . . . abstulit, *took all his* (Periphanes') *cash, cleaned him out.* This refers to the original purchase of Acropolistis, engineered by Epidicus before Stratippocles' return.

353. pater . . . , *quam* (*whom*) *pater credit esse suam natam.*

354. iterum, this is emphatic.

355. inveni, *I have found a way.*

atque, *and even.* **hanc orationem,** *a speech with respect to this.*

356. eius copia, *access to her.*

357. cautorem dedit, *appointed to be my watcher* (or *to check up on me*).

360. crumina, *wallet.*

361. adornat, *praeparat.* **adveniens . . . ,** *ut adveniens maritus fias extemplo domi.*

363. adempsit, *ad-emerit,* future perfect.

364. ad lenonem domum, equivalent to *ad lenonis domum.*

367. quippe ego quî, *quippequî ego, because I.* **dinumeravi,** *paid the bill.*

369. Ibi, *then.* **sceleratum,** in Latin comedy slave dealers are always villains. **imprudens,** *unwittingly.* **caput alligabit,** *take oath.*

371. versutior . . . , *more nimble than a potter's wheel.* **parabo,** *get.*

372. nummo, *for a trifling sum.*

374. simul, *secum.*

375. permeditatam, *well-rehearsed* (or *-versed*) *in.*

378. nimis doctus, *very clever.*

380. abs te intus, *from your house.*

Special Note on the Plot Development

In this scene Epidicus gives only a hasty and sketchy outline of his plans. Not only is he in too much of a hurry for details, but he rather enjoys mystifying Stratippocles and keeping him in suspense. Had Epidicus had the time to reveal his plans in full, the conversation with Stratippocles might have been somewhat as follows:

Ep. (*to Stratippocles*) In the first place, I have advised your father to get your sweetheart, Acropolistis, out of the way.

St. Very good. That suits me perfectly.

Ep. Knowing very little about Acropolistis (least of all, that he already has her in his own house), he has now commissioned me to purchase her; and he intends to whisk her away to the country out of your reach. (That's how I got the fifty silver pieces I just gave you.) I shall now hire another music girl from the forum for just a few hours, and coach her in the rôle of Acropolistis. Before your father has time to carry *her* off to the country, I'll arrange for her to slip out of the house and disappear.

St. Well done, Epidicus! I approve of everything.

Ep. In the second place, your father is going to get you a wife—you are to be married at once.

St. Nothing doing! No one shall ever separate me from my new love.

Ep. Don't worry, I've looked out for that too. You will not have to marry. Now that you have the money to free the captive maiden, you shall make her your mistress. Under those circumstances your father will find no one willing to marry his daughter to you; and if he tries to take your new sweetheart away from you, you can refuse to give her up on the grounds that he himself ordered me to buy her from the slave dealer for fifty silver pieces. Meanwhile I'll tip off the slave dealer to back me up in this, but to say nothing further. He'll only have to swear that he received fifty silver pieces for a music girl, which he really did—I paid him that amount day before yesterday for Acropolistis! Just make sure that your father does not see your mistress; he will not suspect that she is another. He will take her to be the runaway music girl, whom he mistakenly believes to be Acropolistis! Should he vent his anger on me for the miscarriage of his plans, I'll have to bear it. But I shall have good grounds on which to defend myself, for I shall only have carried out his orders! And if your supposed sweetheart has eluded his clutches, that won't be *my* fault.

St. Epidicus, you're a genius! . . .

Such are Epidicus' plans, and he now thinks everything is pat. But there is one crucial fact he does not know—i.e., the identity of Stratippocles' captive maiden—, for he has not yet seen her, and Stratippocles has not chanced to mention her by name. In comedy, as in the detective story, some insignificant oversight like this always leads to the downfall of the malefactor. But comedy is also akin to the novel of roguery, in which the crook is the hero, who triumphs in spite of setbacks.

Act III, scene 3

382. oris causā, *for the face.* **aequum fuit,** *it would be a good thing.*

385. qui, ablative, *one in which.* **cordis copiam,** *their mental abilities.*

386. cogitarent, the subjunctive expresses the idea of *should* or *might.*

387. ut, *how.*

391. delinquo, *do wrong.* **med erga,** *erga me.*

392. solida, *real.*

394. praeda, Acropolistis (as he thinks).

395. mercatorem, said only in fun.

397. suppetunt, *agree with.*

398. istanc, *her.*

400. siris (from *sino*), *siveris.*

401. copulari, *associate.* The subject is *hanc* (the new arrival).

402. aediculam, *room.*

403. divertunt, *are different.* The subject is *mores.* **mores . . . ,** *the characters of a maiden and of a harlot.*

406. istam, *her.* **temperi,** *just in time.*

408. iam dudum, *a while ago, just now.*

409. Hanc rem, the purchase of Acropolistis (which they think they have just forestalled).

410. Ne, an affirmative particle used only with personal pronouns, *you certainly have.* **graphicus,** *ideal.*

411. auro contra, *worth his weight in gold.*

413. Apoecides did not know that she was laughing *at* him.

415. dixit, the subject is *he* (Epidicus); the object, *her.* **esse,** with *facturum.*

416. redierit, the subject is *he* (Stratippocles). **rectam institit,** *he took the right path.*

417. illi, the slave dealer.

421. com-bardus, *fool.* A delightful list of words with this meaning occurs in Plautus' *Bacchides* (l. 1088): *stulti, stolidi, fatui, fungi, bardi, blenni, buccones.*

422. res magna amici, *an important case of a friend of mine.*

425. amico, ablative.

426. tuo, velis, indefinite second person, *one.*

427. adlegassem, *adlegavissem, I had commissioned.*

428. doctum, adjective.

429. os sublitum (from *sub-lino*), slang, *my face would have been smeared*—i.e., *I would have been cheated.* **albis dentibus,** implies a good, healthy, young grin.

432. undantem, cf. *coat tails flying in the wind.* **chlamys** (Greek), *pallium* (see l. 1).

Act III, scene 4

433. praeter-bitas, *praeter-eas.*

434. Platenius, *the Platenian.* Perhaps this refers to some village as his birthplace.

435. Incertus, equivalent to *dum* (*until*) *certus sis.*

441. explices, *deploy.*

442. Prowess in words might be of more advantage here than prowess in deeds!

443. illae [*pugnae*], *the latter* (i.e., *latter's*) *battles.* **de illius** [*pugnis*], *in comparison with the former's.*

445. Nempe quem, *the one whom?*

447. ind-eptum (from *ind-ipiscor*), *adeptum*.

448. manibus dimissis, *with arms outstretched*—i.e., *full speed*.

451. cui . . . , *for whom you may patch up your old rags*—i.e., *tell your old chestnuts*.

452. illi vitio-vertere (idiom), *blame him*.

453. egomet quod, *quod egomet, for what I*.

455. eradicabam, English would say *wore out*.

457. amicam, Acropolistis.

463. tramittas, *transmittas*.

466. Mihi . . . , this is quite an honorable proposal, for the *concubina* might be a foreign-born wife. **absolvam**, *come to terms with*.

469. tuas possidebit ferias, *will occupy your time off*—i.e., when he is not campaigning. **faxo**, *I'll warrant*.

470. atque ita, i.e., *and on these conditions I'll let you have her*.

473. fides (plural), *harp*.

474. accessēre, *ac-cessērunt, went with her*, a legal term.

475. hanc, *her*. **in-temperiae** (plural), the same as *in-sania* (singular).

476. tenebras (slang), compared with his true love—his *lux* (*flame*), etc.—, he can only call this creature a *gloom*.

481. rere (from *reor*), *reris*.

484. peccatum, *erratum* [*est tibi*], *erravisti*.

486. sectari, *attend*.

487. destinavit, *bought*.

488. te . . . concidit (slang), *made mincemeat of you*.

489. Sic, *just*.

490. cerva, *hind* (female deer), just as for Iphigenía in Greek legend—when she was about to be offered as a human sacrifice by her father, King Agamemnon.

491. See note on l. 429.

492. illam, Acropolistis.

493. Eu-ge (Greek), *bravo*. **frugi**, indeclinable adjective, *good*—in a slangy sense here. **'s**, *es*.

494. me emunxisti (slang), *cleaned me out*. **mucidum, minimi preti**, modifies *me; sniveling, worthless*.

496. Fando audivi, lit., *heard in speaking*—i.e., *heard tell of*.

505. admodum, adverb, modifies *incerte*.

508. Periphanaï, genitive. The music girl does not know that she is talking to Periphanes.

513. A literal answer to the music girl's conventional leave-taking.

514. Fides, accusative plural, *my harp*.

516. reddes, the object is *it* (the harp)—for which she will bring a lawsuit against him.

517. qui, the antecedent is *ego* (l. 518). **in tantis . . .** , *placed* (or *mentioned*) *in such important verdicts*—i.e., *whose name appears in such important documents*. He is a man of influence in the community and in the courts.

518. eam, the music girl—who has just insulted his dignity. **impune**, adverb, supply *esse* or *facere*.

518-519. alterum tantum, *the same amount again*.

520. habitum, modifies *me, regarded*. **depeculatui**, lit., *for swindling*—i.e., *easy prey*.

521. [*mihi*] **data esse verba** (idiom), *to have been fooled*.

522. me minoris facio, *I blame myself less*. **illo**, Apoecides.

523. fictor, conditor, *framer and maker*.

524-525. malleum excusso manubrio, *a hammer with its handle knocked off*.

Act IV, scene 1

526. Si . . . , *si quid miseriarum homini est, if anyone is in trouble*.

527. quod miserescat, *so that one is distressed*. **ex animo**, emphatic.

529. me habet, *keeps me.*

532. potita, *fallen into the power of.*

533. peregre, *from foreign parts.*

535. illi usus venit, *she needs.*

536. dare, supply *to anyone* (antecedent of *qui*).

537. Noscito, present indicative active. nam . . . , *nam mihi videor (methinks) vidisse [eam] prius nescio-ubi.*

540. comprimere, *that I seduced.*

544. Sicut, causal. dubia, noun.

545. incerte, *doubtfully.* astu, *cunningly, cautiously.*

546. malitia, *cunning* (noun).

547. Orationis aciem, *the weapon of speech*—i.e., *speech, my only weapon.*

549. quod credidisti reddo, *I repay you what you entrusted to me* (viz., a salutation)—i.e., *I give you tit for tat.*

550. animum inducam, *persuade myself.*

551. Inique iniuriu's (*iniurius es*), *you are very unfair.*

552. interpretari, *act as interpreter for.* commode, *fittingly.*

554. guttula, *just a drop* (of comfort).

556. me levare, indirect discourse, depends on *meministin* above. *Me* is the subject.

557. obsevisti (from *ob-sero*), *plant.*

563. postquam ilico, *as soon as.*

565. adeo, *moreover.*

566. utut, *although.* impense, *very.*

567. Canthara, an old family nurse.

Act IV, scene 2

575. Tu ne, *yes, you.*

579. This is a homely proverb: *Lions' whelps smell very different from those of pigs.*

580. Ne, *affirmative.*

581. Quod . . . , interrogative, *what slave business . . . ?*—i.e., *am I*

(unwittingly) becoming a slave dealer? alienas, *strange women.*

584. fuat, equivalent to *sit.*

585. matris filia, *my mother's daughter, myself.*

586. Non, with *aequum 'st.*

590. Non, with *'st* (*est*).

591. didici, from *disco.*

592. plaustrum perculit, a homely proverb, *he has upset the cart.* English might say: *he has upset the apple cart* (or *spilled the beans*).

599. Quid . . . esset, *even if your servant had disagreed with you*—i.e., as to the girl's identity. nosse, *recognize her.*

604. Circam, an obscure allusion to Circe—perhaps because, like Topsy, she did not know her father and mother.

605. relictis rebus, *relictis ceteris negotiis.* operam dabo, *devote myself to.*

606. faciam hunc diem ut fiat, *faciam ut hic dies fiat.*

Act V, scene 1

607. male morigerus, *very disobliging.*

609. caperrat, *is wrinkled.*

614. Quid agis, *how are you?* commoditas, *convenience, benefit*—i.e., *my helper.* Quod miser, [*ago*] *quod miser* [*agit*], i.e., *I'm feeling very badly.*

615. mi adornas viaticum, *provide me with traveling money.*

616. defloccati, *fleeced.* This is a remarkable identity of ancient and modern colloquialisms.

617. copulas, *lora* (l. 612).

618. in mundo sita (idiom), *in readiness.*

619. illi, *they* (Periphanes and Apoecides).

620. gravastellus, *gray-beard.*

624. consimilis . . . (colloquial), *isn't she like as when?*

624. signum, *picture.*

625. ex tuis verbis, *judging from what you say.* **corium,** *hide.*

626. Apella, Zeuxis, the two most famous Greek painters. But the reference here is to Periphanes and Apoecides, who are artists with the elm switch.

627. Sici-n, *sic-ne.* **iussi,** supply *ut.*

628. qui . . . , *qui [fuisse], he who is said to have had feet of lead* (identity unknown).

630. id quod, *as much as.*

632. Per-numeratum, i.e., he has the exact amount ready. **in-de,** imperative of *in-do.* **Sapienter,** *wisely provided.*

634. Sati'n, a mere interrogative particle. **oculis utilitatem obtineo,** *do I have the use of my eyes?*

636. satam, *begotten.*

638. Quod, *so far as.* English would add a negative, either: **not** *so far as,* or: *so far as . . .* **no.**

640. These are diminutives of *luna, ānus* (ring), *aureus,* and *digitus* —although *anellus* (finger ring) had lost its diminutive connotation.

642. ut fiat, *how could he be?* She knows that she is her mother's only child.

643. liquido, *serene.*

647. Siquid . . . , *should any coin be suspected of being counterfeit or clipped*—more usual in ancient times than now.

648. aeque, *equally well as I.*

649. suum, *her kin* (brother).

651. tu-te, *tu.*

653. quod ames, *a girl to love.* **fidicina,** Acropolistis. She can now be Stratippocles' sweetheart, as Epidicus had originally planned before Stratippocles fell in love with the captive maiden.

655. huic, Telestis. **aquam,** for the bath.

657. Thesprio, see Act I, scene 1.

659. suppetias, *auxilium.* **cum sorore,** *you with* (i.e., *and*) *your sister.*

660. istâc per hortum, *by the garden gate*—a back way.

661. dudum, *before.*

663. eâdem, *at the same time.*

664. certum 'st [mihi], *I am resolved.* **neque haud,** single negative.

665. pedibus provocatum, *challenged to a race*—by running away!

Act V, scene 2

666. Sati'n, a mere interrogative particle. **illic homo,** Epidicus.

667. habes, *keep.*

670. misero [mihi] in genua, *into my poor knees.* **flemina,** *swellings.*

671. exemplis, *modis.*

673. apage (Greek), *away with!*

674. aestu . . . , *he scorches you.*

675. Duodecim dis, ablative of comparison. The phrase is humorously exaggerated: lit., *more than there is* (or *are*) *of immortal gods by twelve gods*—i.e., a total of twenty-four. This is double the usual number.

677. Quicquid, *however much.*

678. Apolactizo (slang), borrowed from the Greek, *kick off.*

679. Dum, *provided.*

680. hunc, Apoecides.

683. There is a line missing in the manuscripts between ll. 681 and 683.

684. conliga, supply *me.*

685. Ilicet (from *ire+licet*), *it's all over, I give up.* **vadimonium facit,** *he gives bail.* As a matter of fact Epidicus does even more—he surrenders himself.

686. mancipium, *servus.*

687. nil moror, with an infinitive, *I don't care to have you do so and so.*

688. agis, colloquial use of the present for the future. **arbitratu,** *wish* (noun).

689. haec, supply *manus.*

690. tragulam, *javelin,* metaphorical here. **adornat,** *praeparat.*

693. mos geratur, lit., *let him be humored.*

694. Cédo, *cĕ-do.* **Morantur,** the

subject is *they* (i.e., my hands).   **artē,**
adverb.

695. Obnoxiose, *timidly, not hard
enough.*   **facto,** *done, finished.*   **arbi-
tramino,** imperative.

696. bene habet, *bonum est.*

697-698. quae . . . , *dicere* [*eam*],
quae empta 'st (Acropolistis) *meam
filiam esse.*

699. da pignus, *make me a bet,
what will you bet me?*   **filia,** Epidicus
means *a daughter;* Periphanes under-
stands *your daughter.* It is impossible to reproduce the catch in English.

700. "mater," Philippa—her alleged mother.   **matris filia,** *her mother's daughter.*

701. Epidicus' ridicule of Periphanes is heightened by his offer not
to *give,* but to *accept,* odds—i.e.,
doughnuts to dollars (not *dollars to
doughnuts*).

702. amica, Acropolistis.

705. Īs, *iis,* with *minis.*   **tetigi**
(from *tango*), slang.

706. Quomodo, *just as?*   **ludos
facere** (idiom), *ludificari.*   **fidicina,**
the (unnamed) music girl—who was
palmed off on Periphanes by Epidicus and unmasked by the Rhodian
soldier in scene 4 of Act III.

708. postremo, adverb.   **argento,**
with the money.

709. maligno, *stingy.*

710. malum, a swearword.

712. vise, *go and see.*

714. témere, adverb.

716. cuius . . . , *cuius operā hodie
haec filia.*

718. ut, *how.*   **mali,** *ill treatment.*

719. Quam-ne, *the one whom?*

720. reperire, quaerere, English
would use a participle here.

721. isti, *for him* (Epidicus).

721-722. me . . . facere, lit., *I appreciate thot he has deserved of me that
I may be allowed* (*liceat*) *to treat him*
(*facere*) *in accordance with his deserts.*

722. ut, *let me.*

724. supplicium, *satisfaction, am-
ends.*

727. quod pappet (slang), *some pap
to eat.*

728. orassis, *oraveris, beg my per-
mission.*

732. Grex, the whole theatrical
company—as it steps to the front of
the stage and pronounces the epiloque.

733. lumbos porgite, *stretch your
loins.*

ENNIUS

ANNALES

Fragments

[1]

He smashed his brains with a stone,
or (to preserve the pseudo-tmesis): *he
knocked the stuf- with a stone -fing out
of him.*

[2]

in suam do-mum.

[3]

O Tite Tati tyranne, *O King Titus
Tatius.*   **tu-te,** *tu.*   **tanta,** neuter plural, object of the verb.

In the second line the subject is
machina minax maxima; the object
is *multa,* neuter plural.

[6]

[b] **is . . . ,** *is dictus est ab illis
civibus olim.*   **delibatus,** *culled, choic-
est.*   **suadae medulla,** lit., *of persua-
sion the marrow* (i.e., *pith* or *essence*).

[7]

[a] *The strength of Rome lies in her
laws and in her men.*

[b] **re,** *property, wealth.*

[c] **noenum,** *non.*   **post-que magisque,** a strained but forceful expression.
viri, Fabius.

[8]

1. dederitis, perfect subjunctive of *dare,* expresses prohibition.

2. cauponantes, *haggling over, trafficking in.*

3. vitam cernamus, *decide the issue of life or death.*

4. [h]era Fors, *Dame Fortune,* the subject of both *velit* and *ferat*—i.e., *virtute experiamur, utrum vos an me regnare Fors velit, quid-ve Fors ferat.*

6-7. Lit., *to spare the liberty of* (i.e., *to grant liberty gratis to*) *those whose valor the fortune of war has spared.*

7. certum 'st [*mihi*], *I am resolved.*

8. Dono, verb. **ducite,** *take them.*

[9]

faxit, equivalent to *faciat.* **virum,** *virorum.*

CATO

DE AGRI CULTURA

Chapter I: On Buying a Farm

1. parare, *get, acquire*—a colloquial meaning which occurs in all periods of Latin literature. **uti ne,** *ut ne.* In Ciceronian Latin the *ut* would be omitted.

1-3. Praedium . . . circumire, *when you consider acquiring an estate, bear in mind not to buy too eagerly, not to spare pains in inspecting it, not to be satisfied with going over it only once.*

2. opera, accusative plural of *opus,* direct object of *parcere.* In Ciceronian Latin *parcere* takes the dative. **vĭsĕre** (from *viso*), complementary infinitive.

4. quod, *that which.* **pacto,** *modo.* **niteant,** lit., *be sleek*—i.e., *prosper.*

5. Et uti . . . , exhortation or advice, expressed by an independent *ut*-clause with the subjunctive.

5-6. eo . . . uti, *to such an extent* (*or in such a way*) . . . *that* (result).

Et . . . possis, *see to it that you go in and look about you in such a way that you can get out*—i.e., *don't commit yourself to a bargain until you are sure.*

7. siet, *sit.* **solo** (from *solum*), *soil.*

7-8. Uti . . . valeat, *let it have good climate, not be subject to storms, and have the advantage of naturally good soil.*

8. sua virtute, *inherently, naturally.*

10. aquarium, *watering place* (for cattle). **validum,** *thriving.*

11. quâ, *where.* **celebris,** *frequented.*

12-13. Siet . . . vendidisse, *let it be in the neighborhood of farms that do not often change hands. Let those who sell estates thereabouts be reluctant to sell.*

14. alienam disciplinam, *another's skill.*

15. colono, *husbandman.*

17-18. Ad . . . esse, *when you come to the buildings, see whether the presses and storage jars are many; where they are not, know that the produce will be correspondingly small.*

19. Instrumenti . . . bono siet, lit., *that it may not be a farm of large equipment, let it be in a good location*—i.e., *a good situation will compensate for meager equipment.*

19-22. Videto . . . multum, *see to it, that it be not a farm of meager equipment and expensive to operate. Know that a farm is the same as a man; though it be a good earner, if it is a heavy spender, there will not be much surplus.*

23-24. Praedium . . . centum, *if you ask me what kind of farm ranks first, I shall say: one of varied character and excellent location, one hundred iugera* (about sixty-five acres) *in extent.* **de omnibus agris,** *composed of all kinds of lands.* Cato advises against single-crop farming.

24-28. Vinea . . . silva, *the vineyard ranks first, if the quality or quantity of the wine is good; in second place comes a well-watered truck garden; third, a willow plantation; fourth, an olive grove; fifth, a meadow; sixth, cornfields* (i.e., *grainfields*)*; seventh, timberland; eighth, an orchard; ninth, an acorn forest* (for hogs).

TERENCE

ADELPHOE

Date of the Play and Details of Its Performance

Accurate records of the performance of plays in this "classic" period of the drama were later compiled by Roman scholars, of whom the chief was M. Terentius Varro, a contemporary of Cicero's. A so-called *didascalia* (a technical term borrowed from the Greek) was prefixed to each of the plays. These *didascaliae* were written in archaic style, somewhat after the fashion of a "playbill" of Terence's own time. Fortunately the *didascaliae* of Terence's plays have been preserved in the manuscripts of his works. The record of the *Adelphoe* is as follows:

INCIPIT [1] TERENTI ADELPHOE: ACTA [2] LUDIS FUNERALIBUS L. AEMELIO PAULO, QUOS FECERE Q. FABIUS [3] MAXUMUS P. CORNELIUS [4] AFRICANUS: EGERE [5] L. AMBIVIUS TURPIO L. HATILIUS PRAENESTINUS: MODOS [6] FECIT FLACCUS CLAUDI TIBIIS SARRANIS TOTA: [7] GRAECA MENANDRU: FACTA VI [8] M. CORNELIO CETHEGO L. ANICIO GALLO COS. [9]

Prologue

With Terence, a prologue is a kind of author's foreword. It is not part of the play proper and was spoken by an actor who wore a special costume, different from any of those worn in the play itself. The prologues of Terence are concerned chiefly with the

---

[1] **INCIPIT,** *here beginneth.*

[2] **ACTA . . . ,** *performed at the funeral games for Paulus.*

[3] **FABIUS,** son of Aemilius Paulus, for whom the funeral games were celebrated; but adopted by the famous Q. Fabius Maximus Cunctator, a hero of the Second Punic War.

[4] **CORNELIUS,** son of the same Aemilius Paulus and adopted grandson of the famous P. Cornelius Scipio Africanus, who defeated Hannibal at the close of the Second Punic War. The Cornelius mentioned here in the *didascalia*—namely, P. Cornelius Scipio Africanus Minor—was the patron of Terence and other authors who formed the Scipionic Circle. At the time of their father's death, both sons were curule aediles and thus in a position to pay notable public tribute to their father's memory.

[5] **EGERE** [*fabulam*], *presented the play*—i.e., they were the actor-managers, but not simultaneously: L. Ambivius Turpio was the manager of the original performance; L. Hatilius Praenestinus and his company presented the play at some subsequent date. The actor-manager owned a troupe of players and contracted with the aediles for a performance.

[6] **MODOS . . . ,** *Flaccus, slave of Claudius, composed the music on Sarranian* (Tyrian) *pipes.*

[7] **TOTA,** *throughout*—i.e., *in the whole play.*

[8] **VI,** sixth (and last) of Terence's plays.

[9] **COS.,** *consulibus.* The date of their consulship was 160 B.C.

literary discussions and feuds of his
day. Referring to himself in the
third person, as "the author," Terence defends his literary practices
and ideals.

Following a general introduction,
the prologue to the *Adelphoe* discusses
two charges—first (ll. 6–14): *contaminatio*, or patchwork methods—
i.e., the piecing together of scenes
from different plays, or the borrowing
of a scene from one play and its inser-
tion into another—, a sort of mild
plagiarism; second (ll. 15–21): the
charge that Terence did not write his
own plays (see p. 110 above). Terence's answer to each of these hostile
criticisms is clever and guileless. He
laughingly says that the scene he
borrowed from a play by the Greek
poet Diphilus and inserted into
Menander's *Adelphoe*, was discarded
—i.e., by Plautus—, and that his use
of it could therefore not be called
plagiaristic. He merely toys with the
second charge, saying that *if* it is
true that his plays are composed by
noble Romans and not by himself, he
is honored and not disgraced!

1. poeta, Terence. **scripturam,** collective noun, *his literary work.*

2. observari, *scrutinized, criticised.*

3. rapere in peiorem partem, *forcibly misinterpret, insist on misinter-
preting.* **sumus,** there is a gap here
of one or two lines. All we know is
that the antecedent of *quam*, some-
where in the next line, was *fabulam*—
i.e., *the play that we are now going to
act.*

4. indicio erit, *he will give evidence.*

5. laudi-n, *laudi-ne, whether praise-
worthy.* **duci,** *to be considered.* **id
factum,** *the following fact.*

7. Com-morientis, Plautus' translation of the Greek title, *Syn-
apothnescontes.* It might be rendered
in English as: *United in Death.* **fabulam,** *play.*

8. in Graeca [*fabula*], the Synapo-
thnescontes. **eripit,** *kidnaps from.*

9. in prima fabula, *in the first part
of the play.*

10. reliquit integrum, *left un-
touched* (or *unused*)—i.e., did not include it in his translation of the play.
Hence Terence wittily implies that it
was abandoned property and could
be appropriated by anyone.

11. expressum, *translated.* **extulit,**
set forth.

12. eam [*fabulam*], the *Adelphoe.*
novam, *for the first time.*

13. furtum, *plagiarism.*

15. Nam quod, *now as for what.*

16. hunc, Terence, the object of
adiutare.

17–18. quod . . . eam, *id . . . quod,
that . . . which. Eam* is substituted
for *id* because of the proximity of the
predicate noun, *laudem.*

18. cum, *since.* **placet,** the subject
is *he* (Terence). **illis,** the great
nobles who were supposed to be help-
ing Terence. According to one tradition they were: Scipio Africanus,
Laelius, and Philus; but this is impossible, for these men—though
patrons of literature—were not yet
civil and military leaders (ll. 19–21).

20. opera, *help, generosity.*

21. superbia, *without stint* (on the
part of the nobles).

22. dehinc, *here*—i.e., in the following lines of the prologue.

23. aperient, *tell.*

24. facite, *facite* [*ut*]. **aequanimitas,** *good will, favor.* There is a gap
here in the manuscripts, probably of
only one line, as ll. 24 and 25 may
easily be run together as follows: [*ut*]
aequanimitas [*vestra*] *augeat poetae
industriam ad scribendum.*

Scene 1

1. Storax, a slave—probably an
adversitor, or gentleman's escort.
This particular *adversitor* was one—

perhaps the oldest and most responsible—of those who had accompanied Micio's son to the dinner party the night before. To avoid public scandal, Micio calls the name of the slave, rather than that of Aeschinus. **cena,** *dinner.*

2. ne, *for fear lest.* **alserit** (from *algesco*), *take a chill, catch cold.*

[3]. See note on l. 1 of Plautus' *Miles,* p. 253. **ceciderit,** from *cado.* **os,** *a bone.*

4. 'st, see note on l. 17 of Plautus' *Miles,* p. 253.

5. Dissimili, i.e., from me. **is,** *frater meus.* **studio,** *ingenio, moribus.* **'st iam inde,** *has ever been.*

7. isti, *people.*

8. Ille . . . , [*fecit*] *omnia contra haec.*

9-10. agere, habere, narrative infinitives; *egit, habuit.* These infinitives do not differ in connotation from *duxit* and the other perfect indicatives that follow.

13. item me habeat, *regard me in the same way*—i.e., *return my affection.* **contra,** adverb; *on the other hand, in return.* **facio,** *strive.*

14. praetermitto, *overlook faults.*

15. clan-culum, *clam,* preposition, governs *patres: behind their fathers' backs.*

15-17. *postremo, consuefeci filium, ne me celet ea, quae alii adulescentes clanculum patres faciunt.*

16. quae (neuter plural accusative) **fert adulescentia** (nominative singular), *which things youth produces* (or *engenders*)—i.e., all sorts of escapades.

19. satius, *better.*

22. adulescentem, Aeschinus. **nobis,** *nostrum.*

23. sumptum suggeris, lit., *supply the cost*—i.e., *pay the bills.*

25. praeter aequum, *beyond what is right.*

29. patrium, *fatherly*—i.e., *a father's duty.*

30. alieno metu, *fear of another.*

31. Lit., *in this a father and a master is different.* **nequit,** supply *facere.*

34. nescioquid, *somewhat.*

35. iurgabit, *he will scold.* **advenire,** in town. The entire phrase is a merely conventional greeting however.

36. gaudemus, *gaudeo.* In Latin the first person plural is constantly used for the first person singular, even when it is neither editorial nor regal. **quaerito,** the present indicative active of *quaeritare* (not the longer imperative form of *quaero*).

37. ubi, *when, since.*

38. siet (sit) **nobis,** *we have on our hands.* **Dixi-n,** *dixi-ne.*

41. tenere se, *binds him.*

42. modô, *just now* (see p. 31). **designavit,** *perpetrated.*

44. familiam, *servants, household.*

45. mulcavit, *punished, cudgeled.*

47-48. *quot homines hoc dixerunt mihi advenienti.*

48. in ore 'st . . . , *it is the talk of the town.*

50. rei dare operam, *pay attention to business.*

51. huius, *on his* (Ctesipho's) *part.*

53. imperito, *ignorant.* **iniustiu'st,** *iniustius est.*

55. Quorsum, lit., *whither?*—i.e., *what are you driving at?*

57. scortari, *to wench.*

59. siit (from *sino*), *sivit.* **egestas,** *inopia* (l. 60), *poverty.*

60. laudi, dative of the noun, equivalent to *laudabile.*

61. esset, supply *nobis*—i.e., *if we had the wherewithal.*

62. tuum, supply *filium.*

66. ausculta, *listen.* **obtundas,** *deafen.*

69. illî, *therein.* **maximam . . . ,** *take the chief blame.*

70. obsonat, *lives high, is an epicure.* **de meo,** supply *est*—i.e., *it comes out of my purse.*

72. excludetur, i.e., by his sweet-heart.

73. di-scidit, *has torn.*

74. re-sarcietur, *patch, mend,*

75. est unde, supply *mihi*—i.e., *I have the wherewithal.* **molesta,** *burdensome*—i.e., *beyond my means.*

77. consiliis, *by virtue of wise guidance.*

78. Tu-n[e], supply *facis.* **pergis,** *continue.*

80. Curae (dative) **est mihi,** lit., *he is for a care to me*—i.e., *I care for him.*

83. dedisti, supply *adoptandum.*

84. quid istîc, colloquial idiom, expresses exasperation and reluctant assent—e.g., *oh very well!* **istuc,** see note on l. 16 of Plautus' *Miles,* p. 253.

86. non nil, *very.* **molesta,** *annoying, disturbing.*

86-87. *nolui illi ostendere, me aegre pati (that I am worried).*

89. Quam, *what girl?* **omnium,** neuter plural, *the whole business.* He has sown enough wild oats and is now ready to settle down.

90. taedebat [*eum*], impersonal, *he was tired of.*

92. Nisi (colloquial), *anyhow.*

93. hominem, *him* (Aeschinus).

Scene 2

95. in-opi, *helpless.* **ilico,** *on the spot.*

97. istam, *her;* supply *tenebo, abducam,* or some such verb.

98. 'st, the subject is *he* (Sannio). **committet,** *risk.* **vapulare,** *be beaten.* This is active in form and passive in meaning.

101. solves, *pay* (or *atone*) *for.* **quod,** *that which.*

102. Abi prae (adverb) **strenue,** *proceed boldly.* **hoc,** *what I say.* **nili facis,** *make light of, care nothing for. Nili* is the genitive of value.

106. in-nuo, *nod at.* **pugnus,** *fist.* **mãla,** *his jaw.*

108. geminabit, *double*—i.e., *repeat the blow.*

109. peccato, imperative, *err.*

111. ornatus, *decorated, treated.*

112. Nostin, *novisti-ne.*

113. tui, genitive of *tuum, of yours.*

114. Quî, *how.* **meam,** supply *slave girl.*

115. abripiêre, *you shall be haled.*

116. operiêre, *you shall be covered.* **lorum,** *lash.* **liber,** *a free man.*

117. Hîc-i-ne, *hîc-ci-ne,* *so here,* sarcastic. (See note on l. 38 of Plautus' *Miles,* p. 254.)

118. debacchatus, *vented your spleen.*

121. modô, *dummodo,* supply *dicas.*

122. minis (from *mĭna*), Latinized form of the Greek *mna,* an Attic coin; call it: *pieces of silver.*

123. dabitur, supply *tibi*—i.e., *I'll pay you the same for her.*

124. vendendam, supply *illam esse* —i.e., *that she is salable.*

125. liberali causâ, *in a lawsuit for freedom.* **illam adsero manu,** *I am going to claim her.*

126. meditari . . . , *work up your case*—merely a picturesque way of saying: *go to law.*

128. ipsum, Sannio. **faxo,** see note on l. 224 of Plautus' *Miles,* p. 257.

129. bene, with *actum, well treated.*

130. nescioquid concertasse, *had a little tiff.*

133. amica, *sweetheart.*

135. dicam, *I could say.* **quin,** *but that.* This is correlative with *ita*— i.e., *quin virtus tua superet id.*

136. rem, *advantage.*

137. homini nemini esse, *no man has.* **principem,** *master of.* This voices rather vague (but enthusiastic) eulogy.

138. Ellum, *em illum, ecce illum* (or *eccillum*).

139. Festivum caput, *a splendid fellow.* **omnia sibi,** *all his own affairs.*

140. omnia sibi, *all his own affairs.*

post (adverb) . . . **prae** (preposition), *of minor importance . . . compared with.*

142. **pote,** *potis,* supply *est esse.*

146. **illam,** *tristitiem* (or *tristitiam*).

148. **adsentandi,** genitive of purpose, *adsentandi causā.* **quo,** *because.* **gratum,** supply *te, dear.*

149. **inepte,** vocative. **norimus,** *noverimus.*

150. **nos,** *I.* **rescisse,** i.e., about your love affair. **rem,** *affair.*

150-151. **in eum locum redisse,** *reached the point.*

152. **pudebat,** *embarrassed, too shy* (not *ashamed* in the moral sense). **parvulam rem,** his reticence (or shyness).

153. **e patria,** supply an exclamatory infinitive—e.g., *exire.* Desperate lovers always went away to a distant country. **istaec,** neuter plural.

154. **illam,** Bacchis.

155. **At,** supply *oro* or *obsecro.* **reddat,** *pay,* the subject is Aeschinus. **modō,** *just.*

158. **aliquā,** *in some way, somehow.* **permanet,** from *permano, -are.*

159. **'s,** *es,* imperative.

160. **lectulos,** *dinner couches.*

161. **re,** *the business*—i.e., the financial dealings with Sannio. **obsonium,** *provisions for the feast.*

162. **hoc,** *things so far.*

Scene 3

164. Supply *anyone* as antecedent of *quam* and *qui.*

167. **Nunc illud est cum,** *now is the time when.*

168. **malo,** *trouble.* **salutem,** *a remedy.* **adferant,** *could bring.*

169. **circumvallant se,** *range themselves around.* **emergi,** impersonal passive, *one cannot emerge.*

173. **animam,** *breath.*

174. **actum 'st** (slang), *it's all up.*

177. **id occulte fert,** *keeps it dark.* **eripuit,** supply *her.*

179. **credas,** indefinite second person, *you* or *one.* **nostrum-ne,** *ne* introduces exclamations as well as questions. **Aeschinum,** accusative of exclamation.

180. **vitam,** *support, livelihood.* **omnium,** *of us all.*

181. **hac,** *her* (Pamphila). **victurum,** from *vivo.*

182. *in sui patris gremio.* *Se* is Aeschinus and *patris* is Micio, "father" of Aeschinus. **puerum,** his child by Pamphila—whose birth was expected any minute.

183. **Ita,** *thus*—i.e., with (or by means of) the child. **obsecraturum,** supply *esse.*

185. **sanu'n,** *sanus-ne.*

186. **An,** *really.*

187. **alieno animo esse,** *alienari.*

188. **infitias ibit,** *will enter denial.*

189. **si maxime,** *even if.*

190. **hanc,** Pamphila.

191. **quoquo pacto,** *quoquo modo, by all means.*

193. **potis est,** *potest.*

194. **Cēdo,** *I yield.* **ut,** *since.* **quantum potest,** *quam celerrime.*

195. **eius,** *her* (Pamphila's).

196. **Simulus,** Sostrata's husband. **summus,** *best friend.*

Scene 4

199. **disperii,** this has the same colloquial meaning as *perii.*

201. **ganeum,** *brothel, dive.*

202. **ille,** Aeschinus.

203. **siet,** the subject is Ctesipho.

204. **grege,** *gang.*

205. **Carnifex,** *scoundrel* (Syrus).

206. **seni,** *my old man, my boss* (Micio).

207. **haberet,** *esset.*

208. **nil quicquam,** *neminem quemquam.*

211. **argentum,** i.e., to pay Sannio for Bacchis.

212. **in sumptum,** *for (incidental) expenses.*

213. ex sententia, supply *meā* or *nostrā*.

214. Huic, *to him* (Syrus). This remark is addressed to the world in general.

216. rationem, *idea, system, way of living*.

217. ne dicam dolo, *ut dicam vere*.

218. purga, *clean*.

219. congrum, *eel* (a live one at that!).

223. fac ..., *see that these anchovies be well soaked*.

224. The first direct question is introduced by *utrum ... -ne,* the second by *an*. **studio,** *intentionally, purposely*. **id,** *that policy*. **sibi habet,** *holds, entertains, follows*. **laudi,** see note on l. 60.

228. psaltria, *music* (or *chorus*) *girl* (Bacchis).

229. Ellam, *em illam*. **habiturus,** the subject is Aeschinus, whom Demea of course believes to be Bacchis' lover.

230. Haecin, this is the same as *Haecine* (l. 221).

233. per-nimium, *per-* is a superlative prefix.

234. quantus quantu's, *quantuscumque es, howsoever much you are*. This is a sly dig.

235. somnium, *fool*. **tuum,** supply *filium*.

237. olfecissem, the proverbial English phrase for this is *smell a rat*.

238. siet, subjunctive of wish, the subject is Ctesipho.

241. hunc, Demea.

242. Sati'n, *satis-ne,* need not be translated. This is used merely as an interrogative particle. **Oh qui,** the English idiom would be: *What! When I ... ?* **produxi,** *saw him off*.

243. iratum, the continuation of his previous remark—i.e., *Ctesiphonem iràtum produxi*. **admodum,** adverb, *quite, very*.

244. Quid, *why?*

245. Ai'n, *ais-ne*.

246. numerabatur, i.e., as Aeschinus and Syrus were paying Sannio for Bacchis.

247. homo, Ctesipho.

248. admittere, *committere*.

251. suum, *suorum*.

253. unde, *a quo, from whom;* the antecedent *aliquem* is to be supplied as the object of *habuit.* **Fit,** lit., *it is done*—i.e., *I do it*.

261. ei, *they* (the fish). **cautio 'st,** *is my worry*.

262-263. *nobis* [*servis*] *tam flagitium est id* (*this*) *non facere, quam vobis* [*dominis*] *flagitium est illa* (*those things*) *non facere, quae modô dixisti*.

263. quod, *so far as*.

265. *too salty; burned; not washed enough*.

268. patinas, *pans*. This is a parody of l. 255.

269. facto usus sit, *facere opus sit*.

270. nos quae, *quae nos*.

271. morem geras, *humor him*.

272. dari, supply *volo* (in answer to the preceding *vis*).

275. is, Ctesipho. **quam ob rem,** *propter quem*.

277. istoc, Aeschinus.

279. tribulis, *clansman*.

281. Ne, an affirmative particle. **illius modi,** equivalent to *talium,* with *civium*.

283. opperiar, *await*.

285. illan, *illa-ne*. The suffix denotes exclamation.

288. alieno, *outsider, stranger*. **nili pendit,** *doesn't care,* equivalent to *nili facit* (see note on l. 102).

289. hic, refers to *pater eius* (Micio).

290. facient, the subject is *they* (Micio and Aeschinus). **quae,** neuter plural, *what*. **illos,** supply *facere*. **sic auferent,** *get away with it*.

293. ille senex, Simulus, the deceased husband of Sostrata (see l. 465).

296. Salvere . . . , a conventional greeting.

300. officium, the direct object of *functus.* In Ciceronian Latin, *fungor* takes the ablative.

301. noras, *noveras.*

301-302. amicum aequalem, *friend and contemporary.*

303. vitiavit, the subject is Aeschinus.

305. ferendum, *bearable, endurable, excusable.*

307. scit, the subject is Aeschinus.

309. se ducturum domum, *that he will marry.*

310. mensis decimus, *it is nine months since.*

311. ille bonus vir, Aeschinus. **nobis,** *noster.*

312. paravit, *got.* **illam,** Pamphila.

314. in medio, *at hand.*

315. captus, noun, *the general run.*

319. illaec, *she.* **fidem,** *help, protection.*

320. voluntate, *of your own free will*—i.e., not under compulsion of the law. **impetret,** *let her obtain.*

323. non me in-dicente, negative prefix *-in, not without my saying so*—i.e., *I told you so.*

324. defunctum, *all were over, this were the end of it.*

326. evomam (colloquial), this need not be translated literally.

327. quod, *so far as.*

328. consolēre, *consolēris,* same construction as *sis* (l. 326).

330. Si est, ut is facturus sit, *if it so be that he . . . .*

332. respondeat, i.e., now, as soon as he meets him.

Scene 5

333. Dic sodes, *do tell!* **sodes** (from *si odes*), *please. Odes* is the vulgar Latin pronunciation of *audes,* which here has its original meaning of *wish* (not *dare*). Cf. the other word

for *please*—namely, *si's* (from *si vis*), *if you wish* (or *will*). *Audeo* is derived from *avid-eo*—i.e., from the familiar root seen in the English *avid* and the Latin *avidus* and *aviditas.*

334. nunc cum maxime, *right now.*

335. Quod . . . , *provided it be done without harming his health.*

337. istoc rectius, *more properly* (or *thoroughly*) *than that.*

338. misere nimis cupio, *I'm awfully anxious.*

344. nequior, supply *es.*

346. Hisce . . . , *so that you could have had business with them.* **Quae non data sit,** *business which I did not have?*

349. illius, Demea's. **sensum,** *character.* **calleo,** *understand.*

350. ovem, *sheep.*

353. Lupus in fabula, *the proverbial wolf.* The English equivalent is: *speak of the Devil and he appears.*

355. me, supply *vidisti.*

356. Ne, a positive particle.

357. a villa mercennarium, *farm hand.*

360. viso, *I'm coming to see.*

363. cellam, *room* (not *cell*).

365. si sic fit, *if this keeps up.*

368. discidit, from either *di-scindo* or *dis-cĭdo.* **labrum,** *lip.*

370. produxe, *produxisse* (see l. 242). Supply *te* as the subject; the object is *eum.* **venit,** the subject is *he.*

371. Non puduisse, an infinitive of exclamation, *think of his not being ashamed!*

372. modô tantillum, *only so big.* **manibus,** *arms.*

373. patrissas, *you take after your father.* **abi,** exclamatory, *go to!*

374. Ne, positive.

375. cogito, *I wonder.*

377. Dimminuetur . . . , i.e., *I'll knock your brains out.*

378. illius hominis, Micio's supposed friend—whose name Syrus cannot remember.

379. apud macellum, *by the meat market.* **hâc deorsum,** *down this way.*

380. Praeterito, imperative. **rectā plateā sursus,** *straight up the street.*

381. clivus . . . , *the down slope is ahead of you.*

382. sacellum, *shrine.* **angiportum,** *alley.* **propter,** adverb, *near by.*

383. Quodnam, *what alley?* **caprificus,** *fig tree.*

385. cense'n . . . , *you must think me an idiot.*

386. hâc multo propius ibis, *this way is shorter.* **erratio,** *chance of mistake.*

387. ditis, *divitis.*

388. Dianae, supply *templum* or *aedem.*

389. portam, *city gate.*

390. pistrilla, *little bakery.* **fabrica,** *workshop.*

391. lectulos in sole, *garden benches.* **ilignis,** call it *mahogany.* **faciendos dedit,** *ordered made.*

392. Ubi potetis, *where you may carouse*—i.e., on the new garden benches.

393. silicernium, lit., *funeral feast* —i.e., *old bones, death's head,* or some such opprobrious epithet.

394. odiose cessat, *is devilish late.*

397. carpam, *nibble.* **cyathos sorbilans,** lit., *sipping goblets*—i.e., *lapping up a few drinks.*

Scene 6

404. illi, *her.*

407. turba, *muddle.*

409. adeo, *moreover.*

410. exorassem, *I could have prevailed on* (or *persuaded*) *him.* **illas,** Sostrata and Pamphila.

419. dicere, i.e., about his affair with Pamphila.

420. istas, supply *fores pultavi* or *pepuli* (in answer to Micio's question, l. 417).

422. Erubuit, the subject is Aeschinus. **salva res est,** *all is well.*

Aeschinus has not yet lost his sense of shame.

425. advocatum sibi, *as his advocate*—i.e., to help or advise him in a matter of law. At this period such advice was generally amateur, rather than professional.

427. ut, *as.* **te,** the subject of *nosse.* **et certo scio,** *in fact I am sure* —i.e., *that you do not know them.*

430. illi, *to her.* **genere,** *of kin.*

431. *leges cogunt hanc nubere huic* (*him*).

432. avehat, supply *her.*

434. male 'st, supply *mihi*—i.e., *I feel faint.*

435. ipsae, supply *faciunt.* **illas,** supply *facere.*

436. Commenta est (from *comminiscor*), *faked up a story.*

437. eum, refers to *viro* (not to *puerum*).

438. illum, the other lover (Aeschinus). **huic,** the supposed kinsman. **dari,** supply *eam* as the subject.

439. haec, *she* (Sostrata).

440. abducet, the subject is *the kinsman.*

444-445. Quid animi, *what feelings, what state of mind.* **illi misero,** Aeschinus.

445. illā consuevit, *had the affair with her.*

448. quo magis, *therefore.*

449. tui, *in your sight.*

453. id, supply *est* or *erat.*

454. cě-do, *tell me.*

456. te, supply *esse.* **socordem** (*se-cordem*), *thoughtless.*

460. arcessas, the first step in the wedding ceremony, preceding the procession.

462. oderint, a wish.

463. *quam* (*than*) *amas illam* (Pamphilam). **aeque,** i.e., not more, but just as much.

466. quo, *inasmuch as.*

469. quî, *how?* **morem gereret,** *could he be indulgent* (or *kind*).

470. gestandus in sinu, a poetic phrase, *cherished.*

471-472. These words mark the triumphant success of Micio's policy (see ll. 13–19).

Scene 7

474. ut, *utinam.*

479. certum est, *I am resolved.*

480. illis, Sostrata and Pamphila.

484. qui, *qualis.*

489. Salus, the goddess of Salvation.

491. Syr-isce, *Syrush ol' boy.* The suffix -*iscus* is Greek.

494. si's, *if you please.*

497. sapientia, vocative, Syrus' favorite nickname for Demea.

498. Dis, *dives.*

499. rem, *fortune.*

505. parasit-aster, *hanger-on* (cf. *poet-aster*).

507. mastigia, *verbero* (see note on l. 407 of Plautus' *Miles*, p. 260).

508. cerebrum dispergam, see note on l. 377. **Abit,** *abiit.*

509. comissator, *reveler, guest.*

512. villi, diminutive of *vinum.*

518. lites (from *lis*), *a row.* **succurrendum 'st,** supply *mihi* (*by me*).

519. nostrum liberum, genitive plural.

530. Scilicet . . . , *I suppose the occasion requires it.*

532. censeo, *I suggest.*

535. favillae, *ashes.* **pollinis** (from *pollen*), *meal, flour.*

536. molendo, *grinding*—i.e., *faxo* (*I'll see to it*) *sit plena favillae . . . coquendo et molendo.*

537. stipulam colligat, *glean.*

538. excoctam, *sunburned.* Sunburn was never regarded as a mark of beauty until the advent of the twentieth-century athletic girl.

538. carbo, *coal.*

539. cui rei est, lit., *for which thing*

(or *purpose*) *it exists*—i.e., **the day is** meant for joy and merriment.

Scene 8

540. ita bene-subducta-ratione, *so well-balanced* (metaphor taken from the balancing of account books)—i.e., *sure of himself.*

540. ad, *toward.*

541. novi, a partitive genitive with *aliquid.*

545. spatio, *my span of life.*

549. laedere os, narrative infinitive, *he affronted* (see note on l. 9).

552. ibi, *there*—i.e., in matrimony.

553. cura, in apposition with *filii.*

554. facerem, i.e., money. **in quaerendo,** *in the pursuit of gain.*

555. fructi, a second declension form, partitive genitive. **pro,** *in return for.*

556. patria, adjective, agrees with the noun *commoda.*

557. illi, *to him.*

562. possiem, *possim.*

563. hoc provocat, *he challenges me to this.*

564. magni fieri, lit., *to be made of great value.* **postulo,** *expect.*

565. posteriores, supply *partes,* stage metaphor, *second part* (or *fiddle*).

566. deerit, financial term, *there will be a deficit.* **natu maximus,** i.e., he is an old man and has not much longer to live.

568. Quis homo, *who is it?*

572. faxim, perfect subjunctive, equivalent to *faciam, I would do.*

574. huc, next door. **quam mox,** *how soon?*

576. vocare, *vocaris.*

578. spectatus satis, i.e., excellent.

579. tibi, supply *dominum curae esse.*

580. usus, *opportunity.*

582. procedit, impersonal.

583. primulum, *primum.* **facio meam,** i.e., win the favor of.

588. hos-ce, *meos.*

590. tibicina, *flute player.* **qui can-
tent,** *those who are to sing*—i.e., the
chorus (or choir).

591. vi'n, *vis-ne.*

593. maceriam, *wall.*

594. hâc, *that way*—i.e., by the
short cut.

596. Euge, *bravo.*

597. turbam, *mob.* **adducet,** the
subject is *frater* (Micio).

600. illas, Pamphila, Sostrata, and
the whole crowd.

601-602. *cum video te velle.*

602. ex animo factum velle, *wish
it done to suit.*

609. unam, i.e., with ours.

615. operam dare, *urge.*

616. ineptis, verb, *you're absurd.*

618. sine, *allow me.*

619. aufer, supply *manum.* **da
veniam,** *grant it as a favor.*

621. estis auctores, *suadetis.*

622. largitor (from *largior*), imperative.

623. quid si quid maius, *what if
something greater?*

625. prolixe, *generously*—i.e., *be
generous.*

628. hoc cum confit, *cum hoc confit,
since this comes to pass.*

629. Quid, supply *est.*

631. agelli, diminutive of *ager.*
locitare foras, *rent out.*

632. qui, ablative, *quo.* **fruatur,**
have the income of, live on.

633. huic, Pamphila.

635. Frugi, indeclinable adjective,
honest.

636. *esse aequum, Syrum fieri liberum.*

638. istos, supply *filios.*

641. prodesse aequum 'st, *it is
right that this benefit him* (or *stand him
in good stead*). **meliores,** *the better
for it.*

642. hic, Aeschinus.

647. huius filio, the newborn child
of Aeschinus.

648. mammam, *the breast* (as a wet
nurse).

650. quanti 'st, *as much as she is
worth*—i.e., Demea says to Micio:
I will stand the financial loss.

653. prae manu, *cash in hand.*

654. unde (*de quo*) **utatur,** *from
which he may have the income, which
he may use as a loan* (or *borrow*).
Istoc vilius, lit., *the cheaper for that.*
Micio sarcastically thanks Demea for
promising speedy repayment of the
loan.

658. prolubium, *whim.*

659. quod, *because, that.*

662. invisa, *hateful.*

663. iusta iniusta omnia, cognate
accusatives with *obsequor*—i.e., *because I do not indulge you in all things,
just and unjust alike.*

664. missa facio, *I wash my hands
of the whole business.*

665. quae, the antecedent is *haec*
(l. 667).

666. videtis, *understand.* The
verbs *cupitis* and *consulitis* are
parallel, and might be connected with
videtis by *and.* **impense,** *strongly.*

667. me, subject of the infinitives.
in loco, *at the proper time.*

670. habeat, supply *her.* **istac,**
her.

HEAUTONTIMORUMENOS

Act I, scene 1

1-8. Chremes very naturally approaches his melancholy and uncom-
municative neighbor with elaborate
apologies—hence the long and involved sentence.

1. nuper . . . , *notitia* (*acquaintance*)
est admodum (*quite*) *nuper.*

2. This parenthetic line explains
nuper. **inde adeo cum,** *only from the
time when* (or *since*).

3. nec . . . fuit, governed by *quamquam.* The word order is as follows:

nec quicquam rei (any dealings) fere sane (hardly at all) amplius hoc (further than this) fuit.

5. quod, *which fact*—i.e., *vicinitas.* in propinqua parte, *a close second to.* The entire line is equivalent to: *quod ego prope amicitiam puto.*

7. quod, *because.* vidēre, *vidēris.* praeter, a preposition.

8. praeter quam, *otherwise than.* res, *situation.*

11. eo, *than that.*

12. preti maioris, *more costly* (or *valuable*), modifies *agrum.*

13. servos, supply *habes.* proinde ..., [facis] proinde quasi nullus servus siet.

14. tu-te, *tu.* fungere, *fungeris.* At this period of the Latin language the object was in the accusative case —not in the ablative.

15. mane, adverb, *early.*

16. fundus, *farm.*

17. aliquid ferre, *bear some burden.*

19. voluptati, equivalent to an adjective, *agreeable.*

20. Chremes puts into the mouth of Menedemus a possible excuse for his conduct, only to demolish it again immediately (ll. 21–22). Enim [dices], *yes—you will say—but.* paenitet [me], *I am dissatisfied with.* operis, a partitive genitive with *quantum.* fiat, supply *a servis.*

21. quod operae tuae, lit., *what of effort.*

22. sumas, *consumas.* illis, *servis.* agas, *accomplish.*

23. The word order is as follows: *est tibi tantum oti ab re tua (your business)?*

24. aliena ea, neuter plural, equivalent to *rem aliorum, other people's business.*

26. Apologetic in tone—i.e., *just regard all this as a suggestion or a query. Hoc* does not refer to l. 25, but to all that Chremes had said from ll. 1–22.

27. The questions are equivalent to conditions: *if it is right, let me do it too; if it is not right, let me deter you.*

28. usus, *way, habit.* ut opus facto 'st, *as you have need of doing.* face, *fac.*

30. labori, equivalent to an adjective, *painful* (cf. *voluptati,* l. 19). nollem, lit., *I would not wish it* —i.e., *I am sorry.* Despite this apologetic phrase Chremes, being a busybody, nevertheless goes right on to ask the most painful question of all: *What's the trouble?*

31. de te commeruisti, lit., *offended against yourself.*

35. quidem, *yes.* dixi, in l. 34.

36. rastros (plural), *mattock.*

37. adpone, *lay down.*

38. Sine, verb, *leave me alone, let me do what I'm doing.* vocivum, older form of *vacuum.*

38-39. The word order is as follows: *ne quod tempus dem mihi (allow myself) vacuum laboris.*

40. Hui, whistling exclamation. hos, supply *rastros habes.*

43. habeam necne, *whether or not I have.*

44. hîc, at Athens. advena, *newcomer.*

46. haec, supply *erant.*

47. humanitus, *humanely.*

48. The entire line is an adverbial phrase enlarging upon the idea of *humanitus.* animum aegrotum, *lovesick state.*

49. tractare [eum], *to treat him.*

50. hem, exclamation.

50-51. The word order is as follows: *speras, licere tibi haec facere.*

51. vivo, *vivente* (ablative absolute).

54. The word order is as follows: *volo dici (it to be said), te esse meum (mine*—i.e., *my son).*

54-55. tantisper . . . dum, *only so long as.*

56. The word order is as follows: *quod (what) me dignum sit, facere in te.*

57. adeo, *moreover.*

58. istuc aetatis, *ista aetate, at your age.*

60. rem, *fortune.*

61. adeo res rediit, *it came down to this, matters came to a head.*

62. eadem [*verba*], the object of *audiendo.*

63. aetate et sapientia [*mea*], ablatives of cause.

65. regem, the Great King (of Persia). **militatum,** supine of purpose.

67. Ambo, father and son. **illud inceptum,** i.e., the son's decision to join the army.

68. animi pudentis, *conscientious nature.*

69. ei (dative) **conscii,** *his confidants.*

72. soccos, *shoes.*

73. alios, supply *servos.* **lectos,** *dinner couches.*

74. quisque, *each and all. Each* with a plural verb is colloquial.

75. quo, *ut* (purpose).

76. tot, supply *servi.*

76-77, meā solius causā, *for my sake alone.*

78. Sumptus, with *tantos, expenditures.*

80. pariter, *equally (with me), just as much as I.* **uti his,** *enjoy these (luxuries).*

81. quod, *because.* **illa aetas,** i.e., *youth.*

83. Malo, *punishment.*

84. usque dum, *as long as.* **colet,** *live.*

86. interea usque, *just so long.* **illi . . . ,** lit., *I will offer self-punishment to him (as atonement)*—i.e., *I will do penance for his sake.*

88. Ita facio prorsus, *I suit the action to the word, no sooner said than done.*

90. opere rustico, *farm work.*

91. sumptum . . . , *earned their keep.*

93. aedis, accusative plural, *my*

house. **mercede,** *for rent.* **quasi ad,** *close to, about.*

96. fiam, *make myself.*

98. ubi, *when.* **meus particeps,** *as participant*—i.e., *to share it with me.*

99. Ingenio leni, ablative of description.

101. tractaret, supply *him* as the object.

103. illum quanti penderes, *how much you valued (or cared for) him.*

104. *ille est ausus credere tibi* [*ea*], *quae aequum est* [*credere*] *patri.*

106. a me, *on my side.*

107. Menedeme, at, *ah well, Menedemus.* **porro recte spero,** colloquial and epigrammatic, *I hope for the best.*

108. propediem, with *adfuturum; quickly, soon.*

110. Dionysia, the festival of Dionysus—a village kermis, or carnival. This is an excellent opportunity for Menedemus to cheer up and recover his spirits. **apud me sis,** *be my guest.*

112. idem filius, *he too—your son.*

113. Non convenit, qui, *it is not right that I, who.*

114. Sic-i-ne, *sic-ne.*

ANDRIA

Act I, scene 1

2. ad-es, imperative. **dum,** *just.* **paucis** [*verbis*], i.e., *I want to speak to you briefly.* **Dictum puta,** *reckon it said*—i.e., *no need to say it.*

3. haec, the provisions.

4. hoc, *than this.*

6. eis, supply *artibus.*

8–10. Ego . . . scis, in outline this sentence reads as follows: *scis, ut* (*how*), *semper postquam* (*ever since*) *te emi, a parvulo* (*from boyhood*), *tibi iusta fuerit servitus.*

9. apud me servitus, *your service to me*—i.e., *my treatment of you.*

11. servibas, *serviebas.* **liberaliter,**

English cannot possibly reproduce all the connotations of this word; it may be rendered in a general way by *nobly*, or be paraphrased—i.e., *with the spirit of a freeman*.

12. pretium, *reward*—i.e., freedom.

13. Haud muto factum, i.e., *I would not wish it otherwise*.

15. fuisse, indirect discourse, depends on *habeo gratiam (feel grateful)*. **adversum te,** *in your sight*.

16. hoc, what follows. **commemoratio,** i.e., what Simo said (ll. 8–12).

17. immemori benefici, *to one unmindful of kindness*.

22. pacto, *modo*.

24. is, his son (Pamphilus). **ex ephebis,** after his twentieth year. In Athens young men were called *ephēbi* from their eighteenth to twentieth years.

27. aetas, i.e., immaturity. **magister,** generic, *a master*. At one time the master might be his father; at another, his teacher; etc.

28. quod, *that which*.

29. ut . . . adiungant, *namely to take up some hobby*, explains *quod* (l. 28).

30. canes ad venandum, *canes venaticos.* **ad philosophos,** supply *adiungere animum*.

31. horum, neuter, *harum rerum*.

33. Gaudebam, Simo is a typically timid father. **Non iniuriā,** *iure,* adverbial.

34. ne quid nimis, the famous Greek proverb: *mēden agan, nothing in excess*—the principle of the golden mean.

35. Sic, *as follows.* **omnis,** *all* people—i.e., to be affable (or easy-going).

36. quibus . . . cumque, tmesis, *unā cum quibuscumque erat, with whatsoever companions he was*.

39. invenias, indefinite second person, *one wins.* **pares** (from *paro, -are), one makes*.

40. hoc tempore, pessimistic, *in these degenerate times*.

41. parit, *begets.* Sosia reveals his own character by this remark.

43. huc viciniam, *in hanc viciniam*.

46. quid mali, *some disaster*.

49. amans, noun.

50. ita ut, *as*.

51. hominum, *human beings*.

52. accepit condicionem, *she accepted their terms.* **quaestum,** *the profession* (of harlot).

53. filium, with *meum* (l. 54).

55. mecum, supply *loquebar*.

56. habet (slang), *K.O., he's got it in the neck.* This was said when a gladiator received a bad blow. **illorum,** of the lovers (l. 53).

58. sodes, *please* (see note on l. 333 of the *Adelphoe,* p. 285).

61. eho . . . , Simo's second question to the slaves. **quid,** *what about?*

61–62. Quid? symbolam dedit, *oh he gave his contribution* (or *paid his share*). His interest did not go beyond the dinner.

64–65. spectatum satis putabam, *I thought him thoroughly tested*.

66. qui, *he who*.

67. neque commovetur animus, *and his character is not influenced*.

68. ipsum, *he,* the subject of *posse*. **modum,** *control*.

69. Cum, *not only*.

70. dicere, laudare, narrative infinitives; *dicebant, laudabant*.

72. Hac fama, i.e., Pamphilus'.

73. gnatam, Philumena.

74. filio, supply *meo*.

75. Placuit [*mihi***],** *I agreed.* **despondi,** supply *filium meum*.

77. Fere in diebus paucis, *within a few days more or less.* **quibus,** an idiomatic substitute for *postquam*.

79. Beasti, *you have made me happy, I am glad*.

80. frequens, *constantly*.

83. consuetudinis, *acquaintance*.

84. huius, *her*.

85. amasset, supply *eam* (Chrysis).
patri, i.e., when I die—a good example
of egotistic sentimentality.
86. humani, *sympathetic.*
87. officia, *kind deeds.* **Quid multis** [*verbis*] **moror,** cf. l. 72.
88. eius, Pamphilus'.
90. Ecfertur, *she* (the corpse) *is
brought out.* **imus,** *we start* (in the
funeral procession).
98. Percussit animum, *it struck me.*
106. mediam, *by the waist.*
107. te is perditum, *go* (i.e., *try*) *to
destroy yourself.* Simo assumes that
she is trying to commit suicide.
108. consuetum, *well-established.*
facile, with *cerneres.*
111. *nec satis causae* [*mihi erat*] *ad
obiurgandum filium.* **Diceret,** *he could
say.*
113. *prohibui* [*eam*], *quae.*
114. oratio, *plea.*
118. comperisse, (*saying that*) *he
had learned.*
120. negare, *negavi.*
121. ita . . . ut quî, *on the understanding . . . that.* **Quî** is here an
untranslatable particle.
122. gnatum, Simo knows what
Sosia is going to say—namely,
obiurgasti.
123. cědo, *out with it, tell me.*
124-126. Simo gives a sample of
what Pamphilus might say—viz.:
*You have set an end to my days of
freedom* (*by betrothing me*). *Until
my wedding day—when I must live in
accordance with someone else's habits—,
let me live after my own fashion.*
128. amorem, *his amour* (or
liaison).
129. *for the first time this is a
punishable* (*animadvertenda*) *offense on
his part* (*ab illo*).
130. operam do, *I plan.*
131. deneget, *refuse to marry.*
132. Davus, slave of Simo and allied with Pamphilus. **consili,** *scheme.*

133. consumat, *use it up, waste it.*
cum, *when.*
134-135. quem . . . facturum, *he
will strive with might and main.*
135. id, *for this reason.*
137. Quem . . . sensero, an uncom-
pleted threat.
140. con-fore, *con-futurum esse,*
this is used as the passive of *conficio;
that it will be brought about, that I will
succeed.*
143. illo, Davus.

RHETORICA AD HERENNIUM

Preface

1. studio, *study, scholarship.*
2. suppeditare, *give.* **possumus,**
Latin uses *we* for *I* much more freely
than English.
4. ratione, *art.*
6-7. eo . . . quod, correlative, *the
more . . . because.*
8. Non parum, *not a little, much.*
8-9. copia dicendi, *eloquentia.*
11. Graeci scriptores, these are the
pedants and academic theorists
against whom his treatise is directed.
12. reliquimus, *omisimus.* **parum
multa,** *too little, not enough.*
13. conquisiverunt, *have sought out.*
quae nihil attinebant, *unimportant* (or
superfluous) *matters.*
17-18. morem geramus, *humor,
comply with.*
20. assiduitate, *constant practice.*

Selections From Book IV

[1]

The Three Styles

2. consumitur, *is comprised.*
3. extenuatam, *thin, meager*—i.e.,
unadorned; equivalent to *colloquial.*
7. dignitate, *form, style.*

[a] Formal style: *The Traitor*

3. Quod, *what?*

4. In, *in the case of.*

5. violassent, *assaulted.* familias, old genitive form.

6-7. huic facinori, *treason.*

7. singularem, *special, specified.*

8. in, *in the case of.*

9. adfines, *implicated in, guilty of.*

10. consilio, *stroke.* universis civibus, *universae civitati.*

13. quo pacto, *quo modo, how.*

18-19. ad exitum perduxisse, *brought to a conclusion, consummated.*

20-21. Nequeo . . . rei, i.e., *words fail me.*

21. neglegentius, *with less concern.* mei, genitive of *ego, me*—i.e., *my help.*

22. animus . . . publicae, *patriotism.*

23. edocet, *prompts.*

25. spurcissimorum, *most foul.*

[b] Medium style: *The Revolt of the Fregellani*

3. cum, *not only.*

4. norunt, *noverunt.*

5. propinquitatem, Fregellae was in Latium.

6. quid posset, *how powerful was.*

7. deliberassent, *decided.*

9. officio, *allegiance.*

12. praesto esse, adesse. ullam rem, supply *praesto esse.*

13-14. Si . . . gererent, i.e., a local and comparatively insignificant conflict.

15. tamen, *even so.* instructiores, i.e., than they now are.

16-20. nedum illi conarentur, *much less would they attempt.*

19. tantulis, *such slight.*

21. conati sunt, *made the attempt.* Eo, with *minus.* isti, the Fregellani, also the subject of *videbant* (l. 22).

22. illi, the other nations of the earth (cf. l. 17). discessissent, *fared.*

23. rerum imperiti, *the inexperienced.* This is a general observation on human nature.

26. eventis, noun, *experience.* rationibus, *advantage.*

28. quemquam, the object of *tenuisse.*

29. temptare, *assail.*

30. aliquid, i.e., *back of it.*

31. quod dico, i.e., *that the Fregellani were instigated and supported by traitors at Rome—men like Catiline (who lived a generation later).*

[c] Colloquial style: *The Bathhouse Brawler*

1. ut, *when.* balneas, *bath, bathhouse.* perfusus est, *took a cold shower.*

2. defricari, *to rub down.* alveus, *pool.*

3. iste, the brawler. de transverso, *unexpectedly*—i.e., *unjustifiably.*

4. pueri, *slaves.* pulsarunt, *pulsaverunt, jostled.*

5-6. qui . . . , relative clause of cause.

5. id aetatis, *at his tender age.* ignoto, *a stranger.*

7. sine, verb.

8. clamare, narrative infinitive, *clamavit.* vel, *even.* rabulae, dative, *noisy pettifogger.* Except for the sex, *fishwife* might be an equivalent.

9. rubores elicere, *elicit a blush, bring shame.*

10. etiam nunc, *still.* He was only a lad, who had never heard anything worse than the scoldings (*lites*, from *lis*) of his caretaker (*paedagogus*, a servant in charge of the children).

11. imperito, agrees with *cui* (l. 10), *inexperienced of* (with genitive)—i.e., *unaccustomed to.*

12. Ubi, *where?* scurram, *a blackguard* (cf. *scurrilous*). exhausto rubore, descriptive of *scurram, who has lost the power of blushing*—i.e., *impudent.* qui, refers to *scurram.*

13. existimatione, the same as *famae* (l. 14), *reputation.*

[2]

What to Avoid in the Three Styles

[a] Bombast

5. ita ut, *just as.* **tumor,** e.g., an internal tumor may cause an enlargement of the abdomen resembling normal obesity.

6. gravis oratio, predicate nominative, *that seems a lofty style which.*

8. duriter aliunde translatis, *forcibly* (or *awkwardly*) *transferred*—i.e., *awkward metaphors.*

10. perduellionibus, *treasons*—used bombastically for *traitors.*

11-12. Neptunias lacunas, an absurd circumlocution for the sea.

12-13. montes . . . pacis, two ridiculous metaphors.

14. specie, *false appearance, semblance* (cf. *specious*).

[b] Incoherence

1-2. profecti sunt, *aimed at.*

5. sese expedire, *unfold* (or *arrange*) *itself in orderly fashion.*

6-10. The order of words and clauses in this passage rambles; there is a complete lack of *periodic order*—i.e., that artistic, if not artificial, word order affected by classical Latin. According to modern standards, the thought development here is perfectly normal; but in order to hold the hearer's attention, as our author says (l. 11)—or in other words, to *force* his attention by making the thought more difficult to follow—, the passage should be recast as follows: *Socii profecto nostri, cum nobiscum belligerare vellent, si quidem suā facerent sponte neque adiutores, homines malos et audaces, hinc haberent multos, quid possent facere etiam atque etiam essent ratiocinati: qui enim magna volunt agere negotia, diu cogitare solent omnes.*

7. ratiocinati, *would have reflected.*

8. hinc, *from here* (Rome).

[c] Dullness

1. illa . . . , the third style—i.e., artistic colloquialism.

3. exile, *thin, meager*—i.e., *monotonous.*

5. istic, *iste,* the brawler. **hunc,** the shy young man.

7. praesente, this is used as a preposition, *in the presence of.*

9. Frivolus, *insignificant.* **illiberalis,** *uncultured, illiterate.*

10. est adeptus, the subject is *he* (the orator.)

[3]

Definitions and Examples of Familiar Themes

[a] Notatio

1. alicuius natura, *a person's character* (or *traits*).

2. notae, noun, *physical marks* (or *signs*), *earmarks, hall marks.* **naturae,** *to the particular character.* **ut,** *for instance.*

4. Iste . . . , the sham millionaire is supposedly sitting in court—probably in the prisoner's box—and hears the orator's sarcastic description of his personality.

5. praeclarum, neuter. **intueatur,** i.e., he assumes a condescending and supercilious air.

6. darem, *I would be generous to* (or *humor*) *you.*

7. mentum, *chin.* **sublevavit,** *has supported.*

8. gemmae, i.e., in the gaudy finger ring that graces his left hand. **perstringere,** *attract.*

10. puerum unum, *his one and only slave.*

11. arbitror, supply *novisse.*

12. barbari, Sannio is supposed to be a native Italian slave, superior to his barbarian fellow slaves, who are Asiatics or Africans. **ut,** *so that.*

14. lectuli, *dinner couches.*

15. rogetur, *be borrowed.*

16. asturco, *saddle horse.* **falso,** adverb.

17. gloriae, *for ostentation.*

18. numerentur, *the items be reckoned.* He intentionally omits the subject in order to mystify and impress his hearers.

20. transnumerari, *the items to be transferred.*

21. Sane, *all right, very well.*

22. casu veniunt, i.e., accidentally run across him on the street. **hospites,** *out-of-town guests.* **homini,** indirect object of *casu veniunt;* him, *the fellow, our man.*

23. peregrinatur, *was traveling.* **invitarat,** i.e., to visit him.

26. rectâ, adverb, *straight*—i.e., instead of wandering around town and meeting him accidentally.

27. undelibet, *from anyone.*

29. ostentatione, *deceitful show,* *pretense.*

30. villae, *his farm buildings.*

31. accedere, i.e., to the country. **audere,** *desire, wish* (the old meaning).

32. Tusculano, *Tusculan estate* (in Tusculum). **insanire,** *to be foolish.* Jestingly he alludes to the supposedly extensive building operations as *sheer folly.*

34. sodalitium, *guild banquet*—a large and semipublic affair.

35. pro notitia, *by virtue of his acquaintance with.* **ingreditur . . .,** he pretends that the house is his and that he is to be host at the banquet.

37. triclinium stratum, lit., *the dining table set* (or *laid*). We would say *the table decorations.* **servulus,** a servant of the real owner of the house.

38. exire, i.e., *go out*—and wait until the host arrives (a polite hint to leave).

39. frater, supply *meus.* **ex Falerno,** where the best wine came from.

40. decimâ, supply *horā.*

45-46. angiporto deerrasse, *turned down the wrong side street.*

46. ad, *till.* **exspectasse,** the subject is *he;* the object, *them.*

47. negotium dederat, i.e., not the night before, but this very day—for he is now planning to bluff a dinner at his own house.

48. rogaret, *borrow.* **Servulus,** Sannio.

49. concinne, *courteously.*

50. aedes maximas, *his palace*—i.e., the large house (not *really* his, of course) where the guild banquet had been held the night before. In this manner he passes off his own small house as a mere temporary makeshift.

51. commodasse, *had loaned.* **Nuntiat,** quietly whispering in his master's ear. **repeti,** i.e., the owner wants his silver back at once. **pertimuerat,** *had been uneasy about it.*

52. Apage, *tut tut.* In the words that follow he poses as the lender instead of the borrower. **aedes,** his supposed palace.

53. familiam, *servants.*

54. Samiis, *earthenware.*

63. quadruplatoris, *crook.* **studium,** *character.*

64. in medium, *into public view.*

[b] Sermocinatio

2. is, *it* (*sermo*).

2-3. cum ratione, *with regard for.* **dignitatis,** *personality, character, individuality, dramatic value.*

4. Cum, *when.*

5. sago (from *sagum*), *military cloak.* This is symbolical of war, as the toga is of peace.

8. beatus, *prosperous, rich.*

9. Quin, *why not?* **praesto,** adverb, *at hand.* He is assumed to be hiding. **tacetis,** this is said to the assembled household.

13. noli . . . exstinctos, *don't kick a man when he's down.* **mansuete,** *quietly, humbly.* **fortunam,** i.e., *your good fortune* (or *victory*).

14. hominem, *a mere mortal*—neither superhuman nor divine.

15. datis, *surrender.*

16. Illi, *to him* (master of the house).

18. Gorgias, the Greek tutor. **pueros,** the master's young sons.

19. praesto, adverb, supply *est.* The soldier had now walked into the inner part of the house and found the master calmly sitting in his room.

20. Sedes, verb.

22-23. plane victus essem, *had been beaten at every point.*

23. mecum contendere, i.e., on a fair field.

25. victus, concessive. **non peribo,** i.e., he has justice and righteousness on his side and is the moral victor.

26. sententias eloqueris, *moralize.* **ei,** *mihi.*

28. iste, her husband. **quidem,** *really.* **sed tu,** this is addressed to the soldier.

29. et tu, this is addressed to her husband. **amplexare,** i.e., *embrace his knees as a suppliant and beg for your life.*

30. animum, *pride.*

32. Tu, the soldier. **cessas,** governs *eripere.* **mihi,** *from me.*

33. mea morte, *by my death*—i.e., *your murdering me.* **Iste,** the soldier.

34. illi, dative, the master of the house.

36. uni cuique, i.e., speaker.

37. dignitatem, *character.*

CAESAR

I

LETTERS

[1]

2. valde, *very much.*

5. Pompeium, the object of *reconciliarem.* **darem operam,** *try.*

8. reliqui, *all the others.* These were previous leaders of the popular party, especially Marius and Cinna.

16. missum feci, *let go.* **fabrum,** genitive plural of *faber.*

[2]

1. Imp[erator] ... Imp[eratori], the flattery is obvious. **Cum,** *although;* governs *vidissem, potuissem, properarem,* and *essem.* **Furnium nostrum,** *our mutual friend, Furnius.*

2. tantum, *barely.* **loqui,** *supply cum eo.* **audire,** i.e., what he had to say.

5. illum, Furnius.

9. propositum, *my first statement.*

[3]

5. opes, *resources, full support.* **opem,** *help.*

11. triumpho, verb.

13. ut, *only to.*

14. mei similem, i.e., *true to my ideals.*

15. praesto sis, *ad-sis.*

17. nihil iucundius, *neminem iucundiorem.*

17-18. Hanc gratiam ... , *huius rei gratiam, I shall be indebted to him for this* (i.e., your coming to Rome and supporting me).

18. poterit, the subject is *he* (Dolabella). **Tanta,** supply *est.*

19. is sensus, *is [est in me* (accusative)] *sensus, ita de me sentit.* **ea in me,** *talis erga me.*

[4]

3. hominum famā, rumors that Cicero would definitely cast in his lot with the Pompeians—which he did in spite of this letter.

4. ne quô progredereris, *that you should not take any step.*

4-5. proclinata iam re, *now that the balance has inclined* (*in my favor*).

5. integrā [re], *when the balance was even, when the issue was undecided.*

6. amicitiae, supply *nostrae*.

7-11. si . . . condemnavisse, lit., *if* (in joining Pompey) *you shall appear* **not** *to have had an eye to the main chance (fortunae obsecutus), and* **not** *to have approved of his cause (causam secutus),* **but** *to have disapproved of my conduct.*

10. cum . . . iudicasti, *when you chose to hold aloof from their counsels*— i.e., to be a lukewarm supporter of Pompey.

15. cum, *although.*

16–17. amicitiae, collective noun, *amicorum* [*meorum*].

II

DE BELLO GALLICO

2. utriusque, Caesar and Ariovistus.

3. dictum, *agreed.*

4. equis devexerat, *he had brought with him on horseback.* Fearing the Roman infantry, Ariovistus had insisted that only cavalry should accompany the commanders to the parley. Caesar agreed; but, distrustful of the Gallic cavalry at such a time, he mounted his Tenth Legion on the Gallic horses.

8. senatus, genitive.

9. eum, Ariovistus. **quod**, *that.*

10-11. quam rem, this distinction (or honor).

12. hominum officiis, *personal services.* **docebat**, *he* (Caesar) *pointed out.* **illum**, Ariovistus. **cum**, *although.*

13. aditum, *right of audience.*

14. In direct discourse this would read: *liberalitate meā . . . praemia consecutus es.*

15. quamque, *and how.*

16. necessitudinis, *friendship, alliance.* **ipsis**, dative, *Romanis.*

16-17. quae consulta, indirect question, *what decrees.*

18. ut, *how*, depends on **docebat** (l. 15) and states a fact.

20-23. Populi . . . posset, these are Caesar's words in indirect discourse.

20-22. ut . . . esse, a substantive clause in apposition with and defining *consuetudinem.*

21. sui (neuter) **nihil**, *none of their property* (or *possessions*).

22. velit, the subject is *populus Romanus.*

22-23. quod . . . posset, in direct discourse this would read: *quis pati possit id iis (from them) eripi quod . . . attulerunt.* **id quod attulissent**, *what they had brought to*—i.e., their wealth and influence.

24. legatis, *to his envoys*—whom he had sent to Ariovistus about a month before. **in mandatis**, *in their (written) instructions.*

25-27. inferret . . . pateretur, the subject of all four verbs is *Ariovistus.*

27. at, *at least.*

32. ipsis, *Gallis.*

33. stipendium, *tribute.* **capere**, in direct discourse this would read: *ego capio.*

39. velint, the subject is *Galli.* **iniquum esse**, in direct discourse this would read: *iniquum est, it is unjust.* **de stipendio recusare**, *(for the Gauls) to refuse payment of tribute.*

41. sibi, in direct discourse this would read *mihi.*

42. petisse, the object is *it* (friendship).

42-43. per . . . Romanum, *through the agency* (or *at the instance of*) *the Romans.*

43. stipendium remittatur, *the (Aeduan) tribute should be abated* (or *cease to be paid*). **dediticii**, *the (Aeduan) hostages.*

45-46. Quod traducat, *as for his bringing.*

46. sui muniendi [*causā*], *for self-defense.*

47. testimonio esse, in direct dis-

course this would read: *testimonio est,
the proof is.* To us the nominative
testimonium would seem more natural
than the dative. **quod,** *that.*

51. Galliae provinciae, the Roman
province of Gallia Narbonensis (now
Southern France, or Provence).

51-52. Quid . . . venerit, in direct
discourse this would read: *Quid tibi
vis? Cur in meas possessiones venisti?*

52-53. Provinciam . . . , in direct
discourse this would read: *haec
Gallia* (Central Gaul) *est mea provincia.*

53-56. Ut . . . interpellaremus, in
direct discourse this would read: *ut
(just as) mihi concedi non oporteat (no
concession ought to be made to me), si
in vestros fines impetum faciam; sic
item vos estis iniqui, quod in meo iure
me interpellatis (interfere with).*

56. Quod diceret, *as for his* (Caesar's) *statement that.*

56-57. non se . . . esse, in direct discourse this would read: *non ego tam
barbarus sum.*

58. bello . . . proximo, *in the last
war between the Allobroges and the
Romans.*

59. ipsos, the Aeduans.

61-63. Debere . . . habere, this is
double indirect discourse. If both
the statement and the thought within
the statement were put into direct
discourse, the passage would read:
*Debeo suspicari, " quod Caesar exerci-
tum in Gallia habet (as for Caesar's
having an army in Gaul), simulatā amicitiā, mei opprimendi causā [exercitum]
habet."*

63. Qui, Caesar.

65. si eum, *si Ariovistus Caesarem.*

66. gratum, *something pleasing, a
favor.*

66-67. id . . . habere, in direct discourse this would read: *id ego compertum habeo (know for certain).*

**67-68. per eorum nuntios, quorum
omnium,** *per nuntios eorum omnium,
quorum . . . .*

68-69. redimere posset, *he* (Ariovistus) *could win.*

69. discessisset, the subject is
Caesar.

70. se . . . remuneraturum, in direct discourse this would read: *ego te
praemio remunerabor.*

71. vellet, the subject is Caesar.

72. confecturum [esse], the subject
is Ariovistus.

73. in eam sententiam, quare, *to
the effect that.*

74. negotio, his present intention.

75. consuetudinem, the subject of
pati. **uti,** *ut.*

76. esse, *was the property of, belonged to.*

77. superatos esse, this took place
in 121 B.C., when Fabius conquered
Gallia Narbonensis.

79. neque, neque, *neque [eos], neque [eis].*

**80. antiquissimum quodque tem-
pus** (idiom), *priority of time.*

83-84. suis . . . voluisset, *(the
senate) had decreed that it should use
its own laws.*

89-90. sine . . . delectae, *without
any danger to his picked troops* (the
Tenth Legion).

90. equitatu, supply *Germano.*

**91-93. committendum . . . circum-
ventos,** lit., *he thought he ought not to
risk having it said, after he had routed
the enemy, that they had been deceived
by him during a parley under oath.*

93. elatum est, *the report spread.*

93-94. quā arrogantiā, the object of
usus. This participle could just as
well be omitted however, and the
phrase *quā arrogantiā* would then be
construed as an ablative of manner.

94. omni Gallia, *omnem Galliam*
(accusative) would be equally correct:
had forbidden all Gaul to the Romans.

96. eaque res ut, *and how that
circumstance.*

100. uti, *ut.*

101. minus, *non.*

102. causa, *any good reason.*

104. ex suis, *one of his officers.*

107. Procillum, a Gaul whose father had received Roman citizenship—probably an official interpreter on Caesar's staff.

110-111. qua..., *quā [linguā] multā ... utebatur* (idiom), *which Ariovistus spoke fluently.* Incidentally, how were Caesar and Ariovistus able to understand each other? **longinqua consuetidine,** *propter longinquam consuetudinem.*

111. in eo, *in his case.*

111-112. peccandi causa, *any excuse for violence.*

112. Metium, a Roman.

112-113. qui utebatur, i.e., he was a " guest-friend " of Ariovistus.

115. apud se . . . , i.e., when they were brought before him.

117. catenas, *chains.*

CICERO

I

LETTERS

[1]

Letters Written From 65-50 B.C.

[a]

1. Sal., *Sal[utem dicit].*

1-2. L. Iulio ... consulibus, normally this is the method of dating the *year* (the consulship of Caesar and Figulus was in 64 B.C.), but the political events mentioned in this letter took place in 65; furthermore Cicero would give the *day*—not the year—of his son's birth. This phrase therefore means: *on the day of the election of Caesar and Figulus to the consulship.* Consuls regularly took office on the first of January; they were elected in the preceding summer

or autumn. Cicero and Antonius were elected consuls about a year after this letter was written, and took office the following January 1, 63 B.C.

2. filiolo ... (idiom), *that a son was born to me.* **scito,** imperative.

3. Ego ... , *de meis rationibus (affairs) scripsi ad te.*

4. competitorem, rival candidate for the consulship of 63.

5. defendere, Catiline had misappropriated public funds; P. Clodius (in collusion with Catiline) was to prosecute him with a *packed* jury. Thus Catiline would be acquitted, and could then not be retried on the same charge. Cicero's rôle in this shady political game was to be that of counsel for the defense—whether or not he actually played it, is unknown.

6. accusatoris, P. Clodius.

7-8. in ratione petitionis, *in the matter of candidacy.* Catiline and Cicero would support each other's candidacy and be elected colleagues in the consulship.

8. humaniter, *philosophically.*

10-11. The aristocrats were naturally prejudiced against Cicero because of his humble birth, and remained hostile in the early stages of his candidacy.

[b]

1. S.D., *S[alutem] D[icit].*

2. Suis, *his own* (or *dear*), used when the addressees are relatives.

3-4. cum ... tum vero, *not only ... but also.*

5. Quod, *and, but.* **utinam . . . ,** i.e., *I wish I had killed myself.*

6. nihil mali, *no misfortune.*

7. commodi, a neuter adjective used as a noun, *happiness.*

8. minus . . . , *I have erred less, I have not been so wrong.*

9. fixa, i.e., to last forever. **vero,** *then.*

10. mea vita, his wife (Terentia).

15. capitis, *citizenship.* **legis,** *decree* (of exile). This was Clodius' **second** bill, which specifically mentioned Cicero by name.

17. praestaret, *praeberet* [*mihi*].

18. Habebimus, supply *gratiam.*

19. a.d. II, *a*[*nte*] *d*[*iem*] *secundum, the day before*—usually called *pridie.*

20. petebamus, this is the epistolary imperfect, equivalent to the present. The tense of a letter was correct for the **recipient,** rather than for the writer—a usage more natural and logical for the Romans than for us, because of the long time that normally elapsed between the sending and receipt of a letter in those days.

23. confirmes, the subjunctive of command, *promote.*

24. transactum est, *all is over, I am done for.*

27. fiet, with the ablative, *will become of.* Cicero's daughter, Tullia, was now about twenty years of age and had been married to Piso for five years. The use of the diminutive Tulliola is a sentimental endearment.

28. illius misellae, Tullia.

29. serviendum est, *we must have regard for.* Because of financial embarrassment, Cicero had been postponing the payment of his daughter's dowry from year to year; should he now die or go bankrupt, she might be divorced. But as a matter of fact Tullia's husband was devoted both to her and to her family. **Cicero meus,** the six-year-old son.

32. utrum . . . , *whether you still retain some property or have lost everything.* At his banishment, Cicero's house was burned and his country estates were plundered. He does not know whether his wife's private property has been seized or not.

34. de familia liberata, *concerning the freeing of all our slaves.* Evidently Terentia heard a rumor that Cicero had taken this step (in order, of course, to decrease the value of his estate, which might fall into the hands of his enemies). **moveat,** *disturb.*

35. tuis [*servis*], Terentia's own personal property.

38. res . . . , lit., *if my property shall have left my hands* (i.e., been confiscated), *they are to be my freedmen* (i.e., be manumitted)—*provided they can maintain their claim* (i.e., legally maintain their status as freedmen). It was illegal to manumit slaves for the purpose of defrauding one's creditors.

39. pertineret . . . , *should the property remain mine, they shall continue as slaves* (i.e., not be manumitted). **oppido,** *very.*

44. Quas exspectassem, *I would have waited for some.*

45. esset licitum, *licuisset.* **tempestatem,** *good weather.*

49. nisi quod . . . , i.e., *except that I ought to have died.* **ornamentis,** *public honors.*

50. liberis, *children.*

53-55. The three men mentioned here were freedmen.

56. Sica, a friend of Cicero's.

58. Cura, *take care, see to it.*

[c]

1. Ego vero, *yes indeed I.* This confirms what Atticus had written to Cicero.

2. animum, *feeling, emotion.*

2-3. videndum . . . , i.e., *use your political influence to prevent the passage of any* **new** *measure*—which would keep Cicero in his province longer than one year. Of course Cicero's enemies might pass such a measure.

3. desiderium, *separation.*

4. ne plus sit annuum, *be not longer than for one year.*

5. transversum . . . versiculum, lit., *crosswise line of* (or *at*) *the end of your letter*—i.e., a postscript written in the margin.

6-42. The rest of this letter is taken up with Cicero's observations on the domestic bickerings between his brother Quintus and the latter's wife, Pomponia—sister of Atticus. That the domestic discord in this closely related branch of the family failed to cause any rift between Cicero and Atticus, attests to the sincerity of their friendship. Recently Atticus had requested that Cicero admonish Quintus to treat his wife more kindly and tactfully. This Cicero did and believed that his brother had taken the admonitions to heart. He now professes to find Pomponia at fault.

7. Arpinas, third declension adjective, neuter accusative singular; *my Arpinate (estate), my estate at Arpinum.*

10. Tusculano, neuter adjective, *my Tusculan (estate).*

11. in, *towards.* **ut,** result.

12. ex ratione sumptus offensio, *any ill feeling (arising) from the matter of expenditure. Sumptus* is genitive.

12-13. *Ille dies sic* [*erat*].

13. ut . . . , depends on *fecit (effecit)* (l. 14). **Arcano,** his estate at Arcae.

14. dies, i.e., it was a local holiday, and Quintus had to preside over the festivities. **Aquini,** locative, *I (remained) at Aquinum.* **prandimus,** *lunch.*

17. accivero, future perfect, equivalent to the simple future, *I will summon.* It is impossible to see exactly why Pomponia took offense at this apparently innocent remark—no doubt some fancied slight caused her to sulk. **potuit,** supply *facere.*

18. cum, *not only.*

19. hospita, *a stranger.*

20. ex eo quod, *for the reason that, because.*

21. videret, *see to, take care of.* Statius was Quintus' freedman and was probably responsible for the

difficulty between Pomponia and Quintus. Pomponia may have been jealous of Statius, who had a great hold over Quintus.

22. quid . . . , *what did that amount to?*—i.e., it was an insignificant tiff.

23. me ipsum commoverat, *she upset even me.*

25. Discubuimus, *we took our places at the dinner table*—i.e., all but Pomponia, who refused to come. The empty chair threw rather a gloom over the family party.

26. misit, supply *food.*

28. maiori stomacho, *of more annoyance, more annoying.*

31. nec voluisse, *she refused.*

32. eiusmodi qualem, i.e., just as touchy as when.

32-33. Quid quaeris (colloquial), *so there you are!*

33. Vel . . . licet, *you may even tell her.*

33-34. ei defuisse, lit., *was lacking to her.*

36. tuas . . . partes, *that you too have a part to play.*

37-38. mandata exhaurias, *finish my commissions.*

41-42. cui . . . velim, i.e., *tell him (when you see him) that I mentioned him to you.*

[d]

1. Imp[*erator*]**,** Cicero had won this title by his insignificant military victory over the hill tribes in his province. **Aed. Cur.,** *curule aedile.*

3. levia nostratia, *humble native (words)*—i.e., the colloquial diction which Cicero uses in his more intimate letters.

4. sollicitus . . . , Cicero is worried that his term as governor may be extended.

8. accessio, *increase.* **fortuna,** *reversal of fortune, change of luck.*

13. Caelius had requested Cicero to send him a shipment of wild panthers for the arena, as an unusual show during his tenure of the aedileship would advance him politically. **agitur,** *the business is being attended to.*

15. queri . . . , Cicero jestingly says that the panthers are the only persecuted residents of his province.

17. sedulo fit, impersonal, *energetic efforts are being made.*

19. nesciebamus, the epistolary imperfect. English would use the present.

21. Megalensibus, a festival celebrated annually at Rome from April 4–10, in honor of the goddess Cybele. It was under the supervision of the curule aediles.

[2]

Letters Written Early in 49 B.C.

[a]

1. Tullius, Cicero himself. **Cicero,** his son. **Q.Q.,** *Quinti-que, and the two Quintuses*—i.e., Quintus Senior and Junior, Cicero's brother and nephew. **S. Plur. Dic.,** *salutem plurimam dicunt.*

2. opportunitatem operae tuae, *the advantage* (or *convenience*) *of your help.*

4. quartanam, *quartan (fever)*—i.e., intermittent malaria, recurring every three or four days.

4-5. vis morbi, hardly different from just *morbus.*

6. id . . . tuae, *that which is part of your human frailty*—i.e., *as befits your frail health.*

8. ex desiderio, *from homesickness.*

10. suscipias, *be subjected to.*

12. ad Urbem accessi, *approached Rome* (without entering it). **pr. Non. Ian.,** *pridie Nonas Ianuarias.*

13. est proditum, impersonal passive, *everyone* (all his friends) *came out.* Prominent people were met as far as five miles out from the city by a committee of welcome.

14. Cui [*discordiae*], dative, depends on *mederi* (cf. *medicina*).

15. cum, *though.* **possem,** i.e., because he had the friendship and respect of both Caesar and Pompey. **cupiditates,** *passions.*

17. Omnino, *for instance.*

17-20. et Caesar . . . et Curio, *both . . . and,* but *both* is generally awkward in English and is to be omitted.

18-19. minacis et acerbas litteras, his ultimatum—read to the senate on January 1.

19. adhuc impudens, *still self-willed.* **qui . . . ,** relative clause of cause.

20. meus, *my intimate friend.*

21-22. Antonius . . . expulsi, two of the tribunes. They had tried to veto senatorial action and were expelled (without personal violence) from Rome.

23. consulibus . . . nobis, all dative; *pr*[*aetoribus*], *tr*[*ibunis*] *pl*[*ebis*].

23-24. et nobis . . . sumus, *and to us proconsuls.*

24-25. ut . . . caperet, the so-called *senatusconsultum ultimum*—indicating a state of war or imminent danger thereof.

26. improbi cives, the popular party.

27. Omnino, *to be sure.* **ex hac parte,** *on our side* (i.e., the Pompeians). **comparatur,** impersonal, *preparations are being made.*

30. Nobis, *for me.* **senatus frequens,** to be taken with a grain of salt.

31-32. quo . . . faceret, i.e., for selfish reasons (according to Cicero), *in order to make his own services more prominent.* In other words it was Lentulus' inning, and he was not planning to let Cicero stage a side show.

32-33. simul . . . relaturum, all indirect discourse, *said that he would bring the matter up for discussion as soon as he had settled important problems of present policy.*

33. Nos, *ego*.

34. pluris, *worth more*. **regiones**, special districts for military administration.

39. D..., *Datum pridie Idus Ianuarias*.

[b]

2. exirem, i.e., from Rome.

2-3. lictoribus laureatis, his guard of honor, or proconsular lictors, wore laurel wreaths because of Cicero's "victory" in his province. Having thus marched "up" to Rome, Cicero did not want to make a laughing stock of himself by marching "down again" (like the grand old Duke of York).

5. nostri, of the Pompeians. **amentissimi consilii**, *senseless policy*. **quid**, *why?*

6. Gnaeus, Pompey.

7. coartatus, *confined*.

8. stupens, *dazed*. **consistet**, the subject is *he*.

9. consilii res, *a matter for deliberation, an open question*.

10. incaute, supply *fecit*.

10. vel quod, *whatever*.

11. buccam, *mouth*.

[c]

1-2. All the family greetings are given in full—Cicero's to his wife and daughter, and Cicero Junior's to his mother and sister.

4. Romae-ne, *utrum Romae*.

6. Dolabella, Cicero's son-in-law and a Caesarian.

11. nostrorum . . . praediorum, *consists of* **my** *towns as well as estates*. Cicero owned the estates and controlled the towns.

12. multum, temporal adverb. **cum abieritis**, *when you leave me*—e.g., whenever Cicero has to go on a tour of inspection, or is especially busy.

12-13. commode esse, *be comfortably situated* (cf. *bene esse*). **nostris**, supply *praediis*.

13. utrum, i.e., to stay in Rome or come to Campania.

14. isto loco, *of your station*.

17. Philotimus, Cicero's steward in Rome.

18. tabellarios, *(private) letter carriers*.

20-21. VIIII. K. Formiis, *at Formiae, on the ninth day before the Kalends (of February)*.

[d]

1. amico nostro, Pompey.

2. omne, *utter*.

2-4. At nemo . . . , Deseret . . . , these two sentences represent Atticus' incredulous replies.

4. talem civem, Domitius. **unâ**, *with him*.

8. quem fugiam, Caesar.

9. Quod enim tu meum laudas, *as for that (remark) of mine which you praise*. The remark (*malle . . . vincere*) follows, governed by *quod dixerim (for I said)*. **memorandum**, *memorable*.

11. istis, the Caesarians. **ego vero**, *yes I do*.

12-13. cum hoc vero, *with the present (Pompey) however*.

14. nostra, neuter plural, *our cause*.

14-15. si malui, contigit, lit., *if I had my preference (or choice), it has come true*.

15. ista, neuter plural, *his cause* (Caesar's).

17. istum, Caesar.

17-18. mihi . . . carendum, *I must be untrue not only to my (friends) but also to myself*.

[e]

1. Lippitudo, *inflammation of the eyes*. Therefore Cicero cannot write his own letters, but must dictate them.

2. manus, *handwriting*.

3. quod . . . erat, epistolary imperfect, *I have nothing to write*.

4. **nuntiis Brundisinis,** *news from Brundisium* (where Caesar had now closed in on Pompey). **hic,** Caesar.

5. **ille** Pompey. **tramisisset,** crossed to Greece.

6. **quem,** equivalent to *qualem.* English might say: *into what hands.* **hominem,** Caesar.

12. **nummulos,** *shekels.*

14. **nostris,** of us Pompeians.

[3]

Letter Written After Caesar's Assassination

1. **Decimus Brutus** (IMPERATOR, CONSUL DESIGNATUS), one of the assassins of Julius Caesar—though he is not to be confused with Marcus Brutus. He was now a champion of the constitutional party, led by Cicero at Rome. Brutus' army had defeated Antony at Mutina a month before, causing the latter to flee headlong over the Alps. But Brutus made the mistake of not following up his victory, and Antony was now assembling stronger forces than ever north of the Alps. Before the year was out first Brutus, then Cicero, was destined to fall a victim to the nefarious deal between Antony and Octavian (the future Emperor Augustus).

10. **inermis,** from the form *inermus-a-um.*

15. **alii facti sunt,** lit., *have been made other* (*than they were*)—i.e., *have changed their opinion, have reversed their decision.*

16. *persecuti non sitis* [*Antonium*], [*Antonium*] *opprimi potuisse.*

17. **populi,** *characteristic of the populace.*

18. **in eo . . . ,** lit., *abuse their freedom in the case of him through whom* —i.e., a statesman who frees his people will be the first on whom they will turn in hostile criticism.

22. **mălo,** verb.

II

ESSAYS

[1]

Essays on Oratory

[a] De Inventione

The faculty of eloquence—a blessing or a curse to mankind?

1. **boni-ne . . . ,** *utrum plus boni* (genitive singular neuter) *an mali.*

2. **copia dicendi,** *eloquentia,* the subject of *attulerit.*

3. **studium,** also the subject of *attulerit.*

3-4. **nostrae . . . detrimenta,** the youthful Cicero first notices what is nearest and closest to him—namely, the calamities brought upon his own country in his own lifetime by demagogues. With these he associates similar calamities in the past.

5. **disertissimos,** *most eloquent.*

6. **invectam . . . ,** *non minimam partem incommodorum invectam* [*esse*].

6-11. **cum autem . . . ,** his pessimistic reflections on conditions in contemporary Rome and elsewhere have been offset by his study of Greek history and philosophy, replete with democratic ideals and theories.

8. **litterarum monumentis,** alludes primarily to Greek literature. **repetere,** *recall.* **multas,** the main clause begins here: *multas urbes constitutas* [*esse*] *. . . intellego.*

10. **cum . . . tum,** *not only . . . but also.* **animi ratione,** *by reason*—i.e., the power of mind over body. The word *ratio* is overworked in this paragraph, appearing in many different meanings—an evidence of youthful awkwardness of style.

12. **ratio ipsa,** *logic.* **potissimum,** adverb.

12-13. **ut existimem,** repeats the phrase *hanc sententiam* in a form that can more readily be linked with what follows.

13. parum, adverb; *little, slightly.*

14. nimium, *much* (not *too much*).

16. rationis et officii, *logic and ethics*—the two chief branches of philosophy (at least for Cicero's purposes).

17. exercitatione, *the mechanics, the practical side.*

18. alitur, *is reared as, is brought up to be*—i.e., *makes himself.*

20. rationibus, *exigencies, needs.*

21. amicissimus, *patriotic.*

Oratory—the chief civilizer of the human race

2. artis . . . , the four genitives are in apposition with *rei.*

4. rationibus, *principles.*

6-7. victu fero, *on wild food, on the bounty of nature.*

7. ratione animi, *reason.*

9. ratio, *idea, principle.*

10. certos . . . , i.e., no one knew whose children were whose; there was no family life, which is the basis of civilization.

11. non acceperat, *nor had anyone learned.* **ius . . . haberet,** this is an indirect question, of which *ius* is the subject: *quid (quantum) utilitatis ius aequabile haberet.*

11-14. Ita . . . satellitibus, an awkwardly constructed sentence, not up to the standard of Cicero's later and maturer style. *Cupiditas,* the main subject, is in apposition with *dominatrix* (or vice versa, if one prefers), and *satellitibus* with *viribus* (*powers* or *forces*).

15. cognovit, *realized, discovered.*

16. animis, *intelligence* (singular in English).

18. homines, accusative. **in agros,** depends on *dispersos.*

19. ratione quadam, whether this phrase means *by a kind of reasoning* or *in a certain way, somehow,* this is the weakest point in Cicero's theory.

22. reclamantes, agrees with *eos* (l. 20). **rationem atque orationem,** this is a very effective play on words, but of course *oratio* is not derived from *ratio.*

23. ex, *in place of.* **reddidit,** *rendered them.*

24-25. nec tacita . . . sapientia, *neither a silent nor a dumb wisdom*—i.e., wisdom could not have accomplished this were she either silent or incapable of speech.

26. rationes, *system, plan, scheme* (singular in English).

27. ut, depends on *fieri* (l. 31)—i.e., *how could it be brought about that?*

28. aliis [*hominibus*], dative.

30. commodi, noun. **amittendam,** *should be sacrificed.*

31. qui, *how?*

33. cum, *when.*

34. plurimum posset, *was supreme.* **ad ius sine vi descendere,** *descend to mere right without might.* This is spoken ironically, from the point of view of the savage. **ut,** *so that.*

35. excellere, by physical prowess.

36-37. quae . . . , a relative clause of cause.

37. naturae, *natural law.* **vim obtineret,** *had the meaning (force* or *validity).* **vetustatem,** *long continuance.*

40. versata, *has been concerned with.*

41. sine ratione, *without regard for.*

42. ingenio, *native ability, cleverness* (without higher ideals).

43. malitia, an abstract, used as a collective noun—i.e., *the wicked, the powers of evil.*

The decline of oratory—causes

2. infantes, *dumb.* This is a relative term, of course.

3. versari, *to be engaged in.*

3-4. ad . . . accedere, *enter upon, take up.*

7. a, *on the side of.*

8. assiduitas, *frequency.*

9. superiores illi, the *magni ac diserti homines* mentioned in ll. 3–4.

9-10. iniurias civium, an objective genitive, *wrongs done to their fellow citizens.*

10. resistere, depends on *cogerentur* (to be supplied, with change of number, from the following clause). **audacibus,** *upstarts*—i.e., the pettifoggers. **opitulari,** *help.* **necessariis,** *clients, dependents.*

13. comparasset, *had acquired.*

14. fiebat, *it came to pass.* **multitudinis,** parallel with *suo*—i.e., *et multitudinis [iudicio] et suo iudicio.*

15. videretur, the subject is *he* (the upstart).

16. gubernacula, *helm.* **temerarii . . . ,** *demagogues.*

18. Quibus rebus, an ablative of cause.

20. ex . . . vita, i.e., politics, statesmanship.

22. postea, the most emphatic word in the sentence, modifies *enituisse; later, subsequently*—i.e., after the decline of oratory. **cetera studia . . . ,** poetry and philosophy.

23. optimis, *gentlemen.* **enituisse,** *blossomed forth.* **hoc** [*studium*], eloquence.

24. quo, *when.*

Nobler ideals of oratory—the need for fostering them

1-3. quo . . . eo, *the more . . . the more.*

3. illis [*hominibus*], dative.

4. consulendum, here, as often, *consulere* means *protect* (or *defend*). **Quod,** *which fact.*

4-5. nostrum illum, *our famous countryman.*

5. fugit, *escaped the notice of.*

6. Africanum, Scipio.

12. eo vehementius, supply *eloquentiae studendum est.* **mali,** supply *homines.*

15-16. hoc, hoc eodem, these are ablatives of means.

16. fiat, this is parallel to *sit* (l. 14), and is therefore governed by the same *cum*-causal. **hinc,** *from eloquence.*

19. amicis eorum, *for the friends of the orators.*

21. homines, *mankind*—a general statement. **cum,** *although.*

[b] De Oratore

Selections from book II

1. Postero die, on the second day of the discussion. Each book of the dialogue represents one day. **secundā,** the second hour of the day (i.e., after sunrise).

2. Crassus, the host, and Antonius are the chief speakers.

2-3. Sulpicius and Cotta were young men, students of oratory.

4. Catulus, Q. Lutatius Cátulus (consul in 102 B.C.) and C. Iulius Caesar Strabo were half brothers; both were prominent aristocrats and distinguished orators.

5. omnes, the assembled company.

6. *causam eorum adventus* (genitive) *esse maiorem aliquam* (*something of major importance*). The political situation at Rome was tense.

8. Qui, Crassus, the host, greeted Catulus and Caesar, the newcomers. **ut . . . ferebat,** *as their intimacy led them.*

9. vos, supply *agitis.*

10. novi, genitive singular, *news.*

11. Nihil, i.e., of interest. **ludos,** *carnival time* (from September 4–12). During popular holidays of this sort, the aristocracy retired to their estates.

12. licet putes, *though you think, at the risk of your thinking.*

13. ad me in Tusculanum, *to my*

Tusculan estate. Tusculum was a famous suburb of Rome.

14. Scaevolam, Q. Mucius Scaevola, the Augur—now an old man of seventy—, had taken part in the first day's discussion, but had gone home in the evening.

14-15. a se esse conventum, *had been met by him* (Caesar). **hinc,** from the villa of Crassus.

15. ex quo, *from whom* (Scaevola).

16. dicebat, the subject is Caesar.

16-19. te . . . disputasse, indirect discourse, depends on *audisse* (l. 15). These are the marvels (*mira*), which Caesar said he had heard about from Scaevola. **te,** Crassus. **ego,** Catulus.

17. permulta, neuter plural, the object of *disseruisse.*

18. schola, *philosophic company.* This is a technical Greek term denoting the groups that gathered about famous philosophers to receive their oral instruction, in more or less Socratic fashion.

19. frater, his half brother, Caesar.

20. ne ipsum quidem nimis abhorrentem, lit., *though not even myself quite averse* (or *disinclined*). *Ipsum* is in apposition with *me.*

22. ut, depends on *exoravit* (l. 20).

23. aiebat, the subject is *Caesar.* **bonam . . . ,** indirect discourse, depends on *dicere.*

29-30. quaevis quam, *any other in the world than.*

30. mallem fuisset, *I would prefer that it had been.*

32. adeo, *however, yet.* **facilitate,** *because of my good nature.*

33. adulescentibus, Sulpicius and Cotta—at whose urgent request Crassus had held forth.

35. doctrinā, a definite, cut-and-dried department of learning—not fit for philosophical discussion.

37. partibus, *rôle.*

39. et, *also*—i.e., *I too* (as well as Catulus).

40. perpetua, *uninterrupted.*

41. minus, *non.* **vel,** *even.*

42. experiar, *I will make trial, I will see what I can do.* **ut ne,** introduces a negative clause of purpose.

45. impertias, *impart, bestow.*

45-46. tibi minus (*non*) **licebit,** this is more polite and deferential than *non potes.*

46-47. neque committam ut iudices, lit., *nor shall I act in such a way that you will think.* *Committam ut* is superfluous in English; the whole sentence may be translated as follows: *Nor will you, in trying to avoid being discourteous, have occasion to think me discourteous*—i.e., *I shall not overurge you.* **dum vereare,** *while you dread, in dreading, in trying to avoid.*

47. esse, supply *ineptum.*

48. Caesar, vocative.

48-49. ex . . . verbis, equivalent to a partitive genitive.

49. huius verbi, i.e., *ineptus.* **vim,** *force, meaning.* **vel maximam,** *quam maximam, quite the most significant.*

50-51. ab hoc ductum, *derived from the following fact.*

53. tempus . . . videt, *non videt quid* (accusative) *tempus* (nominative) *postulet.* What Crassus is driving at in these definitions is of course *tact, urbanity.* **plura,** *too much.*

55. rationem, *consideration* (or *regard*) *for,* with genitive. **genere,** *respect.*

56-57. Hoc . . . natio, this is an unfair criticism of the Greeks in general—as the next speaker immediately points out—but a fair criticism of the host of Greek *pedants* who had flocked to Rome.

58. vim, the English equivalent is *existence.*

59. Ut, *though.* **omnia,** English would say *everywhere.*

60. quomodo, i.e., what the Greek word for *ineptus* is. Crassus claims there is none—but ethical arguments based on vocabulary and idiom are not worth much.

62. nulla, from the English idiom we should expect *ulla.* **illi,** the Greeks.

63. visum est [*illis*], *they take the notion.*

65. adulescentibus, Sulpicius and Cotta. Crassus says this playfully, not seriously.

67. Graeci qui . . . , the classic Greeks of old.

69. horum Graecorum, depends on *similes; the present-day* (or *contemporary*) *Greeks.*

72. temporis, depends on *rationem.*

72-73. *si* [*ei*] *tibi 'inepti' videntur, qui . . . .*

75. haec ipsa, agrees with *porticus.* **palaestra** (Greek), *athleticfield.* Crassus had his own private athletic field on his estate, just as a wealthy American might have private golf links; the *public* athletic fields of Greece had become as much the haunt of loungers and "philosophers" as of athletes (see ll. 85–88 below). *Porticus, palaestra,* and *sessiones* are all subjects of *commovent* (l. 77).

76. gymnasiorum (with *memoriam*), used as a general synonym of *palaestra.* **Graecorum,** masculine, does not agree with *disputationum.* All the aristocratic Romans of Cicero's time traveled and studied in Greece to acquire old-world culture—just as we Americans do in Europe—, and they looked back with a thrill of pleasure on the romantic days spent in Athens. On returning to Italy, their efforts to ape Greek ways were sometimes rather banal.

77. importunum, supply *est.*

78. quod, supply *otium.* **per-optato,** adverb; *desirably, much to our liking, in answer to prayer.*

79. aut [*sunt*] **homines,** the present company.

80. ii, *such.*

81. ducamus, *credamus.*

82. Omnia ista, the three factors which Catulus alleged were favorable for a philosophical discussion—namely, the place, the time, and the company.

83. qui, *for I.* **primum,** *firstly.* Here begins his elaborate rebuttal of the first point (to l. 92). **sedis,** accusative plural, *sessiones.* **porticus,** accusative plural. **ipsos,** with *Graecos.*

84. exercitationis, *physical exercise.*

85. ante . . . quam, *before* (conjunction)—not to be construed as a preposition governing *gymnasia.*

86. garrire, *prate.*

87. discum, the thud of the discus striking the ground.

88. qui, the discus.

90. unctionis causā, i.e., to take part in the sports. Anointing with oil was a necessary preliminary.

91. ipsi, supply *Graeci.*

92. Otium, here Crassus begins his rebuttal of the second point.

93. Verum, *but.* **contentio,** *exertion* (not *contentment*).

94. socero, Scaevola.

95-100. This anecdote is far more unusual in *Roman* life than it would be in modern; a Roman aristocrat's dignity was very precious to him, and boyish gambols were eschewed.

99. umbilicos, the meaning is uncertain, probably *pebbles* of some special sort—e.g., *lucky stones.* **Caietam, Laurentum,** seashore resorts near Rome. **consuesse,** *consuevisse.*

100. ludum, perhaps leapfrog and tag.

101. sese habet, *est.* **ut,** *namely that.* The statement thus introduced is a lengthy simile, of which the first half occupies ll. 101–104 (*quemad-*

modum . . . volitare, just as we see the birds . . .) and the second half, ll. 104–106 (*sic . . . labore, so our minds . . .*). **volucris**, *avis*, accusative plural, the subject of *effingere*.

103. nidos, *nests.* **easdem,** supply *volucris.*

106. gestiant, *exult.*

107. illud quod dixi, English uses the plural, *those famous remarks I made.* **causa Curiana,** i.e., the noted case of Coponius vs. Curius. Defending Curius, Crassus won the case. **Scaevolae,** dative. Scaevola was counsel for the plaintiff.

107-108. non secus ac, *not otherwise than, exactly as.* The exigencies of a case *often* force lawyers to plead contrary to their true convictions, but not so Crassus in this instance.

109-116. Scaevola upheld the letter of the law, while Crassus based his argument on equity; Crassus is here ridiculing Scaevola's legal erudition. The case concerned the interpretation of a will.

115-116. For Crassus' present argument, the point of the quotation lies wholly in this last remark.

115. liber . . . , i.e., *he cannot call his soul his own.*

116. nihil agit, i.e., *takes a vacation.*

117. cum, *whenever.*

118. agere, cessare, infinitives used as neuter nouns, the subjects of *delectat.* **cessare,** *stop work, knock off.* **Nam,** here Crassus begins his rebuttal of Catulus' third reason for holding a discussion (see notes on ll. 83 and 92). **quod,** *what,* correlative with *id* (l. 119).

121. ut, *as,* correlative with *sic* (l. 127). **C. Lucilius,** the first Roman satirist. Together with Terence and others, he was the protégé of Scipio Africanus and Laelius (the Scipionic Circle).

122-124. neque . . . ipse, indirect discourse, depends on *dicere.*

123. alteri, the *indoctissimi.*

124. de quo, *about which.* **etiam scripsit,** i.e., his actual words were.

125-127. The two halves of the quoted line, united, make an eight-foot trochaic. **legere,** supply *me* as object. **volo,** supply *legere me.*

128. ad, *compared to.*

129. nolim, supply *disputare.*

130. vos, who are *doctissimi.*

133. navasse operam, *accomplished my purpose.*

135. Antonius was slated to lead the discussion on the second day, as successor to Crassus.

136. partis, singular in English; *part, rôle.* **quem-que,** *and whom.*

138-140. A playful threat, not meant to be taken seriously. Getting the spirit of it, Catulus interrupts with feigned alarm.

139-140. impetraro, *impetravero.*

142. I.e., *stay here as my guests.* Note that *sitis* is plural, addressed to both Catulus and Caesar.

143. ille, Catulus. **promiserat,** *was engaged to, had an engagement with*—probably for dinner. Dinner was included by Crassus in the invitation.

144. Iulius, Caesar Strabo (half brother of Catulus).

145. ista . . . vel ut, *even on condition that.* English omits *ista.*

145-146. I.e., the charm of your companionship alone (without any speechifying) is enough to hold me.

148. neque, correlative with *et.* Such correlation is stilted in English. **neque domi imperaram** [*ut veniret*], lit., *I, when we were at home, had not bade him come*—i.e., to call on Crassus. The suggestion had been made by Caesar, and Catulus (as his guest) would not be so discourteous as to propose a change. All this suave urbanity on the part of these cultured Roman gentlemen is quite in the modern French manner.

149. hic, Caesar. **eram futurus,** as
guest.

150. promisit, *accepted the invitation* (of Crassus).

151. omnes, supply *homines.*

152-160. With engaging humor,
Antonius assumes the manner and
style of an itinerant declaimer in the
market place—a soap-box orator.

152-153. hominem de schola, *a
schoolman.*

153. eo, *the more.*

155. *nos* [*solemus*] *Latini sermonis*
[*subtilitatem elegantiamque concedere*].

158. accessit os, *cheek* (*boldness* or
effrontery) *has been added.*

159. id . . . didici, an example of
cheek. **omni genere,** *the entire topic*
(or *subject*).

160. res . . . , [*eloquentia*] *mihi
videtur esse res.*

161. facultate . . . mediocris, lit.,
(*made*) *outstanding by natural ability,*
(*but*) *mediocre by technique.* **Ars,**
technical skill.

162. earum rerum est, *is a matter of,
is concerned with those things*—a general statement.

162-163. oratoris . . . , nowadays we
would say: *oratory is not an exact
science.*

163-164. apud eos, *before those*
(juries and assemblies).

165. illi, the juries and assemblies.
alias aliud, lit., *one thing at one time,
another thing at another time. Alias*
is an adverb of time.

166. contrarias causas, *the opposite
sides of a case.* **ut,** result.

168. cum, *though, whereas.*

168-169. uterque . . . defendat,
the same individual may take first one
and then the other side of the same
general question. He may not
change sides in the middle of a case,
of course—that would be illegal.

169. uno, *than one side.*

170-172. Ut igitur . . . ita dicam,
lit., *I shall so speak as in a subject*
which . . .—i.e., *I shall speak on the
assumption that it is a subject which . . .*

172. aucupetur, *aims at.*

173. causam esse, *there is any
reason.*

176. Exorsus es a veritate, *you began with the truth* (or *plain facts*).

177. nescioqua dignitate, *with any
pretensions to authority.*

178. Ut de ipso genere, *although
concerning the whole matter, although
on the general question.*

180. pertractandos, *swaying.*

181. excipiendas . . . , *winning their
good will.*

182. magnam quandam, *a really
great*—but not *supreme* (*maximam*).
The latter is denied both generally
and specifically.

[2]

Philosophical Essays

The Tusculan Disputations—Book V

[a] Dialogue between the *magister*
and the *auditor*

3. One of the disciples states this
negative proposition merely to have it
refuted by the master. **mihi videtur,
credo. satis posse,** *suffices.* The subject is *virtutem.*

3. ad *beate* **vivendum,** the whole
discussion, or sermon—for it soon
becomes that—, turns on the distinction between the baser and nobler
meanings of "happiness" and the
"happy life." The baser meaning is
"pleasure," the nobler is "beatitude,"
"bliss," or "blessedness"—which may
exist along with suffering and pain.
The nobler or philosophic connotation of *beatus* passed over into
Christianity, becoming a synonym
for *sanctus* (e.g., *Beatus Paulus*—St.
Paul); to "beatify" is to "sanctify";
and the Sermon on the Mount consists of the "beatitudes," beginning
with *beatus ille,* or *blessed is he.*

5. The *magister* is Cicero himself, thinly disguised; he plays the part of a professional "philosopher," holding a *schola*, at which he offers to discuss any topic which his disciples may care to bring up. **Bruto**, the famous assassin of Julius Caesar; a professed philosopher and intimate friend of Cicero's.

5-6. A playful *argumentum ad hominem*—which the disciple neatly parries in his next speech.

6. pace ... , a conventional phrase of courtesy; *by your leave, if you'll pardon my saying it.*

7. nec, *but* . . . *not*. **tu** . . . , *quantum tu illum ames.*

8. quod ... **sit**, *quod dixi videri mihi quale sit*, as to which I have stated my opinion (or *how it seems to me*). *Mihi* goes with *videri* (not with *dixi*); there is no ambiguity in Latin, for *mecum dixi* (not *mihi dixi*) would be the Latin idiom for *I said to myself*. The phrase *mihi videri quale sit* is like the old English: *I know thee who thou art;* the Latin could just as well follow the English idiom: *quod dixi quale mihi videatur esse.*

13. recte, honeste, laudabiliter, define the nobler concept of *beate*. The disciple admits that these constitute "goodness," but denies that they have anything to do with "happiness."

16-17. *Potes igitur aut dicere eum, qui male vivat, non [esse] miserum, aut negare eum, quem bene [vivere] fatearis, beate vivere?*

18. Quidni possim, repeats *potes* from the beginning of the previous speech.

19. vivi potest, impersonal passive, *one can live.*

20. dicam, *mean by*. **Dico**, *mean*.

21. Haec, *these qualities*—i.e., *constantia, gravitas*, etc., represented by the adverbs *constanter, graviter*, etc. The qualities are rather vaguely personified.

22. eculeum, diminutive of *equus; the rack*. **con-iciuntur**, *are placed with* (or *accompany*) one. **quô**, *whither, to which.*

23-26. The personification of the virtues, begun by the disciple, is amplified by the master into an allegory.

23. *Sola-ne.*

27. facturus, *accomplish*. **nova,** new arguments.

28. ista, what you have already said. **minime, *non*.**

30. gustata, *sipped*—i.e., they are good enough to dabble with, but are only superficial.

31-32. pictura imaginibusque, *allegory and personifications.*

32. rem, *plain fact.*

33. hoc, this question.

35. agere, *discuss, treat the problem.*

36. te, the subject of *praescribere*.

37. actum, *accomplished*. **superioribus diebus**, the four previous days of discussion—during which it had been established that death, pain, grief, and all "mental disturbances" were to be despised by the true man.

40. profligata, *clinched*. **haec**, with *quaestio*.

43-45. motus . . . **repellentes**, a philosophic definition of human passions and emotions.

44. rationem, *reason*.

45. vitae, dative. **partem**, *function*.

47. non, *otherwise than.*

48. idem, masculine. **quod**, *as*.

52. Quid qui, *how about one who?*

53. eôdem, *thereto*.

54. orbitates, *bereavements*. **qui**, *he who.*

55. non, *otherwise than.*

55-59. illum . . . , the debauchee.

57-58. quo-que affluentius, *and the more abundantly.*

59. sitientem, i.e., for pleasures. **dixeris**, *call him.*

60-61. The reveler.

61. miserior, supply *est*.

62. hi, illi, supply *sunt.* **metus,** nominative plural.

64-65. exultantes languidis voluptatibus, modifies *quos* (l. 11), the personal object of *liquefaciunt* (*weaken*).

66. nullā ... commovente, ablative absolute expressing time—i.e., the sea is understood to be tranquil, when ...

67. status, noun, the subject of *cernitur.*

68. queat, the subject is *it* (*animus*). **est, qui,** *there is anyone who.*

70. ducat, *putet.* **ex quo,** *so that.* **idemque si,** *and if he.*

71. inani, ablative.

72. quid est, *what reason is there?* **haec,** *these results.*

[b] Excerpts from the master's sermon

[i] Which was the happier—the despot Dionysius or the mathematician Archimedes?

2. cum, *inasmuch as.* **quinque ... annos,** *at twenty-five.*

4. servitute oppressam tenuit, verbal phrase, *held in bondage.* The phrase has two objects: (1) *urbem,* modified by *qua pulchritudine praeditam;* and (2) *civitatem,* modified by *quibus opibus praeditam.*

5. bonis, i.e., reliable. **accepimus,** *we have heard, we know.*

7. virum, [*eum fuisse*] *virum.* **eundem tamen** [*fuisse*], *and yet that he was.*

8. Ex quo, *wherefore.*

8-9. omnibus videri miserrimum, lit., *that to all he seem wretched*—i.e., *that all men regard him as wretched.*

9. Ea, neuter plural accusative, the object of *consequebatur.*

10. omnia posse, *had unlimited power.*

11. Qui cum, *although he.*

12-13. alius ... tradidit, i.e., accounts differ.

13. aequalium, lit., *those of his own age.* **consuetudine,** *companionship.*

15. iis, quos servos, *iis servis quos.* **familiis,** *households.*

15-16. quibus ... detraxerat, i.e., *quos manumiserat*—illegal and despotic action, as the *ipse* suggests.

16. convenis, *refugees.* Political exiles and fugitives from justice were always numerous in the Greek states.

18. dominatus, genitive singular.

19. By hedging about, he hedged himself in.

21. sordido ... artificio, lit., *by a sordid and menial craft*—i.e., *exercising a sordid and menial craft.*

22. tonstriculae, *barberettes.*

23. ab his, *from them* (his daughters). **ferrum,** *the steel* (*razor*).

24. candentibus ... putaminibus, *glowing walnut shells* (or *husks*).

25. adurerent, *singe off.*

26. Cum, expresses neither time nor cause, but mere attendant circumstance. English therefore uses the present participle.

27-28. sic ... ut ante, *only when.*

28. fossam, *moat.*

29. cubiculari lecto, *nuptial bed.*

29-30. transitum coniunxisset, English says *construct a way across* or *join the two sides,* but not *join a way across.*

30. ligneo, *wooden.* **eum,** the drawbridge.

31. Idem, *he.*

32. suggestis (from *suggestum*), *platforms.*

33. cum, *whenever.* **pila,** *ball.*

34. poneret, *took off.*

36. dixisset, i.e., to Dionysius. **huic,** the *adulescentulus* (or *adulescens,* as he is called at the end of this line).

37. utrumque, *ambos.*

38. interimendi sui, *ad se* [*Dionysium*] *interimendum. Sui* is genitive of the pronoun *se.*

39. dictum id, *that remark.*

40. doluit, *suffered from remorse.*
nihil ut, *ut nihil.*   **quem,** *the one whom.*

42. impotentium [*hominum*]*,   the uncontrolled.*

43. ipse iudicavit, i.e., he tacitly passed judgment on himself.

43-44. quam beatus, *as to how happy.*

46. dominatus, genitive singular.

47. aedium regiarum, *his palace* (singular in English).

48. inquit, the subject is Dionysius.

50-51. *ille dixisset se cupere,* [*Dionysius*] *iussit.*

51. abacos, *sideboards.*

52. argento auroque, dishes.   **caelato,** *engraved, chased.*

53. eximiā formā, modifies *pueros.*

54. intuentīs, agrees with *eos.*

57. lacunari, *ceiling.*   **saeta,** *a hair.*

58. aptum, a participle, agrees with *gladium; tied to, held by.*

59. cervicibus, *neck* (singular in English). Damocles is reclining; consequently the sword is like the knife of a guillotine.

61. defluebant, *were slipping off*— probably because Damocles was shaking with fright.

63. Satisne, *nonne,* a mere interrogative particle.   **ei,** *for one.*

64. ei, Dionysius.   **integrum,** *open, free*—i.e., *possible.*

66. redderet, *restore.*

66-67. iis, ea, *such. Iis* belongs with the noun *erratis.*   **improvida aetate,** *at that short-sighted time of life,* in loose apposition with *adulescens.*

| **67. inretierat,** *entangled.*   **salvus** ..., identical in substance and phraseology with Christian belief in "salvation."

69. Quantopere, *how greatly.*

70. in ... **illis,** *in the case of the two famous Pythagoreans* (Damon and Pythias). The more correct, but less familiar, form of the latter is Phintias.

71-72. [*Dionysius*] *alterum* (*Damonem*) *vadem mortis* (*as a death*

proxy) *accepisset, alter* (*Pythias*), *ut vadem suum* (*Damonem*) *liberaret* . . . . Pythias, who had been condemned to death for his share in a conspiracy, was released from the death cell when Damon voluntarily took his place.

72. praesto fuisset, *adfuisset,* depends on *cum* (l. 71).

73. *inquit* [*Dionysius*].

74. Quam, *how.*

75. victus, noun, genitive singular.

75-76. homini docto erudito, in apposition with *huic* (l. 74).

77. perstudiosum, poetam, supply *Dionysium.* These accusatives are left suspended with no verb to govern them after the long parenthesis that follows.

77-78. quam . . . **rem,** *how good a poet* (*Dionysius was*), *has nothing to do with the case.*

78. genere, *field.*   **nescioquo pacto,** *somehow.*

79. suum, *his own work.*

80. Aquinio, a poetaster.

86. qua, *than which.*   **taetrius,** *more hideous.*

89. a . . . **radio,** *from his dust* (or *sand*) *and rod.* Thus the great mathematician made his diagrams; we would say: *from his blackboard and chalk.*

90. excitabo, *summon* (as a witness or example).   **qui** . . . , Archimedes lived a century and a half after Dionysius.

91-92. ignoratum, saeptum, vestitum, agree with *sepulchrum* (l. 93). **esse,** *that it existed, that there was any.*

92. vepribus et dumetis, *brambles and thickets.*

93. Tenebam, *had possession* (or *a copy*) *of.*   **senariolos,** *brief verses* (iambic or trochaic *senarii,* or six-foot lines).

94. acceperam, *learned, heard.*   **qui,** the verses.

97. portas, singular in English, one of the gates of Syracuse.

100. principes, *leading citizens.*

101. falcibus, *sickles.*

102. multi, a gang of workmen.

103. adversam basim, *the face of the pedestal.*

105. dimidiatis, modifies *partibus*, *half.*

107. Arpinate, adjective; the nominative form is *Arpinas, from Arpinum*—i.e., Cicero, whose birthplace was Arpinum.

110. humanitate, *culture.*

112. modum, *measure*—i.e., *standards.*

113. quaerimus, *look into.* **alterius,** of Archimedes. **rationibus,** *problems, theories.*

114. cum . . . , *along with the satisfaction of skill (proficiency or intellectual achievement).* **qui,** *which,* agrees with *pastus*, but equivalent to *id quod.*

115. animorum, English uses the generic singular, *the mind.*

116. confer, *bring* (or *put*) *together.*

118-119. pars optima, *mens.*

119-120. illud optimum, *that "highest good."*

120. sagaci, with *mente.*

121-122. bono, bonum, these are nouns.

122. hac, *virtute.*

127. existere, *arises from.* **sequitur,** *it follows* (logically). **honestate,** a synonym of *virtute.*

[*ii*] Socrates, Xenocrates, and Diogenes— despisers of wealth and power

1. pompa, probably a religious procession, in which precious images were carried.

3. talenta . . . , of course not a bribe, but a benefaction.

6. tantum quod, *only as much as.*

7. cui numerari iuberet, *to whom he bade it be paid*—i.e., his treasurer, or purser.

9. triginta minas, i.e., a mere handful of silver coins, whereas fifty talents is a princely fortune. The talent was not a coin, but a *weight* of precious metal.

11. liberius (ut Cynicus), *more frankly, being a Cynic.* Frankness was the Cynics' ideal and they carried it to absurd lengths, regarding all conventions as sham.

11-12. roganti ut diceret si, *requesting him to say whether.* Alexander's words to Diogenes in his tub, were: *"Dic mihi, si quid tibi opus sit ";* and Diogenes' reply to the conqueror of the world was: *" Yes, move a little to one side; you're cutting off my sunlight"!*

13. offecerat, [*Alexander*] *offecerat* [*Diogeni*] *apricanti (sunning himself).* **hic,** Diogenes. **disputare,** i.e., when he held his regular lectures.

14-16. sibi, se, . . . , the various reflexive forms refer to Diogenes, the lecturer; the various forms of *ille* and *is*, to the Persian king.

16. suas [*voluptates*], the object of *consequi.*

17. eum, the subject of *consequi.*

[*iii*] Simplicity—the source of true happiness

1-2. inquinatam, *polluted.*

3. sitiens, esuriens, *thirsty, hungry.*

4. peragranti Aegyptum, while escaping incognito from his enemies— like King Alfred, when he let the cakes burn. It is not known which Ptolemy this was.

5. cibarius, *common.* **casa,** *hut* (of a peasant).

7. ferunt, *they say.* **contentius,** *rather briskly.*

9. obsonare, *was spicing.*

11. Victum, noun, *the fare.* **phili-**

tiis (Greek), *their messes* (in the military sense).

13. iure, *broth.* **caput,** *mainstay.*

16. cursus ad Eurotam, *footraces to the river Eurotas.*

19. ut quicquid, *whenever anything.* **obiectum est,** i.e., to eat.

19-20. quod modô, *dummodo id.*

25. vestrae (not *tuae*) **cenae,** *the banquets of you philosophers.*

27. Quid quod, *what of the fact that?* Or it may be rendered simply by *moreover,* which changes the rhetorical question to a statement.

28. completi, *when filled.*

29. Dionis propinquos, Dionis' kinsmen were in Syracuse. Plato wrote to them from Athens on his return from Syracuse, where his experiences had been very disappointing.

30. quô, *thither* (to Syracuse). **quae ferebatur,** lit., *which was reported*—i.e., *the so-called. Beata* is here used in the vulgar sense of which Plato does not approve.

31. Italicarum, South-Italic—proverbial for *luxurious.*

35. Quae natura, *what character* (or *soul*). **tam mirabiliter,** *in such a remarkable* (or *extraordinary*) *way.* This is ironical. **temperari,** *be properly regulated.*

40-41. These are hexameters. The epitaph of the voluptuary who brags that no one can deprive him of the pleasures he has had—they are his only certainty, incontestably and forever his.

41. illa relicta, *those things I have left.* This is in contrast to *haec* (l. 40). **multa et praeclara,** *though many and fair.* **iacent,** *are done for, are of no use.*

43. habere se mortuum, *that in death he still has.*

47. Aperta, *obvious.*

48. egeat, the subject is *she* (Nature).

LUCRETIUS

DE RERUM NATURA

[1]

Invocation

1. Aeneadum, *Romanorum.* Venus, mother of Aeneas, was the divine ancestress of all the Romans. **divom,** *divorum.*

2. signa, constellations.

3. quae, *thou who,* translate before *caeli.*

4. concelebras, *dost haunt* (or *fill*) *with thy presence.*

5. exortum, *when born,* agrees with *genus.*

7. pangere, *compose.*

8. Memmiadae, patronymic, *Memmio, for Memmius.* He was Lucretius' patron. **nostro,** *my friend.*

10. Quo magis, *wherefore.* **dictis,** *my words.* **leporem,** *charm.*

11. moenera, *munera, works.*

14. Mavors, *Mars* (lover of Venus).

17. nos, *ego.* **agere hoc,** *set to my task.* **iniquo,** *troubled.*

18. Memmi propago, *Memmiades,* supply *potest.*

19. *in such circumstances* (i.e., war time) *to desert the commonwealth.* Consequently he will have no time for philosophy. **desse,** *deesse.*

[2]

The Mission of Epicurus

1. cum, *when.* **ante oculos,** supply *omnium.*

2. in terris, *in the mire.* Life was swinish!

3. quae, refers to Religion (personified).

4. super, with *mortalibus.* **instans,** *impending.*

5-6. *oculos tollere ausus est.*

7. deum, *deorum.*

8. compressit, this has three sub-

jects: *fama, fulmina,* and *caelum.*
murmure, *thunder.*

9. inritat, the subject is *it* (referring
vaguely to *caelum,* etc.). **animi virtutem,** *mind, spirit* (of Epicurus).

9-10. arta, adjective, agrees with
claustra (*bars*).

12. moenia . . . , "*the fiery orb of
ether that forms the outer circuit of the
world.*" So astronomers are often
poetically eulogized for penetrating
(in spirit) the realm of the stars.

12-13. processit, peragravit, the
subject of these verbs is *he.*

13. immensum, *boundless space.*

14. refert, *brings tidings.*

14-16. quid . . . , these were
questions solved by the "discoveries"
of Epicurus—viz.: (1) *quid possit oriri*
—i.e., what phenomena can arise
(according to the atomic theory of the
universe); (2) what phenomena cannot arise; and (3) what are the physical *laws* of the universe.

15-16. finita . . . , *denique qua ratione cuique* [*rei*] *potestas finita sit
atque* [*quis sit cuique rei*] *terminus.*

16. alte haerens, *deeply fixed.*

[3]

**Religion, What Crimes are Commit-
ted in Thy Name!**

1. rearis, from *reor.*

2. te, the reader. **rationis elementa,** *grounds of reasoning.*

3. indu-gredi, *ingredi.* **Quod contra,** lit., *contrary to which.* **illa,** with
Religio.

5. Aulide, locative. **quo pacto,**
quo modo, even as. **Triviaï,** *Dianae.*

6. Iphianassaï, genitive, with *sanguine.*

7. prima virorum, a Greek idiom,
primi viri (nominative plural). *Prima*
is neuter plural nominative.
Danaum, *Danaorum, Graecorum.*

8-9. *as soon as* (*simul*) *the head-
band, placed around her* (*cui*) *maiden

locks, hung down (*profusa 'st*) *equally
(*pari*) on each side of her cheeks
(*mālarum*).*

11. hunc propter, *beside him.* **ministros,** the subject of *celare.*

12. aspectu suo, *at the sight of her.*
civīs, the subject of *effundere.*

13. petebat . . . , *sank down faint-
ing.*

14. miserae, refers to Iphianassa,
dative with *prodesse.* **quibat** (from
queo), the subject is *it.*

15. quod, *that.* **princeps,** *prima.*
She was his oldest child. **patrio
donarat nomine,** *she had presented the
king with the name "father."*

16-17. The pathos of the picture is
heightened by the fact that *sublata*
and *deducta,* in addition to their
literal meanings, connote *wedding
ceremonies*—viz., lifting the bride
over the threshold and escorting her
to her new home. Iphianassa found
herself the bride not of Achilles, but
of Death!

16. virum, *virorum.*

17. sacrorum, *wedding ceremonies.*

18. comitari hymenaeo, *be accompanied by the wedding song.*

19-20. casta inceste hostia, *as a
chaste victim foully* (i.e., *unrighteously*).

20. mactatu maesta, *blasted by the
cruelty.*

21. This is a purpose clause.

[4]

The Difficulty of Lucretius' Task

1. animi, locative, need not be
translated. **reperta,** used as a noun.

3. multa, neuter plural, the direct
object of *agendum sit* (gerund). Cicero
would use the gerundive: *multa sunt
agenda, must be treated* (or *expressed*).

4. rerum, *themes, subject matter.*

5. tua, this is addressed to Memmius.

7. inducit, supply *me* (with which
quaerentem agrees).

8. dictis quibus, *by what words.*
9. praepandere, *spread before.*
lumina, disregard the plural number.
10. quibus, refers to *lumina,* *by which.* **res,** accusative plural.

[5]

The Two Basic Laws of Nature

1. Hunc, *the present.*
1-3. *Necesse est ut non radii sed species . . . discutiant terrorem.*
3. naturae species ratioque, *the form and system of nature*—i.e., the knowledge of nature's laws.
4. *the foundation thereof, in our opinion (nobis), shall thus (hinc) begin.*
5. nilo, *nihilo.* This first principle flatly refutes the opening words of the Bible: *In principio creavit Deus caelum et terras.*
6. ita continet, *so constrains.*
7. quod, *because.*
7-8. multa . . . quorum operum, *multa opera (operations) . . . quorum.*
11. sequimur, *seek.*
13. quaeque, *each and all.* **operā sine,** *without the aid of.*
[14]. See note on l. 1 of Plautus' *Miles,* p. 253.
15. discidio, *by dissolution.* **corpora materiaï,** *first bodies of matter*—i.e., atoms.
16-27. Lucretius' proof of the indestructibility of matter is developed with true poetic feeling: the fructifying rains sink into the lap of Mother Earth and disappear, but from them spring all living things in unbroken sequence. Cf. Omar Khayyam:

I sometimes think that never blows so red
The Rose as where some buried Caesar bled;
That every Hyacinth the Garden wears
Dropt in her Lap from some once lovely Head.

And this reviving Herb whose tender Green
Fledges the River-Lip on which we lean—
Ah, lean upon it lightly! for who knows
From what once lovely Lip it springs unseen!

16. pereunt, *pass away*—i.e., *seemingly.* They disappear but do not die, for they fructify the earth.
19. ipsae, *the trees themselves.*
20. hinc, from vegetation.
22. canere, *resound.* ·
23. fessae pingui (noun), *wearied with fatness.*
27. mentes perculsa novellas, *thrilled in their young hearts.*
29. alid, *aliud.*
30. adiuta, *requited,* agrees with *natura.*

[6]

The Composition of Matter

1-2. Nec corporeā stipata tenentur naturā, *are not held rigid by matter*—i.e., there is void everywhere, both within and between things.
2. inane, noun.
3. Quod, *which fact.* **cognosse,** *cognovisse.*
4. According to Lucretius, food *permeates* the body; he has no idea of the chemistry of digestion, either in animals or in plants.
5. arbusta, *arbores.* **tempore,** *season.*
6. totas, supply *arbores.*
8. Inter saepta, *through barriers.*
10. Quod, *which thing,* the subject of *fieri* (l. 11). **inania,** *empty spaces.* **sint,** Cicero would use *essent.* **quā,** *where*—i.e., via the empty spaces.
12-13. alias res praestare aliis rebus, *some things excel others.*
13. nilo, *nowise,* equivalent to a simple negative. **figura,** *size.*

14-15. tantundem corporis, *just as much matter.*

14. lanae glomere, *a ball of wool.*

15. plumbo, i.e., of the same size. **par est,** *it is natural, it must.*

16. *quoniam est corporis officium (function) premere omnia deorsum*— i.e., to gravitate.

17. inanis, genitive, depends on *natura.* The circumlocution *natura inanis* simply means *void.*

18. quod, *that which.*

19. plus esse sibi, *se habere plus.* **inanis,** genitive, depends on *plus.*

20. contra, adverb. **gravius,** nominative, *the heavier thing.*

21. dedicat, *avows.*

22. Est, *there is.*

23. admixtum, *something mixed with.*

CATULLUS

I

PRELIMINARY BRIEF SELECTIONS

[1]

The Non-Lyric Meters

[a] Hexameter

[i] The wedding song

1. Vesper, *the Evening Star.*

1-2. Olympo lumina tollit, lit., *lifts its light from*—i.e., *hangs over*—*Mt. Olympus.* The evening star does not rise!

3. pinguīs mensas, the wedding banquet.

4. virgo, the bride.   **dicetur,** *be sung.*

5. The refrain of the wedding song is heard.

6. Ut, *as,* correlative with *sic* (l. 12).

7. aratro, *plow.*

10. cum, *when.* **defloruit** (from *defloresco*), *droop.*

12. Over a hundred years later, Quintilian commented on this line in his *Institutes of Oratory* as follows: *Prius "dum" significat "quoad," sequens "usque eo."*

16. vidua vitis, *unwed*—i.e., *unsupported* (or *unpropped*)—*grapevine.* The "marriage" of the clinging grapevine to the supporting elm was a commonplace.

17. uvam, *grapes.*

19. Root and top shoot (*flagellum*) practically touch when the vine lies flat on the ground.

20. accoluēre, *cultivate, tend.*

24. par, *right, proper.* This is a variation of the regular legal phrase *iustae nuptiae.*

[ii] The *epyllion*

1. Peliaco prognatae vertice, modifies *pinus* (nominative plural), *sprung from Mt. Pelion.* This **miracle** of the first ship—how leafy trees were converted into vessels—was one of which the Roman poets never tired.

3. Phasis, a river in the Land of the Golden Fleece. The ruler of this land was Medea's father, Ae-ē-tēs (a mellifluous name)—whence the adjective *Aeētaeōs.* Spondaic lines were much more frequently used by the Hellenistic word painters than by Homer.

4. cum, *when.* **robora,** this is in apposition with *iuvenes.*

5. avertere, *carry off as loot.* **Colchīs,** *from the Colchians.*

7. verrentes, *sweeping.* **abiegnis,** *of fir wood.* **palmis,** *paddles, oars.* Since this also means *hand,* it suggests personification of the noble ship.

[b] Elegiac

[i] Misplaced *h's*

2. Arrius, supply *dicebat.*

4. quantum poterat, *as strongly as possible.*

5. liber, a dig at the low and servile origin of Arrius—he had *one* uncle who was free.

7. Hoc, ablative, *he* (Arrius).

8. audibant, this is the old form of the fourth conjugation. **leniter ... ,** supply *pronounced.*

11. isset, *ivisset.*

[*ii*] A curt rebuff to Julius Caesar

1. nil nimium, *not overmuch.* **tibi,** with *placere.*

2. albus an ater, a proverbial expression of indifference.

[c] Limping Iambic

On the one failing of Suffenus

2. venustus, dicax, *pleasant, witty.*

3. idemque, *and yet he.* **longe plurimos,** i.e., he holds the long-distance record.

4. milia aut decem, *milia aut decem* [*milia versuum*]. **esse illi,** *illum habere,* i.e., in his bookcase.

5. tu, indefinite *you.* **bellus,** this is not used in any disparaging sense, but as a synonym of adjectives in l. 2.

6. unus (colloquial), the indefinite article—as in the Romance languages. **caprimulgus, fossor,** *goat milker, ditcher.* These are general equivalents of *clodhopper, boor, etc.*

7. abhorret, *varies, is inconsistent.*

9. ac cum, *as when.*

11. Nimirum, *of course.* **idem,** neuter singular, cognate accusative with *fallimur*—i.e., *have the same failing.*

12. Suffenum, generic, *a Suffenus.*

13. attributus, i.e., by fate or the Creator.

14. manticae ... est, *that part of the load which is behind our backs.* An ancient grammarian said: *Aesopus tradit homines duas manticas habere* (*all men carry two packs*), *unam ante se, alteram retro; in priorem aliena vitia mittimus* (*put*), *ideo et videmus*

facile; in posteriorem nostra, quae abscondimus et videre nolumus.

[d] Regular Iambic

[*i*] Six-foot iambic with substitutions

The world is going to the dogs!

1. I.e., there is nothing left for an honest man to do but die.

2. struma, in apposition with *Nonius,* a term of abuse that may be rendered by *wart.*

3. Per, *by.* **pérjĕrat,** this is the same as perjūrat, *swears falsely*—implying that he **never** keeps his oath. A consul might very naturally swear by his sacred office.

[*ii*] "Seven-foot" iambic with substitutions

To a light-fingered and effeminate dandy

1. involasti, *stole.*

2. sudarium, *handkerchief.* **catagraphos,** *writing tablets*—perhaps made of some rare carved wood.

3. quae, *which things* (the stolen goods). **palam habere,** *to use openly, to display brazenly.* **avita,** an adjective used as a noun; *ancestral possessions, heirlooms.*

5. laneum, i.e., soft as wool.

6. inusta, lit., *burned*—i.e., *flayed.* Latin metaphorically called any painful abrasion of the skin—e.g., frostbite, chilblains, blisters—a "burn." **flagella,** the subject of *conscribillent.*

7. insolenter, *in an unaccustomed manner.*

7-8. aestues ... , *writhe—like a skiff tossing in an angry sea.*

[*iii*] "Pure" iambic

The yacht's epitaph

1. Phasellus, lit., *kidney bean*—i.e., a light and graceful vessel. The epitaph was inscribed on a model of the yacht, or perhaps on the old hull of the yacht itself—provided it could be brought up the Po to Catullus' estate. **hospites,** *friends, passers-by*—i.e., you who stop to read my epitaph.

2. ait fuisse celerrimus, a Greek construction, *ait se fuisse celerrimum* (cf. l. 6).

3. Amastri, a Greek vocative, *O Amastris on the Black Sea.*

5. ultima, *earliest.*

6. Again the *miracle* (as in the case of the Argo)—the metamorphosis of trees to ships. **dicit stetisse,** a Greek construction, *se stetisse.*

7. impotentia freta, *wild waters.*

8. erum, the object of *tulisse.* The subject is the ship.

9-10. Iuppiter secundus, *a favorable wind.* **utrumque simul incidisset in pedem,** lit., *struck each sheet* (or *sail rope*) *simultaneously* (or *evenly*)—i.e., *blew dead astern.*

12. sibi, dative of agent, *by the yacht.* Vows to the shore gods were made only in fear of shipwreck.

13. novissime, *finally.*

16. Castor, vocative. **gemelle Castoris,** Pollux. The twin gods, Castor and Pollux, were the patron saints of sailors.

[2]

The Lyric Meters

[a] Hendecasyllabic

[*i*] Humble thanks to Cicero

1. Romuli nepotum, *descendants of Romulus* (all the Romans).

3. post, *hereafter.*

6. tanto, *by as much.*

7. patronus, *advocate.*

[*ii*] To Julius Caesar

2. immerentibus, mock humility. **unice,** ironical. Caesar called himself *imperator,* but he acted as if he were *rex!*

[*iii*] Overheard in the crowd

1. modô, *just now.* **corona,** *audience.*

2-3. Vatiniana crimina, *the charges against Vatinius.*

4. manus tollens, a gesture of wonderment.

[*iv*] Ill winds

1. As if in answer to a query from Furius, Catullus laughlingly confesses to the true "situation" of his villa. The whole point of the epigram lies in the double meaning of *opposita*—either *placed toward* or (as a technical term of finance) *mortgaged for.* **Austri,** local names for winds predominate in Latin. The winds here mentioned are approximately south, west, north, and east.

2. flatus, accusative plural.

4. *15,200 sesterces.*

5. ventum, punsters may translate this by *draft.*

[*v*] An invitation to a Barmecide feast

2. si tibi di favent, this slyly suggests the humor of the situation: *God willing, you'll get a good dinner.*

4. candida puella, *a handsome dancing girl.*

5. sale, *wit.* To the Greeks and Romans *salt* proverbially meant *wit* (cf. the English *spice of life*). **omnibus,** *all kinds of.* **cachinnis** (from *cachinnus*), *laughs, laughter.* The English derivative of this is *cachinnation.*

6. noster, vocative, equivalent to *mi* (l. 1).

8. sacculus, *little sack, purse.* **aranearum,** *cobwebs.*

9. contra, *in exchange*—i.e., for what he brings. **Meros Amores,** a perfume, *Essence of Love, Djerkiss.* In ancient Greece and Rome, just as among many peoples today, men used perfume quite as much as women did.

10. quid, *whatever.*

11. unguentum, perfume. The modern method of preserving perfumes in distilled alcohol was unknown to the ancients, because they had no alcohol; they used only oils and salves —like our hair oil and cold cream. **puellae,** *sweetheart.*

12. donarunt, *donaverunt.* **Veneres Cupidinesque,** *the Loves and Cupids.* The plural is a feature neither of Greek mythology nor of Roman religion, but of Alexandrian sentimentality—whence come our valentine Cupids.

[*vi*] *Cherchez la femme*

4. libellis, *bookshops.*

6. Magni Ambulatione, *the Portico of Pompey* (Cn. Pompeius Magnus).

7. femellas, diminutive, *lasses.* **prendi,** *prehendi.*

8. None of them acted guilty.

9. Avens, *cupiens.*

10. Supply *reddite* or *demonstrate.*

11. te, the object of *ferre* (*endure*). The infinitive clause is the subject of *est; Herculi* is genitive; *labos* is another form of *labor.*

12. te-n[e] negas [*nobis*], *te occultas?*

13-14. This is a witty repetition. The object of *ēde, committe,* and *crede* is *it* (the secret).

14. committe, supply *nobis.*

17. fructus, *advantages.* **proicies, perdes,** a witty jibe—i.e., *what's the use of having a secret love affair, if you don't tell everyone all about it?* Similarly Catullus twits a certain Flavius on a secret amour in these words:

Flavi delicias¹ tuas Catullo
(ni sint² illepidae atque inelegantes)
velles³ dicere—nec tacere posses!⁴
Immo quicquid habes boni malique,
dic nobes. Volo te ac tuos amores
ad caelum lepido vocare⁵ versu.

[b] Lyric Strophes

A festal hymn to Diana

This hymn is to be sung by a choir of boys and girls.

1. fide, *protection.*

5. Latonia, *daughter of Latona* (or *Leto*), Diana.

7. quam, *whom* (Diana). **mater,** Latona.

8. deposivit, at birth. To the pagan Greeks, Latona was the wandering and homeless madonna who had no place to put her babe.

9. ut, *purpose.*

11. This line is hypermetric; contrary to usual practise the last syllable is elided before the vowel at the beginning of the next line.

13-14. *thou art called Juno Lucina by women in childbirth.* Diana had many and diverse functions, because, in the evolution of pagan religion, she was a composite of many minor local divinities.

15. Trivia, Hecaté—goddess of magic and the black art. **notho,** *false, borrowed.*

16. According to Catullus, *luna* is derived from *lumen*—although her light is not her own.

17. cursu . . . , i.e., waxing and waning.

18. iter annuum, *circuit of the years*—i.e., simply *the year.*

---

¹ **delicias,** *sweetheart.*

² **ni sint,** *unless she is.*

³ **velles,** *you should want* (or *long*) *to.*

⁴ **posses,** *you ought not to be able to.* This is the climax. .

⁵ **ad caelum vocare,** *make you famous.*

19-20. The moon—as superstitious farmers still say—brings good crops.
21-22. Sis sancta, *be thou hallowed*.
22. This line is hypermetric.
22-24. Romuli gentem, *Romanos*.
24. sospites, verb. This has the same construction as *sis* in (l. 21). ope, *help*, *aid*.

[c] Lyric Long-Lines

(In honor of Priapus)

2. quâ, *where*.
3. ora, the whole shore region and all its cities—not Lampsacus alone.
4. ostriosior, *more oystery*.

II

THE CARMINA

[1]

Vers de Société

[a] On Presenting a De Luxe Edition of His Verses to Cornelius Nepos

1. dono, *donabo*.
2. modô, *just now*, with *expolitum* translate it *freshly*. One of the marks of an expensive book was its polished paper.
3-4. *solebas putare meas nugas* (*trifles*) *esse aliquid*.
5. iam tum cum, *eo tempore quo*. ausus es, *ventured*. Nepos had published a brief universal history—one of the most difficult tasks an historian can undertake.
6. omne aevum, *the whole of time*—i.e., a history of the world. chartis, *sheets of paper*. *Three sheets* is a pardonable exaggeration, due to friendly enthusiasm. The work was in three "books"; when unrolled, a papyrus "book" makes one long sheet of paper.
7. Iuppiter, a mild oath.
8. habe, *cape*.
8-9. quicquid . . . , *hoc libelli* (*this

bit of a book*), *quicquid* [*et*] *qualecumque* [*est*]. This is a modest reference to his own work.
9. quod, *id*.
10. maneat, a prayer.

[b] After a Merry Evening

The friendship between Catullus and Calvus (the *salaputium disertum*) was a famous one; Calvus however was devoted only his leisure time to poetry.
1. otiosi, supply *nos*.
2. lusimus, equivalent to *scripsimus*—when applied to the lighter kinds of verse.
3. ut convenerat, *when it had been agreed*. delicatos (colloquial), *merry*, *jovial*.
5. ludebat, *componebat*. numero, *meter*. modô . . . modô, temporal.
6. reddens mutua, *returning like for like*, *giving tit for tat*—i.e., they were matching, or capping, verses extemporaneously.
8. incensus, *enamored*.
9. ut, result.
11. toto, with *lecto*. indomitus furore, of course he exaggerates his insomnia.
12. lucem, *daylight*.
17. dolorem, *plight*—i.e., infatuation for you.
18. audax, *haughty*, *toplofty*. nostras, *meas*, *my desires and requests* (for further meetings of the same sort).
19. oramus, *oro*.
20-21. Mock solemnity.
21. vemens, *vehemens*.

[c] I'll Get Even With You Yet!

1. Ni, *nisi*. plus oculis, the traditional and conventional Latin phrase.
2. munere, an ablative of cause. English uses *for*.
3. Vatiniano, *Vatinian*, *of a Vatinius*—who had no love for his political enemy and prosecutor, Calvus.

5. male (colloquial), *damnably.*

6. Isti, with *clienti,* a dig at Calvus —for lawyers were forbidden to receive fees, but could accept "gifts." **di mala multa dent,** a real oath.

7. tantum impiorum, *tot impios* [*poetas*], a humorous exaggeration. To Catullus there was no greater crime than writing bad verse.

8. repertum (colloquial), *recherché. Novum ac repertum* may be rendered by *newfangled.*

9. Sulla, not the famous Sulla, but a poverty-stricken schoolmaster— another dig at Calvus and his clientele.

10. male est mi[*hi*], a favorite colloquialism, here *I am downcast.* The meaning depends somewhat on the context; it often is *I am sick.*

11. dispereunt, *go for nought* (or *unrewarded*).

12. Di, an oath. **libellum,** an exclamation in the accusative.

14. misti, *misisti.* **continuo,** adjective, *eodem.* **periret,** the subject is Catullus.

15. Saturnalibus, in apposition with *die.*

16. salse, vocative, *you wag!* **non hoc tibi abibit,** the corresponding American colloquialism uses a personal verb: *you will not get away with it.*

17. luxerit (from *luceo*), *day shall dawn.* This is mock-serious.

18. scrinia, the ancient equivalent of *bookcases.* Actually they were round bandboxes that held the papyrus rolls. **Caesios,** generic plural.

18-20. Catullus will repay Calvus in kind—i.e., with a Latin anthology to match his Greek one.

19. Suffenum, the sudden shift to the singular suggests that Suffenus is in a class by himself.

22. illûc, although he does not specify exactly where, we may conjecture that it is to Limbo. **pedem,** a pun.

[d] An Epistle

1-3. *Velim, papyre* (vocative), [*ut*] *dicas Caecilio, poetae tenero . . . .* [*ut*] *Veronam veniat.* Catullus addresses his letter paper as though it were a messenger carrying a verbal message. **tenero,** *gentle.* **sodali,** *comrade.*

3-4. **Novum Comum,** the present town of Como.

4. Larium, the present Lake Como.

5. cogitationes, *problems.*

6. accipiat, *hear, consider.* The subject is Caecilius. **sui meique,** *mutual—provided* the phrase is to be taken literally. Perhaps Catullus is cryptically referring to himself!

8. From here on Catullus twits his fellow poet on a little love affair.

8-9. *miliens revocet* [*Caecilium*] *euntem.*

11. quae, the antecedent is *puella.*

12. deperit, slang, *amat*—as in Plautus. **impotente,** *passionate.*

13-14. quo tempore . . . ex eo, *ever since.* She seems to have fallen in love with him for his poetry—as Lesbia did with Catullus (see p. 238 ff). **incohatam,** lit., *begun.* We would say *the beginning of.*

14. "**Dindymi dominam,**" these are probably the opening words of Caecilius' poem—just as the Aeneid is called "*Arma virumque.*" **misellae** dative, supply *puellae.*

15. ignes, *amor.* **medullam,** *marrow*—popularly believed to be the seat of passion.

16-17. Sapphicâ Musâ, Sappho herself—the tenth Muse.

18. Caecilio, dative of agent. "**Magna Mater,**" this is probably the title of Caecilius' poem.

[e] Absent-Minded!

1. amores, this is singular in meaning, *sweetheart.*

2. visum, supine, *to visit.* **otiosum,** with *me.*

3. scortillum, diminutive of *scortum,* in apposition with *amores; wench, baggage, jade.* In reality this is a coarse word, but it is used *jocosely* here.

4. illepidum, with *scortillum.*

5. ut, *when.*

5-6. incidēre . . . varii lit., *various topics of conversation came to us*—i.e., *we conversed about various matters.*

6. in, *among.*

6-8. quid . . . quo . . . quonam . . . , these are the questions discussed. **quid,** i.e., what sort of place.

7-8. haberet . . . profuisset, the subject is Bithynia.

8. aere, from *aes*—i.e., *how much money I had made there.*

9. erat, i.e., the truth.

9-10. nihil neque ipsis [*Bithyniis*] **nec cohorti fuisse,** *nec ipsos Bithynios nec cohortem quicquid habuisse.* The two negatives, *nihil neque,* do not make a positive.

10. hoc praetore, an ablative absolute, *under the present governor.*

11. unctius, *sleeker.* **referret,** *bring back home.*

12. irrumator, another coarse word, lightly used—e.g., *son-of-a-gun.*

13. faceret pili, *care a straw for.* The subject is *praetor.*

14-15. quod . . . esse, i.e., the product of the country, in apposition with *homines* (l. 16). Slaves exported from Bithynia were reputed to be the best chairmen (*ad lecticam homines*).

15. comparasti, *bought.*

17. me facerem, *make myself out.* **beatiorem,** *rich.*

18. maligne, *badly off.*

19. quod, *just because.* **mala** (colloquial), *rotten.*

20. octo, eight slaves to one chair would be some turn-out! **rectos** (colloquial), *proper, strong.*

21. nullus, *nemo.*

22. pedem grabati, *leg of a sofa.*

24. Hîc, *hereupon.* **cinaediorem,** another coarse word, *shameless hussy.*

26. commoda, *lend.*

27. mane, the final *e* is not elided, but loses half its quantity.

28. istud, *that remark* (l. 20). The gist of the remark is now repeated, with *me habere* standing for *parare.*

29-30. In his embarrassment, Catullus flounders. **fūgit me ratio,** *I got mixed up.* The metaphor is taken from arithmetic—i.e., *the sum escaped me.*

31. utrum, supply *homines sint.*

32. *Utor* [*Cinnae servis*] *tam bene quam* [*si*] *mihi paraverim.*

33. male (colloquial), *mighty.* **vivis, es.**

34. per quam, lit., *through*—i.e., *thanks to*—*whom.* The antecedent is *tu* (l. 33). **non licet,** *one may not.*

[f] Farewell to My Villa

Meter: limping iambic.

1. noster, vocative, agrees with *funde, my estate.* It was on the *outskirts* of fashionable Tibur (Tivoli), and so far from the town that Catullus' enemies sneeringly referred to it as his "Sabine shack"—for, like Bar Harbor, Tibur was on the edge of the backwoods.

1-2. Tiburs, Tiburtem, these are adjectives, *Tiburtine.*

2. te, the estate. **autumant,** quibus, [*ii*] *dicunt, quibus.*

2-3. quibus . . . laedere, Catullus' friends. **non est cordi,** *non placet.*

3. quibus . . . est, Catullus' enemies.

4. quovis pignore contendunt, *wager anything*—viz. [*fundum*] *esse Sabinum.*

6. suburbana, only Tibur could be called suburban.

7. malam, *accursed.*

7-9. *tussim, quam meus venter mihi* (*non immerenti*) *dedit, dum appeto sumptuosas cenas,* this does not mean that he actually had intestinal grippe,

but that his illness was a punishment
for his *gluttony*—he had lusted after
the fleshpots of Sestius' banquet.

10. Sestianus, a possessive adjective, used for the genitive, *Sestian*
(for *of Sestius*).

11. petitorem, *a candidate for office.*

13. gravedo frigida, *a stuffy cold.*

14. in tuum sinum, *in te, Villa.*

15. urtica, *nettle.* How this was
administered as a remedy, we do not
know.

16. tibi, the villa. **grates**, *gratias.*

17. quod, *because.*

18-19. Nec deprecor . . . **quin**, this
is virtually a double negative, equivalent to *precor* . . . *ut.*

19. recepso, *recepero.*

20. An unexpected and witty turn.
From ll. 16–19 one would expect
merely *mihi det frigus*—i.e., *I don't care
now if I do get a cold from the frigid
speeches of Sestius, for I'm sure to be
cured at my villa;* but instead Catullus
says: *I don't care now if Sestius gets a
cold from his own speeches!*

21. vocat me, *invites me to dinner.*
tunc . . . **cum**, *only when.*

[g] "Come, Landlord, Fill the Flowing
Bowl"

Note the suggestion of alternating
rhyme in the jingle *-er -i -er -i* (l. 1)
and in the final syllables *-es -ae -is -ae*
(ll. 2–5)—a tendency in the direction
of the modern drinking song, or
tavern ditty.

1. Minister puer, vocative. **puer**,
servant, slave, garçon.

2. inger, *ingere*, imperative; *pour
in, fill up.* **calices**, *cups.* **amariores**,
bitterer, sourer—because **stronger.**
The revels began with diluted wine
and worked up gradually to *neat.*

3-7. Postumia, *mistress* of the
revels. She has just commanded that
the wine be drunk unmixed, so Catullus shouts: *Away with water!*

3-4. *Postumiae, ebriosioris* (*tipsier*)
ebrioso acino (*than the tipsy grape*).

5. vos lymphae, vocative, *ye waters.*

6. pernicies, in apposition with
lymphae. **severos**, *Puritans, teeto-
talers.*

7. Thyonianus, *Bacchus* (son of
Thyone)—i.e., *wine.*

[h] To Marrucinus Asinius

1. sinistra, a sneak thief proverbially used his left or "sinister" hand.

3. tollis, *lift, steal.* **lintea**, *hand-
kerchiefs.*

4. salsum, *witty.* **fugit te** (colloquial), *you're wrong.*

5. quamvis, *very.*

7. fratri, supply *tuo.* **vel**, *even.*
The talent is a fabulous sum—more
than anyone would actually pay.

8. mutari, *to be redeemed*—i.e., his
brother is willing to pay hush money.
est, the subject is *he.*

**8-9. disertus puer leporum ac face-
tiarum**, this is general eulogy in rather
colloquial language, *a clever and delightful chap.*

12. aestimatione, *money value.*

13. mnemosynum (Greek), *sou-
venir, keepsake.*

14. sudaria, *lintea.* **Hiberis**, *Iber-
ia, Spain.*

16-17. *necesse est* [*ut*] *haec* [*sudaria*]
amem, sicut amo Veraniolum . . . .

[i] Advice to Egnatius

Meter: limping iambic.

2. ad, with *subsellium.* **rei**, from
reus (not *res*). **ventum est**, an impersonal passive, *when people have
come* (not *when he has come*).

3. excitat fletum, i.e., in the jury.
It was then the duty of friends to appear in mourning and display their
anxiety and grief.

5. lugetur, an impersonal passive;
there is mourning, people mourn.
unicum, supply *filium.*

10. Urbanus, *Roman.* This is quite different from *urbanum,* meaning simply *urbane* (l. 8).

10-14. The long catalogue of nationalities to which Egnatius does *not* belong wittily prolongs the suspense.

15. tamen, *still.*

17. nunc, *as it is.* **Celtiber,** *a Spaniard.*

18. quod quisque minxit, *urina.* **mane,** *next morning.*

19. dentem, gingivan, these are collective; *teeth, gums.*

20. ut, *so that, therefore,* expresses result. **iste vester dens est,** *are the teeth of you Spaniards. Vester* is plural, and as such can never be substituted for *tuus* in classical Latin—although *noster* is regularly substituted for *meus.*

20-21. quo expolitior . . . hoc amplius, *the more gleaming . . . the more* (or *larger amount of) tooth wash.*

21. praedicet, the subject is *dens.* Since the latter is collective, the verb must be translated by *they show* (or *indicate).* **bibisse,** this is sarcastic exaggeration. **lotium,** *urine.*

[j] Scurvy Politicians

1. Porci, vocative.

4. verpus Priapus, Piso. *Verpus* means *circumcised.*

5. lauta, *elegant.*

6. de die, *by day*—a sign of extravagance.

7. in trivio, lit., *at the crossroads.* **vocationes,** *invitations.*

[k] Welcome to the Wanderer

1. omnibus . . . amicis, *alone of all my friends.*

2. antistans mihi, *worth more to me than.* **milibus trecentis,** this is a humorous exaggeration.

4. anum, adjective, *aged.*

6. Hiberum, the genitive plural; with *loca, etc.; Iberians, Spaniards.*

8. applicans [*tuum*] **collum,** *pulling toward me.* English would say: *throwing my arms around.*

10. quantum est hominum, *quot sunt* (i.e., *omnes) homines.*

11. Catullus means *quis me laetior est,* but the neuter is colloquial and jocular.

[l] Homeward Bound

1. e-gelidos, lit., *thawing.*

3. silescit, this is equivalent to the passive, *is silenced by.* **auris,** from *aura.*

4. Linquantur campi, this is equivalent to *linque campos.*

5. uber, *fertile.*

6. urbes, e.g., Ephesus, Miletus, etc. (in Asia Minor). Catullus plans to go sightseeing. **volemus,** from *volare.*

7. avet, *cupit.*

8. vigescunt, *quicken.*

9. coetus, the vocative plural, *gatherings.*

10. *quos, longe a domo simul profectos.* **simul,** *together*—all came from Rome at one time. This is in contrast with *diversae* (*separate)* and *variae* (*of different kinds).*

[m] Home Again

Meter: limping iambic.

1. It was hard to tell whether Sirmio (on Lake Garda) was an island or a near-island (peninsula).

2. ocelle, *gem.* **stagnis,** *lakes.*

3. fert, as though the water bore islands on its surface. **uterque,** mythology has only one Neptune, but in this way Catullus wittily distinguishes between fresh and salt water.

4. quam, *how.*

7. solutis curis, *than release from care.*

11. pro, *worth.*

12. ero, *for your master.*

13. Lydiae, Etruscan.

14. *ridete omnes domesticos cachinnos* (cognate accusative).

[n] When Cupid Sneezes

1. Acmen, accusative. **amores,** *sweetheart.*

3-7. This is a lover's vow; the main clause begins in l. 6.

3. ni, *nisi,* with *amo* and *sum paratus.* **perdite,** adverb.

5. pote, supply *est;* **perire,** *amare.* The whole clause is therefore equivalent to: *tantum quantum is qui potest plurimum amare.*

7. caesio, a traditional epithet for lions, perhaps *gray-eyed.* **veniam,** a wish.

11. ebrios, *love-sick.*

12. purpureo, *crimson* (never what we call *purple*). **saviata,** *kissing.*

13. sic, *so surely.*

14. domino, Love. **serviamus,** a wish.

15. ut, *as.*

20. *amant* [*et*] *amantur.*

21. misellus, *pining.*

24. facit, *finds.* **libidines,** *pleasure.* English uses the singular.

25. homines, *human beings.*

26. Venerem, *a love.*

[2]

Epithalamia, or Wedding Songs

For Manlius Torquatus and His Bride

1. Collis, genitive.

2. cultor, lit., *inhabitant.* **genus,** *offspring.*

3. virum, *bridegroom.*

6-10. Although a male god, Hymen is dressed in the symbolic bridal costume.

7. amaraci, *marjoram.*

8. flammeum, *bridal veil.*

9. gerens, *wearing.*

10. luteum, *yellow.*

16-18. *Vinia* [*talis*], *qualis Venus, like unto Venus when she came . . . .*

17. Idalium colens, *dwelling in Idalium* (Idalian Venus).

18-19. Phrygium iudicem, the judgment of Paris.

20. alite, *omen.*

21-25. Vinia is like a young myrtle tree.

22. Asia, adjective.

24. ludicrum, *as a plaything.* **rosido,** *dewy.*

26. aditum ferens, *adveniens.*

30. Aganippe, a spring—here personified.

33. revinciens, *binding.*

34. hedera, *ivy.*

37. virgines, bridal chorus of girls.

38. par dies, their wedding day. **agite,** *come!* **in modum,** *to the measure* (musical).

42. se, *himself.* **citarier,** *citari.*

43. munus, *duty, office.*

44. dux, Hymen.

46. pandite, spoken to the attendants.

47. ut, *how.*

48. comas, i.e., of sparks.

52-53. I.e., be in the land of the living.

69. En . . . , this is spoken to the bride—who has now reached her new home. **ut,** *how.*

71. sine . . . , *let it* (the household) *serve you.* The wife will be *materfamilias* and *domina.*

74-75. movens tempus, *shaking the temples* (i.e., *head*).

75. anilitas, *old age.*

76. I.e., with the palsy.

79-80. transfer pedes, *lift your feet over.*

81. rasilem, *polished.*

84. bracchiolum teres, *smooth arm.*

85. praetextate, *boy escort.* He is wearing the *praetexta,* garb of boyhood.

86. cubile, *bed.*

89-90. I.e., never divorced, true wives. These are the *pronubae,* matrons of honor who bed the bride.

97. parthenice, call it *lily*.
98. papaver, *poppy*.
112. nomen, *house* (the Torquati).
indidem, *from the same* (*stock*).
124-126. I.e., may the glory of having a good mother bring credit to his stock, just as . . . .
132. munere, *performance of duty*.

[3]

Elegies

[a] On the Death of His Brother

[*i*] From an epistle to Manlius

1-2. Quod mihi mittis hoc epistolium, *the fact that you send* . . . .
3. ut, *begging me to.* **naufragum,** Manlius.
5. quem, Manlius.
6. caelibe, *widowed*.
7. I.e., he can get no consolation from the classic poets, such as Sappho.
9. id, refers to *quod* . . . (l. 1).
10. hinc, *from me.* **munera . . . ,** a poem dealing with conjugal affection.
12. hospitis, *amici*.
13. accipe, *audi.* **quis,** *quibus*.
15. I.e., ever since he put on the toga of manhood.
16. aetas, supply *mea.* **ver,** *its springtime*.
17. multa satis (colloquial), *quite a lot!* **lusi,** *scripsi*—when referring to love poetry. **dea,** Venus.
19. studium, *inclination*.
21. fregisti commoda, i.e., *destroyed my happiness*.
26. studia, as in l. 19.

[*ii*] From an epistle to Allius

2. virum, *virorum*.
3. -ne, exclamatory.
4. mihi, *from me*.
4-8. Cf. the epistle to Manlius (ll. 20–24). The repetition of these lines is probably due to the lack of revision

of certain poems by Catullus before his death.
5. lumen, *life*.
9-12. *Quem* (the brother) *nunc aliena terra detinet*.
9. inter nota sepulchra, i.e., in the family burial plot.
10. cognatos cineres, *cognatorum cineres.* **compositum,** *laid to rest.* The Romans practised cremation, but buried the ashes in a tomb.
11. Troiā, a locative ablative.
12. solo, noun, *soil*.

[*iii*] At his brother's tomb in the Troad

1. vectus, *traveling.*
2. inferias, *ritual* (for the dead).
3. munere mortis, *boon of death*—i.e., the gift due to the dead.
4. The Roman burial service ended with the *conclamatio*, or last call to the dead—like our custom of playing taps over a soldier's grave. The words generally used were: *salve, ave, vale,* or some variation thereof—Catullus works them into his poem in l. 10.
7. haec, i.e., offerings (flowers, wine, salt, etc.). **parentum,** *ancestors*.
8. tristi munere, *as a sad duty*.

[b] To Calvus—On the Death of His Wife, Quintilia

1. mutis sepulchris, dative, the dead.
2. nostro, of the living.
3. quo desiderio, an ablative of means, defines *dolore*.
4. missas, *lost*.
5. dolori, dative of the noun, used as an indeclinable adjective (cf. *cordi*), *grievous*.
6. Quintiliae, dative; *Quintilia non tantum dolet, quantum gaudet.* The philosophy of this poem is worth reflecting on: (1) Do the dead live? (2) Do they miss the joys of earth? (3) Are the dead conscious of us?

(4) What do we gain by mourning? (5)
How does our grief affect the dead?

[4]

Poems to Lesbia

[a] Innamoramento

1. Ille, some rival who is having a
tête-à-tête with his beloved. **par,**
equal.

2. fas, *not sacrilegious.*

3. adversus, *opposite.*

5. quod, *which thing.*

6. sensus, noun, accusative plural.
simul, *as soon as.*

7. Lesbia, naturally this word does
not appear in Sappho's poem from
which Catullus translated. **est super,**
superest, remains.

8. vocis in ore, these words are
conjectural. There is a gap in the
manuscript at this point, but knowing
the thought from the Greek original,
we may assume that Catullus wrote
either: *vocis in ore, gutture vocis, quod
loquar amens*—all modern conjectures
—, or something similar.

10. suo-pte, *their own.*

11-12. gemina lumina, *oculi ambo.*

[b] Symptoms

[i] Telltale irritability

1. viro, *her husband.* **mi mala dicit,**
speaks ill of me.

3. Mule, vocative, her husband.
nostri, *of me* (genitive of *nos*).

4. sana, *heart-free.* **gannit,** *growls.*

5. meminit, *thinks (of me).* **acrior,**
more pointed (or *significant*).

6. uritur, *loves.*

[ii] Telltale garrulity

2. dispeream (*hang me!*) *nisi Lesbia* (*if Lesbia doesn't*) *me amat.*

3. sunt . . . mea, *mea* (*my feelings*)
sunt totidem.

[c] The Heyday of Love

[i] Life is short

2. rumores, *gossip, disapproval.*
severiorum, *puritanical.*

3. assis (from *as*), *farthing.*

4. Soles, *suns, days, light of day.*

5. nobis, *for us mortals.* **lux,** i.e.,
of life.

6. nox, i.e., in death.

7. basium, *kiss.*

11. sciamus, supply *how many
there are.*

12. invidere, *cast an envious spell.*

13. tantum basiorum, *tot basia.*

[ii] How many kisses?

3. The answer to the question
asked in l. 1 is not a single statement,
but a series of comparisons: lit., *how
many grains of sand lie in the desert,
how many stars look down on earth, so
many kisses* . . . . **Libyssae,** *Libyan*
(in the desert of Sahara).

4. Cyrenis, locative, *at Cyrénae.*
laserpici-feris, *laserpicium-bearing.*
This is a humorous mock-heroic
epithet—*laserpicium* being the chief
agricultural product of the country.

**5-6. inter oraclum Iovis et sepul-
crum Batti,** these are two well-known
landmarks of the region. **Iovis,** Juppiter Ammon.

10. ve-sano, *ve-* is a negative prefix.

12. lingua, supply *possit.* **fascinare,** *bewitch* (cf. l. 12 of *Life is Short,*
p. 240).

[iii] Enviable sparrow!

1. Passer, vocative. **deliciae,** vocative plural, *pet.* **puellae,** genitive.

2. quicum, *quo-cum.*

3. primum digitum, *finger tip.*
appetenti, *pecking.*

4. solet, the subject is Lesbia.
morsus, noun.

5. cum, *when.* **desiderio,** *sweetheart.* **nitenti** (from *niteo*), *beautiful.*

6. carum nescioquid iocari, a cognate accusative. Anything that Lesbia does is "dear" to Catullus.

7. solaciolum, vocative, *sweet solace.* Catullus flatters himself that Lesbia needs solace when he is not there. **doloris,** *longing.*

9. The main clause expresses a wish.

[iv] The sparrow is dead!

1. Veneres Cupidinesque, *Loves and Cupids* (as in l. 12 of the *Invitation to Fabullus,* p. 218).

2. quantum est hominum, lit., *as much as there is of men*—i.e., *quot sunt homines, as many men as there are, all ye men.* **venustiorum,** *tender-hearted.*

6. norat, *noverat.*

7. ipsam (colloquial), *mistress, owner.* This is a synomyn of *dominam* (l. 10).

11. Qui, *he.*

12. illûc, to Hades or Orcus (l. 14).

13. malae, vocative, *accursed.*

14. bella, adjective.

[v] Quintia is fair, but Lesbia is charming

1. multis, *to many, in the opinion of many.* She was probably a reigning belle. **longa,** *tall.*

2. sic, i.e., *so far and no farther.* **singula,** *the separate features* (or *details*).

3. Totum illud, *the totality, the combination.*

4. mica salis, *grain of spice.* Quintia was evidently of a statuesque type of beauty; Lesbia, petite and charming.

6. omnibus, *from all.* **Veneres,** *charms.*

[vi] To Ameána—who claimed to be as fair as Lesbia

1. puella, vocative.

1-4. minimo naso . . . , the charms

Ameana does *not* possess are of course the very ones Lesbia does possess.

4. elegante lingua, *refined speech.*

5. *mistress of the bankrupt of Formiae* (Mamurra—a notorious grafter and henchman of Julius Caesar.)

6. Ten, *te-ne.* **Provincia,** *Cisalpine Gaul* (Catullus' birthplace).

[vii] Warning to a would-be rival

1. mala mens, *infatuation.* **Ravide,** pronounce it *Rávid'* or *Raúde.* Some metrical license is permitted with proper names.

2. in, *against.*

3. advocatus, *invoked.*

4. ve-cordem, *ve-sanam, in-sanam.* The *cor* is the seat of intelligence.

5. An, *perhaps.* **in ora,** i.e., *as a laughing stock or byword.*

6. notus, *notorious.*

7. Eris, supply *notus.* **amores,** *sweetheart.*

8. cum longa poena, *to your everlasting regret.*

[c] A Falling-Out

Regrets are vain

Meter: limping iambic.

1. desinas, this is the subjunctive of command.

2. quod, *what.* **perisse** (from *pereo*), *periisse.* **ducas,** *consider, regard as.*

3. candidi soles, *happy days.*

4. ventitabas, *ventitare* is the iterative verb derived from *venire.*

6. iocosa, e.g., *caresses.*

9. iam non, *no longer.* **impotens,** *fool.*

10. sectare, imperative; *nec sectare [eam] quae fugit.*

13. rogabit, *woo.*

14. rogaberis nulla (colloquial), *non rogaberis.*

15. This is mock-serious.

17. Cuius, *whose sweetheart?* **dicē-ris,** *will you be said* (i.e., *famed*). The renown of being Catullus' beloved must have been a strong inducement for Clodia.

[d] Reconciliation

Unhoped-for joy

1. cupido, adjective. Note the hiatus. **optanti,** adjective.

2. insperanti, this is used with full participial force, equivalent to *cum non sperat.*

3. carior, vocative, Lesbia.

6. lucem, *diem.* **candidiore notā,** an ablative of quality. Happy days were recorded with white marks, unhappy days with black ones.

[e] Doubts

[i] All things are fleeting

1. vita, vocative, *sweetheart.*

3. facite ut, *grant that she.*

6. amicitiae, *affection.*

[ii] Writ in water

2. se petat, *woo her.*

[f] Steadfast Devotion

[i] To a scandalmonger

1. vitae, *sweetheart.*

4. tu cum Tappone, *tu et Tappo.* Neither of the two talebearers is otherwise known. **monstra,** *prodigies, marvels*—i.e., *you make everything out to be ominous, you make mountains out of molehills.*

[ii] To Allius—in memory of happier days

1. deae, *Muses.* **re,** *respect.*

2. officiis, *favors, kindnesses.*

3-6. I.e., *when I was a passionate lover, "sighing like a furnace."* Catul-

lus wittily describes his own first pangs of love in the conventional romantic manner.

3. Trinacria rupes, *Sicilian crag* (Mt. Etna—the volcano).

4. lympha, *water* (the Hot Springs of Thermópylae—between Mt. Oeta and the Mālian Gulf).

5. *neque maesta.* **lumina,** *my eyes.*

6. imbre, i.e., *tears.* **madere,** an infinitive, depends on *cessarent.*

7. *Is* (Allius) *patefecit* (*made accessible*) *latum limitem* (*way*) *ad clausum* (*forbidden*) *campum.*

8. nobis, *mihi.* **dominae,** Lesbia. Unfortunately the word *mistress* has two meanings in English and it is impossible to distinguish between *amica,* the ordinary Latin word for *mistress* (in the sense of *paramour*) and *domina,* which is a stronger term (analogous to the English)—not to mention *era* (l. 20), the strongest term of all—implying the *slavery* of the lover.

9. ad quam, *at which.* The antecedent is *domum.*

11-12. plantam innixa, *resting her foot.*

12. argutā, this undoubtedly meant something very definite to Catullus, but our lexicons give it more meanings than almost any other adjective in the Latin language. One may choose from: *sprightly, slender, bright, creaking,* and *sly.* **constituit,** *stepped.*

13. *ut* (*just as*) *quondam coniugis amore.*

13-14. advenit domum, *ducta est domum, came to be married* (to Protesilaüs).

15. *cui* (to Laodamía) *tum digna aut nihil aut paulo concedere* (*yield* or *take second place*). Laodamia was an ancient heroine like Helen of Troy, with whose beauty moderns can hardly compete.

17-18. No doubt the winged god also sneezed occasionally—as in the idyllic poem on the loves of Septimius and Acme.

19. Quae tamenetsi, *although she* (Lesbia). **uno,** *alone*—i.e., she now has other lovers.

20. feremus, *feram, I shall patiently endure.* **verecundae,** so Catullus professes to believe! **furta,** *peccadillos.*

21. molesti, *disagreeable*—i.e., a kill-joy.

22. caelicolum, *caelicolarum.*

23. coniugis, Juppiter. **concoquit,** *digests.* The common English metaphor is *swallows.*

24. omnivoli (from *omni-volus*), *omnes puellas volens.*

26. venit, in lawful wedlock. **odore,** *incense* (associated with wedding festivities).

29. nobis unis, *me alone.*

29-30. *is dies datur, quem.*

30. illă, *she.*

33. vita, *sweetheart.*

34. nos, *ego.*

34-36. domina, lux, Lesbia.

[g] Bitterness and Pain

[i] Successful rivals

[a] **1.** *si vis Catullum debere tibi oculos* (his life).

3. ei, *from him.*

3-4. [id] *quod multo carius est.*

[b] **1. mihi credite,** vocative, lit., *thou believed by me.*

2. magno cum pretio, *to my great cost.*

3. sicine, *sic-ne.* **subrepsti,** *subrepsisti* (from *subrepo*), *stolen into* (or *taken*) *me unawares.* **intestina perurens,** *burning into* (i.e., *gnawing at*) *my vitals.*

4. misero, *from poor me.* **bona,** *blessings* (Lesbia's love).

5. venenum, vocative, *thou bane* (Rufus).

6. pestis, vocative.

[ii] Unsympathetic friends

[a] **1. Male est Catullo,** *Catullus aegrotat.*

2. ei, Catullo. **laboriose** [*est ei*], *laborat morbo.*

4. quem, relative, Catullus.

6. meos amores, *my affection,* supply some such verb as *habes* (*regard*).

7. Paulum adlocutionis, *parvam adlocutionem,* supply *mitte* or *da.* Even English omits the verb in such appeals—e.g., *just a word!*

8. lacrimis Simonideis, *than the tears of Simónides* (a Greek poet, famous for his dirges).

[b] Meter: greater Asclepiadéan (see p. 221).

2. amiculi, Catullus.

5. quae, *which principles* (those implied in the negative answer to l. 4, beginning with *num*).

7. tu-te, *tu.* **iubebas** . . . , *bade me give you my heart.*

9-10. omnia . . . **sinis,** *sinis ventos ac nebulas ferre omnia irrita.*

10. irrita ferre, *bring to naught, blow away.*

11. at, *nevertheless.*

12. quae (*Fides*) *postmodo faciet* (*efficiet*) *ut te paeniteat facti tui.*

[c] Meter: limping iambic.

1-3. *Did a lioness or Scylla give you birth?*—i.e., *are you a monster?*

1. Libystīnis, *Libyan,* African.

2. As snakes grew out of Medusa's head, so mad dogs grew out of Scylla's groin.

3. mente durā, an ablative of quality, modifies *te* (l. 1).

4. supplicis, Catullus. **novissimo,** *last, supreme.*

5. corde, an ablative of quality, *thou of cruel heart.*

[d] **1.** *Desine velle benemereri* (*to deserve well*) *quicquam* (*in anything*)

de quoquam (*of anyone*)—i.e., by being kind to anyone.

2. [*desine*] *putare aliquem posse fieri pium* (*loyal*).

3. **nihil** [*est*] **fecisse,** *it is no use to have acted.*

5. **mihi,** supply *obest.* **urget,** *pains.*

6. **quam qui modô,** *than he who.*

[*iii*] Despair

1-2. *turpe* [*tibi est*], *Veronae esse.* Catullus should return to Rome and defend his honor.

2. **hîc,** at Rome. **de meliore nota,** *of higher social standing* (the aristocrats).

3. **deserto cubii,** supply *tuo.*

[*iv*] Disillusionment

1. *te* (subject) *nosse* (*novisse*) *Catullum solum*—i.e., *Catullus was the only man for you.*

2. **prae,** *in preference to.* **velle,** supply *te* as the subject. **tenere Iovem,** i.e., as your husband (see the poem entitled *Writ in Water,* p. 244).

3. **Dilexi,** the use of *diligere* rather than *amare* here, is very significant. **tantum,** *only.* **vulgus,** *the common herd, hoi polloi.*

7. **Quî,** *how?* **Quod,** *because.*

8. **bene velle,** *respect.*

[h] Struggle and Self-Mastery

[*i*] Hate and love

2. **fieri,** *that it is so.*

[*ii*] Reproach

2. **Lesbia mea,** vocative.

3. **ullo foedere,** *in any bond.*

4. **amore tuo,** *my love for you.*

[*iii*] Impasse

1. **mens,** *my heart.*

2. **officio suo,** *by its devotion.*

4. **omnia,** i.e., even the worst things.

[*iv*] *Apologia pro amore suo*

2. **pium,** *true.*

4. *divum* (*divorum*) *numine abusum* [*esse*] *ad fallendos homines.*

9. *quae omnia, credita menti ingratae, perierunt.*

11-12. **que** . . . **et,** lit., *both* . . . *and.* English may omit *both.*

12. **dis invitis,** ablative absolute.

16. **pote,** *possible,* supply *est.*

17. **vestrum,** *your habit.*

21. **ut,** *how.*

23. **illa,** Lesbia.

26. **reddite,** *grant.*

[i] Loathing

[*i*] To M. Caelius Rufus

4. **angiportis,** *alleys.*

5. **glubit,** a short and ugly word. Lesbia has become a whore—a common streetwalker! **magnanimi,** *lordly-minded.* **nepotes,** *descendants.* These are degenerate by contrast with the Romans of early times.

[*ii*] Clodia and Clodius

1. **Lesbius,** Clodius. **quem malit,** *cum eum malit.*

3. **vendat,** *may sell* (into slavery). **cum gente Catullum,** *Catullus and all his tribe.*

4. I.e., *if* he can find three friends willing to kiss him (the usual salutation). He is universally loathed and shunned.

[j] Scorn

The final word

1. Lesbia had made tentative advances for a reconciliation through two acquaintances whom Catullus cordially hated. Catullus addresses his reply to these two go-betweens, dallying ironically (ll. 1–10) with the idea of their supposed devotion to him and concealing that was really in his mind, until with withering suddenness he delivers his curt message to Lesbia (l. 17).

2. penetrabit, the subject is Catullus.

3. ut, *where.*

5. molles, this is a stock epithet for most Orientals.

7-8. *sive* [*ad*] *aequora, quae Nilus colorat* (i.e., with mud).

9. omnia haec, i.e., perils.

9-10. voluntas caelitum, *fate.*

10. *parati* (Furius and Aurelius) *tempĺare* (*to risk*) *simul* [*cum Catullo*]. *Parati* is vocative.

13. valeat, this is colloquial—as in comedy: *to* **hell** *with her.*

15. nullum, *neminem.* **identidem,** this echoes l. 3 of his *first* poem to Lesbia, *Innamoramento,* p. 239.

16. ilia rumpens, a horrid phrase, suggesting that Clodia is a sort of vampire who drains the life blood of her victims.

17. respectet, *exspectet.*

18-19. ultimi prati, *of the furthest part* (i.e., *the edge*) *of the meadow.* Elide the final *i* of *prati.*

Epilogue

1-2. Si qui eritis, *vos quicumque eritis.*

2-3. manusque . . . nobis, i.e., Puritans might shun him and his works.

4-5. *me* [*esse*] *parum-pudicum* (*impudicum*).

5. hi, *versiculi.*

7. versiculos, supply *castos esse.* **nihil,** *non.*